T0308216

TSUSHIMA

PRAISE FOR *TSUSHIMA*

'Rotem Kowner's *Tsushima* constitutes a *tour de force* treatment of this epic battle and its multiple legacies. He establishes remote and immediate contexts, provides accurate description and informed analysis, and delves deeply into aftermath.'

Bruce W. Menning, Professor of Strategy (ret.), U. S. Army Command and General Staff College

'A book of remarkable originality, daring, and openness of mind. Professor Kowner presents a skilful account of Tsushima which for the first time equally embraces Japanese and Russian sides of the battle and its consequences.'

Dmitrii V. Likharev, Far Eastern Federal University, Vladivostok, Russia

'A penetrating and comprehensive study of the most consequential naval battle fought between Trafalgar (1805) and Pearl Harbor (1941). Where Kowner's work shines brightest is his insightful analysis of this battle's military, political, and cultural legacy for both participants and the wider world. *Tsushima* is masterful.'

J. Charles Schencking, Author of *Making Waves: Politics, Propaganda, and the Emergence of the Imperial Japanese Navy, 1869–1922*

'Rotem Kowner's *Tsushima* presents a comprehensive account of the Battle of Tsushima Strait in 1905. It skilfully describes how and why it occurred and ended with a decisive and one-sided victory by the Imperial Japanese Navy. Among other things, this book is about the big battleships and guns. Well prepared and trained, the IJN made the best use of them against the Baltic Fleet and earned well-deserving glory and acclaim. However, the memory of decisive victory at Tsushima also planted in the minds of generations of IJN's leaders hubris, arrogance, and inflexibility to adjust and change IJN's naval doctrine until its last days in 1945. Kowner, as a true historian, re-enacts the days of the big battleships and guns, and beckons us all to return to the seas again.'

Naoyuki Agawa, Author of *Friendship Across the Seas: The US Navy and the Japan Maritime Self-Defense Force*

GREAT BATTLES

TSUSHIMA

ROTEM KOWNER

OXFORD
UNIVERSITY PRESS

OXFORD
UNIVERSITY PRESS

Great Clarendon Street, Oxford, OX2 6DP,
United Kingdom

Oxford University Press is a department of the University of Oxford.
It furthers the University's objective of excellence in research, scholarship,
and education by publishing worldwide. Oxford is a registered trade mark of
Oxford University Press in the UK and in certain other countries

Published in the United States of America by Oxford University Press
198 Madison Avenue, New York, NY 10016, United States of America

British Library Cataloguing in Publication Data
Data available

Library of Congress Control Number: 2021946671

ISBN 978–0–19–883107–5

DOI: 10.1093/oso/9780198831075.001.0001

Printed and bound in the UK by
Clays Ltd, Elcograf S.p.A.

FOREWORD

The phrase 'great battle' carries four immediate connotations. The first relates to time. The standard narrative, whether applied to Marathon or Waterloo, Salamis or Trafalgar, assumes that the events occurred on a single day, or at most over two or three days. Secondly, a battle has to be on a scale large enough not to be deemed a skirmish. Fighting may characterise war but fighting itself does not constitute a battle. If the forces involved are too small or the commitment to engage by one or both sides too slight, then what happens is not a great battle. At least one side, and possibly both, must want to fight. Third, a battle occurs in a defined, and in some cases confined, space. On land it is sometimes so geographically limited that it takes its name from an otherwise little-known geographical feature, such as Bunker Hill, or an obscure village or hamlet. At sea, its name may be more capacious but as often it gains precision by adopting the name of the nearest landfall. Lastly, a 'great battle' implies that the consequences are commensurate with the commitment; in other words, that the result proves decisive.

The infrequency with which all these four conditions have been met helps explain why 'great battles' have been rare. Great battles need to be infrequent or they lose their cachet. Calling some forms of combat battles may be no more than a rhetorical device, coined for effect, or, more pragmatically, to give shape to otherwise seemingly inchoate episodes. Since the nineteenth century the word battle has been applied to events that are not concentrated in time and space. Persistent fighting in all seasons and all weathers combined with techno-logical innovation and full social and economic mobilisation to make outcomes more cumulative than singular. In the Second World War, the 'battle' of the Atlantic was decisive, both in the economic war and in enabling the D Day landings, but it was not clearly defined in time or space. It lasted nearly four years and, although largely restricted to the North Atlantic, still embraced an expanse of sea larger than any major continent.

At sea especially, battle in a traditional sense was rarely decisive. As the British seapower theorist, Julian Corbett, observed in 1911, man lives upon the land, and so 'it scarcely needs saying that it is almost impossible that a war can be decided by naval action alone'. The Greeks may have checked the Persians at Salamis in 480 BC but they did not topple the Persian empire. The Christian victory over the Turks at Lepanto in 1571 was similarly a great defensive success, which checked the Ottoman advance into the Mediterranean but not into continental Europe. On 21 October 1805 Nelson 'decisively' defeated the French and Spanish fleets at Trafalgar but war with France continued for another decade. While Nelson's victory gave the Royal Navy command of the Mediterranean and secured British trade routes in the Atlantic, it did not end Napoleon's freedom of manoeuvre within Europe. Just over six weeks after Trafalgar, the French emperor won possibly his greatest victory, defeating the armies of Austria and Russia at Austerlitz on 2 December 1805. However, even in land warfare 'decisiveness' can be a relative, rather than an absolute, term. The continental alliance which he had smashed in 1805 was resuscitated in 1813. For many then and since, the final defeat of Napoleon at Waterloo in 1815 embodies the concept of decisiveness, not least because it introduced nearly a century of comparative European peace, but its outcome too rested as much on the exhaustion of France, and of its enemies, after two decades of conflict as it did on the results of a single day on a confined battlefield, however sanguinary the fighting.

In Corbett's day, the ability of warships to cope with adverse weather conditions enabled by the invention of steam power and the end of sail ought to have made naval battle more possible, but it did not necessarily do so, partly because improved navigation and advanced technology opened up more of the world's oceans and so created greater space in which an opponent could hide. Since the beginning of the twentieth century, war at sea has been increasingly fought under and over the surface, as well as on it. In the Second World War 'great battles' were fought in the Pacific at sea and in the air—at Pearl Harbor in December 1941, the Coral Sea in May 1942 and Midway in the following month. Each was conducted at scale and was limited in time, if less so in space. Each was more clearly a 'great battle' in the classical definition than the whole of the battle of the Atlantic, but the war against Japan was also won by sustained economic warfare conducted by submarines and by island-hopping amphibious assaults. The Second World War did not end in a climactic battle like Waterloo in 1815.

For those who practise war in the twenty-first century the idea of a 'great battle' can seem no more than the echo of a remote past. The names on regimental colours or the events commemorated at mess dinners bear little relationship to patrolling in dusty villages or waging 'wars amongst the people'. Contemporary military doctrine down-plays the idea of victory, arguing that wars end by negotiation not by the smashing of an enemy army or navy. Indeed it erodes the very division between war and peace, and with it the aspiration to fight a culminating 'great battle'.

And yet, to take battle out of war is to redefine war, possibly to the point where some would argue that it ceases to be war. Carl von Clausewitz, who experienced two 'great battles' at first hand—Jena-Auerstedt in 1806 and Borodino in 1812—wrote in On War that major battle is 'concentrated war', and 'the centre of gravity of the entire campaign'. Clausewitz's remarks related to the theory of strategy. He recognized that in practice armies might avoid battles, but even then the efficacy of their actions relied on the latent threat of fighting. Winston Churchill saw the importance of battles in different terms, not for their place within war but for their impact on historical and national narratives. His forebear, the Duke of Marlborough, fought four major battles and named his palace after the most famous of them, Blenheim, fought in 1704. Battles, Churchill wrote in his *Life of Marlborough*, are 'the principal milestones in secular history'. For him, 'Great battles, won or lost, change the entire course of events, create new standards of values, new moods, new atmospheres, in armies and nations, to which all must conform'.

Clausewitz's experience of war was shaped by Napoleon. Like Marlborough, the French emperor sought to bring his enemies to battle. However, each lived within a century of the other, and they fought their wars in the same continent and even on occasion on adjacent ground. Winston Churchill's own experience of war, which spanned the late nineteenth-century colonial conflicts of the British Empire as well as two world wars, became increasingly distanced from the sorts of battle he and Clausewitz described. In 1898 Churchill rode in a cavalry charge in a battle which crushed the Madhist forces of the Sudan in a single day. Four years later the British commander at Omdurman, Lord Kitchener, brought the South African War to a conclusion after a two-year guerrilla conflict in which no climactic battle occurred. Both Churchill and Kitchener served as British Cabinet ministers in the First World War, a conflict in which battles lasted weeks, and even months, and which, despite their scale and duration, did not produce clear-cut outcomes. The 'battle' of Verdun ran for all but one month of 1916 and that of the Somme for five months. The potentially decisive naval action at Jutland spanned a more traditional twenty-four-hour timetable but was not conclusive and was not replicated during the war.

Clausewitz would have called these twentieth-century 'battles' campaigns, or even seen them as wars in their own right. The determination to seek battle and to venerate its effects may therefore be culturally determined, the product of time and place, rather than an inherent attribute of war. The ancient historian Victor Davis Hanson has argued that seeking battle is a 'western way of war' derived from classical Greece. Seemingly supportive of his argument are the writings of Sun Tzu, who flourished in the warring states period in China between two and five centuries before the birth of Christ, and who pointed out that the most effective way of waging war was to avoid the risks and dangers of actual fighting. Hanson has provoked strong criticism: those who argue that wars can be won without battles are not only to be found in Asia. Eighteenth-century European commanders, deploying armies in close-order formations in order to deliver concentrated fires, realized that the destructive consequences of battle for their own troops could be self-defeating. After the First World War, Basil Liddell Hart developed a theory of strategy which he called 'the indirect approach', and suggested that manoeuvre might substitute for hard fighting, even if its success still relied on the inherent threat of battle.

The winners of battles have been celebrated as heroes, and nations have used their triumphs to establish their founding myths. It is precisely for these reasons that their legacies have outlived their direct political consequences. Commemorated in painting, verse, and music, marked by monumental memorials, and used as the way points for the periodization of history, they have enjoyed cultural afterlives. These are evident in many capitals, in place names and statues, not least in Paris and London. The French tourist who finds himself in a London taxi travelling from Trafalgar Square to Waterloo Station should reflect on his or her own domestic peregrinations from the Rue de Rivoli to the Gare d'Austerlitz. Today's Mongolia venerates the memory of Genghis Khan while Greece and North Macedonia scrap over the rights to Alexander the Great.

This series of books on 'great battles' tips its hat to both Clausewitz and Churchill. Each of its volumes situates the battle which it discusses in the context of the war in which it occurred, but each then goes on to discuss its legacy, its historical interpretation and reinterpretation, its place in national memory and commemoration, and its manifestations in art and culture. These are not easy books to write. The victors were more often celebrated than the defeated; the effect of loss on the battlefield could be cultural oblivion. However, that point is not universally true: the British have done more over time to mark their defeats at Gallipoli in 1915 and Dunkirk in 1940 than their conquerors on both occasions. For the history of war to thrive and be productive it needs to embrace the view from 'the other side of the hill', to use the Duke of Wellington's words. The battle the British call Omdurman is for the Sudanese the battle of Kerreri; the Germans called Waterloo 'la Belle Alliance' and Jutland Skagerrak. Indeed, the naming of battles could itself be a sign not only of geographical precision or imprecision (Kerreri is more accurate but as a hill, rather than a town, it is harder to find on a small-scale map), but also of cultural choice. In 1914 the German general staff opted to name their defeat of the Russians in East Prussia not Allenstein (as geography suggested) but Tannenberg, in order to claim revenge for the defeat of the Teutonic Knights in 1410.

Military history, more than many other forms of history, is bound up with national stories. All too frequently it fails to be comparative, to recognize that war is a 'clash of wills' (to quote Clausewitz once more), and so omits to address both parties to the fight. Cultural difference and even more linguistic ignorance can prevent the historian considering a battle in the round; so too can the availability of sources. Levels of literacy matter here, but so does cultural survival. Often these pressures can be congruent but they can also be divergent. Britain enjoys much higher levels of literacy than Afghanistan, but in 2002 the memory of the two countries' three wars flourished in the latter, thanks to an oral tradition, much more robustly than in the former, for whom literacy had created distance. And the historian who addresses cultural legacy is likely to face a much more challenging task the further in the past the battle occurred. The opportunity for invention and reinvention is simply greater the longer the lapse of time since the key event.

All historians of war must, nonetheless, never forget that, however rich and splendid the cultural legacy of a great battle, it was won and lost by fighting, by killing and being killed. The battle of Waterloo has left as abundant a footprint as any, but the general who harvested most of its glory reflected on it in terms which have general applicability and carry across time in their capacity to capture a universal truth. Wellington wrote to Lady Shelley in its immediate aftermath: 'I hope to God I have fought my last battle. It is a bad thing to be always fighting. While in the thick of it I am much too occupied to feel anything; but it is wretched just after. It is quite impossible to think of glory. Both mind and feelings are exhausted. I am wretched even at the moment of victory, and I always say that, next to a battle lost, the greatest misery is a battle gained.'

Readers of this series should never forget the immediate suffering caused by battle, as well as the courage required to engage in it: the physical courage of the warrior, the soldier, sailor or airman, and the moral courage of the commander, ready to hazard all on its uncertain outcomes.

HEW STRACHAN

PREFACE

The Battle of Tsushima was fought between Japan and Russia in 1905 and has left a deep and indelible mark on both. The two belligerents have used different names for this naval clash (Jpn. 日本海海戦 *Nihonkai kaisen*; Rus. Цусимское сражение *Tsusimskoe srazhenie*), and have ascribed varying degrees of importance to it through the years. After all, one of them won and the other lost. But in both, this largest naval engagement of the Russo-Japanese War is still debated, still devotedly commemorated, and still triggers pride or pain more than a century after it ended. At the same time, the Battle of Tsushima has exerted an unmistakable significance far beyond the realm of these two nations. Among other things, the strong echoes of this first modern naval victory of an Asian power over a major European power were heard across the entire colonial world and shocked its rulers. Likewise, from a naval perspective, this most devastating defeat suffered by the Imperial Russian Navy in its entire history was also the only decisive engagement between two battleship fleets in modern times.

On the eve of the battle, both sides believed that an engagement of their fleets would determine the final outcome of the war. A Russian victory could lead to Tsarist control of the seas around the Japanese home islands and to an immediate interruption of the flow of personnel and materials to the Asian mainland. This, in turn, might have allowed the Imperial Russian Army to crush the Japanese land forces in Manchuria and thus decide the war. A defeat, however, could end any Russian hope of altering the course of the war and possibly oblige the Russians to negotiate peace. And indeed, the Russian government's hopes of reversing the military situation in East Asia were dashed in

the battle's aftermath. It was now compelled to enter into peace negotiations, which resulted in the Treaty of Portsmouth, signed just over
three months later. In the subsequent years, the influence of this battle
was commemorated and the symbolic victory of an 'Eastern' power
over Tsarist Russia using modern technology was celebrated in both the
Western and Colonial Worlds. Similarly, and in both Japan and Russia,
the Battle of Tsushima had a prolonged impact on the fates of these
nations' respective navies and on their ambitions, which lasted for at
least four decades.

This is not the first attempt to tell the story of the battle. It has been
told over and over again since 1905 in many languages and forms.
However, these endeavours rarely relied on archival and primary
sources associated with *both* belligerents alongside sources originating
from contemporary neutral powers, let alone the vast repository of
digital sources that are presently available to scholars. The present
book seeks to provide a broad and balanced picture of the battle while
employing an extensive and diverse array of sources. Moreover, it is
the first scholarly account to evaluate the battle's short- and long-term
consequences in the political, social, and naval spheres, as well as the
way it has been commemorated by the two nations involved. The
main argument of this book is that the battle has exerted wide and
lasting impact far beyond its immediate arena. It brought about the
end of the Russo-Japanese War and affected dramatically the two
belligerents' geopolitical vision and naval outlook for decades. Likewise, its shock waves affected European affairs, American strategic
plans, and the naval development during the decade before the First
World War. For this profound impact, as well as for its scale and
decisive results, the Battle of Tsushima deserves to be considered one
of the greatest naval battles in history.

ACKNOWLEDGEMENTS

The Battle of Tsushima caught my attention many years ago, and for a good reason. Initially, as a young naval cadet, I was impressed by the way an ostensibly inferior naval power overcame a superior foe. As a student, I became fascinated by the battle's impact on naval development, and in later years I became intrigued by the battle's broader repercussions, and especially by its positioning as a landmark in the rise of imperial Japan. Thus, when I was offered an opportunity to write an entire book about this battle, the project was like a sandbox for a bored child, a kind of dreamy kingdom where the global, the regional, and the local entwine, and where my past and present interests could merge. It is for this reason, but also for his advice and encouragement throughout the project, that I am first and foremost indebted to Hew Strachan.

Still, in writing a work of such a broad angle, one inevitably incurs many more debts of various sorts. A host of colleagues and friends have helped, stimulated, and encouraged me in different ways, for which I am immensely grateful. Putting down their own work, Agawa Naoyuki, Felix Brenner, Shaul Chorev, Inaba Chiharu, Dmitrii Likharev, Bruce Menning, Andreas Renner, Sven Saaler, J. Charles Schencking, Ronald H. Spector and two anonymous reviewers read early drafts of this book, and supplied invaluable leads and constructive criticism. Likewise, John Breen, William Clarence-Smith, Cord Eberspächer, Ofer Shagan, and Daqing Yang responded to my queries and shared with me their profound knowledge. It goes without saying that errors of facts and interpretations are bound to mar this sort of book—these are all my own. I wish to thank also my colleagues, at the

University of Haifa, for their friendship and for creating the atmosphere that makes dedication to research possible. Nimrod Chiat was essential as ever in making the text more perspicuous. Special thanks go to Luciana O'Flaherty and the devoted staff of the Oxford University Press for their patience and constant encouragement.

I gratefully acknowledge the financial support granted by the Japan Foundation, which facilitated research visits to libraries and archives overseas. A few words of gratitude are also due to my family that had to put up with this project, notably, Jasmine, Emmanuelle, Narkisse and Amos. I am particularly indebted to my life partner, Fabienne, for all that she does by the way of inspiration, and for so much else.

CONTENTS

LIST OF FIGURES

LIST OF MAPS

LIST OF TABLES

CONVENTIONS

The writing of this book involved some difficulties in transliteration. Not only is the script of each belligerent's language not Latin, but also the battle was waged in the vicinity of China and Korea, where other non-Latin scripts are in use. Furthermore, in the century that has elapsed since the war, some of the territories around the site of the battle have changed hands and regimes, and many of the place names have changed, often more than once. Place names in Manchuria and Korea during the early twentieth century posed perhaps the greatest problem for this book, as they do for any historian who wishes to write about the war. Each belligerent often had its own name for the various localities; the English-speaking world had a third name. Many of these names were changed after the war, for political reasons or due to a change in the transliteration system.

Names of People

The names of people mentioned in the book follow several transliteration systems. Transliterations of Russian names, written originally in the Cyrillic alphabet, adhere to the modified form of the US Library of Congress. Exceptions are names so familiar in English that they are written in the commonly accepted way so as not to mislead the reader (e.g. Nicholas II rather than Nikolai II); likewise, Russian names of German origin appear in the form usual in that period in the English literature (with the original German name in brackets). The diacritic marks for the unpronounced soft and hard sign of the Russian alphabet are omitted. Japanese names are written according to the Hepburn Romanization system and in consultation with the *Kodansha*

Encyclopedia of Japan (1983 edition). The macron used in some of the Japanese names indicates a long vowel. Chinese names are written according to the Pinyin transliteration system, while Korean names follow the recent Revised Romanization of Korean system. As commonly accepted in the East Asian tradition and in academic writing in English, all East Asian names appear with the family name first, followed by the personal name.

Names of Places

Place names in Japan are written according to the Hepburn transliteration system, in consultation with the *Kodansha Encyclopedia of Japan* (first edition) and the *Kenkyusha Japanese–English Dictionary* (fourth edition). Names of locations in Manchuria and China are written according to the Wade–Giles transliteration system. While today the Pinyin transliteration system is in growing use, most books in European languages dealing with this period, and certainly all books written during the war itself and in the half a century that followed, apply the Wade–Giles Romanization system or similar traditional systems. Finally, names of places of current special importance are written in the present transliteration, such as Tokyo (which a century ago was written Tokio and is transliterated fully as Tōkyō) and Beijing (Peking, Peiping).

Dates

The dates in the book are written according to the Gregorian calendar (the calendar which is commonly used today in the West and most of the world, including Russia), rather than either the Julian calendar, which was used in tsarist Russia until 1918, or the modern Japanese calendar, which is still in use today. The Julian calendar, used in many books on Russian history, was 12 days 'behind' the Gregorian calendar during the nineteenth century and 13 days 'behind' during the twentieth century. Japan adopted the Gregorian calendar in 1873 but also began about that time to number years serially from the year in which a reigning emperor ascended the throne (the entire era). Therefore, the date of the outbreak of the Battle of Tsushima, which occurred on 14 May 1905 according to the Julian calendar in Russia, and on the 27th day of the fifth month of the 38th year of the Meiji era in Japan, appears in this book as 27 May 1905. With regard to the timeline of the battle, the time kept by the Russians was about 19 minutes earlier than the time kept by the Japanese. Whereas the former used the solar time during their entire voyage, the latter used the Japan Standard Time (JST), which is based on the location of the city of Akashi, Hyōgo Prefecture, at exactly 135 degrees east longitude, and is nine hours ahead of Greenwich Mean Time (GMT). This book follows the Japanese time.

Measurement Units

The units of measurement in this book are given by the metric system. Still, the description of the battles at sea pose a special problem because most fleets, including those of countries that had long since switched to the metric system, continued using traditional non-metrical units of measurement. Therefore, units of measurement that have additive professional meaning and were used for general description (e.g. distance in nautical miles) are provided in brackets. The displacement of ships is given in long tons, known also as displacement tons (1 ton = 1,016 kg), even though no accepted unit for measuring and recording the displacement of battleships existed prior to the Naval Conference in Washington in 1922. Therefore, all measurements of warships were related to 'normal' displacement or to the displacement at the planning stage, whereas the measurements of auxiliary ships are in gross register tonnage.

Armament and Armour

Technical data regarding warships and guns are written in abbreviated form and follow the metric system. Thus, the inscription 305-milimetre gun means a gun of bore diameter 305 millimetres. Traditionally, guns' calibre was referred to in inches, as follows:

76-millimetre calibre = 3 inches
120-millimetre calibre = 4.7 inches
152-millimetre calibre = 6 inches
203-millimetre calibre = 8 inches
229-millimetre calibre = 9 inches
240-millimetre calibre = 9.4 inches
254-millimetre calibre = 10 inches
305-milimetre calibre = 12 inches
320-milimetre calibre = 12.6 inches

Ranks

Ranks of military figures are given according to the British system at the beginning of the twentieth century. This is done to simplify the usage of different terms for the armies and navies referred to in the discussion, and to adhere to the names of the ranks as they appear in the contemporary literature in English on the war.[1]

ABBREVIATIONS

Throughout the text, the following abbreviations are used:

IJA   Imperial Japanese Army (*Dai-Nippon teikoku rikugun*)
IJN   Imperial Japanese Navy (*Dai-Nippon teikoku kaigun*)
IRA   Imperial Russian Army (*Russkaia imperátorskaia ármia*)
IRN   Imperial Russian Navy (*Rossiyskiĭ imperatorskiĭ flot*)
Jpn.   Japanese language
Rus.   Russian language

1

Background

The Battle of Tsushima was the most notable naval battle in the early twentieth century and one of the most decisive naval clashes ever. From a broader historical perspective, however, it could also be seen as a flashpoint in prolonged frictions between two expanding powers. Both belligerents were growing empires that were seeking additional territories, the mastery of the seas in their vicinity, and national greatness. Of the two, Russia had greater experience in foreign expansion. It had been encroaching eastward into Asia for centuries, whereas the Japanese Empire had been striving to expand in the opposite direction for only a few decades. These differences notwithstanding, the clash between them in 1904–5 was fierce and vital, to the extent that it would serve as the opening shot of an armed struggle that would last for another 40 years. In attempting to understand this complexity, the present chapter aims to provide the historical background of the Russo-Japanese War, the road to the battle, and the evolution of naval warfare in the years before the battle.

The Russian yearning for territorial expansion in the East can be traced back to the late sixteenth century. It began when a group of Cossacks first crossed the Ural Mountains in their search for furs and territorial gains. Beyond was Siberia—a vast region populated by tribal peoples who were unable to stem Russian intrusion. A decade after Cossacks started pressing into Siberia, Japanese forces under the command of Toyotomi Hideyoshi strove to seize Korea (1592–8) and dreamt of getting hold of China. The failure of these ventures ended

Japanese involvement in Asian affairs for almost three centuries. During the 1630s, the desire to create a sphere of influence outside the Sinocentric world, alongside fears of Christian meddling in Japan's internal affairs, drove the third shogun of the new Tokugawa dynasty to a policy of semi-isolation. Thereafter, and during the long 'secluded nation' period (Jpn. *Sakoku*, 1640–1854), Japan maintained a policy of non-involvement in Asian affairs and restricted economic ties with its neighbours. In the meantime, Russian explorers arrived at Kamchatka in 1697, and soon encountered Japanese castaways. The Russo-Japanese intercultural encounter intensified in 1739, when a Russian vessel approached the north-eastern coast of Honshu and came into contact with local officials. By the end of that century, a renewed interest in Japan resulted in the arrival of a Russian embassy in Nagasaki in 1804. Following the failure of their long negotiations to obtain permission to enter the country regularly, the Russians were deeply frustrated. On their way back, the embassy attacked Japanese settlements in the Kuril Islands, which evoked tension between these two nations for the first time exactly a century before the Russo-Japanese War.[1]

The bilateral tension calmed down in the following half-century despite the Japanese bar on Russian visits. Eventually, Tsar Nicholas I dispatched another delegation to Nagasaki in 1853, but it did not complete its mission due to the outbreak of the Crimean War. Its timing, however, was exceptional, as an American flotilla under the command of Commodore Matthew Perry succeeded in forcing the shogunate to end the country's semi-isolation several months later. One year after the opening of the country, Russia and Japan signed the first of three pre-war Russo-Japanese Treaties which included a temporary compromise regarding the division of Sakhalin. In 1868, a revolution known as the Meiji Restoration broke out in Japan, during which the shogunate was replaced by an oligarchy of samurai from the periphery acting in the name of restoring imperial rule (under the young Emperor Meiji, reigned 1867–1912). Thereafter, the country engaged in an accelerated process of modernization that included the establishment of a national army and navy. The Japanese oligarchy was quick not only to examine ways to prevent the conquest of Japan by Western forces but also to strengthen its position in the eyes of the West by beginning a process of territorial expansion overseas.[2]

During much of the second half of the nineteenth century, Russia and Japan maintained fairly stable relations while strengthening their hold in the region. In 1860, Russia founded the city of Vladivostok on the southern edge of its Pacific shore. The waters in this port freeze during the long winter which, at the time, prevented it from being an all-year-round naval base. In 1875, Japan and Russia signed the second pre-war Russo-Japanese Treaty (the 'exchange agreement') that set out their common borders once again. In the mid-1870s, Japan expanded its territory by annexing the Ryukyu Islands in the southwest, the Bonin (Ogasawara) Islands in the south, and the Kuril Islands in the north, as well as forcing the opening of Korea. Japanese military activities worried the Chinese, who decided to restore their now-weakened influence on the Korea Peninsula. Viewing this area as its future 'living space' during the 1880s, Japan began to regard any foreign endeavour to take control of Korea as a *casus belli*.[3] The first such attempt was made by China and followed by Russia. Japan reached an agreement with the former with respect to Korea in 1885, but its status quo with the latter began to show cracks in 1891. During that year, St Petersburg started laying down the Trans-Siberian Railway from European Russia to the Pacific Ocean, a distance of about 9,934 kilometres.[4] Russian decision makers often referred to this mammoth project as a cultural mission—bringing civilization and Christianity to the peoples of Asia—but it was its political and military ramifications that changed the face of East Asia.[5]

The Crucial Decade: The First Sino-Japanese War and Its Aftermath

Japan declared war on China over their clash of interests in Korea in July 1894. The circumstances ostensibly resembled their crisis 10 years

3

earlier, but now Japan was ready for an armed conflict. Although relatively small, its army and navy were modern and well trained.[6] The two nations mobilized their forces and hurriedly landed on the peninsula but soon Japan gained the upper hand. Two months later, the Imperial Japanese Navy (IJN) defeated the Chinese Beiyang Fleet in the Battle of the Yalu River and secured mastery of the waters around the Korea arena.[7] Thereafter, Japanese forces completed the conquest of Korea and crossed the Yalu River into Chinese territory in Manchuria. They landed on the southern tip of the Liaodong Peninsula and took over the fortress of Port Arthur. The turning point in the war came in January 1895, when Japanese forces executed landing operations in the Shandong Peninsula and began to threaten Beijing. The ensuing destruction of the Chinese fleet at Weihaiwei in February broke Chinese resistance and led the two sides to negotiate terms. In April 1895, they concluded a peace treaty, but less than a week later Russia managed to obtain the support of France and Germany. Consequently, these three powers jointly relayed a message 'advising' Japan to restore to China the territories it had conquered in southern Manchuria. Under this explicit ultimatum, known as the Three-Power Intervention, Japan was forced to withdraw its forces from the Liaodong Peninsula and Port Arthur. Despite this final blow, the First Sino-Japanese War was in fact highly successful for Japan.[8] In naval terms, it offered a useful lesson on the importance of mastering the seas during a war on the Asian continent and on the need for a strong ally to isolate future opponents.

With China's defeat, Russia became Japan's main rival. This was not only because of the political vacuum this created but also due to Russia's own expansionist ambitions.[9] Thereafter, the Trans-Siberian Railway became an even greater source of stress in Russo-Japanese relations. Once completed, it could allow the rapid mobilization of Russian forces and thereby thwart Japan's ambitions in East Asia. Back in Europe, Japan's victory gave rise to grave fears about its growing influence. During the war, the German emperor, Wilhelm II (reigned 1888–1918), invented the term 'yellow peril', which quickly entered the international vocabulary, as the hidden threat posed by East Asians against Western civilization.[10] Moreover, Russia, together with the United States, objected to Japanese demands for exclusive rights in Korea. In early 1896, King Gojong of Korea (reigned 1863–1907) sought sanctuary in the Russian legation in Seoul. Many Koreans interpreted their monarch's 'internal exile' as a call to rebellion against the Japanese presence in the country and began to act accordingly. In the year following the First Sino-Japanese War, the Russian involvement in Korea was thus greater than ever before and soon expanded to China too.[11]

Reeling from the impact of its recent clash with Japan, China concluded the Li–Lobanov Treaty with Russia in 1896. Although the core of this agreement was mutual aid in the event of Japanese aggression, it also included a Chinese concession allowing Russia to build a significant shortcut for the Trans-Siberian Railway line across Manchuria. The landing of German troops in Jiaozhou (Kiachow) Bay in the southern part of the Shandong Peninsula a year later impelled the Chinese to allow the Russians to occupy Port Arthur, and especially make use of its ice-free and protected harbour. Fearing the loss of its influence in Korea, Japan then formulated the doctrine of Manchuria–Korea exchange, which soon led to the Nishi–Rosen Agreement of 1898.[12] Russia, nonetheless, was unwilling to relinquish its interests in Korea, although the Boxer Uprising that broke out in northern China in late 1899 dampened the simmering Russo-Japanese rivalry.[13] As both countries dispatched troops to quell the uprising, Russia used this opportunity to occupy Manchuria. With the joint intervention over in 1901 and the railway project approaching completion, Japan was determined to establish its control over Korea while pushing for a Russian evacuation of Manchuria.[14] Although their negotiations with the Russians soon proved futile, the Japanese were more successful in their talks with Great Britain. The Anglo-Japanese Treaty, signed in early 1902, provided Britain with a strong Asian ally that could assist it in the struggle against Russian expansion on several fronts across Asia.[15] For Japan, the treaty ensured that Russia would be partly isolated in the case of a conflict with it.[16]

The discovery of activity by a Russian enterprise on the Korean side of the Yalu Delta in spring 1903 caused an uproar in Tokyo and required firm action from the government. In St Petersburg, hardliners were getting the upper hand too.[17] A month later, in a meeting between Russian and Japanese representatives in Tokyo, the former offered to turn the northern part of Korea into a neutral zone in return for removing Manchuria from Japan's sphere of interest while omitting any obligation regarding the withdrawal of Russian forces. The Japanese negotiators responded with amendments to the Russian proposal, but the Russians were trying to buy time and delivered their own response late and with no significant changes. In Tokyo, militant opposition factions grouped together against Katsura Tarō's government as the ruling oligarchy was beginning to build a broad consensus for war over Manchuria if the proposals on Korea were rejected.[18] War now seemed a strong possibility and the preparations for it continued unabated. In December, the IJN reformed the Combined Fleet—a temporary force formed for the duration of a conflict.[19]

In St Petersburg, decision makers, and the tsar in particular, wanted to avoid war. They assumed that time was in Russia's favour, especially since the Trans-Siberian Railway would soon be fully functional. At the same time, there was a general sense of confidence as to Russia's power to withstand a Japanese attack. On 6 January 1904, St Petersburg delivered another message reiterating the need to create a neutral zone in Korea and asking that Japan should recognize Manchuria as being outside its sphere of interest. Before the Boxer Uprising, such a response would have satisfied the Japanese oligarchy, but the latter now distrusted Russia and was reluctant to see it maintain a firm hold in Manchuria. On 12 January, another meeting of the Imperial Council in Tokyo determined that Russia had made no significant concessions over Korea and was unwilling to enter into negotiations regarding Manchuria while trying to build up its military strength there.[20] The message it dispatched reached St Petersburg on 16 January but was not understood as an ultimatum. On 2 February 1904, the Japanese ambassador to Russia informed his government that St Petersburg had no intention of replying. Coincidentally, this was the same day on which the tsar approved a counter-response which contained no significant change from the message of 6 January. This counter-response reached Tokyo on 7 February but to no avail. A day earlier, the Japanese ambassador had already announced the rupture of diplomatic relations and begun preparations for leaving the Russian capital.[21]

Naval Thought and the Balance of Power on the Eve of the War

The final decade of the nineteenth century marks an exceptional period in naval history. This was the zenith of a hectic era that began when France launched the first steam-propelled ironclad warship in 1859.[22] The brief panic over this French trump card was followed by an extended naval race for larger, faster, and more armoured warships.[23] In 1889, Britain laid the keel of the first ship of the *Royal Sovereign* class—the harbinger of a new age of battleships. With its high turret and its improved protection, it was a prototype for most of the battleships built up to the end of the Russo-Japanese War. At the beginning of the twentieth century, the typical battleship displaced around 15,000 tons, was heavily armoured, and boasted a primary battery placed on two rotating turrets, each customarily equipped with two barrels of 305-millimetre guns (Figure 1). With these formidable guns, as well as an impressive secondary battery, battleships were designed to lay down great firepower on their enemy while withstanding as much damage as possible, and in this manner dominate the naval arena. However, because of their high cost and technological sophistication, only a few nations could afford them and even fewer could build them.

The rise of the battleship also raised some doubts. During the 1880s, the leading navies held intensive debates as to the role of this warship in future naval operations. Her exorbitant price tag and the constant improvement made to the torpedo—a self-propelled, underwater explosive device that was invented in the 1860s and could sink any

Figure 1. The prime product of a recent naval evolution: the new Russian battleship *Kniaz Suvorov*, the flagship of the Baltic Fleet (below) and the Japanese battleship *Asahi* (above)

warship in a single hit—led politicians and naval experts alike to question the rationale underpinning the frenzy of their construction.[24] France was probably the most sceptical country in this respect. In the mid-1880s, it saw the emergence of a radical naval approach known as the Jeune École (Young School).[25] Adding fuel to the fire, its thinkers suggested the use of swarms of small vessels armed with torpedoes to counter the British Royal Navy's superiority in battleships. Instead of a single battle, they also stressed the importance of an extended campaign of raids on the enemy's sea lanes until its economy was suffocated.[26] In 1890, Alfred Thayer Mahan (1840–1914), a United States naval officer and historian, entered the fray with his book *The Influence of Sea Power Upon History*.[27] Mahan did not conceive a new grand strategy, but his views on 'blue-water strategy' were the diametrical opposite of the French school, since he argued that naval operations were chiefly to be won by large fleets fighting a decisive battle or imposing a blockade. Indeed, by articulating clearly the rationale behind the contemporary naval dogma which the Jeune École had attacked, Mahan won widespread popularity among the world's leading navies, and his works were soon translated, inter alia, into Russian and Japanese.[28]

On the other side of the Atlantic, the retired Royal Navy officer and historian, Vice Admiral Philip Howard Colomb (1831–1899), extolled Britain's battleship-centred high-seas fleet and the great weight it carried in defending the empire almost unaided.[29] Single victories cannot give command of the sea, Colomb stated, 'unless the force defeated has also been annihilated'.[30] In view of the impressive build-up of French naval power in the early 1880s, Britain declared a two-power standard (in the 1889 Naval Defence Act) and adopted greater expansion programmes, with the intention of being able to face any combination of two of the other largest fleets. For this purpose, it appropriated large budgets that allowed the rapid construction of additional battleships, ending by late 1905 with an unmatched force of 47 pre-Dreadnought battleships. Britain was not alone. On the eve of the Russo-Japanese War more than one hundred battleships of pre-Dreadnought design were sailing the seas, flying the flags of nine navies, including the Imperial Russian Navy (IRN) and the IJN.[31] But with no battle to validate the battleship's effectiveness, the utility of this enormous investment in battleship construction, much like the acrimonious debate in this respect, remained unresolved. Although no great power could take the risk and abandon the battleship, all expected the imminent clash in the Pacific to provide a clear-cut answer in this regard.

Cruisers were another major type of warship that was to take part in the coming war between Russia and Japan. This multi-purpose principal warship, smaller but faster (18–25 knots) than the battleship, came into existence in the latter half of the nineteenth century. Since the 1880s, and at the time of the Russo-Japanese War, cruisers were split into three main categories: armoured cruisers, protected cruisers, and unprotected cruisers (Figure 2). These categories differed according to the size of the ships and the armour with which they were protected, as well as in the armament they carried, with unprotected cruisers being the lightest and least armed, and armoured cruisers the heaviest and most armed. The latter type was almost the size of a contemporary battleship (8,000–13,000 tons) and could join major engagements as well as cruise the oceans and disrupt enemy commerce.[32] In addition, contemporary navies made use of torpedo boats and destroyers. Armed with torpedoes, these two small types of warship could turn into giant killers, if used daringly. The first were small (50–200 tons), fast (20–30 knots), and inexpensive vessels designed to hit large ships with their torpedoes while swarming around them. By the late 1880s, France began to regard the swarm of torpedo boats as a viable challenger to the battleship's dominance, and subsequently even small navies procured this vessel.[33] To counter the torpedo boat's threat, Britain developed a new type of warship called the 'destroyer'. In this capacity, the destroyer assumed the role of the defender and 'long arm' of battleship squadrons. On the eve of the Russo-Japanese War, the destroyer was fast (25–30 knots), somewhat larger (240–400 tons) than an ordinary torpedo boat, and carried several light 57–76-millimetre guns, as well as torpedo launchers (Figure 2).[34]

The navies of both Russia and Japan constituted an integral part of recent global naval competition. Both had undergone rapid development in the two decades that preceded the battle and both were

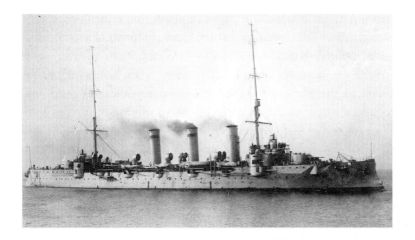

Figure 2. Sidekicks in the major battles of the early twentieth century: the Russian protected cruiser *Oleg* (above) and the Japanese destroyer *Shirakumo* (below)

considered modern and major naval powers. Of the two, the IRN was older, with greater experience and a deep-rooted tradition. In the aftermath of its poor performance in the Russo-Turkish War of 1877–8, the IRN had undergone reorganization, and, starting in 1882, was boosted by a massive 20-year construction programme.[35] By the mid-1880s, the IRN was the world's fifth-largest naval power, possessing no less than 138 First Class torpedo boats—more than any other naval power. Initially, the new emphasis on capital ships, first armoured cruisers and then battleships, did little to change Russia's contemporary geostrategic limitations. Apart from its relatively short shorelines, Russia's two main fleets—one in the Baltic Sea and the other in the Black Sea—could not combine, since the latter was confined to its sea by the London Straits Convention of 1841. With Tsar Alexander III's premature death in 1894, his son, Tsar Nicholas II (reigned 1894–1917), began to focus his attention on north-east Asian affairs. A year later, he approved an inter-ministerial resolution to maintain a substantial fleet in the Pacific.[36] Assisted by the leasing of Port Arthur from China and the progress made on the Trans-Siberian Railway, this resolution led to the deployment of a powerful third Russian fleet in the north-west Pacific as early as 1898. But despite this sudden strategic development, the new fleet would wither away even faster than it had materialized.[37]

The rise of the IJN was even more spectacular, as no one considered Japan a naval power even two decades before the war. Established in the early 1870s, the IJN depended at first on shogunal vessels captured in the civil war that engulfed Japan during 1869–9. From the outset, its leaders emulated the British Royal Navy, and so copied its procedures and traditions in full. The establishment of the Ministry of the Navy in 1872 made the IJN an independent branch of presumably equal power to the Imperial Japanese Army (IJA).[38] In reality, however, the former was of secondary importance during the first decades of its existence, and this position alongside limited resources forced it to rely on an array of old vessels and to focus on coastal defence. Against the backdrop of growing motivation for imperialistic expansion, an eight-year naval programme was announced in 1882, based on 22 torpedo boats and a number of large cruisers. The outbreak of the Sino-Japanese War of 1894–5 found the IJN ready for its first significant clash despite being significantly smaller than its rival. The navy's combat success boosted its confidence while providing seminal experience and a model for future engagements. It also raised its assertiveness vis-à-vis the IJA in terms of allocations and independence.[39] Strategically, the navy proved its central importance in any future war Japan would fight in Asia, and so it won autonomous command even in wartime in 1903. With Russia becoming Japan's main rival, the IJN abandoned its adherence to the Jeune École doctrine, and instead presented an ambitious 10-year programme for its expansion. Financed largely by Chinese indemnities for the war, this programme was headlined by six British-made battleships and six armoured cruisers that gave the service the nickname of the 'Six-Six Navy'. On the eve of the war against Russia, the IJN was also able to purchase two new Italian armoured cruisers. Renamed *Nisshin* and *Kasuga*, they were the only reinforcement the IJN obtained during the war.[40]

In terms of manpower, the IJN was able to emulate centuries-old naval traditions of instruction and training developed in the West within a few decades. Its officer corps was drawn predominantly from the ex-samurai class.[41] Following careful selection, candidates enrolled in the Imperial Naval Academy in Etajima and took up a demanding four-year course. After graduation, they had to pass an examination before any commission and their promotion was based on performance.[42] The typical Japanese sailor came from a peasant family and volunteered for service. He had to pass a physical examination and to demonstrate basic literacy. The minimum service for sailors was four or six years, but many chose to continue until retirement age, depending on their rank. The IRN maintained a far longer naval tradition, although the selection and training of its manpower was based on similar lines as in Japan. Its officer corps was drawn from the aristocracy and families of naval officers, and was also educated in a four-year course at the Naval Cadet Corps in St Petersburg. Promotion was based largely on performance, but it was rigidly regulated, burdened by nepotism, and slower than in Japan. The sailors were conscripts drawn initially from the maritime provinces and, by turn of the century, preferably from the urban working class rather than the peasantry. They served for seven years (with three more years in the reserve) and were paid and fed poorly, and hardly any were promoted. With these conditions, it is little surprise that tradition did not solve the IRN's chronic shortage of sailors or their low quality and poor relations with their officers.[43] For these, the differences between the sailors of the two navies was marked. The Russians served shorter time and tended to be less literate, less disciplined, and especially not as motivated as their Japanese counterparts. Among the officers, the differences were not as evident but the Russians were apparently less trained, were less inspired, and had shorter sea time than their adversaries.[44]

By early 1904, both the IRN and the IJN were among the world's largest naval forces. They were equipped with some of the most sophisticated naval systems available, including battleships, cruisers of all sorts, destroyers, and torpedo boats. Between the two, however, Russia was unequivocally superior. With its vast resources, three-fold population (146 vs. 47 million), five-fold gross national product, and much greater military expenditure, Russia's infrastructure was markedly stronger.[45] Militarily speaking, it was significantly more powerful both on land and sea.[46] Whereas its land forces were the largest in the world, its navy was the world's third or fourth largest.[47] The IJN was significantly smaller and occupied sixth place.[48] No wonder, then, that in purely numerical terms, Japan's venturing into war against Russia was often likened to David facing Goliath. However, when the military balance is examined locally, Japan's prospects did not seem so poor. The presence of Russia's land forces was limited in the East Asian arena and its Pacific Fleet was roughly of similar strength to the IJN. In the entire arena, however, the IRN had a single main base in Port Arthur, whereas its secondary and only other base in the arena was Vladivostok, some 2,430 kilometres away by sea. The fleet had seven battleships (all part of the Port Arthur Squadron) compared to Japan's six and 25 destroyers to Japan's 20, but was inferior in all other categories, especially when the geographical dispersal of its two bases is taken into account (Table 1). Despite this slight overall inferiority, Russia could bring reinforcements, and—in a protracted war— could even build additional warships, including battleships, while

Table 1. The naval balance on the eve of the Russo-Japanese War, 8 February 1904

Warships	Imperial Japanese Navy	Russian Pacific Fleet	Imperial Russian Navy
Battleships	6	7	17
Armoured Cruisers	7	4	10
Protected Cruisers	13	10	12
Coastal defence/ obsolete battleships	3	–	16
Unprotected Cruisers/ Gunboats	19	12	44
Destroyers	20	25	49
Torpedo Boats	90	11	90
Aggregate displacement (warships)	260,000t	190,000t	c.500,000t

Notes: These figures do not include the Japanese armoured cruisers *Kasuga* and *Nisshin*, which arrived in Japan on 16 February 1904, joined the 1st Battle Division on 15 April, and within a month replaced the two sunken battleships *Yashima* and *Hatsuse*. For a similar aggregate of the two rival fleets in the Pacific (246,206 vs. 191,000 tons) see <<<REF: BK>>>Kaigun rekishi Hozonkai, *Nihon kaigun-shi* (Tokyo, 1995)<<<REFC>>>, 7:150–1. For an aggregate of the IRN's total displacement on 1 January 1905, see 'Sea Strength of the Naval Powers', *Scientific American* 93, no. 2 (8 July 1905), 26.

Sources: For the number of ships: Evans and Peattie, *Kaigun*, 90–1; and Kowner, *Historical Dictionary*, 691–4 (appendix 6). The aggregate displacements were calculated by the author, based on data found in Kowner, *Historical Dictionary*.

Japan could not. Hence, the IJN had to exploit its margin of superiority rapidly and could not afford to fail.[49]

Japan's war plans shaped the course of its battles. While prepared separately by the army and the navy, their first and common premise was that Japan must keep its supply lines unimpeded to allow for the rapid deployment of its forces along the front. This could only be achieved if the IJN dominated the seas separating Japan's home islands from the war theatre. Thus, any war scenario consisted of an opening blow against the harbour of Port Arthur, and if possible of Vladivostok too, in order to put the Pacific Fleet out of action. As its worst-case scenario was the reunion of two or more Russian fleets, the IJN needed to annihilate the Pacific Fleet at all costs and before the arrival of reinforcements. Once this objective was achieved, the IJA was to overrun the relatively small Imperial Russian Army (IRA) units in Manchuria before it could muster any reinforcements via the still unfinished Trans-Siberian Railway. The plan recognized that Japan could not eliminate the Russian threat forever, but assumed that even partial success would bring the Russians to the negotiation table around which Japan could use Manchuria as a bargaining chip.[50]

Russia's war plans were by nature defensive and so allowed for a scenario in which Japan would be the aggressor and would invade Manchuria. First drafted in 1895, the plans were constantly subject to change to the extent that they were still incomplete when war broke out. The updated plans stated that, in the case of a Japanese attack, the IRA would protect both Port Arthur and Vladivostok, and deploy defensively behind the Yalu River with particular emphasis on the Mukden region. With substantial reinforcements arriving in the region via the Trans-Siberian Railway and once numerical superiority was attained, the Russian forces would go on the offensive. Russia's naval plans were also defensive and focused on the domination of the northern part of the Yellow Sea, the prevention of a Japanese landing on the Korean coast in that area, and the disruption of enemy communications. The war was supposed to conclude with an invasion of the Japanese home islands, although there was no detailed plan beyond an initial deployment of the Russian defences (Map 1).[51]

The Outbreak of the Russo-Japanese War and Its First Year

On the morning of 6 February 1904, the day diplomatic relations between Japan and Russia were broken off, the Japanese Combined

Map 1. The land and naval arena of the Russo–Japanese War, 1904–5
Japanese main naval bases and headquarters of naval districts: 1. Sasebo, 2. Kure, 3. Maizuru, 4. Yokosuka; Russian major naval bases on the eve of the war: A. Port Arthur, B. Vladivostok. Main naval battles before the Battle of Tsushima: 1. Naval Attack on Port Arthur (8–9 February 1904), 2. Battle of Chemulpo (9 February 1904), 3. Battle of the Yellow Sea (10 August 1904). 4. Battle of the Korea Strait (14 August 1904). Main railroads: 1. Chinese Eastern Railway, 2. South Manchuria Railway.

Figure 3. The importance of mastering the seas: Japanese troops marching in the Korean capital, Seoul, following their landing in the nearby port of Chemulpo, February 1904

Fleet sailed for the shores of Korea. Appointed commander only six weeks earlier, Vice Admiral Tōgō Heihachirō (1848–1934) led this large force with confidence. He was assisted by two talented and loyal officers from his native feudal domain: Vice Admiral Kamimura Hikonojō (1849–1916), the commander of the Second Fleet, with six armoured cruisers at its core, and Vice Admiral Kataoka Shichirō (1854–1920), the commander of the Third Fleet, with older cruisers. These two would also serve as his deputies in the Battle of Tsushima. Opposite the port city of Chemulpo, in the vicinity of Seoul, the force split into two. Most of the warships made for Port Arthur, while a small naval force under Rear Admiral Uryū Sotokichi (1857–1937) remained to protect the army's landing operations in Chemulpo on the night of 8 February (Figure 3).[52] At Port Arthur, during the same night, 10 Japanese destroyers slipped into the naval roadstead and under the cover of dense fog attacked the Russian warships anchored there with torpedoes.[53] This first large torpedo assault in naval history ended with only moderate damage inflicted, and a subsequent naval bombardment by the Japanese battleships achieved even less.[54] Back in Korea, and on the following morning, First Army troops seized control of Seoul, whereas Uryū's naval force demanded that the Russian naval detachment in Chemulpo exit the neutral port. Following a short engagement outside the harbour, known as the Battle of Chemulpo, the Russian cruiser *Variag* and the gunvessel

Koreets limped to the port.[55] Their crews then scuttled the vessels so they could not fall into Japanese hands.[56]

Despite his initial limited success, especially of Port Arthur, Tōgō would remain the commander in chief of the Combined Fleet throughout the entire war. In this capacity, he would become one of the two main protagonists of the Battle of Tsushima, more than 15 months later. Born into a samurai-class family in the Satsuma domain, from where many of the leading figures of the young Japanese navy came, this 56-year-old officer possessed extensive experience.[57] At 16 he had already taken part in the defence of his city, Kagoshima, against a British naval bombardment and saw combat against shogunal forces as a gunnery officer five years later. After the Meiji Restoration, he joined the new IJN as a cadet and was sent to Britain as a naval student in 1871. On his return to Japan six years later, the 29-year-old Tōgō rose quickly and reached the rank of captain within nine years. During this period, he commanded various warships, but was almost forced into retirement due to poor health. With the hostilities against China looming, he won command of a cruiser and soon was involved in sinking the British transport *Kowshing* en route to Korea—a controversial act that precipitated the First Sino-Japanese War.[58] Subsequently, Tōgō participated in the naval Battle of the Yalu River in 1894, and was promoted to rear admiral by the end of that war. Appointed commander of the Readiness Fleet a short while later, his fame was beginning to spread even beyond Japan.[59] Almost a decade later, this reticent officer was considered not only highly competent but also blessed. Luck was not a crucial factor in Tōgō's war plans but it would certainly be on his side.[60] In spite of these positive attributes, Tōgō had never been the most powerful figure in the IJN nor would be. With the death of the ex-Navy Minister Saigō Jūdō (Saigō Tsugumichi; 1843–1902) in 1902, the true leader became the new minister, Vice Admiral Yamamoto Gonnohyōe (1852–1933), and it was he who appointed Tōgō, four years his senior, as commander-in-chief of the Combined Fleet.[61] In his position as Navy Minister, the former would back the latter throughout the coming war and would also remain the leader of the navy after the conflict.

On 10 February, Japan formally declared war on Russia, whereupon a fierce nineteen-month clash began. On land, Japan had the upper hand right from the outset and its forces occupied the entire Korean Peninsula with virtually no opposition during the first two months of the war.[62] While Russia hoped its foe would be content with this territory, Japan was determined to cross the Yalu River and invade Manchuria. The Battle of the Yalu in May 1904 marked the first time in the modern era where an Asian force overcame a European force in a full-scale clash.[63] The psychological impact of this defeat on the Russian land forces was so great that some writers have viewed it in retrospect as the decisive land battle of the war. Within a month of crossing the Yalu River, four Japanese armies landed successively along the southern coast of the Liaodong Peninsula, where they chose the hills of Nanshan as the place to cut off the garrison in Port Arthur from the rest of the Russian Manchurian Army in the north. Following its victory at the Battle of Nanshan in May, the Third Army under General Nogi Maresuke began to lay siege to Port Arthur while the remaining Japanese forces turned northward en route to the city of Liaoyang.[64]

During the first six months of the war, the Port Arthur Squadron remained a 'fleet in being'.[65] While it hardly left the port, the squadron posed a constant threat to Japan's control of the seas and its capacity to maintain land forces on the front. Unable to annihilate the fleet in the harbour, during the first months of the war the IJN attempted in vain to impose a naval blockade using no less than 21 blockships.[66] It also carried out mining operations that led to the sinking of the Russian flagship *Petropavlovsk* on 13 April (Figure 4). On board this battleship was Vice Admiral Stepan Makarov (1849–1904), the illustrious and recently appointed commander of the Pacific Fleet on the first and last time he left to face the Japanese.[67] One month later, the Russians exacted retribution in a similar operation that caused the IJN to lose two of its six battleships within a single day.[68] The shock

Figure 4. The blockade of Port Arthur: Admiral Makarov's flagship, the battle-ship *Petropavlovsk*, strikes a mine, 13 April 1904

made Tōgō even more prudent and less aggressive. But then, on 10 August 1904, he received a rare chance to face the Port Arthur Squadron and finally master the naval arena. With the Japanese land siege of Port Arthur intensifying, the squadron, including six battle-ships, six cruisers, and 14 destroyers, were ordered to find safe haven in Vladivostok. Shortly after noon, Tōgō, by now a 'full' admiral, sighted his opponents and led the Combined Fleet to intercept them.

The Battle of the Yellow Sea was the largest naval engagement of the war until the Battle of Tsushima, but it was not a 'great' battle.[69] As the Japanese moved in, it became a chase in which the commander of the Pacific Fleet, Rear Admiral Vilgelm Vitgeft (1847–1904), was able to evade Tōgō's manoeuvres, and especially his attempt to cross the Russian T. In this rarely successful tactic, a line of warships crosses in front of a line of enemy ships in a manner that allows it to bring all its guns to bear, usually concentrating on the leading enemy ship, while only receiving fire from the enemy's forward guns. As the chase

Figure 5. The battle of the Yellow Sea: warships of the IJN 1st Battle Division fire at the escaping Russian ships (the battleship *Shikishima* in front), 10 August 1904

continued, both sides kept using their big guns from range of as much as 13,000 metres, but their occasional hits did little to stop each other (Figure 5). But then, after more than five hours of constant engagement and as sunset was approaching, a 305-millimetre salvo (with each shell weighing 386 kilograms) hit the Russian flagship *Tsesarevich* and killed Vitgeft instantly. With her helm jammed, the ship started to turn in circles and the warships behind her turned back immediately and abandoned her. During the night these warships were able to escape the 74 torpedoes launched by Japanese light vessels and return safely to Port Arthur.[70] Miraculously, the *Tsesarevich* too extricated herself and reached a safe haven in the German port of Kiaochow (present-day Jiaozhou) in north-east China, where she was interned until the end of the war.[71]

In retrospect, the battle was a strategic victory for Japan, since the decision to return to the besieged port consigned the Port Arthur Squadron to slow expiration without honour. Tactically, however, the Combined Fleet failed to achieve its mission. Notwithstanding the sudden stroke of luck it enjoyed, Tōgō's caution prevented his force from annihilating its foe. Instead, it allowed the Russian squadron to retain its role as a 'fleet in being'. It was a bitter lesson the Japanese admiral would not forget. Four days later, on 14 August, the IJN managed to win the small but important Battle of Ulsan. At this point, the IJN was at last able to free itself from the menace posed by the Russian Vladivostok Independent Cruiser Squadron. During the previous months, this three-ship unit had daringly sunk 15 transports and succeeded in evading interception. But its luck ran out. Unaware of the fate of the Port Arthur Squadron, its commander, Rear Admiral Karl Iessen, decided to steam south and assist the coming fleet. Off Ulsan, in the Korea Strait, the Second Fleet under the command of Kamimura sighted the cruisers and succeeded in sinking one of them and thus terminating the exploits of this unit until the end of the war.[72] Thereafter, the Japanese actions continued undisturbed by any Russian naval intervention until the arrival of the Baltic Fleet nine months later.

In the meantime, the land campaign intensified. On 25 August 1904, the two armies met in the Battle of Liaoyang—the biggest land engagement so far, with close to 300,000 combatants on both sides. It was here that Kuropatkin, now in his capacity as the commander-in-chief of the Russian Manchurian Army, had set up a new defence line during his 'planned withdrawal' up the Liaodong Peninsula. The battle was not conclusive and ended in a Russian retreat. About a month later, another large-scale land battle broke out near the Sha River (Shaho) after which the Russian line reformed just south of Mukden. After the Battle of the Yellow Sea, the Japanese determination to take Port Arthur at all costs resulted in one of the greatest sieges in history. Altogether, this siege lasted about seven months and once the fort surrendered on 2 January 1905, both sides had over 100,000 casualties.[73] Once Port Arthur fell, the IJN took hold of all the warships in port, including five semi-sunken battleships (Figure 6). It would take many months, however, before these ships could be re-commissioned under a Japanese flag.

Figure 6. The end of the Pacific Fleet: semi-sunken Russian warships in the harbour of Port Arthur shortly after it fell into Japanese hands, January 1905

Following the takeover of the fort, the Third Army headed north for the final major land engagement and the largest single battle of the Russo-Japanese War. Once near the city of Mukden, it joined the main Japanese land forces preparing for a decisive confrontation against the Russian Manchurian Army. The two deeply entrenched forces faced each other for several months, but the Russians were the first to move. Between 25 and 29 January 1905, the two sides engaged briefly in the Battle of Sandepu, which ended in great losses but without significant advances by either side. During the interlude, both forces were reinforced and then redeployed in Mukden on 23 February. Despite the great expectations and the horrific casualties on both sides, this, at its time the largest engagement in military history, ended on 10 March, in another Russian retreat.[74] By then, the Japanese forces lacked additional human resources, and in Tokyo the government began to seek an end to the conflict through negotiation with greater earnest. As war ground to a halt, the world turned its eyes back to the naval arena. The Baltic Fleet was on its way to the Japanese home islands.

The Voyage of the Baltic Fleet

The Battle of Tsushima cannot be separated from the epic voyage of the Baltic Fleet, nor can it be understood without it. The departure of the Russian Fleet for Asia in October 1904 was a game changer. It could determine the fate of the war, and the struggle in its naval arena in particular. By March 1905, the cowardly flight of the Port Arthur Squadron back to its base seven months earlier appeared to be an almost pyrrhic victory for Japan. Had Tōgō annihilated the squadron, Japan might have refrained from the costly takeover of the naval base by abandoning its siege and concentrating its land forces to the north whereas Russia might not have sent reinforcements to save its besieged fleet.[75] But that was not the case. By autumn 1904, the IJN faced a new danger, as the Baltic Fleet, now renamed the Second Pacific Squadron, began its voyage towards the shores of Japan. The initial decision to dispatch the fleet to East Asia was made in June 1904, when the Japanese Third Army began to close in on the fortress of Port Arthur and the vulnerability of warships in the port became evident. The fleet's first units did not depart before 11 October, however.[76] By the time the fort surrendered in January 1905, most of the warships had already rounded the Cape of Good Hope. Nonetheless, their epic voyage continued for an additional five months until they approached the Tsushima Strait, while attracting extraordinary international attention.[77] Even before the fleet's departure, the world's press and naval observers expected it to end in a great battle with the Japanese navy, a clash that might bring the war to an end (Figure 7).

The decision to dispatch the Baltic Fleet was followed by the appointment of Vice Admiral Zinoviĭ Rozhestvenskiĭ (1848–1909) as its commanding officer. He was not the IRN's first choice for the job, but, unlike a few of his superiors, he did not refuse the nomination.[78] Despite being born in the same year as Tōgō, his background and course of life were strikingly different.[79] The son of a physician from

Figure 7. Wild speculations: even before its departure, the voyage of the Baltic Fleet raised high, at times prophetic, expectations in the world press, as seen in this cartoon published in an American daily

the capital St Petersburg, he joined the IRN as a cadet at the age of 17 and, after graduating from the Naval Cadet Corps, began his service as a gunnery officer. He was transferred to the Black Sea Fleet shortly before the outbreak of the Russo-Turkish War of 1877–8, in which the

28-year-old Rozhestvenskiĭ participated occasionally in cruising raids against Ottoman warships. During one such raid, he was credited with saving an armed steamer engaged in a lethal encounter with a superior Ottoman adversary.[80] Unlike his Japanese counterpart, however, this meagre combat experience remained Rozhestvenskiĭ's last. In the following years, he became the commander of a few warships, held appointments as a naval attaché, and gained extensive experience. But at the age of 50, and despite his striking appearance—his 'piercing black eyes' and well-trimmed beard, he hardly seemed destined for greatness.[81] Nevertheless, fate had its own plans for Rozhestvenskiĭ. His pathway to greatness emerged almost overnight, when he was appointed to direct a Russian–German naval review in July 1902. With the tsar and Kaiser Wilhelm II on board his ship, his gunnery performance impressed the German guest and Nicholas's gratitude was readily forthcoming.[82] He was appointed Chief of the Naval General Staff several months later, and promoted to vice admiral in September 1904. Incredibly, this unremarkable officer, who had never been in charge of more than a single ship at sea, was to lead the Baltic Fleet in its most fateful test ever.

After lengthy preparations, the Baltic Fleet left Kronstadt on 30 August 1904 and began manoeuvres in the Baltic Sea. Rozhestvenskiĭ had little say in the composition of his fleet and, unlike Tōgō's deputies, his two flag officers showed no great promise either. His second-in-command, Dmitrii von Felkerzam (1846–1905), had served with him twice before but was now seriously ill, whereas the eminence of the other officer, Oskar Enkvist (1849–1912), stemmed mostly from his family ties: he was Navy Minister Fedor Avelan's (1839–1916) cousin and protégé.[83] During the following six weeks, Tsar Nicholas II vacillated over whether or not to dispatch the fleet; his indecisiveness peaked during October when he changed his mind three times. Finally, he reviewed the armada at the port of Reval (present-day Tallinn, Estonia) and bade it farewell on 10 October 1904 (Figure 8). On the next day, the force of 42 warships and some 12,000 officers and sailors left for Libau (present-day Liepāja, Latvia), and, after

Figure 8. Tsar Nicholas II on board the cruiser *Svetlana* reviewing the Baltic Fleet before its departure from Reval, 10 October 1904

coaling there, departed on a voyage of about 33,000 kilometres (17,800 miles) on 15 October.[84]

Tensions within the fleet rose even before it crossed the strait into the North Sea. Nonsensical rumours of an impending ambush by Japanese torpedo boats triggered a full alert.[85] When the fleet reached the Dogger Bank on the night of 21 October 1904, the Russian warships opened fire on a number of identified vessels and even hit each other.[86] In the morning, the enemy turned out to be British fishing boats and, apart from the sheer embarrassment of sinking one trawler and damaging another five, the matter nearly escalated into an international conflict with Britain.[87] Only the patience and determination of British Prime Minister Arthur Balfour and Foreign Secretary Lord Lansdowne could calm the public outcry for revenge, and the incident was eventually resolved at the International Court in the Hague. In the following weeks, Rozhestvenskiĭ's critical hurdle was logistic. He needed at least 3,000 tons of coal a day but was unable, according to international law, to stop at neutral ports. To Russia's chagrin, the French government had refused to supply the colliers necessary for the voyage or even to let the Russians stop at Metropolitan France, but was persuaded eventually to allow the fleet to anchor briefly at a number of ports in its colonies.[88] Instead, Russia resorted to the services of a German company, the Hamburg–Amerika Line, which leased it scores of colliers for the transport of coal.[89]

The Russian armada was granted their first refuelling at the Spanish port of Vigo and split up at the next stop in Tangier (Map 2). Five of the older and least reliable warships, along with several transports, took the shorter route through the Suez Canal under the command of Rear Admiral Dmitriĭ von Felkerzam while the remaining force steamed southward to circumnavigate Africa. The formal reasoning was the canal's insufficient depth, but the Russians were actually afraid that the British would not maintain their neutrality and seize the ships. On 20 November, the first of two detachments intended to reinforce the armada left Libau under the command of Captain Leonid Dobrotvorskiĭ. Comprising 10 ships and led by the two new cruisers *Oleg* and *Izumrud*, this force took the short route via the Suez Canal. The main force headed undisturbed to Dakar, refuelled there, and then reached Gabon on 1 December, Great Fish Bay six days later, and Angra Pequena in German South West Africa on 16 December. The armada departed on the following day, rounded the Cape of Good Hope, and reached Sainte-Marie Island (present-day Nosy Boraha) off the eastern coast of French Madagascar, on 29 December. Three days later, Port Arthur surrendered, and upon receiving the grim news, Rozhestvenskiĭ could not but immediately understand the implications for his fleet. In fact, the entire voyage's main objective—to join the First Pacific Squadron that was trapped in the port—was no longer valid. The admiral was instructed to wait. He may have expected the fall of the fort but the new situation was certainly confusing.[90]

Despite the sudden stalemate, the tsar displayed atypical resolve. Some three weeks after Port Arthur's surrender, he sent a brief update

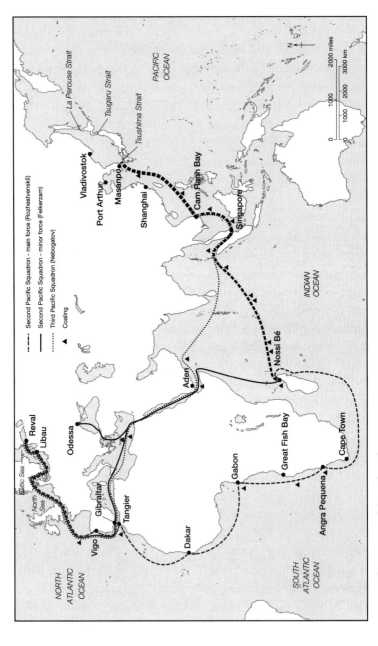

Map 2. The voyage of the Baltic Fleet

Legend:

- ---·--- Second Pacific Squadron - main force (Rozhestvenskii)
- ——— Second Pacific Squadron - minor force (Felkerzam)
- ········ Third Pacific Squadron (Nebogatov)
- ▲ Coaling

La Pérouse Strait
Tsugaru Strait
Tsushima Strait

PACIFIC
OCEAN

Vladivostok
Port Arthur
Masanpo
Shanghai
Cam Ranh Bay
Singapore

INDIAN
OCEAN

Nossi Bé

Odessa

Reval
Libau
Baltic Sea
North Sea

Gibraltar
Tangier
Vigo

Aden

Gabon

Great Fish Bay

Cape Town

Angra Pequena

Dakar

NORTH
ATLANTIC
OCEAN

SOUTH
ATLANTIC
OCEAN

N

2000 miles
3000 km
1000
2000
1000
0

to Rozhestvenskiĭ about his objectives. 'Your mission,' he stated plainly, 'is *not* to reach Vladivostok with several ships, but to *master* the Sea of Japan.'[91] This drastic change of plans forced the admiral to wait in Madagascar. Apart from the urgent need for repairs and some complications in coal supply, his armada required reinforcement to fulfil its new objectives.[92] Earlier, on 9 January 1905, Rozhestvenskiĭ's armada reached Nossi Bé Island (present-day Nosy Be), off the northern coast of Madagascar, where it met Felkerzam's detachment. On 14 February, the entire force was joined by Dobrotvorskiĭ's small detachment too, but the main reinforcement, under the command of Rear Admiral Nikolai Nebogatov (1849–1922), was still in the Baltic Sea. This force, now called the Third Pacific Squadron, finally left Libau only on the next day. Its late departure would delay the Baltic Fleet's arrival in East Asian waters by at least six weeks.[93] While dawdling in the tropical heat, morale among the crews sagged further and the admiral shut himself away.[94] Rozhestvenskiĭ's own anger stemmed mostly from the decision to send him this new reinforcement and so prevent him from proceeding. He believed this force of old and slow warships, despite its additional firepower, would be of no use in the ensuing clash.

Unknown to Rozhestvenskiĭ, Nebogatov would assume an important role in the coming months. Born into the family of a naval officer in the vicinity of St Petersburg, his career within the Baltic Fleet advanced slowly and he only received his first command, of a small gunvessel, at the late age of 39. In subsequent years, Nebogatov was granted the successive command of three cruisers and shortly before the war was appointed chief of the Black Sea Fleet's Training Unit. He was considered an experienced and sensible naval officer as well as excellent executive.[95] The campaign to send reinforcements under his command began in October 1904 and was orchestrated by Commander (Captain 2nd rank) Nikolai Klado (1862–1919) with the support of the press and some leading IRN figures.[96] As Rozhestvenskiĭ correctly assumed, the force was to include the obsolete battleship *Imperator Nikolai I* as a flagship, the three sluggish *Admiral Ushakov*-class coastal defence battleships, the old cruiser *Vladimir Monomakh*, and seven auxiliary vessels.[97] However, with the Black Sea Fleet confined to its sea and the battleship *Slava* still under construction, this assortment of outdated warships was the utmost the IRN could muster.[98]

For Japan, the delay was highly advantageous. This was the first time since the outbreak of the war, and in fact since early 1905, that it did not face any immediate naval risk. It was also an opportunity to maintain and repair its ships after almost a year of continuous use.[99] But the euphoria was temporary, since every Japanese was aware of the slow but constant eastward advance of the Baltic Fleet. Indeed, a network of Japanese agents reported its whereabouts throughout its entire course.[100] As early as December, Tōgō met Navy Minister Yamamoto and Navy Chief of Staff Itō Sukeyuki (1843–1914) in an attempt to implement measures against the advancing enemy. Their main concerns were providing early warning and tools for interception. To this end, the navy intended to deploy a force of auxiliary ships in the Korea Strait and a flotilla of cruisers in the Tsugaru Strait, while patrols were dispatched to the seas south of Japan to search for clandestine enemy vessels serving as an advance guard. The main fighting units were required to increase their readiness by practising communications, torpedo attacks, and especially gunnery on an almost daily basis.[101] Tōgō also chose Jinhae [Chinhae] Bay, on the southern coast of the Korean Peninsula between the port towns of Masanpo (present-day Changwon) and Busan, as the anchorage of his Combined Fleet.[102] Fearing that the Russians might seize a base off the Chinese coast and use it to launch their attack, this anchorage seemed the best choice for keeping the fleet on permanent alert.[103]

Lingering in Madagascar for more than two months, Rozhestvenskiĭ became increasingly impatient. Eventually, and despite the unequivocal instructions to wait for Nebogatov's squadron, he left for Singapore on 16 March 1905.[104] The huge Russian armada passed by this British port in front of thousands of onlookers on 8 April 1905, and six days later it anchored in Cam Ranh Bay (present-day Vietnam). In this last stop before the battle, and while benefiting from the fleeting benevolence of the French authorities, Rozhestvenskiĭ kept waiting for Nebogatov, whose force had passed through the Suez Canal and was proceeding to the Strait of Malacca.[105] During the long stay at this last stop before battle, morale in the Second Pacific Squadron was as low as it had ever been and a mutiny broke out on the battleship *Orël* (*Oryol*).[106] In Japan, the Russian stay off the Indochinese coast led to a storm of anti-French demonstrations and to mounting diplomatic pressure. Paris eventually capitulated and the Russian armada was requested to leave. This became possible on 9 May when the Third Pacific Squadron finally joined the main force. Upon sighting its five ships, one of the waiting officers noted that 'everyone is in a great state of excitement, and rushes to the bridge'.[107] They were aware that the ships were relatively old but their 17 big 229–305-millimetre guns seemed a veritable reinforcement for the coming battle, one that more than adequately compensated for their slow speed.[108]

Plans and the Balance of Power on the Eve of the Battle

By the spring of 1905, the IJN was ready for its imminent clash with the Baltic Fleet. Its strategy and the minute tactics of engagement were conceived and practised repeatedly. Both were the brainchild of Lieutenant Commander Akiyama Saneyuki (1868–1918), a staff officer of the First Fleet now in charge of the Combined Fleet's operational planning. Akiyama himself was a maverick officer.[109] Unable to gain entry to the US Naval War College at Newport, he accepted the advice of Alfred Thayer Mahan and undertook private study. During the Spanish–American War of 1898, for example, he observed naval operations against the Spanish navy with the fleet staff of the North Atlantic Squadron, and now made good use of his broad experience and knowledge in planning operations against Russia. In terms of overall strategy, he planned a two-day battle in which the fleet would defend the southern entryways to the Japanese archipelago while engaging the Russian warships in order to prevent them from reaching Vladivostok. To this end, Akiyama outlined a seven-stage plan of attrition that relied on the daylight engagement of capital ships and on night assaults by the lighter vessels that would begin with the interception of the Russian armada as it approached Japan and ending a day later with its annihilation.[110]

Akiyama completed the Combined Fleet Battle Plan (Jpn. *Rengō kantai sensaku*) in the course of 1903. The plan did not predict the arrival of the Baltic Fleet but aimed broadly against the approach of any large enemy unit, and the Russian Pacific Fleet in particular. Specifically, it defined the objectives and formation of each unit in the fleet along with the key tactics to be used in battle. A fundamental facet of these tactics was the manoeuvre known as 'Crossing the T'. However, the inability to sustain it over time made Akiyama devise a modified formation known as the L-tactic. In this manoeuvre, the enemy column was 'scissored' by two forces.[111] On 10 May 1905, Akiyama submitted a revision to the plan, reflecting the experience of the war and especially of the Battle of the Yellow Sea, in which the Russian force escaped rather than engaged. It was still based on the same tactics but made the L-tactic less dominant. Along with a new emphasis on engagement on a parallel course, he devised the use of traps consisting of four mines attached to 100-metre rope segments. These were to be laid before the oncoming enemy ships by torpedo boats and destroyers upon the onset of the main fleet battle.[112]

The entire Baltic Fleet, too, appeared to be ready at last. Before departing north-eastward, the admirals of the two Russian forces met for the first and last time before the battle. Their talk was brief and did not include extensive planning or definite instructions.[113] Despite Rozhestvenskii's disparagement, Nebogatov had displayed true grit during his voyage, making it without incident in just 83 days. Once his ships joined the main force, the entire armada, now comprising 38 vessels, made its final preparations to leave. The world, too, was waiting for this move. The Russian force's position was no secret, since the voyage received constant coverage by the international press. Japan also made use of its own network of military intelligence along the Russian route, but the IJN did not know the most critical information, namely the Russians' exact course, at this climactic moment. Tōgō and Akiyama assumed that their goal was Vladivostok and that they would accordingly sail the shortest course through the Tsushima Strait. Further to this line of thought, the Japanese planned to dispatch a multitude of ships to locate the Russians as they approached the strait. Rozhestvenskiĭ, too, engaged in an assessment of the pros and cons of the three passages that lead to Vladivostok—the Korea, Tsugaru, and La Pérouse (Soya) Straits.

As the Japanese expected, Rozhestvenskiĭ chose to traverse the Korea Strait en route to Vladivostok. Concealed by low visibility, he chose this rather than the longer routes via the more northern passages of the narrow Tsugaru Strait or the remote and dangerous La Pérouse Strait. His exact considerations remain unknown, since he shared his plan and exact objectives with no one on board, but they seem obvious. The most important of these was the fact that any passage other than the Korea Strait was considerably longer and could nonetheless allow Tōgō's Combined Fleet to intercept the Russian ships.[114] Moreover, the death of Felkerzam from a brain haemorrhage on 24 May left Nebogatov second in command, a state of affairs he, or others, was not informed about, as Felkerzam's flagship *Osliabia* would carry his flag until her demise (Figure 9). On 26 May, a day before the battle, Tōgō was informed that six of the Russian transports had arrived in Shanghai.[115] Several days earlier, the armada had been seen in the same area—off the Saddle Islands and near the mouth of the Yangtze River. For the Japanese admiral, this was more than an indication that his gamble about the Russians' course was correct. However, the armada itself was yet to be detected and a strong feeling of uncertainty prevailed once more.[116]

As the reinforced Russian armada approached the Japanese archipelago, naval experts and the press were divided on each side's prospects. Some, such as the *Washington Times*, predicted a Russian victory. 'Togo is outnumbered', this daily newspaper announced on the day before the battle, although it qualified this by stating that 'the Russian

Figure 9. The leading commanders of the two belligerent forces: Vice Admiral Zinoviĭ Rozhestvenskiĭ (above left); Rear Admiral Nikolai Nebogatov (above right); Admiral Tōgō Heihachirō (below right); and Vice Admiral Kamimura Hikonojō (below left)

Ships are foul, and consequently slow'.[117] *The New York Times* cited a
Russian naval officer, Captain Nikolai von Essen, saying he was 'Confident Togo will lose'.[118] Indeed, the naval force under Rozhestvenskiĭ
had an overwhelming numerical advantage in battleships, which at the
time were considered the supreme and decisive vessel in any open sea
engagement, and in firepower. At the time, only battleships carried the
mighty 305-millimetre guns that had proved so effective some nine
months earlier at the Battle of the Yellow Sea.[119] In this respect, the
Baltic Fleet had eight of these versus only four in the IJN's Combined
Fleet (with an aggregate displacement of 101,446 vs. 57,510 tons). In
addition, the Russians also possessed an evident advantage in very-
large-calibre guns, a factor of decisive importance in naval battles of
the time. Rozhestvenskiĭ had 26 of the largest (305-millimetre) calibre
guns at his disposal, while Tōgō only possessed four battleships and 16
guns of the same calibre.[120] The Russian admiral had an even greater
advantage in other large-calibre (229–254-millimetre) guns: 19 vs. only
one on the Japanese side (Table 2). This Russian upper hand was
substantial and impressed naval experts as well.[121]

Odd as this may seem, many among the Russian crews were not as
impressed.[122] Their pessimism was largely subjective, but there were
also some hard facts to substantiate their feelings. Indeed, when a
comparison of the aggregate displacement of the two fleets is made,
Tōgō's Combined Fleet possessed an unmistakable edge in almost
every measure apart from battleships. It was larger in the aggregate
displacement of all of its warships (218,161 tons vs. 165,266 tons for the
Baltic Fleet), of its warships larger than destroyers (194,963 vs. 161,964
tons), and of its first-line capital ships (130,849 vs. 106,309 tons).[123] By
the same token, the Combined Fleet possessed a definite advantage in
the number of the powerful armoured cruisers, second only to battleships (nine vs. three). It also had many more protected cruisers (14 vs.
five) and lighter warships, such as destroyers (21 vs. nine) and torpedo
boats in particular (39 vs. none). During night attacks, these two types
of small vessels could be used to hassle large warships and even deliver
them a death blow while relying on their numerous torpedo launchers

Table 2. The naval balance between the two forces at the outset of the Battle of Tsushima, 27 May 1905

Warships[a]	IJN Combined Fleet	IRN Baltic Fleet
Battleships	4	8
Coastal defence/obsolete battleships	2	3
Armoured Cruisers	9	3
Protected Cruisers	14	5
Destroyers	21	9
Torpedo Boats	39+	0
Unprotected Cruisers/Gunboats	9+	1
Auxiliary Ships	9+	9
Total number of warships	98+	29
Total number of vessels	107+	38
Aggregate displacement (all ships)	265,000t	229,000t
Aggregate displacement (warships)	218,000t	165,000t
Crews on board the vessels	c.16,000	c.14,000
Armament[b]		
Very heavy (305–320-millimetre) guns	16 (23)	26
Heavy (229–254-millimetre) guns	1 (7)	19
Medium (203-millimetre) guns	30 (34)	14
Lighter (120–152-millimetre) guns	174 (271)	139
Torpedo launchers	153 (246)	25 (99)

Notes: [a] The numbers for the IJN include those ships deployed in the arena of the battle, whereas the + sign indicates that additional ships were available elsewhere. [b] The numbers represent the armament of the warships fighting in the initial engagement (the 1st and 2nd Battle Divisions in the IJN) whereas the numbers in parentheses represent the armament of the entire force. As for torpedo launchers, the numbers represent those aboard destroyers and torpedo boats, whereas the number in parentheses represents the launchers in the entire force.

Sources: [a] The figure for personnel was calculated based on JACAR, 'Meiji 37-8 nen gokuhi kaisen-shi', Section II, 5:70–5. For a slightly larger figure (14,546 men) for the IRN, see Kostenko, Na 'Orle', 490. [b] Kowner, *Historical Dictionary*, passim.

(153 vs. 25 for the Baltic Fleet). In terms of armament, the Japanese had a considerable advantage in the number of medium-calibre (203-millimetre) guns and small-calibre (120–152-millimetre) guns: 30 vs. 14 and 174 vs. 139, respectively.

Another important advantage of the Combined Fleet was its faster speed: at least 15 knots as opposed to the slowest Russian battleship's 12 knots. Furthermore, the Russian force was hampered by its auxiliary ships, and could not steam faster than 9–10 knots if sailing in a single group.[124] Even if we exclude the auxiliary vessels, the Japanese warships were still of greater uniformity and of a higher quality of construction. In terms of human resources, the Japanese crews seemed to exhibit greater motivation and fighting spirit, and to benefit from better training and considerable battle experience, although it was difficult to quantify the exact extent of this difference.[125] On board the Russian ships, quite a few of the crews were sick, either physically or mentally, and the entire fleet trained occasionally in manoeuvres but only once in artillery.[126] At the same time, and in the case of defeat, even partial, the IJN had no means of obtaining reinforcements or replacing its ships, while the IRN could still theoretically muster some additional ships. Ironically, this vital importance of a victory to Japan's war efforts as a whole would turn into one of its biggest assets.

2

The Battle

The tension in both fleets was extremely high on the night of 26–7 May 1905. For weeks, the world and the belligerents had been anticipating a titanic clash with unfounded rumours abounding.[1] As the Russian armada was steaming slowly north-east towards the Korea Strait, its crew and senior officers were acutely aware of the significance of this passage. The coming day was crucial—the culmination of their entire voyage. It was also the ninth anniversary of the tsar's coronation and a unique opportunity to bestow a much-expected victory upon this ruler. Winning the battle could shift the balance of power radically towards Russia, perhaps even end the long war. On the Japanese side, the strain was all the more severe, as the price of defeat could be prohibitively greater than the benefits of victory. Waiting with his main fleet in anchorage in Jinhae Bay, Admiral Tōgō Heihachirō, the commander of the Combined Fleet, was on full alert. Early in the morning of 26 May, he was informed that a number of Russian auxiliary vessels had been seen off Shanghai.[2] A day earlier, Vice Admiral Zinoviĭ Rozhestvenskiĭ had bade farewell to six of his transports in an attempt to free his armada from their vulnerability. He did keep, however, nine other auxiliary vessels, among them the *Orël* and the *Kostroma*, the first hospital ships the Red Cross Society had ever sent with a fighting fleet.[3] For Tōgō, nonetheless, this much-anticipated news was marvellous since it indicated that the Russians were near and probably heading in his direction.

The Japanese admiral had at his disposal some 70 vessels with which to cover the entire area that separates western Japan from the

Korean archipelago. Their first patrol line was situated along the 180-kilometre- (98-mile-) wide passage between the Goto archipelago on the Japanese side and Jeju (Quelpart) Island on the Korean side. Further to the north, near Tsushima Island, there was a second line, in case the Russians somehow succeeded in eluding the first. That night, four Japanese auxiliary cruisers patrolled in the first line, two cruisers in the second line to the north, and another four cruisers were on standby in the vicinity of the Goto islands.[4] Still, a heavy fog covered the seas and the location of the Russian armada had remained unknown for the past few days.[5] As the Russian warships advanced, Tōgō, along with the entire Combined Fleet, was aching for a clue as to their where-abouts and was losing his confidence with every passing moment.[6]

Phase I. Interception

The coveted signal arrived later that night, and the long confusion about the Baltic Fleet's location was finally cleared up. The first vessel to sight a harbinger of the Russian Armada, although without con-firming its identity yet, was the auxiliary cruiser *Shinano-maru* at 2.45 a.m., 27 May 1905. Requisitioned by the IJN as the war began, this largest cargo ship of the Nippon Yūsen Company, armed now with two 152-millimetre guns, had been committed to the search (Map 3). It took almost another two hours before the liaison officer on board, and practically the ship's commander, Captain Narukawa Hakaru,[7] could verify the identity of the silhouette: it was the white-coloured hospital ship *Orël*.[8] At around 4.45 a.m., after catching sight of a number of additional Russian warships, Narukawa was certain, and so reported the armada's location and course using a Japanese-made radiotele-graph transmitter ('Enemy sighted at square 203').[9] It was an epoch-making message, the first interception transmitted wirelessly in naval combat history.[10] Relayed through the cruiser *Itsukushima*, the flagship of the Third Fleet moored at Tsushima Island, the message reached Tōgō shortly after 5.00 a.m.[11] Although the *Shinano-maru*'s crew miscalculated the location slightly and soon lost contact with the

Map 3. The interception of the Baltic Fleet, early morning, 27 May 1905

Notes: A fifth vigilance or patrol line (Jpn. *keikaisen*) was set further in the north, connecting Cape Jizo (near the city of Matsue) on the Japanese coast, the Liancourt Rocks, and the Korean coast. For a map of the entire network of vigilance lines, see Inaba, *Baruchikku kantai*, 214.

large target due to the morning mist, the Japanese admiral did not require more than this brief alert.[12]

Tōgō was at last certain that the Russians were going where he had expected them to go and would soon cross the eastern passage of the Korea Strait, known as the Tsushima Strait. At 6.30 a.m., he led the main force of the Combined Fleet out of its anchorage in Jinhae Bay to face the advancing armada. He headed first eastward and then south-eastward at 14 knots (Figure 10). It would not be long before the

Figure 10. The 1st Battle Division of the Japanese Combined Fleet sails to its ultimate test, morning, 27 May 1905

admiral transmitted his famous albeit cryptic message, drafted by Commander Akiyama Saneyuki, which ended in the sentence: 'Today's weather is fine but the waves are high.'[13] In IJN headquarters, and in later years among the Japanese public as a whole, this was understood as a poetic and glowing description of the tactical conditions.[14] In reality, it was a succinct weather report. But as the fog had just lifted, and the winds were strong and the sea fairly high, the small torpedo boats could not keep up with the larger warships, and so Tōgō ordered them to find shelter in Takeshiki naval base in the middle of Tsushima and wait for a better sea.[15] As it transpired, he was going to need these boats.

By early morning, the Russian armada was still some 70 miles away from the Japanese main force. It sailed in a wedge formation made up of two main columns and a scout division. The starboard column (under the direct command of Rozhestvenskiĭ himself) incorporated the fleet's principal force: the battleships *Kniaz Suvorov*, *Imperator Aleksandr III*, *Borodino*, *Orël*, *Osliabia*, *Sissoi Velikiĭ*, and *Navarin*, and the armoured cruiser *Admiral Nakhimov*; while the port column (under Rear Admiral Nikolai Nebogatov) was made up of the battleship

Imperator Nikolai I, the three coastal-defence battleships, *General Admiral Graf Apraksin*, and *Admiral Seniavin*, and *Admiral Ushakov*, the two armoured cruisers *Dmitriĭ Donskoi* and *Vladimir Monomakh*, and the two protected cruisers *Oleg* and *Aurora* (under the command of Rear Admiral Oskar Enkvist).[16] The scout division, in turn, consisted of the protected cruiser *Svetlana*, the armed yacht *Almaz*, and the auxiliary cruiser *Ural*. In addition, and on either side of the two main columns' leading ship, there was a small scout detachment headed by protected cruisers, the *Zhemchug* and *Izumrud*, each followed by two destroyers. Finally, and behind this large formation, were eight auxiliary ships: four transports, two repair tugs, and two hospital ships. Altogether, this force comprised 38 vessels, of which 29 were warships (see Appendix).[17]

Rozhestvenskiĭ became aware that his force had been detected at around 5.00 a.m. One hour later, he ordered his scout division to move back to the rear in order to protect the auxiliary ships. From this point onwards, sightings of Japanese warships became more frequent. At 06.45, his force noted the presence of a distant vessel on the starboard beam, soon recognized as the Japanese cruiser *Izumi*; shortly after 8.00 a.m., it sighted four Japanese cruisers of the Third Fleet on the port bow; and then, two hours later, another four light cruisers of the 4th Battle Division of the Second Fleet in the same direction.[18] What Rozhestvenskiĭ did not yet know at this point was that he was steaming on a collision course towards Tōgō's main force.[19] At 9.30 a. m. the Russian admiral ordered his ships to move into battle formation, and so most of them regrouped into a single column. An hour later, the force was ready for battle and the first exchange of fire occurred at 11.20 a.m. It was apparently a mistake. The battleship *Orël* fired an 'accidental shot', as it was called, at the shadowing Japanese cruisers on the horizon, which, in turn, responded for a moment. As other Russian warships joined in, it took Rozhestvenskiĭ a few minutes to stop the entire force from wasting its ammunition.[20]

One hour later, the Russian admiral was still oblivious to the presence of the main Japanese force. As he sailed onwards at a speed of 9–10 knots, he was fully aware, however, that a number of Japanese warships were following his fleet and that his whereabouts were known to the enemy.[21] By noon, the Russian formation began to cross the Tsushima Strait west of the island of Iki. It was still shadowed by the four Japanese protected cruisers of the Third Fleet, which reported the enemy's location intermittently. Watching the horizon from the bridge of his battleship *Mikasa*, Tōgō intended to use the 1st Battle Division, made up of the six strongest Japanese warships (the four battleships, the *Mikasa*, *Shikishima*, *Fuji*, and *Asahi*, and two armoured cruisers, the *Kasuga* and *Nisshin*), as his vanguard. Abandoning the idea of attack by torpedo boats, he was prepared now to use this division to deliver the initial blow to the advancing Russians. Leading the six warships south-eastward into a position ahead of the estimated enemy course, the Japanese admiral then turned sharply west to position himself while the enemy approached (Map 4).

At 12.40 p.m., and at a distance of some 28 kilometres (15 miles) from Tōgō's main force, Rozhestvenskiĭ changed the formation of his fleet for the second time. Fearing it might face an attack by torpedo boats or, worse, hit floating mines, he ordered his ships once again to deploy in two columns. The eastern column comprised seven of the fleet's eight battleships, led by the *Kniaz Suvorov*, *Imperator Aleksandr III*, *Borodino*, and *Orël*, as well as a cruiser, while the secondary column, under Nebogatov's command, moved on a parallel course and included all the other vessels led by the battleship *Osliabia*. The Russians sighted Tōgō's main force at around 1.15 p.m. while it was sailing west into the haze. Intending to face the weaker Russian column first, Tōgō ordered his main column to turn south at 1.31 p.m. Eight minutes later, the Japanese column emerged out of the haze, and the two main forces could at last see each other clearly at a distance of about 15–16 kilometres (8–9 miles). Surprised at the sight of the Japanese main force, Rozhestvenskiĭ ordered his two columns to reunite so as to allow all the ships at the head of the column to use their guns without risking each other.

Map 4. Phase I of the battle, 27 May 1905

It was at this moment, at 1.38 p.m., that Tōgō began to display his tactical genius. He instantly ordered his 1st Battle Division to head north-west and then north and thereby withdraw from the Russians. By so doing, he allowed his enemy to maintain its course while entering his trap. At 1.55 p.m., the Japanese admiral turned west at a battle speed of 15 knots to gain even further room. Despite steaming away, Tōgō knew the battle was impending and, under Akiyama's instigation, decided to share his view of the gravity of the moment with the crews of his entire battle division. In an iconic gesture, he ordered the unfurling of the Z flag, following Nelson's celebrated

Figure 11. Admiral Tōgō standing on the bridge of his flagship, the battleship *Mikasa*, during the early phase of the battle, surrounded by his staff officers with the Z flag being hoisted above

signal at the opening of the Battle of Trafalgar. Flown alone, this four-coloured flag meant 'The fate of the Empire rests on the outcome of this one battle; let each man do his utmost' (Figure 11).[22] The crews greeted the flag with excitement. Many of them sensed that their performance in the coming hour would determine the battle and perhaps the war as a whole, but it was not a time for brooding, as the first engagement between the two fleets was now a matter of minutes away.

Phase II. First Engagement

At 2.02 p.m. and at a distance of about 11 kilometres (6 miles) from the first Russian warship, Tōgō ordered another turn. His division headed south-west by south and followed an opposite course to that of the Russian columns. If continued, this course would mean that the two columns would pass each other at a distance, while exchanging fire briefly but with no clear advantage to either of them. Then, at 2.07 p.m.,

Tōgō ordered the most important turn of the entire battle, signalling his division to turn *east-northeast*. It briefly sailed parallel to the Russian column, but due to its faster speed drew closer to the Russian van. While making the turn, the 2nd Battle Division, under the command of Vice Admiral Kamimura Hikonojō, joined the rear of the 1st Battle Division. With this reinforcement of six armoured cruisers (the *Izumo*, *Azuma*, *Tokiwa*, *Yakumo*, *Iwate*, and *Asama*) moving some 500 metres to port, the main Japanese line consisted of 12 warships accompanied by two light dispatch ships (the *Chihaya* and *Tatsuta*).[23] At this point, the line was sailing in the same formation as at the Battle of the Yellow Sea, but its sudden manoeuvre at once brought the two forces to a clash (Map 5).

Tōgō's manoeuvre was neither the arbitrary outcome of whimsy nor an unintentional decision. He had discussed it earlier and was to repeat it three more times in the coming two hours. Naval historians have tended to interpret it as a concrete manifestation of his superior tactical skills. Obviously, the admiral could also decide on a battle turn, as Admiral John Jellicoe would later do in 1916 at the Battle of Jutland, and so expedite the manoeuvre, but then he would leave his flagship at the end of the column or at its middle. The Russians were fleetingly baffled but soon felt elated at the sudden vulnerability of their opponents. "How rash!" one of the officers on the bridge of the *Kniaz Suvorov* exclaimed, 'Why, in a minute we'll be able to roll up the leading ships!'[24] Indeed, and at a distance of 7,000 metres from the Russian flagship, the dozen Japanese ships seemed a perfect target. Not only had they not yet opened fire themselves but also, as long as they turned—each passing in succession over the point at which the *Mikasa* had turned, they presented condensed and slow-moving silhouettes. Observing the unexpected turn, Rozhestvenskiĭ responded immediately and ordered his warships to open fire.[25] The first to do so was Rozhestvenskiĭ's own ship, the *Kniaz Suvorov*, which at 2.08 p.m. targeted the *Mikasa* and *Shikishima*, the first two ships to complete their turn (Map 5).[26] In his field diary, the *Mikasa*'s commander, Captain Ijichi Hikojirō, wrote plainly: '2.07 p.m.: Direction: east by

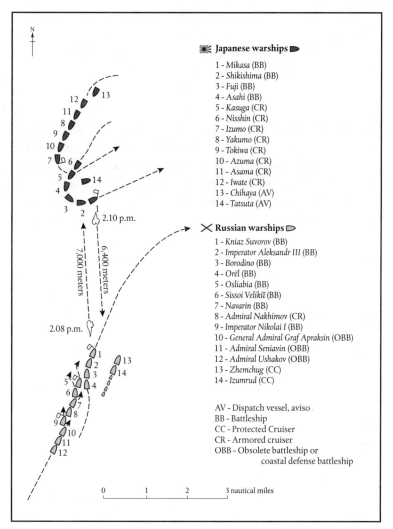

Japanese warships ▶
1 - *Mikasa* (BB)
2 - *Shikishima* (BB)
3 - *Fuji* (BB)
4 - *Asahi* (BB)
5 - *Kasuga* (CR)
6 - *Nisshin* (CR)
7 - *Izumo* (CR)
8 - *Yakumo* (CR)
9 - *Tokiwa* (CR)
10 - *Azuma* (CR)
11 - *Asama* (CR)
12 - *Iwate* (CR)
13 - *Chihaya* (AV)
14 - *Tatsuta* (AV)

✕ **Russian warships** ▷
1 - *Kniaz Suvorov* (BB)
2 - *Imperator Aleksandr III* (BB)
3 - *Borodino* (BB)
4 - *Orël* (BB)
5 - *Osliabia* (BB)
6 - *Sissoi Velikiĭ* (BB)
7 - *Navarin* (BB)
8 - *Admiral Nakhimov* (CR)
9 - *Imperator Nikolai I* (BB)
10 - *General Admiral Graf Apraksin* (OBB)
11 - *Admiral Seniavin* (OBB)
12 - *Admiral Ushakov* (OBB)
13 - *Zhemchug* (CC)
14 - *Izumrud* (CC)

AV - Dispatch vessel, aviso
BB - Battleship
CC - Protected Cruiser
CR - Armored cruiser
OBB - Obsolete battleship or
        coastal defense battleship

Map 5. The order of the two main columns at the moment of opening fire, 2.08 a.m., 27 May 1905

northeast. We are facing the enemy head on, but assuming a position to cut off their front. At this point, the closest enemy ship, the *Osliabia*, turns toward us first and opens fire.'[27] Both sides would later concur that it was effective fire.[28]

Other Russian battleships soon joined what seemed at first to be a turkey shoot, but Tōgō still held his fire. The exultation within the Russian column was momentary. Once they had completed their turn, the Japanese warships, led by the four battleships of the 1st Battle Division, headed quickly to the front of the Russian column. Miraculously, none had suffered serious damage yet, although the cruiser *Asama* was forced temporarily to leave the line due to a hit by a heavy shell.[29] At a distance of 6,400 metres from his enemy, Tōgō ordered the firing of a ranging shot using a 152-millimetre gun, and then, at 2.11 p.m., ordered his entire column to open fire. Sailing almost in parallel to the Russian column, the Japanese did not execute a perfect T crossing (see Chapter 1) as is often described. For one thing, their distance from the Russian column was too close to allow a passage perpendicular to it; and for another, Rozhestvenskiĭ responded aptly, since he understood the implications of the manoeuvre, by turning slightly starboard.[30] Still, by now sailing at 15 knots and being ahead of and faster than their opponents, the Japanese ships could use all their main batteries while the Russians could not, either because of their course or, initially, because they were still seeking to enter a single column in a disorderly fashion. In fact, some of Rozhestvenskiĭ's warships even stopped their engines to avoid colliding with each other, and then steamed at 11–12 knots (with bursts of up to 14 knots), leaving the auxiliary ships somewhat behind, at least for a while.[31]

Tōgō did not lose his advantage. Benefiting from his higher speed, he was able to control the distance from his enemy, staying mostly at 5,500 metres. Although much of the next hour was spent in parallel engagement, his ships took full advantage of the situation. They concentrated their fire on the leading Russian warship, the *Kniaz Suvorov*, and on the *Osliabia*, which sailed at a lower speed in an attempt to enter the single column behind the *Kniaz Suvorov*. Under intense fire, the two columns held their course for about 30 minutes. During this time, shells caused terrible damage to both sides, but those of the Japanese, because they were concentrated on fewer targets, were more accurate and effective. At 2.40 p.m., Rozhestvenskiĭ, recognizing the havoc caused to his column, ordered his flagship to turn slightly eastward and away from the Japanese column. Tōgō responded by turning to the south-east and was able to maintain the close engagement. The fruits of this turn were almost immediate, as the Japanese shells hit the centre of the *Kniaz Suvorov* and its steering mechanism at 2.50 p.m. It was a fatal hit and a turning point in the initial engagement. The Russian flagship began to move erratically and out of control, with thick smoke coming out of its main structure. It would not return to the main column. No less disastrous was the state of the leading figure on board. Struck by splinters that entered the conning tower, Rozhestvenskiĭ was badly wounded, along with the ship's captain. He was taken down below and would no longer take an active part in the battle. From this point on, the Baltic Fleet was practically without a commander.[32]

Despite the extreme damage the *Kniaz Suvorov* suffered, the Baltic Fleet's first loss was not its flagship. At about the same moment when Rozhestvenskiĭ was hit, the battleship *Osliabia* suffered massive damage too, mostly from the armoured cruisers of Kamimura's 2nd Battle Division.[33] She was hit by a large calibre shell at the waterline near the bow. Russian crews noted that 'the entire ship shuddered as if she was a living being and able to feel the pain.' The breach was too large to be repaired and 'water rushed in, in a powerful torrent, flooding the entire compartment.'[34] The same disastrous shell also ripped apart the *Osliabia*'s main electric cable, the one that powered the forward turret. The cable was soon reconnected but the turret remained jammed due to two further hits.[35] Unable to fight and pounded extensively by gunfire, including some ten hits from the heaviest shells at the enemy's disposal, this new battleship abruptly turned southward.[36] With water streaming in rapidly through three holes and filling its compartments, the *Osliabia* was doomed. At 3.10 p.m., and exactly one hour after the Japanese opened fire, she capsized and then sank, bow first, taking 531 crewmen with her.[37] Among the 221 survivors, saved mainly by nearby destroyers and transferred later to the cruiser *Dmitriǐ Donskoi*, 76 were wounded and only 145 remained unharmed (19 per cent of the original crew). Their ordeal did not end as the majority of them would also fall prisoner two days later.

The *Osliabia* was a harbinger of greater losses as the entire Russian column began to scatter south-eastward. Tōgō kept his fire on the *Kniaz Suvorov* but was unable yet to reap the full benefits of the Russian chaos and lack of leadership. The fierce resistance from the Russian flagship could not but impress observers even on the Japanese side, but she was not the only Russian ship to struggle desperately for her life.[38] In a gallant endeavour to save herself, the ship in the lead—the *Imperator Aleksandr III* under the command of Nikolai Bukhvostov— charged straight at the Japanese line.[39] Fearing this could end in a torpedo attack, Tōgō decided at 2.58 p.m. to withdraw temporarily north-eastward, after turning simultaneously and sharply, with the last ship in his division, the *Nisshin*, now sailing in the lead. The *Kniaz Suvorov* was thus saved for the time being, but in her brief sortie the *Imperator Aleksandr III* was also badly damaged with grave implications for her own survival a few hours later. Despite the initial Japanese success, the battle was far from decided. At 3.03 p.m. the Japanese main column split again after almost an hour of operating together, and the 2nd Battle Division, under Kamimura, left southward in search for escaping enemy vessels.[40] Three minutes later, and sufficiently distant from the Russian ships, Tōgō ordered his 1st Battle Division to change its course north-westward in an attempt to resume crossing the T and in so doing was able to force the Russian line to turn away to the south. In the meantime, Kamimura's division found no ships in its sortie and hurried back northward to join the main force. However, its absence for some two hours took its toll by reducing Tōgō's firepower and effectiveness.[41] By then, the range between the ships of the two main columns was occasionally down to about 1,500 metres, but visibility was poor due to the smoke and mist that covered the arena (Map 6).

While the battleships exchanged fire, Japanese and Russian lighter warships engaged each other too. At 2.50 p.m. the 3rd and 4th Battle Divisions of the IJN, comprising protected cruisers, joined the fray and targeted primarily the slow Russian auxiliary vessels.[42] They concentrated their fire on the auxiliary cruiser *Ural*—a large ocean liner with fine saloons the IRN had purchased from Germany a year earlier.[43] Defended fiercely by the First Cruiser Division (the *Dmitriĭ Donskoi*, *Vladimir Monomakh*, *Oleg*, and *Aurora*, and joined later by the *Zhemchug* too), the large steamship was badly hit and the entire Russian line of auxiliary ships fell into disarray. Miraculously, none of them was sunk.

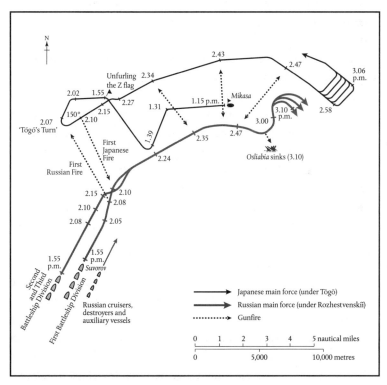

Map 6. Phase II of the battle, 27 May 1905

53

Moreover, the exchange of fire between the cruisers at a range of 6,000–7,000 metres was largely ineffective and no side gained the upper hand. However, as the Japanese force was bolstered by the arrival of cruisers of the 5th and then 6th Battle Divisions shortly before and after 4.00 p.m., it could press home its advantage. The cruisers stopped the two hospital ships *Orël* and *Kostroma* and, after seizing them as prizes, escorted them to Sasebo.[44] In the rising panic that spread among the auxiliary vessels, the *Ural* collided with the *Zhemchug*, while the *Anadir* rammed and sank the tug *Rus*.[45] At about 5.20 p.m., the remaining Russian auxiliary ships, now encircled, suddenly spotted their main column in their vicinity. The Russian battleships inflicted substantial damage upon the cruisers *Matsushima* and *Kasagi* and easily drove off the remaining Japanese cruisers.

During the late afternoon, a blanket of thick fog began again to cover the arena.[46] With this unexpected help, the Russian battleship column got rid of the chasing Japanese, while Enkvist's cruisers and the auxiliary ships slowly rejoined it. Starting at about 5.00 p.m., Tōgō's main force lost contact with its opponents, and a hiatus occurred in the engagement of the two main forces. The Russian column was now able to reorganize, although the *Kniaz Suvorov*, riddled with large holes, and without her mast and funnels, remained outside the line. Taking advantage of the opportunity, the Russian destroyer *Buinii* approached the flagship and steamed away at 5.30 p.m. with the wounded Rozhestvenskii, seven of his staff and flag officers, and an additional 15 crew members.[47] The transfer was designed to move the admiral and his staff to another, more functional battleship and, although that did not happen, it saved them from certain death.[48] With their departure and bereft of her wounded skipper, the position of the *Kniaz Suvorov* was hopeless. Steaming slowly southward under the command of a lieutenant with a single light-calibre gun undamaged, she was left behind at the mercy of prowling Japanese vessels.

At this stage, and as the Russian column briefly headed southward in an attempt to disengage, the four-hour opening engagement was finally over. Scoring an impressive victory, the Japanese were still far from achieving their goal. The Baltic Fleet had been seriously battered and had suffered fairly heavy casualties (close to one thousand dead), but almost all its ships still sailed ahead in a frantic effort to reach Vladivostok. Crucially, even at this point it still had six functioning battleships against Japan's four. The objectives on either side were markedly different, however. While the Russian warships were determined to reach Vladivostok, the Japanese force was at least as determined to prevent them from doing so. With much less damage to his ships, greater speed, and stronger motivation, Tōgō, although unaware of Rozhestvenskii's wounds, knew that the two hours remaining until darkness might be his last chance.

Phase III. Second Engagement

At 5.27 p.m., and after a fruitless search for Russian ships, the main Japanese column began to move northward. Reorganized and having brought its damage under control, it once again included the two battle divisions' dozen warships. Although many were hit, the number of casualties was relatively low. It was not long before the column came across the crippled auxiliary cruiser *Ural* and finished her off by gunfire.[49] Then, at 5.59 p.m., and as the mist was clearing, Tōgō was relieved to rediscover the Russian main column sailing in a parallel course on his port bow. It was the start of a new phase of the battle, and one with a different character. Unlike the initial engagement, in which both sides fought fiercely, this second engagement was characterized by an uneven pursuit and relentless hunt. Furthermore, the Japanese had been ahead of the enemy earlier, but were now behind it. The Russian ships began shooting at a range of about 8,100 metres to repel their pursuers rather than to destroy them. The Japanese would soon do the opposite: destroy rather than be repelled.

With quicker vessels, the Japanese column closed in quickly and opened fire too at 6.02 p.m. The fleeing Russian column, now led by the battleship *Borodino*, was concealed by the sunset but could not avoid enemy shells. The Japanese drew nearer, settling at a distance of about 4,500 metres. Their fire was increasingly accurate, while the Russians' firepower diminished gradually as their guns were put out of action. The first casualty in this evening duel was the battleship *Imperator Aleksandr III*, which received multiple shell hits, including some 12 hits from the heaviest guns.[50] Observers noted that her bow was badly damaged, and that there was a large hole in her forward hull on the port side. At 6.30 p.m., and shortly after fire had resumed, the ship moved out of the line. By then, she was listing so heavily that her guns touched the water and she soon capsized. She sank some 37 minutes later, along with the full complement of her crew of 840.[51]

With the *Imperator Aleksandr III*'s demise, Tōgō shifted his fire to her sisters, the battleships *Borodino* and the *Orël* (Figure 12). At this point, it became a broadside action, with the leading Russian warships slightly forward of the beam of the Japanese flagship, at a range of some 5,500–6,600 metres. The *Borodino*, the lead ship of her new class, was able to advance a few miles further but she too soon met her

Figure 12. The gruesome results of naval artillery: the battleship *Orël* in the aftermath of the two daylight engagements, 27 May 1905

end. On board the cruiser *Aurora*, the ship's surgeon, Dr Vladimir Kravchenko, was watching the exchange of fire from afar. It was simultaneously a dreadful and awe-inspiring scene:

> The courageous *Borodino* stubbornly refused to leave the line or turn to port: she kept leading the squadron in northeast 23° [course]. The sun was setting amid scarlet, blood like rays. In a few moments, it would be below the horizon. The wind had dropped and the sea calmed down. There were some five minutes to go before sunset. Everyone was longing for the night to cover the miserable ship with its protective darkness. Every moment was costing so much, five minutes seemed like an eternity![52]

With the sun setting, visibility increased and accuracy improved despite the fact that the range between the two columns grew to some 7,700 metres. A salvo of 305-millimetre guns from the battleship *Fuji* hit the *Borodino*'s 152-millimetre shell magazine on the waterline and caused a fatal detonation at 6.57 p.m.[53] Subsequent detonations of adjacent magazines blew open her hull and caused her to capsize in several minutes, with her propellers still turning.[54] 'Her underwater part,' Dr Kravchenko described, 'was uncovered and her keel glittered in the ray of the setting sun like the scales of a gigantic fish.'[55] Then, 'she disappeared under the waves even faster than had the *Osliabia*, in no more than half a minute,' leaving behind, as another shocked observer remarked, nothing but 'a patch of white foam!'[56] Only one sailor from the original crew of 855 survived.[57] Watching the *Borodino* sinking, Tōgō's 1st Battle Division fired its last shots at 7.23 p.m. and started retreating south-eastward.[58] Seven minutes later, Kamimura's 2nd Battle Division too called it a day and followed suit in the same direction, and the entire force steered north once it dropped into position behind the 1st Battle Division.[59]

At about the same time, and some 40 kilometres (22 miles) to the south, another sister ship of the *Borodino* class, the crippled *Kniaz Suvorov*, expired too. Sailing together with the auxiliary ship *Kamchatka*, the battleship was harassed by several warships belonging to Vice Admiral Uryū Sotokichi's 4th Battle Division. With more

Japanese vessels joining the onslaught, the *Kamchatka* was sunk first, at 7.10 p.m.[60] The *Kniaz Suvorov* seemed more resistant to the cruisers' gunfire but only for a few minutes longer. Charged by four vessels from the 11th Torpedo Boat Division, she was fatally hit by two torpedoes. As a result, one of her magazines exploded and blew open her hull. The Russian flagship listed further to port, and then capsized and sank with all her surviving crew other than those taken earlier by the *Buinii*.[61] The loss of the *Kniaz Suvorov* had, later testimonies suggested, exerted 'a fatal influence' on morale and motivation in the remaining Russian warships.[62] The damage was also piling up. The Baltic Fleet had now lost four of its mightiest warships at a cost in human lives of some 3,200 dead from these ships alone, or about two-thirds of the total death toll in the battle (Map 7). These ships, all commissioned a year or so before the war, were the backbone of the fleet. Tōgō's decision to concentrate his fire on them was proved right.[63] With the demise of Rozhestvenskii's strongest battle division, the chances of recovery looked nearly impossible. Tōgō for one remained unaware of the full scale of the Russian toll until the next morning.[64] By then, the outcomes of the night's operations would have altered the picture irreversibly.

Phase IV. Night Operations

The sinking of the *Kniaz Suvorov* was the opening act in the night's operations carried out by Japanese destroyers and torpedo boats. Shortly before sunset, Tōgō withdrew his main column northward as planned. Unwilling to risk his large warships in a night engagement, he was going to wait until the next morning near the island of Ulleungdo (Dagelet; Jpn. Utsuryō-tō), some 120 kilometres east of the Korean Peninsula. On the opposite side, the Russian column did not have the leisure to rest. With Vladivostok some 700 kilometres (380 miles) away, the prospects of escape during the night were not bleak. It was now the turn of the battleship *Imperator Nikolai I* to take the lead, with Rear Admiral Enkvist's detachment sailing to her port

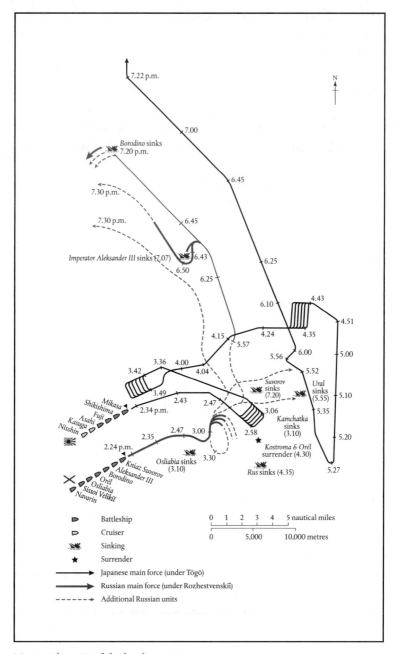

Map 7. Phase III of the battle, 27 May 1905

and the destroyers and the remaining auxiliary ships steaming further behind. The speed of the surviving ships was 11–12 knots, the maximum Nebogatov's flagship could sail.[65] Between 5.35 and 6.05 p.m. the transfer of the fleet's command was signalled by flags along the column.[66] Many in the Russian column believed that Rozhestvenskiĭ had died, but Nebogatov showed little signs of fully assuming his new role.[67] It was as late as 8.40 p.m. when he made his first significant decision by turning north-east and increasing the speed of his ship slightly.[68]

With Nebogatov's warships speeding up, the slow auxiliary vessels began to lag behind, while Enkvist's two cruisers, *Oleg* and *Aurora*, lost contact too. After a few harmless encounters with Japanese torpedo boats and attempts to break northward, these two cruisers turned south-westward at about 10.00 p.m. with some more vessels joining in.[69] A short while later, the group shrank, since, at the 18-knot speed the admiral ordered, only his two ships, the protected cruiser *Zhemchug* and the destroyers *Bodriĭ* and *Blestiashchiĭ*, could keep up.[70] During the following hours, Enkvist changed his mind and decided to escape south, to either Shanghai or Saigon, but the officers on board his flagship *Oleg* opposed his intention and insisted on returning northward. He seemed, the *Aurora*'s surgeon recalled, 'very shaken by the result of the battle'.[71] With tears in his eyes, Enkvist was deeply moved but his conviction to avoid battle remained firm: 'I am already an old man. I do not have much longer to live, but besides me there are 1,200 younger lives which will be able to serve the fatherland. No, dear, tell the officers that though I wholeheartedly share and appreciate their choice, I cannot agree. The whole responsibility will be mine.' He then approached the officers on board the *Aurora* but they did not condone his plan either. The *Oleg*'s skipper, Leonid Dobrotvorskiĭ, came to his rescue and offered to head to Manila. Enkvist concurred at once, apparently assuming that the American authorities might not disarm his warships.[72] However problematic, Enkvist's decision probably saved his cruisers from the wrath of the Japanese light vessels during the night. Tōgō, for one, did not intend to stop his single-minded pursuit.

At this point, it was the Japanese smaller units' chance to shine. Comprising no less than 21 destroyers (in five divisions) and 32 torpedo boats (in ten divisions), they were ordered to intercept the remaining older Russian warships and attack them with torpedoes while blocking the escape routes of the Baltic Fleet's smaller vessels. Although the sea was not as high as in the morning, visibility was limited to the extent that the Japanese small vessels encountered difficulties in locating their enemy, and a few of them even collided with each other in the ensuing chaos. Nevertheless, some did better. The most successful unit was the 4th Destroyer Division under the command of Commander Suzuki Kantarō (1868–1948).[73] Forty years later, in August 1945, and by then a 77-year-old retired admiral, Prime Minister Suzuki would be a key figure in the final days of the Japanese Empire. On the eve of the war against Russia, however, he was still mainly known as the IJN's leading torpedo expert. A year after the battle, Nebogatov had nothing but praise for Suzuki and his comrades:

> The Japanese torpedo craft were extraordinarily energetic and daring in their attacks. For example, my officers spotted one of them launching a torpedo near the *Imperator Nikolai I*. Being forewarned, I somehow managed to turn away and was told that the torpedo passed very close. The attacker audaciously continued firing and hit our secondary battery, wounding several men.[74]

Other torpedoes were more accurate. On the night of 27–8 May, the 4th Destroyer Division's four vessels put Suzuki's knowledge and training to good use.[75] They could approach their opponents under the cover of night and sometimes fire at ranges of less than 100 metres. The Russian warships were largely blind as very few could use searchlights after the earlier bombardment.[76] Torpedo attacks, recalled one of the officers on board the *Izumrud*, came 'for some hours in succession—The penetrating beams of the search-lights—the boom of cannon—the shouts of the Japanese when the illumination revealed one of them! Here was an inferno in panorama!'[77]

At 2.30 a.m., and after an intense search, they tracked down the 10,200-ton low-freeboard battleship *Navarin* some 50 kilometres (27 miles) north-east of Tsushima Island. She was limping northward after being hit earlier by multiple shells and a single torpedo. The sky was now turning clear and starry, allowing the Japanese destroyers to launch three torpedoes, two of which hit her. The destroyers then laid six segments with a total of 24 mines across her bow, of which the battleship struck at least one.[78] In the ensuing explosion, the *Navarin* sank immediately, taking the majority of her originally 622-man crew with her.[79] Apparently some 70 abandoned the ship safely, but only three were alive when found 16 hours later. The next victim of Suzuki's Destroyer Division was the battleship *Sissoi Velikiĭ*, which was similar to the *Navarin* in displacement but not in form. On the eve of the battle, she was second in line after *Osliabia* but quickly sustained multiple gun hits, including five hits from large-calibre (254–305 millimetre) guns that caused many casualties.[80] The *Sissoi Velikiĭ* kept on course, but was hit by a single torpedo that damaged her rudder and propellers. At 3.15 a.m., the flooding in her compartments intensified, and her bow was so submerged that forward movement was no longer possible. Helpless and with no prospects of escape, her crew surrendered on the morning of 28 May, while attempting simultaneously to scuttle the ship. The Japanese succeeded in towing her at first while rescuing 613 of her crew, but she capsized with no further casualties at around 10.00 a.m.[81]

Apart from these two battleships, the Japanese light vessels added two more scores to their overall tally. These were the two old armoured cruisers the *Vladimir Monomakh* and *Admiral Nakhimov*, which were sunk the next day. The former engaged the Japanese cruiser *Izumi* during the initial engagement and suffered limited damage, sustaining one dead and 16 wounded. At 8.40 p.m., however, she was hit by a single torpedo and reportedly sank one torpedo boat.[82] As a result of the damage to her hull, the *Vladimir Monomakh* became heavily flooded in the early morning and her commander, Captain Vladimir Popov, decided to abandon her at a short distance from the northern tip of Tsushima. He transferred some of the crew to her lifeboats and then ordered the ship to be scuttled. The cruiser sank at 10.20 a.m. with most of her crew taken aboard two Japanese auxiliary ships.[83] The fate of the *Admiral Nakhimov* was not much different. Sailing eighth and last in the main column as the battle began, she was hit about 30 times during the first two engagements and lost 91 of her crew members (25 of whom died), but nonetheless succeeded in escaping serious damage.[84] During the night, however, she too sustained a single torpedo hit and was allegedly scuttled by her crew north-east of Tsushima as she surrendered the next morning.[85]

Phase V. Escape, Surrender, and Denouement

By the early morning of 28 May 1905, a few Russian capital ships were still heading together towards Vladivostok. This surviving nucleus of the Baltic Fleet was the former rearguard of the Russian main column under Nebogatov's command. Comprising the new *Borodino*-class battleship *Orël*, the older battleship *Imperator Nikolai I*, the two coastal-defence battleships *General Admiral Graf Apraksin* and *Admiral Seniavin*, and the cruiser *Izumrud*. None of these ships was badly damaged and the number of casualties aboard them was relatively small.[86] In facing them, the Japanese force remained as determined and as unflappable as before. After a night of rest, Tōgō and his two battle divisions, as well as many other smaller vessels, were waiting for Nebogatov's force between Ulleungdo Island and the Liancourt Rocks (present-day Dokdo/Takeshima islands), some 350 kilometres (190 miles) north-east of Tsushima Island. At around 6.20 a.m. one of the 5th Battle Division cruisers spotted the advancing Russian ships and alerted the entire fleet. Less than three hours later, a large portion of the IJN arrived at the scene.[87] At 10.00 a.m., Nebogatov noticed 27 large Japanese warships, excluding destroyers, on the horizon and realized he was surrounded.[88] The exhausted and demoralized admiral felt his slow force had little chance of prevailing over its formidable adversary. 'I had no way to do any harm to the enemy,' he would later claim. His warships lacked ammunition, some of their guns were out of order, and their damage from the first day engagements was massive.[89] One year later, Nebogatov recalled his predicament:

> My situation, obviously, was critical. Naturally, as the commander, I had to think of everybody. They all looked up to me. What was to be done? What adviser did I have? None, there was only one head here. But there were the Regulations. I knew that the Regulations sometimes permit breaking the oath. I turned to the Regulations and read them. Article 354 was the one. I had to decide whether or not I was in the circumstances envisaged in this article... None of my subordinates could see from my face what was going on in my soul...[90]

Before reaching a decision about the best course, Nebogatov did consult his officers. He also contacted the other ships in his force to check their ammunition stocks and, critically, to gain support for this plan.[91] In view of the opposition in his own ship, he made a speech that resembled the one Enkvist had delivered several hours earlier in both content and style. 'I am an old man, 60 years old,' the admiral said, 'and my life has no particular value any more. It is over anyway. I will get shot for this. But you are young people in your prime and you are destined to restore the glory of the Russian Navy. I take responsibility for this step all by myself.'[92] Nebogatov's candid reasoning was not accepted unanimously and a few of the officers charged him with defeatism. Nevertheless, the majority endorsed his decision, with one notable exception.[93] Determined to make for Vladivostok independently, the *Izumrud*'s skipper, Commander Vasiliĭ Fersen (1858–1937), decided to disobey his admiral's resolution.[94]

Unaware of the drama on board Nebogatov's flagship, the armoured cruiser *Kasuga* fired the first shot at the Russian warships at 10.37 a.m. Missing, she immediately fired another and soon the entire Japanese force opened fire at a range of 7,100 metres. The Russian force did not respond but changed its course slightly.[95] Several minutes later, Nebogatov's flagship, *Imperator Nikolai I*, lowered

Figure 13. Rear Admiral Nebogatov's flagship, *Imperator Nikolai I*, upon surrender. The Japanese battleship *Shikishima* is on the far left and the *Orël* behind on her right

her flag and hoisted the Japanese flag instead (Figure 13). Some of the Russian officers opposed the move, including the *Orël*'s acting captain, Commander Konstantin Shvede (1863–1933), but Nebogatov's prerogative prevailed.[96] A decade earlier, the commander of the Chinese Beiyang Fleet, Admiral Ding Ruchang, had faced a similarly hopeless situation against the IJN, but ordered his warships to be scuttled and then took his life with an overdose of opium, as did his deputy.[97] Nebogatov, by contrast, resolved to defend his decision. It took another ten minutes until the Japanese warships noticed their own national flag being hoisted on the other Russian ships and a few more minutes until they ceased their fire entirely. They were undeniably surprised.[98] On board the battleship *Asahi*, an observer noted, 'everybody laughed, not derisively, but from sheer happiness.'[99]

Meanwhile, the *Izumrud* exploited the few moments of confusion to sneak away. It speeded south-east and later changed course northward at 24 knots, and none of the four nearby Japanese cruisers was able to bring her to a halt.[100] The *Izumrud* almost made it. During her anxious flight, she went off course and during the night of 30–31 May ran aground in Vladimir Bay, some 430 kilometres (230 miles) north-east of Vladivostok (Figure 14).[101] After several attempts to get the ship moving and with only 10 tons of coal remaining, Fersen decided to blow the ship up and so keep her out of Japanese hands. Eventually, several days later, the crew reached Vladivostok by land.[102] Nebogatov's capture was not the final blow to Russian pride. Several hours later, Rozhestvenskiĭ too fell into Japanese hands when the destroyer *Bedoviĭ*, to which he had been transferred earlier, capitulated after a short clash with the Japanese destroyer *Sazanami*. Here too, the crew refused to give in but eventually yielded when faced with the admiral's staff officers' persistence. Rozhestvenskiĭ did not take an active part in the surrender decision since he was either delirious or unconscious most of the time.[103]

The slow coastal-defence battleship *Admiral Ushakov* was also close to escaping. During the first day of the battle she was badly damaged

Figure 14. The cruiser *Izumrud* after it was blown up by its crew north-east of Vladivostok

by multiple gun hits but due to her low speed remained behind and so evaded the light flotilla's night-time assault. On the morning of the second day, the Japanese units that encircled Nebogatov's force paid little attention to this plodding ship, but spotted her again at around 3.00 p.m. Two of the Japanese armoured cruisers, the *Yakumo* and *Iwate*, sought to persuade her to capitulate in the same fashion as her two sister ships had done a few hours earlier.[104] This Russian warship was not open to persuasion, however, and began to engage her opponents, who responded instantly, at 5.20 p.m. The misfortune of the *Admiral Ushakov* may suggest the fate of Nebogatov's ships had they not surrendered. Less than an hour later, she was no longer afloat, perhaps also by the hands of her own crew.[105] The armoured cruiser *Dmitriĭ Donskoi* was also initially able to evade the Japanese but eventually was spotted again east of Ulleungdo Island in the morning.[106] In the ensuing clash with several Japanese cruisers (again, mainly the *Otowa* and the *Niitaka*) and a number of destroyers, the Russian cruiser was heavily hit but succeeded in steaming ahead and hid under the cover of darkness near the island's shore.[107] The next morning, on 29 May, her crew scuttled the ship, surrendered, and were brought to Sasebo.[108]

The protected cruiser *Svetlana* was even less fortunate. During the night, she attempted to escape to Manila and then to Vladivostok, but was surrounded by the *Otowa* and *Niitaka* in the morning. Serving in peacetime as a yacht for the General-Admiral Grand Duke Aleksei Aleksandrovich (1850–1908), she fought more furiously than some of the battleships. Her gallantry notwithstanding, the *Svetlana* was sunk in less than an hour after sustaining 16 hits and suffering 167 fatalities, including her captain, who refused to leave the sinking ship.[109] The fate of the *Buiniĭ*, one of the destroyers that accompanied the *Dmitriĭ Donskoi* during the first night, was not much different. Despite her malfunctioning machinery, she kept sailing northward but another technical breakdown forced the crew to scuttle her at around mid-day.[110] Three of her sister ships suffered similar bad luck on the same day: the *Blestiashchiĭ* was hit by shells and eventually sank during her escape south-westward; the *Bezuprechnĭ* was sunk by the Japanese cruiser *Chitose* and the destroyer *Ariake* while fleeing north-eastward; whereas the *Bistrĭ* was scuttled near the Korean coast at 10.40 a.m. and her crew rescued by Japanese warships after a lengthy chase northward. Some 20 minutes later, the *Gromkĭ*, a Russian destroyer of a different class, was sunk too, near the Korean coast and north-east of Ulsan (Map 8). Finally, the transport *Irtish* was sunk by gunfire near the Japanese coast during the morning of 29 May.[111]

A number of Russian warships did, however, succeed in fleeing to neutral ports. The most prominent among these were the cruisers *Oleg*, *Aurora*, and *Zhemchug* under Enkvist's command. This small force sneaked southward through the Korea Strait and arrived in the port of Manila, in the Philippines on 3 June, six days later.[112] Although the American colonial authorities did allow the three Russian warships, as expected, to reload coal in the port and leave, they were eventually interned on 7 June following an order from St Petersburg.[113] More than a week earlier, on 29 May, the tug *Svir* and the transport *Koreia* had safely reached the Chinese port of Wusong in the vicinity of Shanghai and were soon interned by the local authorities.[114] On 4 June, the destroyer *Bodrĭ* arrived in Shanghai. She was towed there by a British merchantman after drifting in the sea for lack of fuel.[115] Then, on 27 June, exactly one month after the battle, the transport *Anadir* arrived in the harbour of Diego Suarez (present-day Antsiranana) in northern Madagascar. By consuming the coal it carried, the ship was able to avoid internment and within little more than another month was able to return to the port of Libau.[116] Eventually, only three vessels of this large armada reached their destination. The first of these was the armed yacht *Almaz*. She succeeded in evading patrols while moving close to the Japanese coast and reached Vladivostok on 29 May.[117] The destroyer *Bravĭ* followed a similar course but due to a fuel shortage arrived at the base during the evening of 30 May.[118] The destroyer *Groznĭ* also made it to the safe haven of Vladivostok. Succeeding in avoiding interception, she rushed northward and by the evening of 30 May reached Askold Island with almost no coal. After a brief

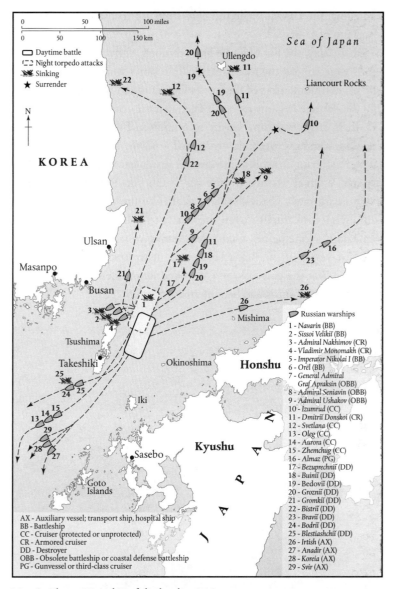

0   50   100 miles
0   50   100   150 km

Sea of Japan

- ▭ Daytime battle
- ⸤⸥ Night torpedo attacks
- ✹ Sinking
- ★ Surrender

N

KOREA

Ullengdo

Liancourt Rocks

Ulsan

Masanpo

Busan

Tsushima

Takeshiki

Mishima

Okinoshima

Honshu

Iki

Kyushu

Sasebo

Goto
Islands

⬟ Russian warships

1 - *Navarin* (BB)
2 - *Sissoi Velikiĭ* (BB)
3 - *Admiral Nakhimov* (CR)
4 - *Vladimir Monomakh* (CR)
5 - *Imperator Nikolai I* (BB)
6 - *Orel* (BB)
7 - *General Admiral Graf Apraksin* (OBB)
8 - *Admiral Seniavin* (OBB)
9 - *Admiral Ushakov* (OBB)
10 - *Izumrud* (CC)
11 - *Dmitriĭ Donskoi* (CR)
12 - *Svetlana* (CC)
13 - *Oleg* (CC)
14 - *Aurora* (CC)
15 - *Zhemchug* (CC)
16 - *Almaz* (PG)
17 - *Bezuprechnyĭ* (DD)
18 - *Buinyĭ* (DD)
19 - *Bedovyĭ* (DD)
20 - *Groznyĭ* (DD)
21 - *Gromkiĭ* (DD)
22 - *Bistryĭ* (DD)
23 - *Bravyĭ* (DD)
24 - *Bodryĭ* (DD)
25 - *Blestiashchiĭ* (DD)
26 - *Irtish* (AX)
27 - *Anadir* (AX)
28 - *Koreia* (AX)
29 - *Svir* (AX)

AX - Auxiliary vessel; transport ship, hospital ship
BB - Battleship
CC - Cruiser (protected or unprotected)
CR - Armored cruiser
DD - Destroyer
OBB - Obsolete battleship or coastal defense battleship
PG - Gunvessel or third-class cruiser

Map 8. Phases IV and V of the battle, 28 May 1905

refuelling, the *Groznĭ* made the final short leg to the port during the morning of 31 May.[119]

On 29 May, the fog of battle grew thinner. Although a few Russian ships were still on the run, preliminary reports were accumulating in the naval headquarters of the two belligerents and rumours surrounding the debacle began to spread. The Japanese could start celebrating. As their large warships began returning to base, the surrendered Russian warships were slowly towed (mostly to Sasebo), and the prisoners brought ashore, the overall result became clear: they had secured a great victory (Figure 15).[120] On the Russian side, some preliminary news of the fleet was cabled by the approaching *Almaz*, although it took the IRN a few more days to track down the remnants of its units. Nonetheless, and by the evening of 31 May, when the third and last vessel of the Baltic Fleet made it to Russian waters, it was apparent that the epic voyage had ended in a cataclysmic failure and that most of its ships had been destroyed.[121]

Figure 15. Russian prisoners of war brought ashore on board the battleship *Asahi*

At the final count, almost every Russian warship was sunk, captured, or interned. This heavy toll includes eight battleships (six sunk and two captured), three coastal defence battleships (one sunk and two captured), three armoured cruisers (all sunk), five protected cruisers (two sunk and three interned), and seven destroyers (five sunk, one captured, and one interned). The Japanese losses, on the other hand, were negligible: three torpedo boats sunk (for a detailed list of the losses, see Appendix). Moreover, and although some of the capital warships were heavily damaged, they were all still combat-ready by the end of the battle.[122] In terms of aggregated tonnage lost, captured, or interned, the imbalance is even more apparent: Russia's total losses were 198,721 tons (92.5 per cent of the entire fleet) compared to the mere 265 tons lost by Japan (a ratio of 749:1). A comparison of the aggregate tonnage of the warships sunk in the battle, 97,000 vs. 265 tons, is no less astonishing (a ratio of 366:1).[123]

The number of casualties in the battle was extremely uneven too. On the Russian side, the losses were appalling: 4,830 dead; 5,917 captured (122 officers and 5,795 ratings), many of them wounded; and 1,862 crew interned in neutral ports. Only 1,227 men, comprising less than 9 per cent of the original force, were able to escape the fate of their comrades above and reach a safe haven. The Japanese losses, by contrast, were small: a mere 117 dead (41 times less than Russia's death toll), 583 wounded, and not a single man falling prisoner or interned.[124]

Analysis: Why Did Tōgō Win and Rozhestvenskiĭ Lose?

With the benefit of hindsight, both contemporary observers and later writers were fairly unanimous about the factors that shaped the battle. They tended to emphasize the Russian shortcomings before the battle ('ill-assorted rabble'; 'a collection of ships') and the Japanese performance during it.[125] And yet the unequivocal outcomes were not self-evident. It took a number of years before the official histories were published, the reports of naval observers compiled, and the eyewitness testimonies made available, thus allowing the entire scope of the engagement to be revealed. The most burning question since the battle has been how the IJN managed to clinch such a remarkable triumph. After all, no expert had predicted a landslide victory for either side on the eve of the battle. The following section seeks to highlight the differences between the two belligerents as revealed in the battle and examine the reasons for the one-sided outcome. These differences touch virtually every dimension of naval warfare, starting from the features of the warships involved and their tactical use, going on via the two combatants' experience and motivation, and ending in each fleet's strategic objectives.

Armament

The use of guns was a key element in the early and decisive phases of the battle. Numerically speaking, the two sides did not differ in the number of guns in a way that could explain the battle's uneven outcomes. In the initial two engagements, both sides relied first and foremost on their heavy guns while using them at ranges unheard of before the war and only used previously, albeit unsuccessfully, in the Battle of the Yellow Sea nine months earlier. These guns were crucial for penetrating the thick armour of the battleships in the lead, silencing their main batteries, and wreaking havoc among the crews on board. But if heavy guns (the standard 305-millimetre and 254-millimetre guns) were crucial, contemporary experts found it difficult to explain how the Japanese, with only 17 guns of this type, gained the upper hand over the Russians who possessed no fewer than 41 such guns. In later years, Soviet scholars argued that the Japanese's higher firing rate and use of larger explosive charges gave them an overwhelming advantage even before the battle started.[126]

The Japanese gunners were able to compensate amply for their numerical deficiency in heavy guns by employing a higher firing rate, greater accuracy, and better projectiles, as well as by their numerical advantage in small-calibre guns. With more than 11,000 shells fired, their use of ammunition was unprecedented in the history of naval warfare up to that point in time.[127] The number of shells the Russians fired is unknown, but according to some estimates was not much lower.[128] Accuracy on both sides was relatively low, but Japanese gunnery was nonetheless significantly more accurate than the Russian. It is likely that some 5 per cent of Japanese shells hit the target (and 15.9 per cent of their heavy-calibre guns!) compared to little more than 1 per cent for the Russians (and 3.5 per cent for their heavy-calibre guns).[129] In view of other naval battles of this era, before and after, the Japanese accuracy was remarkable.[130] It was the outcome of the combat experience the IJN had gained since February 1904, the intensive drills its crews had engaged in before the battle, and also because the battle was fought for the most part at relatively short range.[131]

With a greater firing rate and higher accuracy, the Japanese bombardment was devastating. Unlike the Battle of the Yellow Sea, the havoc was also wreaked by lower-calibre guns, including the 120- and 152-millimetres.[132] Commander Vladimir Semenov (1867–1910), one of Rozhestvenskiï's flag officers aboard the *Kniaz Suvorov* and a hardened officer who had also participated in the Battle of the Yellow Sea, was shocked. 'I had not only never witnessed such a fire before,' he wrote, 'but I had never imagined anything like it. Shells seemed to be pouring upon us incessantly, one after another.'[133] Semenov's impression is magnified by the discrepancy in firing rate and accuracy between the two fleets: the Russian ships were hit by 79 large-calibre (254- or 305-millimetre) shells whereas the Japanese ships were only hit by a mere 43 large-calibre shells (54.4 per cent of the shells hitting Russian ships). This discrepancy was conspicuously larger in the medium- to large-calibre (203- or 229-millimetre) guns: 112 vs. 6 hits (5.6 per cent); and by the quick-firing medium-calibre (120- or 152-millimetre) guns: 367 vs. 81 (22 per cent).[134] Altogether, the Russian warships were hit by 558 shells of various calibres, whereas the Japanese were hit by as few as 130 shells (23.4 per cent).[135]

This is a staggering difference, but it does not end here. The Japanese shells used were also more potent and caused greater damage per hit. The Russians used armour-piercing (AP) shells, which nonetheless tended to burst upon impact rather than penetrate, caused little damage, and quite a few of them were duds.[136] The Japanese, in contrast, relied largely on thin-skinned high-capacity (HC) shells and, to a lesser extent, on high-explosive AP shells.[137] Although the former hardly ever penetrated the thick armoured hull of the Russian capital ships, they did inflict horrendous damage on their structure and crews, and caused numerous fires.[138] Their damage was the amplified by the use of four times the explosive charge of the AP shells,[139] and by their use of Shimose powder—a relatively less unstable explosive than other picric-acid-based explosives available at the time, which generated greater heat and blast power.[140] Altogether, guns of all sorts proved to be a crucial weapon. Throughout the first 15 months of the war, naval artillery had failed to impress, especially since all the large warships sunk were hit by mines or by a mixture of causes, but never by guns alone. Now, at last, naval artillery thoroughly vindicated itself and regained its dominant place in warfare. This happened, however, on the Japanese side alone. It was the outcome of a higher firing rate, an uncommon degree of accuracy, and the efficient use of HC shells.

The Japanese used torpedoes in far greater numbers and with greater effectiveness than the Russians. They fired as many as 64 torpedoes with some 10 hits, whereas the Russian only fired four without a single hit.[141] Despite being one of the greatest disappointments of the war, torpedoes appeared to be quite effective during the Battle of Tsushima. With no less than 15.6 per cent success, the IJN made effective use of them in finishing off large ships. The vast majority of Japanese torpedoes (90.6 per cent) were launched by destroyers and torpedo boats, which, despite the weather conditions, traversed the course of the Baltic Fleet repeatedly once the second engagement was over. Moving in swarms and at high speed, they were extremely valuable in tracking escaping Russian vessels and in administering a short-range *coup de grâce*, occasionally at extremely short range, something only possible under the cover of the night or in conditions of limited visibility. The Japanese boats were apparently less successful against Russian vessels that had not been hit badly by earlier gunfire and also displayed their limitations in the morning due to the high seas.[142] Evidently, the Baltic Fleet was even less adept in using its torpedoes. One reason was that it had many fewer destroyers and not a single torpedo boat at its disposal, for none could have endured such a long voyage. The larger Russian warships too had difficulties in using their torpedoes since the fleet was on the run and so less tuned to facing its enemy for this purpose alone.

Armour and Structure

Some of the Russian battleships did not stand the Japanese fire. The first of them to sink, the *Osliabia*, was evidently substandard in terms of armour, inasmuch as the lead ship of her class had been referred to as 'really an armoured cruiser masquerading as a battleship'.[143] Although commissioned only two years earlier, its design was obsolete with substantial unarmoured areas, especially in her extremities.[144] In spite of this deficiency, armour did not seem to play a crucial role in determining the outcomes of the battle. On the face of it, some of the Russian battleships were better armoured than the Japanese, but reality proved different. Of the Japanese battleships, only the most recent, the *Mikasa*, was protected with cutting-edge Krupp armour, while no less than four Russian battleships, all belonging to the *Borodino*-class, were protected with this steel.[145] After the battle, certain specialists argued that the Russian battleships' armour protection was faulty, or at least did not cover their extremities sufficiently and thus rendered them vulnerable.[146] Nevertheless, recent Russian studies of this aspect suggest that at the very least the four battleships of the *Borodino*-class that took part in the battle were not inferior to their Japanese counterparts, and perhaps even superior at close range.[147]

Whatever the armour advantage of these battleships, it did not materialize in the battle, especially as a significant part of their armour belt was under water. This was partly due to a structural fault but also because all were overloaded with coal.[148] In addition, the recent Russian battleships were characterized by high centres of gravity that contributed to their eventually capsizing. Thus, the IJN British-made battleships eventually proved to be more protected and resistible. These differences notwithstanding, very few shells, including those of the largest calibre, succeeded in penetrating the battleships' belts. Indeed, the ultimate capsizing and sinking of some of the Russian battleships was not necessarily the direct outcome of their armour, but occurred because of their structure and also because their watertight compartments and longitudinal bulkhead were not designed to prevent listing after being breached.[149] Furthermore, none of the battleships of either side was protected by a torpedo bulkhead and effective system for flooding one side of the ship for the sake of balance.[150] Hence, and in conclusion, the quality and thickness of either the IRN's or the IJN's warship armour was not a cardinal cause of either loss or victory in battle.[151]

Speed

This dimension has rarely been as crucial as it was in the Battle of Tsushima, where the two belligerents differed conspicuously in their speed. The difference was not due to a specifically fast Japanese class of vessel, but because of the Russian column's greater heterogeneity. It was slowed down by an odd assortment of sluggish auxiliary ships ('a sore hindrance of all of our ships') and coastal defence battleships, although even its faster warships were burdened by fouled bottoms encrusted with barnacles.[152] Having a relatively homogeneous force characterized by an absence of low-speed ships, Tōgō's main column took advantage of its superior speed from the start.[153] During the initial phases of the battle, this column was able to sail at 15 knots, whereas the Russian main column sailed at no more than 12 knots. His force's faster speed, in turn, allowed the Japanese admiral to maintain his position at will, at times closing the distance from the enemy and at times opening it. His entire opening manoeuvre was based on the awareness that his enemy was notably slower. In other words, this speed allowed him to throw 'the Russian broadsides more and more out of action', as Alfred Thayer Mahan put it, in referring to Tōgō's famous manoeuvre and the four additional turns he later performed during the first engagement.[154] During night operations too, the Japanese light forces benefited from their higher speed. By being able to sail at a maximum speed of 28–30 knots, the Japanese destroyers were much faster than any larger Russian warships and so could easily outmanoeuvre those they intercepted.

Communication and Detection

The IJN equipped its ships with wireless radios and was able to use them effectively. Thanks to the wireless, the early detection of the Russian columns allowed Tōgō ample time to deploy his battle divisions. This newly developed invention, for whose development the Nobel Prize in Physics was awarded four years later, also allowed the Japanese admiral to dispatch his units for an extensive search during the battle and bring them back at will. The advancing Baltic Fleet was less prepared in terms of wireless or visual communication. Rozhestvenskiĭ did not make substantial use of his own wireless equipment either in searching for the Japanese fleet or for blocking their transmissions.[155] Moreover, the dense black smoke the Russian ships emitted, in all likelihood the result of low-grade coal, and their bright yellow funnels made the entire armada particularly visible even in the foggy late May weather.[156]

Leadership and Preparedness

The style of leadership in each fleet differed considerably and eventually had crucial implications for the outcomes of the battle. First and foremost, the two commanders in chief differed in their awareness of each other. Before battle, Tōgō was anxiously concerned about his enemy's dispositions and, once they were discovered, followed them closely, whereas Rozhestvenskiĭ did very little to gather information about them. Mahan's observation that the Russian admiral 'knew nothing' of the Japanese forces is grossly exaggerated, but after his safe passage through the Malacca Strait and off Singapore he indeed scarcely pursued further information on the Japanese positions and plans.[157] No less importantly, Tōgō initiated manoeuvres proactively and daringly in combat whereas Rozhestvenskiĭ responded passively and docilely.[158] Throughout the entire battle, for at least 36 hours, Tōgō remained the ultimate authority in his fleet. Unflagging and unflappable, he led his division through its most gruelling times, but also shared his plans with his commanders, delegated responsibilities, and trusted his subordinates. On the Russian side, the dearth of leadership of this sort was evident. A centralist with a certain aversion to his subordinates, the Russian commander in chief did not share his plans for the battle with his immediate deputies, Nebogatov and Enkvist, let alone the commanders of his ships.[159] In fact, before the battle, he had met his second in command Nebogatov only once and never discussed his strategy or intentions with him. Ultimately, from the time his flagship, the *Kniaz Suvorov*, no longer took part in the battle and he himself was moved wounded to another ship, Rozhestvenskiĭ was late to transfer the command of the squadron and, when he did, Nebogatov barely assumed command.[160] These two leadership styles led to remarkably different outcomes in terms of preparedness. The Japanese crews had practised intensively for the coming engagement while their commanders discussed and practised the tactics it was to involve.[161] The Russian crews spent the long months before the battle in wearing anticipation for additional reinforcements and, of course, in sailing at cruising speed. They spent little time, however, in gunnery practice and their commanders saw no tactical manoeuvres or any other endeavour to prepare for the battle.[162]

Motivation

The two forces differed considerably in their motivation and in their determination to secure victory. The high morale of the IJN was the result of more than a decade of intense indoctrination in patriotism and loyalty developed both through the education system and in the armed forces.[163] Seen in this light, the war marks a watershed in the rise of nationalism in Japan and the popular support lent to the state and its overseas expansion.[164] The determination the IJN displayed stemmed in part from the enormous implications that victory, and even more defeat, had for the nation as a whole. After 15 months of constant fighting, Japan could not risk losing this battle since it could end in Japan losing the entire war. Moreover, with its relatively limited human resources and under-developed economy, Japan could hardly settle for a partial victory. Allowing the Baltic Fleet to reach Vladivostok meant dragging the war on for longer and transforming it into a war of attrition Japan could not afford. Moreover, the presence of a large Russian naval force in the vicinity of Japan, either as a constant menace or as a 'fleet in being', could risk the sustenance of its land forces in Korea and southern Manchuria, and could also put a stop to the provision of essential supplies to the Japanese home islands.[165] Rozhestvenskiĭ himself stated before the battle that, if only 20 of the ships under his command reached Vladivostok, 'the Japanese communications would be seriously endangered'.[166] Keenly aware of these circumstances, the Tōgō of May 1905 was determined to avoid the mistakes he had made during the Battle of the Yellow Sea and, accordingly, was willing to take greater risks than ever before.

Despite his orders, Rozhestvenskiĭ was not as determined as Tōgō to master the waters around Japan. His correspondence suggests he did not necessarily regard the voyage as an operation whose main objective was to achieve ascendancy, but rather as a tool for securing a Russian advantage in the eventual peace negotiations.[167] His lack of determination is also reflected in the decisions made by other senior officers of the Baltic Fleet during the final phases of the battle. Enkvist chose to escape southward and found shelter in Manila, whereas Nebogatov opted for an uncommon surrender. The low motivation in the Baltic Fleet ran deeper than the question of objectives and resolve. The arduous voyage of the Russian armada cannot be separated from the question of motivation. Any fleet embarking on such a protracted odyssey would have experienced lower morale and reduced fighting capacity.[168] Thus, the voyage, the wretched conditions on board the ships, and the treatment meted out by the officers crushed what little motivation the ranks had had upon departure. During their stop at Nossi Be, the tropical heat, the limited provisions, and the general uncertainty stirred enduring dissent and insubordination among the rank and file. No less problematic was the lethargy that characterized many Baltic Fleet officers, although it was a symptom of a broader phenomenon. The passive anticipation for reinforcements that marked high-ranking officers of the Pacific Fleet and highest echelons of the Russian Manchurian Army was not very different. However, whereas the IRA could rely on an almost unlimited supply of soldiers, the IRN's resources were finite.[169]

Tactics

Although the two belligerents engaged in an artillery duel at first, their tactical decisions shortly before and during the battle profoundly affected its outcome. In retrospect, several decisions made by both sides were extremely significant. For the Russians, Rozhestvenskiï's decision to keep the entire armada together was probably the most crucial. The fact that he ordered his auxiliary vessels to sail behind the warships, rather than independently, slowed down the entire column and kept it in constant anxiety for the safety of these vulnerable ships.[170] By so doing, he also wasted the firepower of his cruisers on guard mission rather than taking part in the initial and most critical engagement. Rozhestvenskiï's replacement, Rear Admiral Nebogatov, did not excel in tactics either. His main endeavour, as one historian has summed it up, consisted 'of evading the enemy shells at the battleships' expense, and waiting for the protection of nightfall'.[171] On the Japanese side, Tōgō's mobilization of 58 destroyers and torpedo boats armed with torpedoes during the battle was highly successful, despite the weather conditions and earlier let-downs. During the night operations, these light vessels became the mainstay of the navy even though they did not transform the contemporary axiom, as alluded to by Captain (later Admiral) William Pakenham (1861–1933), that 'numbers can only annihilate'.[172] That said, the 10 out of 58 torpedoes (and the six out of 42 during the night operations) launched by the light flotillas that hit their targets were effective in finishing off limping enemy ships, including battleships. Moreover, their constant presence and incessant attacks demoralized the Russian crews with undeniable repercussions on the fighting during the second day.

Strategy

The overwhelming defeat of the Baltic Fleet calls the strategic considerations that underlay its initial dispatch into question. Nonetheless, its objectives were different before and after the demise of the bulk of the Pacific Fleet when Port Arthur surrendered in early January 1905. The tsar modified the fleet's objectives later that month, but Rozhestvenskiĭ's subsequent actions, and especially those carried out on 27 May 1905, do not appear to correspond to his instructions. While making every effort to reach Vladivostok, he did not seek to master the seas in its vicinity. There is little doubt that Rozhestvenskiĭ should be praised for leading his armada all the way to Tsushima Strait against all odds, but he failed completely in preparing and executing his wider strategy. Tōgō, in contrast, followed his own strategy successfully. By waiting for the optimal time and location for annihilating his enemy, he could prevent it not only from mastering the sea but also from forming a 'fleet in being' in the safe haven of Vladivostok.[173] Above all, the Japanese admiral's choice of place was crucial. The relatively narrow strait and the search plan he devised made the prospects of encounter almost certain. A decade later, the British and German experience in the North Sea would show that even the use of wireless did not prevent large naval forces from missing each other and consequently avoid a decisive battle for most of the war. After Tsushima, the possibility of the IRN recovering its maritime position was, in Julian Corbett's terms, too remote to be a practical consideration, and so the IJN gained 'permanent command' of the seas in the arena for the first time.[174] Moreover, the outcomes allowed Japan to maintain its command on land too and hasten the peace negotiations.

Altogether, the keys to Japan's decisive victory in the battle can be divided into two. During the opening phases, it was the Japanese main column's dozen capital ships that gained the upper hand from the outset. By concentrating their fire on the four most modern and formidable Russian warships, they largely neutralized them and so were able to set the course of the entire battle. More specifically, the Japanese column benefited from better tactical command and faster speed, and also used its gunnery in a more effective way than its opponents, inasmuch as it fragmented its enemy and sharply decreased his capacity to resist. Had the battle ended at 7.00 p.m., on the first day, the Japanese victory would have been outstanding. But it raged for another 24 hours. During its final phases, and especially during the night, it was the successful use of a large number of small vessels, mainly swarms of destroyers and torpedo boats, which contributed to even greater scores and to the ultimate crushing victory. Despite operating after dark, they were able to locate the fleeing Russian ships, forcing them to scatter and escape to neutral ports or sinking them by torpedoes launched at close range. This successful tactical use of the Japanese force was enhanced by an impaired strategic vision on the Russian side. If the Russians had possessed such clear vision, to say nothing of a more aggressive and creative temper, they could have ended the battle on less uneven terms.

3

Japan's Rise to Naval Prominence

Upon hearing the news of the victory, the entire Japanese nation was filled with a sense of exultation. It was nonetheless a sobering joy, and the public was—to the foreign observers' amazement—mostly able to hold back a mixture of exhilaration and relief. Reflecting the proper spirit of day, Emperor Meiji composed a five-line poem that solemnly grieved for the Japanese soldiers lost in the fighting.[1] Still, some could not suppress their elation. For example, over 100,000 people gathered spontaneously to celebrate the triumph in Tokyo's Hibiya Park off the Imperial Palace's moat.[2] Unlike earlier lantern parades—a common sight during the conflict against Russia—the atmosphere was particularly euphoric this time around. Although the newspaper headlines seemed somewhat restrained, the breaking news, following a hiatus of more than two months since the land victory at Mukden, gave the crowd a solid reason to believe that the war was about to end.[3]

These heightened expectations notwithstanding, the Battle of Tsushima did not end the war at once. It did, however, prompt new efforts on Japan's behalf for peace negotiations that were to conclude the war within little more than three months. After the Battle of Mukden, the country was exhausted militarily and financially, even as it achieved more than it had envisaged before the war.[4] It craved a lasting peace that would take its accomplishments on the battlefields of Manchuria into consideration. The Battle of Tsushima merely reinforced this urge. With a splendid victory in its pocket, the prospects of ending the war through peace negotiations were even greater. It was little wonder, then, that Tokyo, rather than St Petersburg, took the first steps towards peace in the wake of the battle. On 1 June 1905, and a mere four days after the government in Tokyo received the full news, its United States representatives approached President Theodore Roosevelt (1858–1919) and asked him to advance 'his own motion and initiative'.[5]

Throughout that month, Japanese negotiators sought, to little avail, to exploit Russia's naval defeat and to bring its leaders to the negotiation table. Eventually, and with Roosevelt's support, the Japanese decision makers resolved to occupy the large island of Sakhalin, the nearest Russian territory. The mission was given to the IJN's Third Fleet under Vice Admiral Kataoka Shichirō and the IJA's newly formed 13th Division.[6] The invading expeditionary force left for Sakhalin on 5 July 1905, and the first landing operations began two days later. The entire island fell into Japanese hands on 13 July although Russian partisan units kept on fighting in the northern part of the island. Not until 1 August 1905 did the Russian garrison finally surrender.[7] In the meantime, the Japanese government remained aware that the international struggle over the two powers' images had not ended with Tsushima. Since the outbreak of the war, it had made tremendous efforts to present both the nation and its military conduct as civilized and even chivalrous.

By early summer 1905, the strategic gains of a supportive world public opinion were evident.[8] Japan's pre-war image improved markedly, and in the United States in particular.[9] It was no time for a momentary distraction or, worse, bravado and hubris. Celebrations of the victory were thus postponed and the Russian prisoners were accorded commendable treatment.[10] This was the lot also of the most famous, the wounded Rozhestvenskiĭ. On 3 June 1905, Tōgō visited him at the naval hospital in Sasebo. As he exemplified the Japanese spirit of chivalry and held Rozhestvenskiĭ's hand in his hands, Tōgō said emphatically: 'Defeat is an accident to the lot of all fighting men, and there is no occasion to be cast down by it if we have done our duty. I can only express my admiration for the courage with which your sailors fought during the recent battle, and my personal admiration of yourself, who carried out your heavy task until you were seriously wounded.'[11] This ostensibly private visit, which took place a mere six days after the battle, was soon immortalized in a multitude of texts and visual records.[12] Two weeks later, and in a similar gesture of civility, the Japanese authorities released the *Kostroma*, one of the two hospital ships which had been captured. She left for Shanghai with wounded sailors on board and then headed for Manila to take also wounded interned sailors back to Russia.[13] As modern wars are also waged in the media, no better scenes and gestures could epitomize the image Japan coveted in 1905: a victorious yet compassionate nation (Figure 16).

Once the takeover of Sakhalin was complete, the road to a peace treaty was short. With President Roosevelt serving as host, the two belligerents sent their representatives to Portsmouth, New Hampshire, where the peace conference was to be convened. Roosevelt had conveyed messages to the belligerents stating his keenness to serve as mediator as early as February 1905, but the Russians were adamant in their refusal despite the Japanese government's announcement of its readiness to negotiate in March. It was only after Russia's defeat in Tsushima and surrender in Sakhalin that both belligerents recognized that diplomacy might be less painful than the continuation of an

Figure 16. Admiral Tōgō pays a visit to his wounded nemesis, Vice Admiral Rozhestvenskiĭ

armed struggle. The change of mind was mostly on Russia's side and its negotiators were willing now to accept the majority of Japanese demands. On Nicholas II's strict insistence, however, they rejected the claim for an indemnity entirely and offered their recognition of Japan's control of the southern half of Sakhalin instead. The Japanese surprised the world by accepting the Russian offer and signing the Treaty of Portsmouth on 5 September 1905, an act which ended the 19-month war.[14] The Japanese public received the news with a shock that exceeded the relief of ending the war. Unaware of the military and economic strain the long war had exerted on the nation, it expected Russia to yield to all Japanese demands. The anger at the terms of the agreement, and the absence of any reparations in particular, was so deep that newspapers used the term 'betrayal' in discussing it.[15] In the port city of Sasebo, Russian prisoners of war were surprised to see 'not a single flag' among people 'so fond of beflagging their houses'.[16] On the day the treaty was concluded, some 30,000 demonstrators gathered in Hibiya Park in Tokyo. Their protest soon turned into a rampage ('Hibiya Riots') and martial law was declared in the capital. Four months later, the lingering public unrest exerted a direct impact by precipitating the collapse of Prime Minister Katsura Tarō's cabinet.[17]

In spite of this sour denouement to the war, few in Japan at the time doubted the war was a success story.[18] When, on 20 December 1905, the Combined Fleet was dispersed, very few military units in Japan were as venerated. If asked, ordinary Japanese pointed to the Battle of Tsushima and possibly to the seizure of Port Arthur as the war's climax. In subsequent years, Japan was also able to capitalize on its victory and to establish an array of mutual agreements with other powers and thus fortify its position in north-east Asia. As evidenced by the renewal of their alliance in 1905 and again in 1911, Great Britain remained Japan's most valuable ally, but, surprisingly the latter also signed an agreement with both France and its arch enemy Russia in 1907.[19] This was also the first time Russia acknowledged Japan's interests in Korea fully and even committed itself to non-intervention, while Japan reciprocated by recognizing Russian interests in Outer Mongolia. The powers thus considered Japan, with its combination of victories in battle and array of diplomatic agreements, a regional power. Thereafter, in the entire Pacific Ocean, only the United States Navy could be seen as Japan's equal. Domestically, however, the first decade after the war was not characterized by any particular public prosperity or national grandeur. It took another 14 years for Japan 'suddenly' to turn into a true power. In January 1919, it was one of the 'Big Five' powers that controlled the Versailles Peace Conference, and it soon won a permanent seat on the Council of the newly established League of Nations.

The Imperial Japanese Navy following the Battle

On 21 October 1905, the Japanese media marked the centenary of Admiral Horatio Nelson's death in the battle of Trafalgar. In Yokohama, a banquet was held for the hero of Trafalgar attended by both a British admiral and by Admiral Tōgō.[20] The sudden public interest in Nelson was self-serving since the domestic media, much like the foreign press, hailed Tōgō as his true heir, thereby placing Japan and Britain on a similar footing.[21] The timing was both perfect and intentional. A day later, on 22 October, and a little more than a month after the war ended, Japan celebrated the triumphal return of its own fleet. By then the public clamour that had erupted in Hibiya had subsided and some of the old humdrum routine was restored. The fleet's return represented the climax of a whole week of celebrations imbued with symbolism, including a visit by Tōgō to the Ise Grand Shrine—Shinto's holiest and most important site.[22] During the first day of the celebrations, Tōgō, on a black horse, passed under a triumphal arch erected in the centre of Tokyo and was welcomed by a huge cheering crowd (Figure 17). On the same day, the admiral also paid a visit to the imperial palace, where he reported on the naval operations during the war to Emperor Meiji. The next day, the emperor and the admiral joined a crowd of more than 150,000

Figure 17. A rare welcome: Admiral Tōgō's triumphal return to the Japanese capital, 22 October 1905

enthusiastic spectators in the city of Yokohama and inspected a triumphal naval review. With 146 warships in attendance, including several captured Russian ships, it was the largest Japan had ever seen.[23]

Sailing on board the imperial yacht, the admiral briefly introduced each ship and its wartime record, and included some of the recently captured Russian battleships (Figure 18). Conspicuously missing in the celebrations was Tōgō's flagship throughout the war, the battleship *Mikasa*. Six days after the conclusion of the Treaty of Portsmouth, and while moored at the naval base in Sasebo, she had been involved in a great mishap. The ship was suddenly engulfed in a fire that led to the explosion of its rear magazines and she subsequently sank.[24] The loss of the ship shocked the nation, as did the deaths of 339 of its crew.

Figure 18. The grand imperial naval review: Emperor Meiji (on the right), Admiral Tōgō (second from the left), and prominent military figures inspecting the Japanese fleet, 23 October 1905

Notes: Lithograph, 1905. Among the other dignitaries (standing to the Emperor's left): Admiral Gerard Noel, Commander-in-Chief, China Station; Admiral Itō Sukeyuki; Admiral Yamamoto Gonnohyōe; Prime Minister General Katsura Tarō; and Field Marshal Yamagata Aritomo. Dimensions: 40×55 centimetres

Rozhestvenskiĭ sent his condolences from his prison camp. Tōgō replied laconically: his grief was inconsolable.[25] The eight who had died on board the *Mikasa* during the battle paled by comparison. It took almost a year until the ship was refloated and another two to bring her back to active service, but she would never regain her earlier position, serving mostly in coastal defence and support duties. Few could imagine then that this victim of a terrible accident would become Japan's primary monument to the battle. This mishap apart, the IJN had much to be proud of. From its perspective, the Russo-Japanese War was a success story and the Battle of Tsushima was unquestionably the conflict's single most important battle. A year later, on 27 May 1906, the IJN celebrated for the first time its Navy Day (Jpn. *Kaigun kinenbi*), and continued to do so until 1945.[26]

The end of the war found the IJN larger than ever. In absolute terms, it increased its size substantially by incorporating several Russian battleships, as well as a number of newly built capital ships of its own.[27] In relative terms, it rose to fifth place among the world's largest naval forces, and thus regained the position it had held between 1901 and 1903.[28] In qualitative terms, too, the IJN gained valuable combat experience and a degree of self-confidence which affected its ambitions overseas and its conduct in subsequent inter-service competition at home. The combat success at Tsushima, and the huge popularity of the navy and Tōgō immediately after the war, induced IJN leaders to promote a navalist agenda, which meant the IJN's further expansion. Highly publicized naval reviews resembled the pattern set in October 1905, and were reinforced by ceremonies held during the domestic launching of warships and in books and journals.[29] Images of the Battle of Tsushima and its participants would remain an important vehicle in the navy's public affairs and memorabilia for years to come.[30]

After 1905, each service had different goals and different sets of priorities. These mirrored a new condition that historian Oka Yoshitake has defined as a 'dissolution of consensuses'.[31] Unlike the IJA, the IJN could no longer regard Russia and its enfeebled naval force as its primary enemy. In its stead, and under the influence of the naval theorist Satō Tetsutarō (1866–1942), the IJN adopted an explicit policy of expansion which treated the United States Navy as its potential rival.[32] In view of the clash in the Pacific in the early 1940s, this choice might appear prescient, especially given the intensifying tension between the two countries which has been interpreted as a protracted cold war.[33] And yet, at least initially, the United States Navy posed very little threat to Japan, and the IJN's view of it was largely as a 'budgetary enemy' created to allow it to reap the fruits of its newly acquired 'Tsushima glory'.[34] After 1905, the IJN began to see itself as the long naval arm of a true power and its numerical and qualitative yardsticks were, respectively, the United States Navy and the British Royal Navy. Accordingly, it hurried to build its own dreadnought battleships and battlecruisers domestically. Likewise, and during the eight years between 1911 and 1918, it completed the construction of 12 capital ships—the same number as its American 'hypothetical rival'— and another two by 1922, the point at which the Washington Naval Conference's restrictions came into effect.[35]

Thereon, the relations between Japan's navy and army turned sour and adversarial. Although the new policy directed the focus of Japan's military away from Russia and towards the United States, the discord over national goals and the corrosion of a central decision making process characterized the following years. The 1907 document on Imperial Defence Policy (Jpn. *Teikoku kokubō hōshin*) was drafted to solve this very problem. It aimed to limit increasing inter-service rivalry by creating a single national defence strategy, but failed to settle the differences between navalist and continental approaches and even gave a certain precedence to the latter.[36] In terms of build-up, the navy formulated a plan for an 'eight-eight fleet', namely, eight new battleships (all dreadnought-type) and eight battlecruisers.[37] Although financial constraints prevented it from eventually fulfilling this plan, the IJN did keep expanding, while procuring or building the largest warships available.[38] With no further battles and with the demise of some of its competitors, Japan became the world's third largest naval force by the end of First World War. Hence, the Battle of Tsushima marked a transitory stage in Japan's naval development. Whereas in 1890 the IJN was a negligible force, by 1920 it could seriously challenge either of the world's two largest naval powers.

This rise became obvious from May 1905, when Japan was first recognized as a true naval power as well as the foremost power in the Pacific (Figure 19). The IJN's proven dominance rendered 'the position of Japan quite unassailable', as one foreign observer noted in 1909.[39] The IJN's budget rose with its reputation. However, despite the larger allocations it obtained, the IJN failed to redefine its purpose after Tsushima. As Tadokoro Masayuki has argued, it was 'too big and

Figure 19. Post-Tsushima Japan as a world naval power: 'No Limit. Japan–I see your cruisers and raise you a dreadnought!' *Puck*, 1909

Note: Artist: Louis M. Glackens (1866–1933).

ambitious' for Japan's immediate strategic needs but also 'too small to achieve the Mahanite dream of naval mastery in the Pacific, if not of the whole world'.[40] Part of this problem of definition was political. The IJN's success during the war, and the Battle of Tsushima in particular, made this service, much like the IJA, highly involved in internal affairs. This phenomenon had pre-war roots and would recede temporarily in the early 1920s, but the war against Russia definitely served as its catalyst. Of the two services, the IJN was the greater beneficiary of the war on account of its intact combat record, but also because it became evident that Japan would not be able to maintain its naval hegemony in the region without large annual budgets. After the war, the Navy began to perceive itself as the Army's equal and vied for a greater share of the state's limited resources.[41] In these new political circumstances, its leaders were now capable of forging a political alliance with members of the Seiyūkai which resulted in a counter-alliance between the Army and parties opposed to the Seiyūkai.[42] During the 1930s, growing inter-service competition exerted a far-reaching and subversive impact on internal politics that was accompanied by greater pressures for imperialist expansion.[43]

Long-Term Naval Consequences

The most profound effect the Battle of Tsushima exerted on the IJN was in doctrine. While the entire war against Russia marked a watershed for Japanese militarism as a whole, the Battle of Tsushima was a defining moment for the navy.[44] Despite fading gradually and turning into a mythical foundation, the lessons of the battle affected the IJN's naval strategy and mindset until its 1945 dissolution, if not later.[45] After all, from a post-1945 perspective, we can safely say that the Battle of Tsushima was the most important landmark in the IJN's 83-year history. While it is possible to argue that the attack on Pearl Harbor on 7 December 1941 was more spectacular, its legacy was short and controversial, as the IJN suffered one of its most painful defeats—at Midway—within six months. In military terms, the clash with Russia had no precedents in scale, and remained Japan's most fateful challenge until the Pacific War (1941–5). As a lesson in history, the battle provided the ultimate and most solid evidence that the Japanese nation and its naval force were invincible. This conviction could not have emerged after its victory over China's Beiyang Fleet in 1894 because of the opponent's seeming inferiority and because the victory had been an isolated case. The triumph over the Baltic Fleet provided the continuity that was required.

The victory also conveyed an unambiguous message. It reinforced an existing belief that Japan's national spirit, and its fighting spirit in particular, could make up for, if not replace, a shortage of manpower and deficiencies in armament. Although the IJN did not suffer an overall inferiority in the battle, it did overcome eight battleships with only four. Furthermore, the battle was the final stage in the destruction of Russia's larger naval force. After the war, the concept of *Yamato Damashii* (Japanese Spirit) became a major factor in comprehending Japan's victory over colossal Russia. This concept had a longstanding historical background in Japan but was now used for military objectives.[46] The concept of a 'Japanese spirit' was partly a myth, and—like all myths—was detached from reality and thorough analysis. After all, the naval victory in Tsushima was not a true 'victory of spirit over matter'. The Baltic Fleet, much like the Pacific Fleet, was much stronger than the Beiyang Fleet 10 years earlier, but the IJN was operating in a state of numerical parity, if not certain advantage, throughout much of the war. The Japanese crews were better trained than their Russian counterparts not only in moral education but also, and mainly, in gunnery and damage control. Ultimately, the emphasis on *Yamato Damashii* bore a catastrophic message that manifested in the military adventures the IJN was to attempt later on and in motivating the rank and file to sacrifice their lives.[47] Given this line of thought, it is little wonder, then, that the initial formation of Special Attack Units (Jpn. *Tokubetsu kōgekitai*; 'kamikaze') in 1944 involving the use of military aviators for suicide attacks took place in the IJN.[48]

In operational terms, the experience of Tsushima exerted a conspicuous effect on the IJN in several spheres that lingered until the IJN's disbandment in 1945. The emphasis on a climactic and decisive naval battle was probably the main, and most harmful, legacy of Tsushima.[49] Thereafter, all naval plans for war against a future enemy, and the United States Navy in particular, anticipated a decisive battle near the shores of Japan—a sort of Tsushima remake.[50] This Decisive Battle Doctrine (Jpn. *Kantai kessen*) called for the use of a strong battleship force to destroy an invading fleet in a single stroke, in a similar manner to the battle in May 1905. There was, however, one important difference: whereas the clash in Tsushima ended the conflict, the future decisive battle would come at the beginning of it.

Numbers mattered too. Soon after Tsushima, IJN planners led by Satō Tetsutarō recognized that the 70 per cent ratio between the defensive (Japanese) force and the offensive force would be the minimum required for viable defence.[51] This ratio planted seeds in 1905–7 which would bear their rotten fruits decades later. It would become the cornerstone of IJN construction projects and of budgetary clashes. Internationally, its role would be even more pivotal. Starting in the 1921–2 Washington Naval Conference and continued during the subsequent 14 years, the IJN would insist on this or a higher ratio in discussing the fixed quotas of battleships (and aircraft carriers) it was to have in relation to the British and American navies. This insistence, against the backdrop of Anglo-American unwillingness to offer more than a 60 per cent ratio, would be the cause of growing tension between Japan and its previous allies alongside extreme frustration at home.[52]

Throughout this period, the Decisive Battle Doctrine was not abandoned. This scenario was supposed to apply when the enemy fleet approached Japan after suffering losses by attrition as it penetrated the nation's perimeter defences. The exact location of this battle changed repeatedly, but large surface battles still held a central place in the IJN's strategic plans even on the eve of the attack on Pearl Harbor in December 1941. The attack on Pearl Harbor was thus not a refutation of this view, but a gamble intended to realize it. Anticipating an American recovery and the regrouping of its naval forces, the principal Japanese scenario for the Pacific War foresaw a decisive naval battle that would lead to the final victory.[53] While the idea did not vanish completely until 1945, it was only the successful use of aircraft carriers in the attack on Pearl Harbor and their dominance in the Battle of Midway that began to render the Tsushima legacy of a big-gun battleship engagement obsolescent.

The Battle of Tsushima represented an enduring legacy for virtually any senior IJN officer who took part in the Second World War. Admiral Yamamoto Isoroku (1884–1943) and Vice Admiral Nagumo Chūichi (1887–1944) may serve as cases in point. For the former, the commander of the Japanese Combined Fleet and the mastermind of the attack on Pearl Harbor, it was the most memorable and formative combat experience he could rely on, at least until December 1941. Thirty-six years earlier, the 21-year-old Yamamoto was an ensign on board the cruiser *Nisshin*, which formed part of the 1st Battle Division. When the ship's forward turret was hit by a Russian shell during the initial engagement, he was injured in his leg and lost two fingers.[54] In subsequent years, Yamamoto maintained the orthodoxy of a single decisive battle dominated by battleships. With this mental imprinting, and despite being the former chief of the Naval Aviation Department, this illustrious admiral, much like the rest of the IJN top echelon, still regarded the ageing American battleships as the key weapon in the impending naval clash as late as the eve of the attack on Pearl Harbor.[55] Thus, he carried on with his pre-emptive aerial strike despite the absence of the American carriers. Obviously, he had other strong motives for this assault but his Tsushima mindset cannot be precluded. Symbolically as well, and in reference to the famous Z flag (Jpn. *zetto-ki*) which Tōgō hoisted on the *Mikasa* in 1905, the attack on Pearl Harbor was referred to as Operation Z during its planning.[56]

The flag was not forgotten during the actual attack too. Under Yamamoto's exhortation, Vice Admiral Nagumo, who 36 years earlier had served as a young officer in Suzuki's 4th Destroyer Division and now was leading Japan's main carrier battle group, ran up the same pennant on his flagship, the carrier *Akagi*.[57] Shortly before, Nagumo read aloud an 'imperial rescript' written before the fleet's departure by Emperor Shōwa. This text, too, was reminiscent of Tsushima: 'The responsibility assigned to the Combined Fleet is so grave that the rise and fall of the Empire depends upon what it is going to accomplish.'[58] Six months later, it was all too symbolic, but somewhat unplanned, that Nagumo chose the 37th anniversary of the battle, Navy Day on 27 May 1942, as the date his fleet would weigh anchor and leave for another battle. Eleven days later, when the Battle of Midway ended, it would become a turning point in the Pacific War and mark the beginning of the IJN's downfall.[59]

The second legacy of Tsushima was the idea of a campaign of attrition against a superior force of bigger and more numerous warships. The IJN throughout its subsequent existence, David Evans and Mark Peattie have concluded, 'remained convinced that the basic strategy and tactics of attrition were the best means of equalizing Japanese and enemy strength in capital ships and fire power prior to the decisive battle.'[60] Another legacy concerns the structure of the fighting force and the stress on its homogeneity and quality in particular. After 1905, the IJN was careful to avoid the adverse repercussions the IRN had experienced due to its use of a heterogeneous force and kept using capital ships of similar form and performance. Possessing a homogenous fleet was a valuable asset, but, as noted by Alessio Patalano, it was 'pursued at the cost of balance among the fleet's different functions and tactical and operational flexibility'.[61]

In terms of weaponry, the IJN was to emphasize offensive capabilities.[62] This, in turn, fostered the use of capital ships, mostly battleships, and in the late 1930s aircraft carriers too, for offensive purposes.[63] This is not to say that the IJN was the only naval force to do so, as battleships remained the mainstay of every large navy until the early 1940s. And yet the IJN's stress on capital ships came at the expense, and at times even neglect, of other vessels, as can be seen in the case of anti-submarine warfare (ASW).[64] In terms of quality, the use of the expensive but seemingly indomitable *Mikasa* proved to be a sound investment. After Tsushima, the IJN kept striving to procure warships with an edge in speed, armour, or gunfire and, if possible, in all three dimensions, over similar classes launched by its opponents. Starting with the four *Kongō*-class battlecruisers, which in all likelihood were the best of their kind at the time of their commission (1913–15), the IJN repeatedly built larger and often better warships than its rivals, reaching its epitome with the construction of the *Yamato*-class battleships. A final, albeit minor, legacy was the reliance on the torpedo as a major weapon in surface engagements. As in 1905, the use of torpedoes in later years would be mostly assigned to small vessels operating at night and so offsetting the IJN's supposed inferiority during the daytime when engaging a superior opponent.[65]

Altogether, the Battle of Tsushima left behind a complex and enduring legacy. It had many positive aspects that made the IJN a formidable fleet with extreme offensive capabilities that shocked the world in 1941–2. At the same time, certain aspects of it were harmful, and even calamitous. This is because they were interpreted as if future wars would be a dress rehearsal of the 1905 engagement and because they forestalled greater flexibility and preparedness for a protracted total war in a changing naval environment.

The Memory of the Battle and Its Significance

As the party that won the war and benefited from it the most, it was only natural that the battle would remain a centre point in Japan's collective memory. Throughout the years before Japan's surrender in 1945, and to a lesser extent even after, the battle continued to be the focus of commemoration and pride, possibly more than any other single battle the country had ever won or lost. Nonetheless, with the passing of time and changing circumstances, attitudes towards the battle witnessed their ups and downs much like the attitudes towards the entire war against Russia.[66] This was not necessarily because of the battle per se but largely due to the winding road the Japanese approach to war and militarism has followed. Accordingly, the history of the battle's memory can be divided into three distinct eras: the final 40 years of imperial Japan; the era of Allied occupation and its aftermath (until 1957); and the subsequent years as a democratic Japan regained its sovereignty.

I. Source of Pride and Jubilation: The Imperial Era (1905–45)

During the forty years that lasted from the end of the Russo-Japanese War to Japan's surrender, Tsushima was construed as the country's ultimate naval victory. Initially, Japan celebrated the anniversary on a large scale, but public interest flagged quite quickly.[67] Moreover, from

1910 onwards, improving diplomatic relations with Russia helped to tone down further the celebrations.[68] Still, in the collective consciousness, the prominence of the battle only grew with the passage of time.[69] Apart from celebrating Navy Day on 27 May every year, imperial Japan also built tangible monuments to the battle. The first of these was a stone memorial erected in 1911 near the Tsushima Island coast in which 143 survivors of the cruiser Russian *Vladimir Monomakh* had landed and were helped by people of the village of Nishidomari.[70] Quoting Admiral Tōgō Heihachirō's four-character poem 恩海義喬 (Jpn. *onkai gikyō*; 'sea of grace, righteousness is high') and praising those villagers' virtue, this first site of memory was also a solemn monument of reconciliation (Figure 20).

More than any monument or ceremony, however, it was Admiral Tōgō who served as a living reminder of the great triumph during

Figure 20. The memorial monument to the Battle of the Sea of Japan in Kamitsushima (1911)

most of this era. With time, his image transcended that of any other figure that took part in the battle and even the entire war, including Emperor Meiji himself. Tōgō's rise to fame was not always as evident. During the first year of the war, the Japanese state and the navy had highlighted the heroism of Lieutenant Commander Hirose Takeo (1868–1904), who had attempted to sink a blockship at the harbour entrance of Port Arthur. Following his death, Hirose received a state funeral in the capital and was made one of the two War Gods (Jpn. *Gunshin*).[71] Alongside Hirose's heroism, the living Tōgō, much like the conqueror of Port Arthur, General Nogi Maresuke (1849–1912), became a symbol of staunch military leadership. After the war, both Tōgō and Nogi received almost every possible domestic honour, including the title of count in 1907, as well as widespread foreign recognition (Figure 21).[72] Tōgō, for one, was also made chief of the

Figure 21. Admiral Tōgō on a visit to the Naval Academy, Annapolis, 1911

Naval General Staff in December 1905, naval councillor in 1909, and *gensui* (equivalent to fleet admiral) in 1913.

After General Nogi's ritual suicide in 1912, Tōgō took charge of the education of Crown Prince Hirohito (reigned 1926–1989). Unlike Nogi, whose victory at Port Arthur was attained with a tremendous loss of life, the admiral's triumph was anything but controversial. This fact, along with Tōgō's longevity, helped to cultivate even further the myth of the battle and of his own personality.[73] A major instrument in promoting his image as the saviour of the nation was Ogasawara Naganari (1867–1958), the de facto official historian of the IJN until its demise in 1945, a prolific writer, and a close confidant of the admiral since the first war against China.[74] Tōgō did not intend to remain a mere symbol and became increasingly militant during the 1920s. Joining the opposition to the Washington Treaty and wielding a strong influence in this regard upon his former disciple, who soon became Emperor Shōwa (Hirohito), the old admiral became even more powerful during the last decade of his life.[75] He was made a marquis on his deathbed in 1934, was awarded a state funeral, only the tenth such ceremony since the Restoration of 1868, and was buried next to a former monarch, Emperor Taishō (reigned 1912–1926).[76] By then, he was considered one of Japan's greatest modern military leaders and its most prominent naval figure of all time.[77] And yet, even the deep reverence for Tōgō and the erection of a monument on the Island of Tsushima were not a genuine substitute for a central memorial site for the battle.

This commemorative function was fulfilled by the battleship *Mikasa*, Tōgō's flagship during the battle. The trigger for the decision to turn her into a memorial site was the Washington Naval Conference of 1921–2. Unintentionally, the Conference's setting of quotas on the aggregated displacement of capital ships in each major fleet brought about the *Mikasa*'s end as an active navy vessel. In fact, the decommissioning of this obsolete ship in 1923 prompted an almost instant media campaign for its preservation.[78] The Mikasa Preservation Society was established a year later with Tōgō as its honorary chairman.[79] Its main aim was to lobby for the ship's transformation into a memorial site and thereby to inspire the public with her historical value and cultivate the national spirit.[80] The year 1925 thus marked a new phase in the Mikasa's annals. The preservation of the Mikasa was now made official government policy and was followed by an appeal to the leading powers to allow the ship to be retained as a monument, despite the requirements for naval reductions.[81] With their approval, the ship was towed to its ultimate berth in Yokosuka, very close to the naval base it had served and about one-hour's ride away from Tokyo, in June 1925. The site's opening ceremony was held on the 12

Figure 22. The opening ceremony of the Memorial Ship Mikasa: Admiral Tōgō and Crown Prince Hirohito, Prince Regent of Japan, on board the ship, 12 November 1926

Notes: The photo was released to the public on the following Navy Day, 27 May 1927. By then Hirohito had become the reigning emperor.

November 1926 in the presence of Crown Prince Hirohito, Tōgō, and some 500 attendees (Figure 22).[82] Encased in concrete, the Memorial Ship Mikasa (Jpn. Kinen-kan Mikasa) instantly became the main commemoration site for the battle and the naval chapter of the war against Russia. Its popularity grew gradually and reached a zenith before the Pacific War when more than 500,000 visitors a year made a pilgrimage to see it.[83]

Another site of memory for the battle was inaugurated in Fukutsu, Fukuoka Prefecture in the year Admiral Tōgō died (Figure 23).[84] Built in a warship-like concrete form with a turret directed at the Tsushima Strait, the monument was a personal initiative of Abe Masahiro, who had served aboard the IJN *Okinoshima* (formerly the IRN *General Admiral Graf Apraksin*).[85] The mid-1930s also witnessed endeavours to revive the memory of the Russo-Japanese War as a tool for enhancing patriotism and militarism.[86] By then, the Battle of Tsushima had

Figure 23. Monument memorializing the Battle of Tsushima, Fukutsu, Japan, 1934

become a dominant theme in moral education and appeared in virtually every school history textbook.[87] Tokyo, however, had to wait a little longer for a monument of its own. It was in this city that Tōgō would be bestowed six years after his death with one of the greatest honours and a relatively rare token of recognition which can be conferred posthumously on a Japanese. He was officially deified and publicly worshipped as a god (*kami*) as part of the newly formed State Shinto-sponsored nationalist pantheon. To this end, and with the help of donations from the public and naval associations, Tōgō Shrine (Jpn. *Tōgō jinja*) was erected in Harajuku District, at the very centre of the capital. The shrine was ceremonially dedicated on the Navy Anniversary Day of 1940 in the presence of Fleet Admiral Prince Fushimi Hiroyasu.[88] The initiative for its construction was the outcome of public pressure on the Navy Ministry, the establishment of an association to this end, and extensive donations. In a period of escalating inter-service rivalry, the IJN was particularly open to persuasion. With a shrine devoted to its greatest admiral, it could keep pace with the honour bestowed upon the IJA General Nogi Maresuke and his wife Shizuko, for whom the Nogi Shrine had been dedicated in Tokyo as early as 1923. Eventually, the two shrines shared a tragic fate. On 25 May 1945, and exactly two days before the battle's 40th anniversary, both were burnt to the ground as a result of an American air raid.[89]

II. Forced Amnesia: The Occupation Era and Its Aftermath (1945–57)

The interest in the battle diminished abruptly upon Japan's surrender in 1945. The nation was at first immersed in basic survival, and its longstanding focus on militarism and heroism was soon replaced by democratic ideals and a pacifist ethos under American indoctrination and censorship. In this respect, the Battle of Tsushima came to be regarded as another stepping-stone on the path leading to the Pacific war and the nation's ultimate defeat. Hence the battle was ignored and its memorial sites neglected during the first decade of post-war Japan. The Tōgō Shrine, for example, remained in ruins and the Memorial Ship Mikasa was pillaged by Allied soldiers upon their arrival in

September 1945. Adding insult to injury, the Allied occupation authorities also decided to remove the ship's masts and some of her guns a
few months later.[90] It did not take long before the ship turned into a
recreational site for US army soldiers with a dancing hall ('Cabaret
Togo') in her central structure, as well as, at a later time, a sea life-
themed aquarium at her stern.[91]

The Japanese government and the municipality of Yokosuka
showed little care for the shrine or for the *Mikasa* even after the
occupation had ended. Nonetheless, the ship's decline reached a turning point in 1955—a year after the establishment of the Japan Self-
Defence Forces. During that year, the editor of the English-language
Nippon Times received a letter concerning the ship's abysmal state.[92]
Interestingly, the writer of this letter was not Japanese, but a Philadel-
phia businessman named John Rubin, who was born in Barrow-in-
Furness in Britain, the town in which the *Mikasa* was built.[93] Observing the ship's launching in 1900 at the Vickers Naval Construction
Yard, Rubin asserted that she was to the Japanese what HMS *Victory*
was to the British. The publication of the letter led to a minor public
buzz about the state of the ship as well as to a detailed response by a
retired admiral, Yamanashi Katsunoshin (1877–1967), the president of
the recently established Japan Naval Association (Jpn. Suikōkai).[94] At
that juncture, the idea of bringing the *Mikasa* back to its pre-war glory
was not only a matter of foreign pressure or personal whim but also
associated closely with prevailing attitudes towards the bellicose
nature of the country's recent past. The first of these perceived the
IJN as having opposed the IJA's rash plans to challenge the West, or at
least as attempting to restrain them. It was the outcome of a simplistic
tendency born soon after Japan's surrender, and which remained
strong even after the end of the Allied occupation, to distinguish
between the 'good navy' and the 'bad army'.[95] The second such
attitude concerned the Russo-Japanese War in particular and viewed
it as the last major conflict Japan fought to achieve justified ends.

In this context, and in his capacity as the president of the Suikōkai,
Admiral Yamanashi saw the restored ship as becoming a major

memorial site for more than the Battle of Tsushima. Instead, by focusing on the service's heyday of international glory, the ship could be a memorial for the IJN as a whole. Aware of the need for public support, Yamanashi handed the public campaign for the restoration project to Itō Masanori (1889–1962), by then Japan's leading naval affairs journalist.[96] A year later, on the 51st anniversary of the battle, Itō launched the campaign with a commemorative article. Published in one of Japan's leading newspapers, it highlighted the ship's significance and the global impact of the victory at Tsushima. Subsequently, Itō and others were able to enlist the support of one of the Yokosuka city councillors, whose naval base had been hosting the United States Seventh Fleet's headquarters since 1945. They also approached a number of leading American naval officers, including Admiral Arleigh Burke (1901–1996), by then the Chief of Naval Operations, and the ageing Fleet Admiral Chester Nimitz (1885–1966), who had felt a deep admiration for Admiral Tōgō since their meeting more than half a century earlier.[97]

III. Pride and Ideal: The Postwar Independence Era (1957–present)

The era of amnesia came to an end 12 years after the end of the war. While naval enthusiasts were busy with their plans for the restoration of the Memorial Ship Mikasa, a film on the Russo-Japanese War heralded a new era. Entitled *Meiji Tennō to Nichiro dai sensō* (*Emperor Meiji and the Great Russo-Japanese War*), it portrayed the major events of the war, including the Battle of Tsushima.[98] Released on the day of the Emperor Meiji's birthday, the film was hailed as the country's first CinemaScope film, and achieved overwhelming box office success.[99] This domestic popularity notwithstanding, American support remained an important factor in the restoration of the ship. In 1959, Japan's leading monthly published an article written by Admiral Nimitz, in which he argued that the *Mikasa* would be a monument to a turning point in Japanese history hailed at the time as such by the world.[100] Nimitz's donation of the fees received for the article to this cause was followed by members of the Seventh Fleet in Yokosuka and matched by domestic supporters.[101] With this enthusiasm and financial support, the ship was subsequently restored and opened to the public on the 1961 anniversary of the battle (Figure 24).[102] By then, the Tōgō Shrine had witnessed a similar recovery. With a flurry of donations, including Nimitz's royalties from the Japanese translation of his book *The Great Sea War*,[103] the shrine was rebuilt alongside a small museum devoted to the admiral's memory and to the Battle of Tsushima.[104] The entire site was reopened in 1962, during the same year as the Nogi Shrine and a year after the Memorial Ship Mikasa's reopening.[105]

A boom of war films and historical fiction novels also helped in bringing the battle back into the Japanese mainstream several years later. In this regard, the harbinger of change was Maruyama Seiji's 1969 film *Nihonkai dai kaisen* (*Great Naval Battle of the Japan Sea*) which focused exclusively on this naval battle for the first time. Although it was probably inspired by the centenary celebration of the Meiji Restoration a year earlier, there was also a financial motive.[106] By featuring the pre-eminent actor Mifune Toshirō in the role of Tōgō, Tōhō

Figure 24. The reopened Memorial Ship Mikasa with the statue of Admiral Tōgō in its front

studios sought to repeat the box-office success of its film *Nihon no ichiban nagai hi* (*Japan's Longest Day*) two years earlier. Given the cult of the 'good navy', naval themes became highly popular, with *Rengō kantai shirei chōkan Yamamoto Isoroku* (*Yamamoto Isoroku, Commander in Chief of the Combined Fleet*) screened a year earlier, the American–Japanese co-production *Tora! Tora! Tora!* a year later, and *Okinawa kessen* (*Decisive Battle for Okinawa*) two years after that (1971).[107]

The most important cultural reference to the battle in this new era appeared in written form. Entitled *Saka no ue no kumo* (*Clouds Above the Hill*), and serialized in the national daily *Sankei Shimbun* between 1968 and 1972, this novel told the story of the Russo-Japanese War while devoting a full volume to the battle.[108] One element in the book's success was undoubtedly the identity of its novelist—Shiba Ryōtarō (1923–1996), Japan's most prominent and popular author of historical fiction to this very day.[109] But additional elements were its content and context. During a period when the Japanese public began to feel confident enough to re-examine its sour past during the so-called Fifteen Years War (1931–45), *Saka no ue no kumo* told the story of a just war and of patriotic officers. Epitomizing Shiba's passion for the *bushido* values of patriotism, loyalty, and selflessness, the novel focused on the lives and exploits of three non-fictional figures: the brothers Akiyama Yoshifuru and Akiyama Saneyuki and their friend, the poet and literary critic, Masaoka Shiki.[110] The storyline follows their life from childhood until the climax during the Battle of Tsushima. Shiba's multi-volume epic triggered a revival of public interest in Tsushima. Tōgō, for example, was the topic of no fewer than three new biographies published within four years.[111] The same year in which Shiba's final volume appeared also witnessed the publication of Yoshimura Akira's (1927–2006) *Umi no shigeki* (*Historical Drama of the Sea*). This novel also told the story of the naval struggle during the war, and of the Battle of Tsushima, in a semi-documentary style, and stressed the Russian perspective even further.[112]

In the past two decades, the most notable literary contribution to the battle's commemoration has been in a form of graphic novels (manga). The first such novel was the work of illustrator Ueda Shin and writer Takanuki Nobuhito and was entitled, *Jitsuroku Nihonkai kaisen (The Record of the Naval Battle of Tsushima)*. This novel focused on the battle and was serialized in 2000.[113] A year later, Egawa Tatsuya's (1961–) *Nichiro sensō monogatari (A Tale of the Russo-Japanese War)* became a sensational hit.[114] The story is concerned with the rise of Akiyama Saneyuki and, despite stopping at the Sino-Japanese War, it hinted at the crowing point at Tsushima a decade later in its subtitle (and Akiyama's famous meteorological message shortly before the battle): 'The weather is fine but the waves are high.'[115] By all accounts, the success of both amplified the popularity of *Saka no ue no kumo* among a new and younger audience. Consequently, a few years later and four decades after its initial publication, Shiba's novel reached a second peak in an adapted visual form. After years of wavering, apparently on account of the novel's militaristic content, NHK, Japan's national public broadcasting organization, decided to produce a TV-special period drama (Jpn. *taiga dorama*) based on it.[116] Airing between 2009 and 2011 and culminating in a final episode entitled *The Battle of Tsushima* (Jpn. *Nihonkai kaisen*), this 13-episode drama was the most expensive and most elaborate period drama NHK had ever produced.[117]

Domestically, and even more so among its neighbours, Japan's modern wars and the period of Asian imperialism have remained controversial issues. And yet, the spectacular economic success and rising confidence the country experienced in the 1980s also revived interest in the pre-war past in official circles. In 1988, the Japanese Ministry of Education included Tōgō in a list of historical figures recommended for primary and secondary school texts.[118] The ministry's decision attracted strident criticism, but the Russo-Japanese War has been gradually accepted as a war of self-defence and the Battle of Tsushima as its glorious centrepiece.[119] Recent Japanese school textbooks on modern history, national and global alike, have followed suit and often refer to the battle and its significance but without the stress on its heroic virtues as was the case with pre-war textbooks.[120] The climax of this post-war fascination with the battle occurred around its centenary in 2005. By then, the Japan Maritime Self-Defence Force (JMSDF) had established the Russo-Japanese War as an ethical epitome of the defensive role this service is expected to fulfil. The pinnacle of that war, in the JMSDF's view, was unquestionably Tsushima. It is not surprising, then, that the JMSDF stood behind the major commemorative events of the anniversary. The two most important of these were held on 28 May (not to be confused with the pre-war Navy Anniversary Day a day earlier): one on board the *Mikasa*, with some 2,000 guests in attendance, and the other at sea, at the site of the battle.[121]

Ever since, brochures sold at the Memorial Ship Mikasa have presented her as one of the 'Three Great Historical Warships of the World', alongside HMS *Victory* in Portsmouth, and the USS *Constitution* in Boston.[122] This international sentiment did not end there. The JMSDF also dispatched its training squadron to Portsmouth, England, to attend the International Fleet Review held off Spithead in the Solent on 28 June 2005, thereby associating the bicentenary celebrations of the Battle of Trafalgar with the centenary of the Battle of Tsushima.[123] The same year witnessed the homecoming of the Z flag which Tōgō had hoisted aboard his flagship *Mikasa*. Some six years after the battle, when the admiral attended the coronation of King George V, he donated the flag to the Thames Marine Officer Training School, in which he studied in the early 1870s. As the centenary celebrations of the battle approached, the Marine Society, which inherited the flag, agreed to lend it permanently to the Tōgō Shrine.[124] By then, the shrine had long regained its position as a major and accessible site of the battle's memory and commemoration. Since its retrieval, the flag has turned into a major symbol of the shrine and copies are its best-selling memorabilia (Figure 25).

In 2006, a new memorial site for the battle was unveiled on Tsushima Island. Known as the Japan–Russia Friendship Hill (Jpn. *Nichiro yūkō no oka*), it is located next to the old Memorial of the Battle of the Sea of Japan. At the centre of this outdoor site there is a huge relief depicting Admiral Tōgō visiting the wounded Rozhestvenskiĭ in

Figure 25. Tōgō Shrine hoisting the Z flag, 2019

Sasebo. In addition, there is a board nearby carrying the names of *all* those killed in the battle, Japanese and Russian alike (Figure 26).[125] Despite this ostensible de-nationalization of the commemoration, the entire site nonetheless emphasizes domestic virtues under the guise of reconciliation.[126] With this renewed emphasis, it can be considered to be a part of a new-old trend, put into motion by the government and followed by local organizations, towards transforming the nation's past militant image by stressing the humanitarian facets of its modern history.[127] Nevertheless, and since the beginning of the 21st century, the commemoration of the battle of Tsushima in Japan has reflected a new amalgam that had been missing in the past and which has succeeded in attracting a new audience.[128]

At present, the battle is presented as a unique episode of self-defence, during which humanitarian acts abounded, and occurring

Figure 26. A monument for 'Peace and Friendship': a relief depicting Tōgō visiting the wounded Rozhestvenskiĭ, Tonosaki Park, Tsushima Island

in an era of a broad international support for the country and its cause.[129] It is arguably the only modern war that Japan can celebrate, memorialize, or remember without real or manufactured war guilt. Indeed, many contemporary Japanese seem to yearn for this early 20th-century state of affairs—a brief period during which their country could project power and display unfettered patriotism while simultaneously being venerated internationally as a David fighting Goliath. Japan later lost this dualism. After the First World War, it was perceived by others as a menacing imperialist power, whereas since the end of Second World War, and under the restrictions of its new constitution, it has largely been seen as a benign state but also as a militarily weak state dependent on others.[130] Thus, the Battle of Tsushima in present-day Japan exists as a reminder that the likelihood of being both strong and venerated is rare but possible.

4

Russia's Shattered Naval Dream

When the news about the battle first reached St Petersburg, the blow was profound. 'Tsushima,' poet Anna Akhmatova (1889–1966) recalled years later, was 'a shock that lasted all my life. And because it was the first, it was especially horrifying.'[1] For the first time since the war started, foreign observers noted, the capital was really moved.[2] Within days, the shockwaves spread across Russia and 'a shadow of gloom and consternation spread over the land'.[3] Only shortly before, expectations in the Russian capital had been high. Although there was no keen anticipation of an overwhelming naval victory, no one predicted a defeat, to say nothing of such a catastrophic debacle. With the news flashing like lightning, Aleksandr Kuprin (1870–1938) wrote in a book published in 1906, 'the word Tsushima was on everybody's lips'.[4] For the Russian media too, the news was a rude awakening that was followed by expressions of anger directed at different targets, depending on the writer's political leaning.[5] The political and literary newspaper *Peterburgskaia Gazeta*, for example, saw history repeating itself: 'They defeated not *us*, but that which was wounded at Sevastopol [during the Crimean War].' It was nonetheless an auspicious time for a change, the article concluded: 'it is absolutely necessary to take heed of the lessons of history.'[6] The lesson most newspapers shared was about the course of the conflict in East Asia. Free of government interference, they almost unanimously demanded an immediate end to the war.[7]

Within the Zemstvo organization of local governments, the Battle of Tsushima led to a sudden, albeit short-lived, unity between the democratic majority and the Slavophile minority.[8] Elsewhere, the crushing defeat did little to unite the Russians. If anything, the opposite is true. A month after the battle, critic and essayist Piotr Boborykin wrote acidly, 'We have only one enemy, and it is not in Tokyo, but much closer.'[9] Hardline revolutionaries rejoiced at every downfall the tsarist regime suffered, and that of Tsushima was no exception. Members of oppressed minorities did not mourn the defeat either, or at best shared mixed feelings about it. Many members of the Jewish community in Russia could not feel anything but hate for the tsarist regime given recent pogroms, but at the same time were concerned about the war since thousands of their brethren fought on the Russian side.[10] Accordingly, Jewish newspapers kept a neutral tone about the outcomes of the battle, and even expressed their hope for the resurrection of 'true Russia'.[11] On the other, Austro-Hungarian, side of the border, however, the joy was evident. The Lviv-based orthodox newspaper *Machsike Hadas* [*the Keepers of Religion*], for instance, saw the Japanese victory as a revenge for the pogrom carried out in the town of Zhytomyr (Rus. Zitomir) a few weeks earlier. Although the newspaper forbade its readers from celebrating, it stated that the defeat was an act of God.[12]

God also played a decisive role in Tsar's Nicholas II's identity and in the legitimation of his regime.[13] But as Russia's absolute ruler, the tsar's own reactions to the battle were of the utmost importance. Upon receiving the initial reports on 29 May, Nicholas 'said nothing. As usual', his cousin, Grand Duke Aleksandr Mikhailovich (1866–1933), recalled years later. He 'went deathly pale and lighted a cigarette'.[14] Perplexed by the fragmentary information, the tsar jotted down the following in his diary during the same evening: 'Today there began to arrive the most contradictory accounts of the battle between our squadron and that of Japan—all about our losses but telling nothing of theirs. Such lack of information is profoundly depressing....'[15] Three days later, on 1 June, he received the full account and wrote:

'Now, at last, the terrible news about the annihilation of almost the entire squadron in the two-day battle has been confirmed. Rozhestvenskiĭ himself taken prisoner, wounded! The weather has been wonderful, which made my anguish even worse.'[16] This is not to say that the tsar held inflated expectations of the armada. By early May, his blatant pre-war hubris had dwindled and his scorn for Japanese military capacity evaporated, but nonetheless his resolve to continue the war remained unshaken. He stated that a naval victory would be a welcome turning point in the war, but conceded that even a defeat would not change the course of the war.[17] Reality proved him wrong, as the Battle of Tsushima was to change the tsar's determination drastically.

The Battle and Russian Policy at Home and Abroad

When the third and last surviving warship arrived in Russian waters, on 30 May 1905, Nicholas assembled the War Council. At that early stage, none of the council members could envisage how pervasive the repercussions of the battle would be for Russia's domestic and foreign policy in the coming decade. Discussing the outcomes, the War Minister, General Victor Sakharov (1848–1905), advocated the continuation of the war, but Grand Duke Vladimir Aleksandrovich (1847–1909) argued passionately for ending it. As the balance among the tsar's advisors was shifting to the peace camp, his earlier resolve for war began to falter.[18] Nevertheless, it was foreign actions and pressure that compelled him to take drastic action. On 3 June, President Roosevelt summoned the Russian ambassador in Washington and discussed his peace plan. Russia's position, the president admonished unrealistically, was hopeless and if war continued it might lose eastern Siberia.[19] Nicholas, for one, was more sanguine than these doomsayers, but with Japan making the first step towards peace the question of national honour was mitigated, and as a consequence he, too, could now see the benefits of the American initiative. On 6 June, Nicholas II once again assembled the War Council. The views at the council were as divided as before, but it nonetheless concluded that 'internal welfare is more important to us than victories. It is necessary to make an immediate attempt to clarify the peace terms and conditions.'[20]

The crucial decision was made on 7 June 1905. During that day, the tsar held an audience with the American ambassador George von Lengerke Meyer (1858–1918), during which he granted him his approval to open the peace negotiations.[21] In their memoirs, leading Russian army generals would often lament the naval debacle and the ensuing peace agreement, arguing that the IRA could fight on. 'Far from assisting our army,' General Aleksei Kuropatkin (1848–1925) stated in his apologia, 'Rozhestvenskiĭ brought it irreparable harm. It was the defeat of his squadron at Tsushima that brought about negotiations and peace at a time when our army was ready to advance—a million strong.'[22] From a purely military perspective, this supreme commander of the Russian armed forces in East Asia until March 1905 was probably correct. But the story of the war in Russia cannot be considered without the concurrent revolution, known also as the First Russian Revolution. Its role as a trigger for the peace negotiations notwithstanding, the battle was not the only factor in the tsar's decision making. For the tsarist regime, the news about the defeat in Tsushima came at the worst moment during the war against Japan, given that the entire country was engulfed in a wave of unprecedented protest at the time. The growing dissent was closely linked to the course of the war and swelled with every staggering defeat. Although the critical sources of the revolutionary movement were political and social questions unrelated to the conflict with Japan, the war catalysed them markedly.[23] Public protest erupted in a workers' march that turned to bloodshed in the capital three weeks after the fall of Port Arthur, and escalated with the retreat in Mukden in March. Now, with the news of the tragic fate of the Baltic Fleet spreading nationwide, the protests reached a zenith, and millions of workers and peasants took an anti-government stand in numerous demonstrations and strikes across the vast country.[24]

The growing dissent in the wake of the battle did not skip the armed forces and the ranks of the IRN in particular. In the Black Sea Fleet, morale was ebbing and radical groups among the crews were plotting simultaneous mutinies. The most conspicuous case of insurrection occurred on board the Battleship *Potemkin* (Rus. *Kniaz Potëmkin Tavricheskiĭ*), exactly one month after the outbreak of the Battle of Tsushima. While training at sea on 27 June 1905, some of her crew refused to eat borscht that was putatively prepared from rotten meat infested with maggots. Their culinary protest soon turned into a full-scale mutiny, in which the 800 rebel sailors killed seven of their officers, including the captain, and took control of the ship. In the following days, the crew's efforts to spread the mutiny within other units of the fleet in Odessa, one of the main bases of the fleet, ended with partial success. Eventually, the *Potemkin* sailed to the Romanian port of Constanţa, where the crew was granted asylum and later scuttled the ship. In Odessa, contemporary estimates of the death toll in June alone, mostly at the hands of government troops, ranged from one to two thousand.[25]

During the summer, the 1905 Revolution spread further. With close to one million soldiers mobilized to northern Manchuria, the tsarist regime had to make tough choices about the places to police.[26] In early October, when fears of an impending bankruptcy gripped the government, a strike among railway workers in Moscow also developed into a general strike in the capital. By 26 October, some two million workers were on strike and the entire railway system ground to a halt. In discussing the situation, more and more Russians were now uttering the traditional term *smuta* (lit. 'trouble'), a reference to the political crisis and anarchy during the last years of the Rurik dynasty some three centuries earlier.[27] No less alarming for the regime was the disproportionally high number of riots in the non-Russian provinces, Poland, and the Baltic region in particular, and the mounting inter-ethnic confrontations throughout the Caucasus. In later years, some would associate the fiasco in Tsushima with this ethnic strife. The famous conservative journalist Mikhail Menshikov (1859–1918) is one example. As an ex-navy officer and advocate of conspiracies against Russia, Menshikov found it difficult to believe that the Russian debacle was due to Japanese superiority.[28] In one of his articles published in *Novoe Vremia* in 1908, he blamed the 'subversive' Poles, among whose ranks he listed Rozhestvenskiĭ, alongside people of German ancestry, such as Foreign Minister Vladimir Lamsdorf, for the naval disaster.[29]

Nevertheless, the seemingly mounting crisis that peaked with the defeat at Tsushima did not escalate further after September 1905. Hence, as Jonathan Frankel has suggested, the conclusion of the Portsmouth Peace Treaty 'can be ranked as a major turning point in the course of the 1905 Revolution'.[30] With peace established and the reservist troops rapidly released, the prospects for a mutiny among the armed forces diminished considerably. Thus, in retrospect, it was the end of the war against Japan that came to the rescue of the tsarist regime. Liberated from the burden of war and having the benefit of limited coordination among the revolutionaries, Nicholas II could now focus on the dire predicament within. In view of the dangerous situation and under pressure from his inner circle, he was at last prepared for unprecedented reforms that could appease the masses. Their architect, Sergei Witte (1849–1915), suggested the creation of a legislative parliament (Imperial Duma), the granting of civil liberties, and the formation of a cabinet government. The two had never collaborated so swiftly as in this case. On 30 October, the tsar issued a document (known as the 'October Manifesto') that would serve as the harbinger of the first Russian Constitution of 1906. This carrot came with a big stick, however, as the regime was able to mobilize the Cossacks as well as regular army units to crush the revolutionary forces gradually in the course of the next few months. The terror and violence continued throughout 1906 but the tsarist regime survived.[31]

The Battle of Tsushima exerted a similar but even more enduring impact on Russia's foreign affairs. For decades, St Petersburg had displayed an eastward orientation that culminated with the de facto takeover of Manchuria, but the battle, as Sergei Witte noted, 'was a death blow to our ambitions in the Far East'.[32] Another contemporary observer was even more pessimistic, regarding the battle as putting 'an end, perhaps for centuries, to all aspirations of Russia towards naval predominance in the Far East, and has closed to her the long-sought outlook upon the Pacific and the China Seas which was her ambition— who shall say not her necessity?—with future consequences for Europe and Asia which no man can measure.'[33] In the short run, both were correct as Russia did turn westward soon after the war. Having lost most of its blue-water navy and been pushed away from Manchuria and Korea, the tsarist regime shifted back to its traditional involve-ment in European affairs, and the Balkans in particular. Obviously, it did not return as a victor. The war's detrimental effect on its image and confidence could be detected as early as June 1905, during the peaceful separation of Norway from Sweden, and more explicitly a month later when it concluded (but did not ratify) a treaty with Germany in Bjørkø, Finland.[34]

After Tsushima, and in the wake of the Portsmouth Peace Treaty, Russia entered the road to the First World War.[35] Its strategic plight and perceived military weakness opened the way to a mixed assort-ment of failures inconceivable before May 1905. In 1908, for example, Foreign Minister Aleksandr Izvolskiĭ conveyed the tsar's approval for the Austrian annexation of Bosnia and Herzegovina, which subse-quently became a cause for further humiliation. Russia gave this consent in return for another Tsushima-related issue, since it needed Vienna's support for the revocation of the clauses of the 1878 Berlin Treaty preventing the opening of the Bosphorus to the Black Sea Fleet—the IRN's sole surviving unit.[36] The resulting Bosnian Crisis of 1908–9, historian Robert Seton-Watson concluded, 'converted the Southern Slav Question and the relations between Austria–Hungary and Serbia into an international problem of the first rank', and it remained so throughout the Balkans Wars of 1912–13 and until it triggered the outbreak of the Great War a year later.[37]

Despite this dramatic development, Russia also witnessed a much-needed improvement in its position in European affairs. The most evident legacy of the war against Japan, and the Battle of Tsushima in particular, was its position in the new alliance system that emerged in Europe by 1907. Germany's determination to achieve political hegemony over Europe—so evident during the war, the rapprochement between Britain and France, and Russia's own naval weakness—drove the tsar into the arms of Britain. An alliance between these two, who had been arch-rivals for most of the nineteenth century, and still unimaginable in early 1904, could consolidate the Russian position in Europe and in Asia alike, as well as facilitate rapprochement with Japan in 1907.[38] That year, St Petersburg and Tokyo signed a secret convention in which they divided Manchuria into two spheres of influence, the northern and the larger one to Russia, thereby stabilizing their relations for an entire decade.[39] Overall, with the signing of the Anglo-Russian Entente in 1907 and the balance achieved in East Asian affairs, a new de facto balance of European powers came into existence and remained in force until the outbreak of the First World War.

Consequences for the Imperial Russian Navy

With the revolution subsiding, it became apparent that the Battle of Tsushima had exerted a considerable but brief impact on Russia as a whole. Its repercussions upon the IRN, however, were profound and long lasting. Although they cannot be separated completely from the entire war against Japan, the battle markedly exacerbated the already disastrous impact of the first 15 months of the naval campaign. By the night of 28 May 1905, the service had lost two complete fleets out the three it had had on the eve of the war. Thus, in terms of sheer size and motivation, the war affected the IRN far more than the IRA. Whereas the latter ended the war with close to a million men in northern Manchuria who could sway the conflict if put to battle, the former remained with very few functioning units. During the war, the IRN lost no less than 14 battleships, three coastal defence battleships, five armoured cruisers, six protected cruisers, and an additional 35 smaller warships. These losses essentially left it with the Black Sea Fleet alone.[40] Apart from this demoralized and strategically restricted fleet, it now only possessed two battleships and two armoured cruisers of any fighting value.[41] In terms of manpower, the IRN lost about one-fifth of its entire personnel alongside a considerable part of its able officer cadre.[42] Hence, the year of 1905 marked the eclipse of the IRN. Within the first five months of this *annus horribilis* for Russia, this once great naval power took a radical nosedive. It dropped from third place among the world's largest naval forces on the eve of the war, and fifth on the eve of the battle, to sixth or even seventh place and a pronounced marginality for decades to come.[43] The Battle of Tsushima alone was responsible for about half of Russia's naval losses during the war, but while previous losses were suffered bit by bit, they now came in a single blow.

The recovery of Russian naval power required time, and initially only one recourse was available. One member of this once venerable force expressed the general mood within its ranks: 'So bitter was the defeat, so painful to all, so many hopes were dashed to the ground, that the natural outburst of many was: Find and point out the guilty person! It cannot be that no one is guilty!'[44] With this outcry and in this charged atmosphere, the two highest-ranking figures in the navy resigned in June 1905. Grand Duke Aleksei Aleksandrovich, the general-admiral of the fleet, resigned first, and the post he held for 22 years was eliminated. Two weeks later, the Navy Minister Fedor Avelan resigned too and was stripped of his rank. These resignations, however, neither relieved the furious outburst nor enabled the IRN to draw any lessons about the defeat and its causes. In this impasse, the government established a Special Investigative Commission which soon began to probe into the matter. The Commission interviewed hundreds of witnesses, many of whom had taken part in the battle and recently returned from Japanese captivity. While stirring only limited public interest, the conclusions reached by the Commission were forthright but far from blunt or unorthodox and did not refer to the political sphere, let alone the tsar. As the main technical cause of the debacle, the Commission highlighted the overloading of the warships and the obsolescence of the guns. By the same token, it found fault with the heterogeneity of the Russian warships, their low speed, and the insufficient number of armoured cruisers. It also criticized the Navy Ministry's lack of a clear war plan and its choice of Vice Admiral Rozhestvenskiĭ as the commander of the fleet, and had harsh words for the latter's preparations during the voyage and his decisions and functioning in the battle itself. Following the Commission's recommendations, the IRN decided to adopt more severe measures to punish those deemed responsible for the defeat. As one might have expected, these attempts to cleanse the proverbial Augean stables were largely confined to surviving officers of the Baltic Fleet, while leaving untouched the higher-ranking officers at home.[45]

The fate of Vice Admiral Zinoviĭ Rozhestvenskiĭ was telling. Although in later years opinions about his personality, but not his performance in battle, would vary considerably, Rozhestvenskiĭ came to personify the Russian defeat from the outset.[46] It nonetheless remained unclear whether and how he would be punished. Recovering in a Japanese hospital, he left Japan after a four-month internment and returned to St Petersburg via the Trans-Siberian Railway. Despite the revolutionary fervour throughout the country, throngs of admirers welcomed the admiral along his way in early December 1905.[47] Upon his arrival, he was reinstated in his previous position as the Chief of the General Naval Staff.[48] However, the press soon began to ask for his head, perhaps under the crown's instigation.[49] The admiral sought to fight the accusations. He talked about his vision for naval reforms and also pointed his finger at Britain for intending to use its warships in Weihaiwei against his fleet had the Japanese failed.[50] His provocations caused uproar in the Russian capital while disapproval kept mounting to the extent that Rozhestvenskiĭ decided to resign from his post on 21 May 1906. Six weeks later, he faced a court martial in Kronstadt along with 11 of his subordinates (10 officers and a single mechanic) who had been with him on board the destroyer *Bedoviĭ* (Figure 27).[51] The six-day trial did not deal with the entire fiasco

Figure 27. Vice Admiral Rozhestvenskiĭ on trial before the Naval Council of War at the naval base in Kronstadt, 21 July 1906

but focused solely on the humiliating surrender of the *Bedoviĭ*. Rozhestvenskiĭ assumed full responsibility for the surrender but the judges thought differently.[52] While sentencing four officers to death (including the *Bedoviĭ*'s captain, Nikolai Baranov), they acquitted the admiral on account of his being unconscious at the time of his capture.[53] A free man once more, Rozhestvenskiĭ remained in the city but lost his purpose. He died of a heart attack at the age of 60, exactly three years after his return from captivity. 'Now it's over! The admiral is dead!' Vladimir Semenov lamented soon after his funeral, but the memory of the battle was to prevail over this, or any other death.[54]

Rear Admiral Oskar Enkvist was only slightly more fortunate. He stayed in Manila with his three warships until the end of the war and then made the voyage back to Libau. On his return, he was subjected to criticism as quite a few officers believed he had disobeyed Rozhestvenskiĭ's order to break through for Vladivostok.[55] Still, Enkvist was not prosecuted and was even promoted to vice admiral in 1907. He was then dismissed from the service and died within five years. The full catharsis the IRN waited for anxiously was Rear Admiral Nikolai Nebogatov's trial. Unlike his two colleagues, Nebogatov was not even greeted upon his return from captivity, since there was a consensus that his conduct had been far more disgraceful. After all, neither Rozhestvenskiĭ nor Enkvist had capitulated to the enemy of their free will as he did. Worse, in summer 1905, three of the warships under his command were re-commissioned under the Japanese flag and a fourth, the new battleship *Orël*, would follow suit in two years. Furious with Nebogatov's conduct, the tsar had stripped him of his rank even before he returned. Eventually, in December 1906, he too faced a court-martial in Kronstadt, together with a number of his subordinates, including the four captains of his ships, and was charged with having improperly surrendered his force.[56] The navy regulations were indisputable—warships could only be surrendered upon sinking or burning and when all other means of defence were exhausted. This was not the case on the morning of 28 May.[57]

Nebogatov's defence, nonetheless, was that defective ships, guns, and ammunition made effective resistance impossible. 'I would not have hesitated,' he stated, 'to sacrifice the lives of 50,000 men if it could have been of the least use, but in this case why should I sacrifice the lives of young men? It would only have been suicide.'[58] During the trial, the admiral retracted and took responsibility for his own ship alone, while arguing that the other skippers could have disobeyed him. The court held that his conduct rather than the condition of his ships was the issue, and sentenced him to death, together with three of his captains.[59] Elsewhere, Nebogatov's conduct was not considered a triumph of humanism or a precedent for naval conduct, but on the contrary, a symbol of the weakness and ill-training of the entire branch. The sin of surrender and its punishment was learnt all over again.[60] As Holger Afflerbach observed, it was both the first and last case of a major naval surrender in the entire 20th century.[61] Nebogatov was not executed. In recognition of the extenuating circumstances, the court petitioned Tsar Nicholas II for leniency, and the admiral's death sentence was commuted to a 10-year confinement, the same as the sentence of Lieutenant General Anatolii Mikhailovich Stessel (1848–1915), the acting commander of the fortress of Port Arthur at the time of its surrender.[62] So was his captains' fate. Due to his ill health, Nebogatov was released in May 1909, moved to Moscow and disappeared into obscurity.[63]

The ongoing trials did little to change the navy's public image. Unlike the army, the service became the butt of popular sarcasm and jokes soon after the war. Among other, and even worse, epithets, it was referred to as 'Tsusimskoye Vedomstvo' (Tsushima Department) and its warships as 'Samotopi' (self-sinkers).[64] In this ebb, the leaders of the IRN were astute enough to look for positive models from the battle and to make heroes of the few officers who had defied the enemy. Three junior officers on board the *Kniaz Suvorov* who reportedly chose to go down with their ship won now public accolades (Figure 28). As for living heroes, the Battle of Tsushima had Vasiliĭ Fersen, the *Izumrud*'s captain who disobeyed Nebogatov's orders to surrender. The way in which he was recognized resembled that of Captain Vsevolod Rudnev, the cruiser *Variag*'s commander, during the first year of the war.[65] Despite his insubordination and the fact that his ship was eventually wrecked off the Russian Pacific coast, Fersen was not punished but promoted to the rank of captain in the same year in which Nebogatov faced trial. Within another seven years, he was promoted to vice admiral and retired in 1917 after serving, ironically, as a member of the naval court.

In like manner, the crew of the *Admiral Ushakov* was considered the apogee of collective heroism and resistance. Upon returning from captivity, the surviving crew of the ship, 325 men altogether, were awarded the Decoration of the Military Order of Saint George for their collective struggle against a superior enemy force. The officers waited for another year, but were eventually also decorated with the more prestigious Order of St Vladimir, 4th degree. The endeavours within the IRN to purge its ranks did not undo the necessary reforms, nor did they stop the heated debates about the battle and its implications. In

Figure 28. The heroes of the *Kniaz Suvorov*: a memorial photo of officers who chose to go down with their sinking warship

Notes: Photographer: A. Kieff, St Petersburg. The text reads: 'Kursel Virubov Bogdanov; Tsushima 14 May 1905; As witnessed by Commander Kolomejtzev, Lieutenants of the battleship Virubov and Bogdanov, as well as Ensign Kursel, having full possibility to be rescued have refused to go over to a destroyer and, remaining true to their duty, with other officers and sailors of the *Suvorov*, as it became apparent later, have heroically perished.'

April 1906, the tsar issued a rescript that ordered the Navy Minister to establish the Naval General Staff as a new department within the ministry.[66] Three months earlier, a discussion circle within the navy had begun to meet. Receiving the approval of the Navy Ministry, it aimed to identify the scientific principles required for a reformed navy.[67] Alongside these closed-door discussions, debates over naval reforms had also raged in the public sphere as well. Most notably, several prominent newspapers and magazines based in the capital carried a large number of articles on this and related topics.[68] For naval officers, and the Naval General Staff in particular, the most urgent objective was the quick reorganization of the Baltic Fleet, while maintaining only a symbolic presence and no blue-water capacity in the Pacific.[69]

In view of its total destruction, some believed the Baltic Fleet should be a defensive fleet, with torpedo boats, submarines, and mines; whereas others insisted on an offensive fleet, which would once again rely on capital ships in the spirit of Mahan. Outside the IRN, the preference was unequivocal. Meeting in December 1906, the State Defence Council maintained explicitly that 'the Baltic Fleet should not be seen as an offensive fleet in the broad sense of the term, but should limit itself to the defensive role decreed by Imperial authority.'[70] Four months later, however, this defensive scheme was slightly revised. Reflecting his ministry's view, the new Navy Minister, Ivan Dikov (1833–1914), reiterated the council's view but also added a somewhat vague objective. The fleet, Dikov stated, would also be 'a free-ranging naval force for the protection of the interests of the Empire in foreign waters'.[71] Within the State Duma, the views on fleet reconstruction were far from uniform, but the tsar's support for the vision presented by the Navy Ministry was crucial. The unceasing ruminations on the future and nature of the post-Tsushima navy hindered Russia from starting to rebuild its warships. Ultimately, two years elapsed after the battle before the tsar endorsed the 'Programme for the Development and Reform of the Armed Forces of Russia' in June 1907, which, inter alia, provided the means for a small-scale reconstruction of the Baltic Fleet.[72]

Two years later, with the echoes of the Bosnian crisis still reverberating and Russia's economic growth starting to take off again, the 'Small Shipbuilding Programme', as it was widely known, underwent significant revision. Instead of building mostly small vessels, the new 10-year 'Big Shipbuilding Programme' focused on the construction of battleships and the resurrection of the Pacific Fleet.[73] The recent plans for this fleet, alongside the fresh memories of the protracted voyage of the Baltic Fleet, revived now earlier interests in the Northern Sea Route.[74] The voyage via the Northeast Passage, connecting Europe with north-east Asia along the Arctic coasts of Norway and Russia, had been a dream since the early days of the Age of Exploration.[75] In 1910, the Arctic Ocean Hydrographic Expedition on board the IRN icebreaking steamers *Taimir* and *Vaigach* left Vladivostok for first systematic survey of this route. During the next five years, the expedition charted the eastern section of the Northern Sea Route, and, ultimately, in September 1915, the two ships completed the entire route from Vladivostok to Arkhangelsk. Although credited with the discovery of the archipelago of Severnaia Zemlia, the outbreak of the Great War and the fall of the tsarist regime precluded further exploration. It was not before the early 1930s that the Soviet government reinstated efforts to open the route resulting in its use for military purposes during the Second World War and its growing commercial use in recent decades.[76]

As for the Baltic Fleet, its operational plans hardly changed following the implementation of the new 10-year programme. In 1912, its plans included detailed defensive operations but very little on offensive ones.[77] This limited operational vision did not preclude the construction of new battleships. Based on the lessons of the recent war, and the Battle of Tsushima in particular, the Naval General Staff concluded, much like other leading navies, that its new battleships must carry as many heavy guns as possible, while sailing at a faster speed than earlier battleships.[78] Eventually, Russia's first all-big-gun battleship was commissioned as late as December 1914. This first of the four IRN *Gangut*-class dreadnoughts joined the Baltic Fleet exactly eight years after the British Royal Navy had commissioned its own first new type battleship, the HMS *Dreadnought*, and considerably behind every other major naval power.[79] Their design was poignantly coastal. However delayed and partial, Russian efforts to rebuild a substantial naval force fleet in the years between the Battle of Tsushima and the outbreak of the First World War were exceedingly expensive. Between 1908 and 1913, the shipbuilding portion of the Russian budget quintupled, and battleships once again occupied a large portion of it. Similarly, the IRN's share of the nation's defence budget increased appreciably during the same period, rising from 17 per cent of the budget in 1908 to no less than 28 per cent in 1913.[80]

The outbreak of the First World War found the IRN still weakened by the war against Japan.[81] It was, however, in the midst of an ambitious shipbuilding programme, although it did not take long before the great conflict would once again shatter the rising dreams of naval greatness. This second rude awakening, however, was not in the violent manner experienced at the Battle of Tsushima.[82] The shadow of the Russo-Japanese war loomed over operations in the Baltic Sea. Due to the nature of the unfolding war, the lingering relative weakness of the Baltic Fleet, and the fear of losing capital ships in the wake of Tsushima, the IRN remained peripheral at best. It avoided offensive operations and, apart from a successful mine blockade of the German coast, did little to affect the nation's war efforts.[83] Repeated defeats on land and changing priorities stopped most of the pre-war shipbuilding project. Finally, with Russia ceding hegemony over the Baltic States to Germany at the Treaty of Brest-Litovsk in March 1918, the Baltic Sea largely became a German lake to all intents and purposes. The end of the war was not the nadir of Russian naval power. It reached that in the early 1920s due to the radical activity within its ranks. The suppression of the 1905 revolution had not prevented the navy from remaining an ideological hotbed for radical activities which continued even after the Bolshevik revolution. Eventually, it was the suppression of the large-scale mutiny at the naval base of Kronstadt in March 1921 and the execution of thousands of navy personnel which inflicted a final blow to the navy in general and the Baltic Fleet in particular. It resulted in a lingering distrust and in limited allocations to this service in the succeeding years.[84]

Thereafter, the Soviet Navy entered into an extended period of relative paralysis and decline. Mikhail Frunze (1885–1925), who became the People's Commissar for Military and Naval Affairs in early 1925, found the state of the navy so wanting that he stated: 'In sum...we had no fleet.'[85] In the mid-1930s, Joseph Stalin (1878–1953), by then General Secretary of the Communist Party of the Soviet Union, began to envisage a huge ocean-going fleet but, once more, the outbreak of an all-out war in Europe brought his deep commitment to a halt.[86]

By summer 1945, the Soviet Navy possessed no more than 'two old and several-times-refloated ex-tsarist dreadnoughts in the Baltic, one leased Royal Navy battleship of the same age in the Northern Fleet...two more dreadnoughts in the Black Sea...[and] had no battleships in the Pacific Fleet at all.'[87] Ultimately, it was not until the 1960s that a truly large naval force would emerge in the Soviet Union. By then, it was evident that the Battle of Tsushima was not necessarily the source of every evil that had happened to the navy since 1905. That said, the battle was unquestionably the most significant milestone in its decline and a trigger for some of the worst setbacks Russia's naval forces would experience in the decade after 1905, if not longer.

The Ever-Changing Memory of the Battle

The memory of the battle in Russia has been painful and lasting. Over the years, however, the pain has worn off and, with the changing political climate, the memory, much like that of the entire war, followed an exceptionally winding path.[88] Similarly to the situation in Japan, this path can be divided essentially into three distinct eras, each matching broader political developments and characterized by somewhat contradictory attitudes to those that came before. These eras include the remaining dozen years of tsarism, the Soviet era that followed the Bolshevik revolution of 1917, and the period that began with the rise of the Russian Federation in 1991.

I. Shock and Lament: The Tsarist Era (1905–17)

The first years after the battle were characterized by a few initial commemoration endeavours, undertaken with little enthusiasm since tsarist Russia regarded the war against Japan with distaste and sorrow. It was, as some writers referred to it, a 'sinister and dismal conflict' amounting to a 'total bloody nightmare'.[89] Reflecting on the war, contemporary Russians had very little to be proud of, but it was still *their* war, a debacle in which their own fathers and sons had sacrificed their lives. The Battle of Tsushima was therefore not very different from other defeats during the war, but the feeling of disappointment it evoked was particularly strong. This was, in part, the result of the contrast between the long duration and high tension of expectations before the battle and the abrupt intensity and unambiguity of the climax itself. So extreme was this feeling that many writers now began to use the very name Tsushima ('like Tsushima' or 'worse than Tsushima') to denote a humiliating failure in politics and especially in naval affairs.[90] After the battle, even advocates of pacifism could not but express their despair at the loss of lives. In a diary entry written on 1 June 1905, the 77-year-old Leo Tolstoy (1828–1910) found war in general to be incompatible with Christian beliefs. It was the reason, he explained, 'why, in any war with a non-Christian people for whom the highest ideal is patriotism and military heroism, Christian peoples must be defeated.'[91]

By the same token, the battle became a symbolic edifice, with a brief but manifest effect on contemporary Russian literature and poetry.[92] For the poet Viacheslav Ivanov (1866–1949), for example, the battle offered a springboard for the resurrection and purification of the Russian psyche. Written on 31 May 1905, his famous four-stanza poem 'Tsushima' was inspired by the latest news of the miraculous arrival of the Almaz in Vladivostok. 'The Russian armada sailed further,' Ivanov opened his poem, 'into enchanted sea...—the last of all our hopes,' while reaching a catharsis in the fourth and final stanza: 'Rus', baptize yourself with fire! Burn; And save your Diamond [Rus. Almaz] from the blackened pyre! In the hands of your leaders your helms are shattered; See, in the heavens there are greater helmsmen yet.'[93] More commonly, however, the battle became a prophetic emblem of Russia and its impending doom. The Symbolist writer Andrei Bely (1880–1934) referred to the battle in this very context in his novel Petersburg (1913), which many still regard as one of the Russian masterpieces of the 20th century.[94] For Bely, Tsushima, like the River Kalka where several Rus' principalities had been defeated by the invading Mongol hordes in 1223, symbolized the threat posed to the Russian nation by the East.[95]

Accounts of the battle during this brief era ranged from personal memoirs to critical analysis, and often contained both. One of the most internationally renowned and fiercest critics was Commander Vladimir Semenov, who faced a court martial together with Rozhest-venskiĭ and was subsequently acquitted. A man of literary aspirations, he considered himself the chronicler of the voyage and of the battle in particular. Following his retirement in 1907, Semenov devoted the subsequent three years, until his untimely death, to complete the writing of his wartime experience.[96] His criticism benefited from his rare experience, since he was the only high-ranking officer to take part in the two most significant battles of the war, first as a senior officer on board the cruiser *Diana* in the Battle of the Yellow Sea and then as a flag officer on the *Kniaz Suvorov* in the Battle of Tsushima. Commander Nikolai Klado was another high-profile critic with a respectable naval background. Standing behind the media campaign to dispatch the Baltic Fleet to East Asia, he joined the voyage but had to leave at Vigo to represent the fleet at the international commission settling the Dogger Bank incident. An influential naval analyst, his writings on the war against Japan and the battle were promptly translated into English, French, and German. Klado's criticism lambasted the Baltic Fleet's combat performance but did not prevent him from being reinstated in the navy in 1906 and being appointed as a professor of naval strategy in the Naval Cadet Corps four years later.[97]

However disastrous and humiliating this defeat, it warranted also a measure of commemoration. Understandably, the plans to pay homage to the fallen sailors by erecting monuments were neither as immediate nor as grandiose as in Japan. Before launching any commemorative project, the prisoners had to return home, the court martials had to end, and the initial trauma had to be dispelled. The first monument to the battle was a large granite obelisk erected in the surrounding gardens of St Nicholas' Naval Cathedral (Rus. *Nikolskiĭ morskoi sobor*), in central St Petersburg. Known as the 'Tsushima obelisk', it was inaugurated on 28 May 1908, on the third anniversary of the battle, to commemorate the crew of the battleship *Imperator Aleksandr III*

Figure 29. Monument to the heroes of the battleship *Imperator Aleksandr III*, St Petersburg

(Figure 29). This specific vessel was chosen because it had been the only Russian warship to sink without a single survivor. The deaths of its crew were the ultimate testimony of their loyalty to the tsar and their commemoration matched the regime's new desire to valorize ordinary sailors and soldiers in the wake of the revolution. Journalist Mikhail Menshikov was quick to capitalize on this notion. Two days before the monument was unveiled, an article he wrote for the popular daily *Novoe Vremia* noted that 'The overwhelming majority of Russian sailors did not surrender and did not run away.'[98]

Another early plan was to build a memorial church. During the same year in which the monument was erected, a committee was established to raise money for this purpose under the auspices of Queen Olga of Greece (1851–1926). The imperial family soon joined in to help financially, as it had done with the obelisk.[99] Built along the Admiralty Channel in St Petersburg, the Church of Christ the Saviour (*Tserkov Khrista Spasitelya*), also known as the Temple of Salvation on the Waters, was opened in 1911. The church was conceived shortly before the battle, but its walls were inscribed with the names of fallen Russian sailors and became Russia's central monument of the battle. Elsewhere across the tsarist empire, several other small-scale monuments were erected, usually in towns related to the voyage of the Baltic Fleet. Kronstadt, for instance, the Baltic Fleet's home port, erected a monument devoted to the sailors who perished in the battle in Petrovskiĭ Park, while two large boards with the names of sailors who died in the battle were placed on the wall at the Church of Aleksandr Nevskiĭ in Reval (present-day Tallinn, Estonia), the fleet's first station.

These sites notwithstanding, the cultural lament over Tsushima and the endeavours to commemorate its victims were relatively short-lived. Following the 1905 revolution, the country was engulfed by internal unrest and Japan was no longer considered an arch enemy upon the conclusion of Russo-Japanese agreement of 1907. For quite a few, incredibly, it became again a source of cultural fascination and occasionally even identification.[100] Crucially, with the outbreak of the First World War, new defeats and much greater losses nearer home quickly overshadowed the memory of the conflict in East Asia a decade earlier.[101] In early 1916 and under growing strain, Russia repurchased three of the warships, including two battleships, which Japan had captured in 1905. Given this turn of events, the religious service for the dead of Tsushima, which still took place in 1915, ceased outright and, similarly, the plans for erecting a national memorial monument to the war, or even to the battle, were also abandoned.

II. Condemnation and Warning: The Soviet Era (1917–91)

With the outbreak of the Bolshevik revolution and the establishment of the Soviet Union, the memory of the Russo-Japanese War, and even more so of the Battle of Tsushima, faded almost completely. During its first years in power, the Soviet regime was occupied with civil war and internal strife, and public memory was largely concerned with the terrible toll during the First World War and the ensuing civil war. By then, condoning the war against Japan meant supporting the tsarist regime and rejecting the revolution.[102] Diehard revolutionaries had objected to the war against Japan even while it was ongoing. Upon the fall of Port Arthur in 1905, Vladimir Lenin (1870–1924) himself declared that 'the proletariat has its reasons to rejoice.'[103] Five months later, some 10 days after the destruction of the Baltic Fleet, he pointed out elatedly the significance of the event: 'Everybody understood that the definitive outcome of the war depended on the naval victory of one of the belligerents.'[104] In this spirit, the Soviet regime exploited the memory of the war and the defeat at Tsushima in particular as additional means for condemning the tsarist regime and its inept military leadership. Despising the weak naval officers that led the fleet, the Bolsheviks emphasized initially the heroism of radical sailors at home during 1905.[105] The hatred for the naval officers of the tsarist regime, and Admiral Aleksander Kolchak (1874–1920) in particular, stemmed also from their active role they had played in the counter-revolutionary movement. Thus, their defeat at Tsushima became an integral part of their legacy.

It did not take long before the Soviet regime sought to eradicate the remaining tangible traces of the tsarist fiasco at Tsushima. The principal victim of the new policy was the Church of Christ the Saviour—the main tsarist commemoration associated with the battle. It was closed down on 8 March 1932 and, despite the protests of thousands of St Petersburg residents, it was soon blown up.[106] During the same year, the Soviet Union hailed the publication of the first volume of *Tsushima*—the most notable Russian novel of the battle.[107] Its first volume especially enjoyed phenomenal domestic success, selling 925,000 copies in its first edition.[108] Translated within a few years into several foreign languages, the novel described the heroism of IRN sailors and a few officers, and the extent of their revolutionary activity during the voyage of the Baltic Fleet alongside the high command negligence that led to the fiasco.[109] The author, Aleksei Novikov-Priboi (1877–1944), had been a sailor aboard the battleship Orël and was taken prisoner following its surrender. During his captivity in Japan, he began to write his own memoir and to gather the personal accounts of his fellow prisoners. He set out to publish his account upon his return to Russia but, due to their explicit criticism of the way the war had been handled, it was banned by the tsarist authorities and Novikov-Priboi himself fled to Finland and then moved to Great Britain. He did return to Russia shortly before the First World War but could not resume the writing of his novel under the tsarist regime. Novikov-Priboi's second volume received the Stalin Prize, but was also increasingly subjected to the authorities' criticism for its demoralizing impact in a period of naval revival. Although often regarded as a genuine account based on personal experience, the book should be read with more than a grain of salt. Later critics pointed out that it is fraught with multiple factual inaccuracies that stem in part from the author's ideological bent as well as from discrepancies between earlier and later versions due to the changing political circumstances after its initial publication.[110]

Paradoxically, the success of Novikov-Priboi's Tsushima heralded a transition in the Soviet attitude to the battle. Deteriorating Russo-Japanese relations and escalating military tensions during the latter half of the 1930s did affect the change but not exclusively.[111] Assuming a more imperial posture, and shifting from the strategy of world revolution to building socialism in one country, Stalin started to rehabilitate the military history of the pre-revolutionary ancien régime. This policy, alongside a growing anticipation of a second war with Japan, gave rise to a more objective and dispassionate examination of the war, as seen in various analytic studies and literary works. Conspicuous among the former were the comprehensive studies of Nikolai Levitskiĭ (1887–1942) and Aleksander Svechin (1878–1938), and the most prominent of the latter was Aleksandr Stepanov's (1892–1965) Port-Artur (1940–2).[112] Winning the Stalin Prize for each of its two volumes, Stepanov's book was reprinted in large numbers in 1944 and gained immense popularity.[113]

Levitskiĭ offered a rather balanced perspective of Tsushima that took account of the fundamental Russian disadvantages. With Port Arthur's surrender, he asserted, it was evident that the Baltic Fleet was no match for the Japanese, but the government pushed Rozhestvens-kiĭ to make headway.[114] On the eve of the battle too, and despite the reinforcement of Nebogatov's ships, the Japanese Combined Fleet had a definite advantage in almost every aspect, and especially in fire-power.[115] This Russian inferiority was exacerbated by Rozhestvens-kiĭ's command, his passivity in particular.[116] Altogether, Levitskiĭ concluded, 'the campaign of the 2nd Pacific Squadron was adventur-ous. It was launched out of political rather than military consider-ations in the hope of saving part of the empire.'[117] In 1942, Captain Pëtr Bikov (1890–1963), a lecturer in naval history, devoted an entire book to the naval operations during the Russo-Japanese War. His observations and conclusions followed Levitskiĭ's approach closely. Bikov, too, asserted that the Baltic Fleet was not strong enough to face the Japanese Combined Fleet and that its dispatch originated in the idea it would operate jointly with the Port Arthur Squadron.[118] Based on a comparison of several critical parameters, Bikov demonstrated that Nebogatov's reinforcement did little to change Russian inferiority on the eve of the battle.[119] His final conclusions were harsh but fair.[120] 'The defeat at Tsushima,' he wrote, 'was due to the technical back-wardness of the ships of the Russian fleet and their weapons, as well as the tsarist naval command's failings and mediocrity.'[121] Strategically, Bikov found, 'the dispatch of a technically backward and unprepared fleet, with no single base all the 18,000-mile way from Kronstadt to Vladivostok, was essentially an adventure and could not but lead to disaster.'[122]

This new outlook on the Tsushima fiasco permitted the Soviet government to seek revenge for the humiliation endured in May 1905. The victories over the IJA in the undeclared border conflicts of 1938–9 and the Battles of Khalkhin Gol in particular laid this sentiment bare.[123] A case in point is a cartoon that appeared in the Soviet satirical magazine Krokodil in late 1939. Displaying a group of Japanese and Soviet soldiers standing in front of a map of north-east Asia, its caption was explicit: 'thirty-five years ago: We [Japanese] marked Mukden, Port Arthur, Tsushima. Nowadays: We [Russians] mark Volochaevka, Spask, [Lake] Khasan.'[124] Despite these bitter memories, the two nations avoided war during the subsequent six years. In the meantime, the regime refreshed the memories of its soldiers at the front by distributing millions of pamphlets and books about Tsushima and Port Arthur alongside the recent Soviet success in Khalkhin Gol.[125] Eventually, the Soviet Union revenged Tsushima, among other humiliating defeats, when its armies swept into Manchuria and recaptured Port Arthur in August 1945. The victory over Japan was turned at once into the climax of a 40-year struggle. Stalin himself acknowledged that, 'Our people believed and hoped that a day would come when Japan would be smashed and that blot effaced. Forty years we have waited for this day.'[126]

In spite of this retribution, the Soviet Union did not hesitate to erase tokens of Imperial Russia's defeat at Tsushima even after its victory. In early September 1945, Soviet representatives in Japan led by Lieutenant General Kuzma Derevyanko (1904–1954) were delighted when Admiral William Halsey Jr, the commander of the United States Third Fleet, handed them the ensign hoisted on the Mikasa's stern. The ensign did little to loosen Derevyanko's animosity for the memorial ship. During the course of Japan's disarmament, he argued repeatedly that the Mikasa was a fortress and as such should be destroyed. Although the ship was eventually spared due to American and British insistence, this Soviet pressure contributed towards the stripping of the ship's pre-war status as a memorial site.[127] Back home, the battle remained a stain on Soviet honour. In 1954, at the 50th anniversary of the battle of Chemulpo, the state decorated surviving veterans of this brief engagement with a medal and two years later unveiled a statue of the Variag's commander Rudnev in Tula, where he had retired. The veterans of Tsushima, and even those who were wounded and fought

Figure 30. The cruiser *Aurora* as a museum ship and major tourist attraction, St Petersburg

to the bitter end, were ignored.[128] Similarly, when the cruiser *Aurora* became a museum ship in Leningrad (present-day St Petersburg) in 1957, it was for her role in the Bolshevik revolution rather than for her part in Rear Admiral Enkvist's detachment in 1905 (Figure 30).

By the late 1960s, the Soviet Union had further relaxed its attitude towards the tsarist era and its military heritage. This new trend for retrospection, if not sheer nostalgia, was propelled by a wave of films and novels that no longer focused on Russian heroism during this period.[129] The war against Japan and the Battle of Tsushima were no exception. The popular writer, Vladimir Pikul (1928–1990), for example, wrote several novels that dealt with the war, including in 1981 *Tri vozrasta Okini-san* (*The Three Ages Okini-san*), which comes to a climax at Tsushima. With détente between the Soviet Union and the West in the late 1960s, relations with Japan improved as well.[130] And yet the Soviet government still opposed any Japanese attempts to jog its memory of the battle. When the Japanese businessman Sasakawa

Ryōichi (1899–1995) sought to salvage the wreckage of the cruiser *Admiral Nakhimov* off Tsushima in 1980 in order to search for the alleged gold the ship had carried, Moscow protested strongly but to no avail. When divers brought back precious metals from the wreck, a Soviet diplomat approached the Foreign Office in Tokyo and laid claim to whatever would be found. Sasakawa announced his willingness to comply but asked in return for the four Kuril Islands the Soviet Union had been occupying since 1945, and on this note the affair quickly faded away.[131]

III. Nostalgia and Fascination: The Russian Era (1991–present)

The collapse of the Soviet Union in 1991 and the rise of the independent Russian Federation in its stead set free the recent interest in the Russo-Japanese War in general and the Battle of Tsushima in particular. One of the first signs was the 1990 establishment of a foundation to rebuild the Church of Christ the Saviour. Thirteen years later, the church was opened on the same spot where the original church stood and in the same exact form.[132] With the rise of Vladimir Putin (1952–) in 1999, interest in the battle grew further. Putin has repeatedly stressed the importance of historical memory and glorified myth, and in a 2003 meeting with historians demanded that 'textbooks should develop pride for the country and her history among Russian youth.'[133] The outcomes of this pressure were soon visible. A study published in 2015 found that history textbooks published in Russia during the previous decade shifted their attention from the tragic aspects of the war against Japan to the heroism displayed by Russian soldiers.[134] The Battle of Tsushima was no exception, as the Russian seamen taking part in it were said to display 'heroism and self-sacrifice'.[135]

Despite this new approach, Russia's willingness to collaborate with Japan in commemorating the battle has remained limited and calculated. While the memory of the past is important, Putin's Russia has not shown the slightest intention to relinquish any of its territorial assets. When the Russian national team lost to Japan in the 2002 FIFA

World Cup, the website of 'Aziatskaia biblioteka' (Asian Library) betrayed the national mood with the following headline: '"Tsushima". Japan–Russia: 1:0. Yet, we will not return the islands back.'[136] In February 2005, for example, the Russian Navy declined a Japanese invitation to take part in the centenary commemoration of the battle. Although the two fleets had cooperated in previous years and Russia did not necessarily rebuff the commemorations of other war-related events, it stayed away from a joint event commemorating Tsushima.[137] A year earlier, Russian representatives did hold an event off the South Korean port city of Inchon to commemorate the centenary of the Battle of Chemulpo, the first naval engagement in the war, but they did not invite Japanese representatives although they did ask South Korean military representatives.[138]

On other occasions, however, the Russian government was more cooperative, possibly due to the far-reaching political implications these events could exert on Japanese public opinion.[139] In this respect, representatives of the Russian embassy in Tokyo took part in the ceremony on board the Mikasa on 27 May 2005, and the Russian government supported the erection of the board carrying the name of all those killed in the battle (97.6 per cent of whom belonged to the IRN) on a hill overlooking the site of the battle on the Tsushima coast. It also covered the costs of creating the huge relief next to it (Figure 26) and the entire place was renamed the Japan–Russia Friendship Hill.[140] Notwithstanding these efforts and the boom of new books on the subject, the war against Japan had become a distant and fading memory for most Russians by the time of its centenary.[141] In a poll conducted in Russia in 2005, 72 per cent of the respondents could not name a single site of memory of that war. Still, among the sites recalled, Tsushima was the first.[142]

The battle of Tsushima exerted a profound impact on tsarist Russia during the years before the First World War. Although it only briefly exacerbated the revolutionary protest, it gave rise to a long-term effect on Russia's foreign and naval policies and its plans for expansion in north-east Asia. Moreover, the Russian and later Soviet Navy required decades to recover its position as a reliable and top-quality service committed to the nation's security. As for the battle's domestic commemoration, this has changed considerably with the years but has retained its status as one of the nation's most devastating defeats and as a bitter but useful lesson for the future.

5

Worldwide Reactions and Assessments

A s the news of the Japanese victory spread, the Battle of Tsushima became an instant sensation worldwide. It was a period when news began to travel quickly, and yet, even in later years there have been very few battles that attracted such a degree of public attention at the time they were fought. The interest in this titanic clash was global, ranging from Europe and the United States to virtually any other location linked to an emerging worldwide news network. The public fascination with the battle had begun months before it raged and was sustained long after it ceased, but it naturally culminated with the first reports of the events. In spite of this sensational news, the way the world interpreted the outcomes was not uniform. For many, the news marked a watershed: some regarded it as a harbinger of hope whereas others saw it as spelling impending doom. Given this array of responses, assessments, and prophecies, the international reaction to the battle is intriguing. In making sense of it, the present chapter is concerned with three layers of attention: the mass media, state-level decision makers, and naval experts.

Media Response

In 1905, large swathes of the globe were already connected to each other by an extensive network of land and undersea telecommunication cables. The war zone was also linked to this global network to the extent that the Russo-Japanese War was 'the first full-fledged war of modern communication'.[1] The contemporary mass media was almost entirely made up of newspapers. Capitalizing on news transmitted quickly with the help of news agencies, newspapers flourished even in small provincial towns across the Western hemisphere and in every major city elsewhere. It was therefore hardly surprising that the world press had been following the war in north-east Asia closely since 1904. The land battles in Manchuria and the plight of the Pacific Fleet trapped in Port Arthur attracted a passionate interest among the educated strata of society. In satisfying this interest, dozens of war correspondents representing leading newspapers in the West arrived in the arena, mostly via Tokyo.[2] The Japanese authorities were not overly cooperative, censorship was tight, and wireless telegraphy still unreliable, but these correspondents were able nonetheless to stir a great deal of interest.[3] The fascination with the Baltic Fleet was even greater. Its voyage not only seemed to lead to a gigantic naval engagement but also generated a sense of suspense with respect to its progress. Its story had evidently reached epic dimensions by the time the Russian armada entered Asian waters. That said, the media knew very little about it on 27 May 1905 and for many hours after the battle had ceased.

In Britain, Japan's closest ally, the press followed the voyage of the Baltic Fleet and the impending battle closely. The reports, however, came in at a slight delay as long-distance telegrams still travelled rather slowly in 1905.[4] The headlines on 27 May 1905, the day the battle began, still reported the location of the Russian ships as being off the Chinese coast and dealt with Vice Admiral Rozhestvenskiǐ's possible routes to Vladivostok.[5] On that day, the illustrated weekly *The Sphere*, for example, devoted its front page to the Russian commander and speculated, under a large image of him, that he would be replaced upon arrival in Vladivostok (Figure 31).[6] The following day was Sunday, so actual news of the battle broke on Monday, 29 May. 'The Great Naval Battle,' announced the *Newcastle Evening Chronicle*, 'Japanese Victory; The Russian Fleet "Practically Annihilated",' whereas the *Liverpool*

Figure 31. A dated image: by the time Vice Admiral Rozhestvenskiĭ appeared on the front page of *The Sphere*, he was lying wounded in his flagship, 27 May 1905

Echo had a similar headline in the opposite order: 'Rodjestvensky's Fleet Annihilated. Victory for Admiral Togo.'[7] *The Times* of London was more cautious and reserved. Its tiny headline read: 'Reported Japanese success. Five Russian Warships sunk.' It was only on the following day that this newspaper announced unreservedly: 'Great Japanese Victory. Russian Fleet Shattered.'[8] Indeed, by 30 May, the British public could read detailed reports of the battle, albeit still partial and replete with inaccuracies.[9] Emotionally speaking, the British press did not embrace the victory immediately, but on 2 June, when the outcomes were incontestable, *The Times* referred to Tōgō's appeal to his crews 'as identical with that of our own Nelson'.[10] Other British newspapers also sided clearly with the Japanese and stressed their success, although the news of the battle rarely occupied their first page, and remained mostly, as in *The Times*, in the 'Colonial and Foreign Intelligence' section.[11]

The interest in the battle in the United States was at least as high as Britain's. On the day of the two fleets' encounter, and based on a dispatch by a Reuters correspondent in Tokyo, a few American newspapers reported that the Russians were passing the Tsushima Strait.[12] Although one provincial newspaper mistakenly informed its readers that the Russian fleet had succeeded in evading the Japanese, the vast majority opted to wait for official reports rather than rely on rumours.[13] The tension seemed to reach new heights on that day: 'Naval Battle is Expected,' announced one newspaper, 'News of meeting of Russ [*sic*] and Japanese fleets hourly expected at St. Petersburg.'[14] By 28 May 1905, the day the battle ended, the American press was still oblivious to its occurrence, let alone its outcomes. It was a Sunday and more than a few newspapers still reported the Russian fleet as passing through the Korea Strait. During the day, and under tight Japanese censorship, the Tokyo Associated Press released some preliminary reports of a major naval battle that had taken place in the Tsushima Strait. Hours later, American morning papers, including the *New York Times*, either speculated on the battle or were already able to report its occurrence while disclosing that further details were still being withheld by Japanese authorities.[15] Only one newspaper, the *Los Angeles Times*, whose time zone allowed it some leeway, came close to printing the true story. And yet, even this paper had little to reveal to its readers: 'The world will probably have to wait another day to learn even the skeleton facts of the stupendous drama.'[16]

As in Britain, news of the battle appeared on Monday, 29 May 1905, some two days after the two fleets had first engaged. It was an instant sensation that appeared on the front pages of almost any American newspaper with large headlines followed by photographs and maps. The reports of the Japanese triumph overshadowed any other news— local, national, or international—including the sinking of an American merchantman in Chinese waters. The *San Francisco Call*'s headlines, for example, exclaimed 'Russian Fleet Destroyed,' and on another page asserted that 'Togo's Strategy Surprises the Naval Experts' (Figure 32).[17] Similarly, the *New York Tribune*'s headline announced: 'Japan Wins at Sea: The Entire Russian Fleet Reported Disabled or Dispersed,' but cautioned about 'Rumors of Running Action in the Sea of Japan.'[18] In the American capital, the *Washington Times* reported 'Togo Sweeps Foe from the Sea: Russia's Once Formidable Ships Put out of Commission.'[19] By Tuesday, 30 May 1905, further details became available, including the number of sunken Russian ships and the fact that only two of them made it to Vladivostok.[20] During that day, the battle still occupied the headlines of all the leading newspapers, although they were yet to provide a conclusive report or analysis.

A great deal of the initial reports was based on facts known before the battle, such as the comparative strength of the two fleets and their plans.[21] Since not a single journalist was assigned to either side's warships, and Japan was maintaining tight control of the news, the newspapers were obviously still speculating. The first newspaper to offer a detailed account of the battle was the *Baltimore Evening Herald*.[22] Its young editor, H.L. Mencken (1880–1956), was thrilled. 'Like every managing editor of normal appetites,' he would later recall, 'I was thrown into a sweat by this uncertainty.'[23] Based on the earliest

RUSSIAN FLEET DESTROYED

TOKIO, May 29, 2:15 p. m.----It is officially announced that Admiral Rojestvensky's fleet has been practically annihilated. Twelve warships have been
sunk or captured, and two transports and two destroyers have been sunk.

Many Russian Warships Are Sunk and Japanese Fleet Loses Cruiser and Small Craft While Running
Fight Continues Northward on the Sea of Japan.

Figure 32. Sensational news: *The San Francisco Call*, 29 May 1905

fragments of information, this future famous essayist fabricated a full
story about the battle fought off Tsushima, thereby giving his newspaper, as he wrote in later years, 'a bit on the world, and what's more, a
bit that lasted for nearly two weeks'.[24] With authentic information
overflowing, readers of the *Baltimore Evening Herald*, or any other
newspaper for that matter, were unable to notice its special merits,
and, fortunately for Mencken, the gist of his fabricated article was
ultimately not far from reality.

The human element in the battle was not lost either. For the American press, it manifested itself in a clash between 'Togo' and 'Rojestvensky' and it thus paid special attention to the former's upbringing and family and to the latter's tragic fate.[25] Within days, Admiral Tōgō was to be compared to Nelson. In fact, this was not the first time the two were linked, as the Japanese admiral had been crowned occasionally as 'The Nelson of Japan' since the outbreak of the war.[26] Now, however, the comparison became standard practice, even more so than in Britain. With Tōgō's portrait adorning every front page, Tsushima became synonymous with Trafalgar (Figure 33).[27] The concern for Vice Admiral Rozhestvenskiĭ seemed genuine, as did the admiration expressed for his adversary. As early as 29 May, for example, the *Washington Times* speculated that 'Rogestvensky [sic] May Be Dead; Down to Death With Ship,' and then specified 'His Fate is in doubt; Eight captains of his command chose a hero's fate; Many prisoners taken.'[28] A day later, the same newspaper related that 'Rogestvensky is Wounded But Safe at Vladivostok: Paris Hears that Russian Admiral Has Been Rescued; Picked up out of Sea.'[29] Readers now also familiarized themselves with the name of Rear Admiral Nikolai Nebogatov.[30] He appeared to be among the prisoners, the news of 29 May announced, but his surrender was reported for the first time during the following day.[31] Soon, Nebogatov became the villain in this heroic saga, with his surrender depicted as 'a contemptible spectacle'.[32] The interest in Rozhestvenskiĭ remained on 31 May too. During that day, it was reported that his skull was fractured and that he had been transferred to the destroyer *Buiniĭ*. Then, on 1 June, it finally became patently clear that the Russian admiral had survived and been taken prisoner.[33]

In France, Russia's main ally, the media followed the voyage of the Baltic Fleet with moderate interest.[34] Apparently, the public dissonance between the desire to support an ally and the need to keep strict neutrality towards its struggling fleet was not easy to resolve. Moreover, certain French intellectuals supported Japan's cause in the war due to either cultural and ethical considerations or their antagonism

TAKING HIS PLACE

Figure 33. 'Taking His Place': Admiral Tōgō climbing the podium shared by great admirals, with Britain's Horatio Nelson and the United States' George Dewey on his two sides, in a cartoon at the *Chicago Tribune*, 30 May 1905

towards Russian autocracy.[35] Nevertheless, this general apathy changed abruptly on 30 May 1905, when the electrifying news about the battle first appeared in France. As could be expected, the headlines concentrated on the Russian debacle ('disaster' or 'catastrophe') rather than on the Japanese victory. *Le Petit Parisien*'s front page, for example, announced 'A Russian Disaster: Rodjestvensky's Squadron Annihilated,' while producing a photo of Rear Admiral Tōgō Masamichi

(1852–1906) under the title *L'amiral Togo* instead of his more senior namesake.[36] Paris's *Le Journal* also announced a Russian disaster, and both newspapers mentioned that Admiral Nebogatov had fallen into Japanese hands.[37] On 31 May, and with more details now available, the magnitude of the Russian disaster became clear.[38] On that day, the daily Roman Catholic newspaper *La Croix* concluded, or pleaded, that 'The War Must End.'[39] The official Japanese report of the battle was cited widely in early June, and many of the French newspapers, like their counterparts in other Western countries, displayed an evident concern for Rozhestvenskiĭ's uncertain fate. Nonetheless, French interest in the battle subsided conspicuously by 3 June, and further reports were placed in the back pages.[40] Thereafter, domestic news, such as 19-year-old King Alfonso XIII of Spain's visit to Paris or the death of the French financier Alphonse James de Rothschild, attracted a far greater degree of attention.

In Germany, the earliest news of the battle appeared on 29 May 1905. 'Roschdjestwensky Beaten!' was the liberal *Berliner Tageblatt*'s headline, whereas the *Berliner Volks-Zeitung* announced: 'The Baltic Fleet Destroyed!'[41] The following day's headlines were less sensational, but provided a more detailed account of the battle, including maps of the arena.[42] Reading the news, a 16-year-old Austrian youth named Adolf Hitler 'jumped with joy'. In later years, Hitler was to remember that already back then, in 1905, he had thought of German–Japanese collaboration.[43] The German press displayed a less discernible bias for either the Japanese or the Russians than could be found in Britain and France, although it did show a similar concern for the human tragedy involved, and especially for the fate of the Russian admirals. On 31 May, for example, the *Berliner Tageblatt*'s headline asked 'Roschdjest-wensky, Fölkersahm and Nebogatow Captured?'[44] By 1 June, the press began to lose interest in the event even as it summarized its repercussions. Some newspapers evidently felt pity towards the people of Russia and particularly towards the tsar and his admirals.[45] It took time, however, until the full political repercussions of the battle were reviewed. During the war, the Munich weekly magazine *Simplicissimus* ran a number of cartoons that poked fun at Britain's exploitative relations with Japan. Almost five months after the battle, the magazine carried a cartoon of a tweedy gentleman representing Britain telling the Japanese 'Your reference may be recent, but you can fight all my wars from now on.'[46]

Beyond Europe and North America, the Asian and African press greeted the Japanese victory in Tsushima with great enthusiasm. Against the background of Western colonialism that was reaching its apex, this press hailed the outcomes of the battle as the first true triumph of the East over the West in modern times. It was also a sign, for some, that the 'white man's' dominance was not indefinite.[47] Considering the Russian Empire an enemy, the media in Muslim countries and the communities in its vicinity, such as the Ottoman Empire, Iran, and the Caucasus, welcomed the Japanese triumph in particular.[48] News of the battle also attracted widespread attention in more remote parts of the Muslim world, such as Egypt and the Dutch East Indies, where Japan was seen as an anti-colonialist power.[49] In India, too, the public followed the war excitedly, and the Japanese victory at Tsushima was perceived as a harbinger of liberation.[50] In Calcutta, for instance, the Persian-language magazine *Habl al-Matin* asked rhetorically: 'What could have caused the victory except divine help, a reminder for their justice.'[51] In China, many newspapers, and notably Shanghai's *Dongfang zashi*, regarded the battle as a final blow to white racism and as the zenith of a war that made the 'yellow people' defend themselves 'and stand with pride'.[52] The memory of the battle and the recognition of its wider significance in Asia have been long-lasting. Almost a century after the clash at Tsushima, *Time*'s Asian edition would select it as the first of five major battles that 'changed the continent'.[53]

Decision Makers' Reactions

The sweeping Japanese victory also attracted the attention of many public figures and decision makers. They recognized almost instantly the geopolitical implications of the battle, particularly for their own countries. Apart from the two belligerents, the country most concerned about the battle was the United States. The world's largest economy in 1905, it was also a rapidly growing naval power with recent stakes in the Pacific and East Asia. The Philippines—its recently acquired colony—was not far from the theatre of war. Throughout the first year of the war, President Theodore Roosevelt felt no contrition about the mutual attrition endured by both Russia and Japan. But a Japanese or Russian victory in the impending battle, Roosevelt realized, could ruin the precarious balance of the entire region and affect American interests too, and so he followed the news closely. He believed the Japanese may have the upper hand three days before the battle, but he had 'no conception, and no one else had any conception,' as he confessed in a private letter some three weeks later, 'that there would be a slaughter rather than a fight, and that the Russians would really make no adequate resistance whatever.'[54] On the face of it, the American president was startled by the Japanese naval performance. He was quick to praise Japan in a message he sent to its minister in Washington, Kaneko Kentarō, on 31 May 1905. 'Neither Trafalgar nor the defeat of the Spanish Armada,' he commended, 'was as complete—as overwhelming.'[55]

Still, the immediate implication the battle had for Roosevelt was not historical but strategic.[56] Japan was becoming too strong, he conceded, while recognizing that the battle not only 'decided the fate of the Japanese empire' but also decided that of the United States in the Pacific.[57] Thus, almost overnight, Roosevelt came to believe that a stable balance of power in East Asia, rather than an incessant and one-sided conflict, would best serve American interests.[58] Russia's position had to be retained in order to check Japanese imperial aspiration in north-east Asia, and efforts towards peace had to be resumed to this end. The American president wasted no time. During the subsequent three months, he acted as a perfect broker and was able to cajole, and at time also coerce, the two parties to gather around the negotiation table (Figure 34). Once brought to the relaxed

ROOSEVELT : Assez ! — Enough ! — Genug ! (Collection T. Bianco)

Figure 34. An impartial umpire? President Roosevelt mediating between Emperor Meiji and Tsar Nicholas II (with a bandage inscribed *Tsushima* on his head) on a French postcard, 1905

Note: Painter: T. Bianco. Lithograph with hand colouring; ink on card stock; dimensions: 8.8 × 13.8 centimetres.

ambience of Portsmouth, New Hampshire, the two belligerents were able to conclude a sustainable peace agreement in less than a month.

For this achievement, Roosevelt was awarded the 1906 Nobel Peace Prize. But beyond this benevolent activity, the American president was genuinely worried that his own navy might find itself in a similar situation to that of Rozhestvenskii's. This fear was neither sudden nor dissociated from his earlier activity.[59] During his entire presidency, Roosevelt was the guiding spirit behind the rise of the United States Navy and American imperialistic ambitions in the Pacific.[60] In a letter sent to the British ambassador in Washington, Cecil Spring Rice, three weeks after the battle, he confided:

> I wish to see our navy constantly build up each ship at the highest point
> of efficiency as a fighting unit. If we follow this course we shall have no
> trouble with the Japanese or anyone else. But if we bluster, if we behave

badly to other nations ... and if at the same time we fail to keep our navy
at the highest point of efficiency and size—then we shall invite disaster.[61]

Britain was less ambivalent about the Japanese victory. As Tokyo's
closest ally and the main supplier of the IJN's warships, the outcomes
were self-complimentary. 'The battle-worthiness of the ships is a
tribute to the efficiency of the British yards,' *The Time*'s influential
war correspondent, Charles à Court Repington (1858–1925), boasted,
'while the havoc wrought by the guns made in England appears to
justify us in the belief that we can hold own with the best.'[62] More
importantly, the battle had significant and mostly positive repercussions on Britain's global strategy. Perturbed for more than a decade by
the Franco-Russian Alliance and its naval implications, the news about
the battle's outcomes was stunning. On 7 June 1905, the senior diplomat Arthur Henry Hardinge (1859–1933) sent a message to the Secretary of State for Foreign Affairs, the 5th Marquess of Lansdowne
(1845–1927), with regard to the 'catastrophe in the Korean Straits'.
Hardinge assessed correctly that the battle eliminated the Russian
naval threat for the foreseeable future.[63] Indeed, what London hailed
as 'the Trafalgar of the East' could provide the basis not only for
ending the war but also for a new strategic alignment in Europe.
With Japan pulling Britain's chestnuts out of the fire in Tsushima,
the IRN no longer posed a danger to the Royal Navy. In hindsight,
Whitehall's policy of containment during the war, that is 'being more a
neutral and less an ally' to Japan, was sensible, at least in relation to
Russia.[64]

Once defeated and no longer a menace to Britain, Russia could
reciprocate and amend its own policy on Britain. Although it did not
abandon its interests in East Asia completely, the Tsarist Empire now
temporarily retired from an almost century-long wide-ranging border
conflict with Britain across Asia (whimsically referred to as 'the Great
Game').[65] With their animosity contained at last, the two empires
would consolidate an alliance two years after the war.[66] From a global
perspective, Britain can also be regarded as the true beneficiary of the

new situation, at least for a while. While its rapprochement with France in 1904 exerted a greater significance, its establishment of Russia as an ally three years later and its securing of relations with Japan as early as 1902 meant that Britain's 'Splendid Isolation' was evidently over. This is not to say that Russia and France did not reap some benefits from this unexpected alliance. They did, and by 1907 the three new allies' common concern was no longer secret. 'An entente between Russia, France and ourselves would be absolutely secure,' stated Britain's new Foreign Secretary, Sir Edward Grey, unhesitatingly as early as 1906. 'If it is necessary to check Germany it could then be done.'[67]

For France, the fiasco associated with its foremost ally brought an end to its remaining hopes for Russian victory in the war. The news about the battle came as a shock but also as a welcome relief. Maurice Paléologue (1859–1944), special assistant to Foreign Minister Théophile Delcassé, regarded the battle as marking 'the end of Russian domination in Asia', much as Philip II's armada debacle had brought about the decline of Spanish dominance in Europe in 1588.[68] More than a year earlier, Russia's first defeats in its war against Japan had surprised French decision makers, but they were dismayed to realize with each additional disaster just how weak and unreliable their ally's armed forces actually were.[69] This weakness, alongside the rise of German military might, contributed to France's diminished position in European affairs after 1904. In an attempt to refrain from jeopardizing its new ties with Britain following their *Entente cordiale*, France found itself in a difficult position during the voyage of the Baltic Fleet. Among other things, French officials asked the Russian government to route it via Cape Horn and thereby avoid coaling in French ports. After the war, Franco-Russian relations experienced a temporary deterioration.[70] Nonetheless, Paris's commitment to St Petersburg did not end with the battle. In fact, it facilitated diplomatic and strategic gains that could not have been expected in early 1905. Aware of the changing balance of power before the Russo-Japanese War even began, the Quai d'Orsay urged St Petersburg to limit its military activities in East Asia and concentrate its power in Europe as a counterbalance to Germany's burgeoning aspirations.[71] Heavily invested in various projects in Russia, France also provided its ally with much needed loans in 1906. The most important gain, however, occurred a year later, when France entered into the unofficial Triple Entente with both Russia and Britain, and thereby completed its vision of a formidable countermeasure against German ambitions.

In Germany, another neutral bystander and ostensible ally of Russia, the Japanese victory was received with shock and curiosity. As the war broke out, Kaiser Wilhelm II enthusiastically declared: 'Now we must use all means to grab the whole of East Asia, particularly on the Yangtze.'[72] He also fervently supported the dispatch of the Baltic Fleet and expressed confidence about its prospects.[73] After Tsushima, his tone altered radically. On 3 June 1905, the day President Roosevelt introduced his peace initiative, the Kaiser made a move too. He sent the tsar an affectionate letter in which he expressed his concern that the internal strife might end with the tsar's death if the war with Japan did not cease. He strongly advised Nicholas to seek peace.[74] The benefit to Germany, at least in terms of its position in Europe, was obvious, and the two leaders concluded the Treaty of Björkö two months later. This was a secret mutual defence accord and a soon-to-be abortive exercise in personal diplomacy on the part of Wilhelm II that attempted to exploit Russia's post-Tsushima weakness.[75] The full repercussions of the conflict for Germany began to unfold in September 1905 when the belligerents concluded a peace treaty. By then, the Kaiser's geopolitical aspirations had reached maturity and were recognized fully by his neighbours. In this sense, the battle served as a discernible stage in, or even a final catalyst to, the rise of German ambitions towards becoming a world power, as well as a wielder of hegemonic power on the continent.[76]

Beyond the confines of the Western world, personal reactions to the Japanese victory were overwhelmingly ebullient. Like the entire Turkish public, the young Ottoman officer Captain Mustafa Kemal (Mustafa Kemal Atatürk, 1881–1938) was overjoyed when he heard about the victory in provincial Damascus.[77] In the capital, Istanbul, Sultan Abdul Hamid II responded in the same manner. He praised the victory, stating: 'The success of Japan pleases us. Its victory against Russia should be valued as our victory.'[78] In South Africa, the young Indian lawyer and civil-rights activist Mohandas Gandhi was also impressed. Two weeks after the battle, Gandhi wrote about it in his own newspaper: 'Japan's star seems to be in the ascendant.... In this war Japan has not known defeat. What, then, is the secret of this epic heroism?'[79] In British India, another writer carried the lesson learnt in the battle one step further: 'If the rice-eating Jap is capable of throwing into utter rout and disorder the Russian soldiers, cannot the rice-eating Indians also if properly trained, do the same?'[80] For 16-year-old Jawaharlal Nehru (1889–1964), India's first prime minister after independence, the battle was a landmark in his political awareness. The news caught him in Britain and put him in 'high good humour'.[81]

Sun Yat-sen (1866–1925), the provisional first president of the Republic of China in 1912, was also in Britain at the time news of the battle began to spread.[82] To his surprise, the British public expressed a certain consternation which he attributed to racial fears. 'Blood is thicker than water', he concluded.[83] His sentiment of racial pride and reprisal was shared by numerous East Asians. It ran so deep that even Koreans, who at the time were anxious about Japan's colonial plans for their country, were filled with a sudden sense of achievement.[84] This rising racial sentiment among Asians was not lost on Europe and North America. Quite a few observers, including leading decision makers, could not but see the triumph in Tsushima, and the war as a whole, as 'the victory of a non-white people over a white people.'[85] The implications of this heightened racial awareness were not limited to specific bilateral relations or even regional conflict but were global and long-term. Many predicted now a protracted struggle for liberation along racial lines, perhaps even an end to 'the territorial expansion of the white races'.[86] Japan, with its military and technological edge, was expected to be in the vanguard of this historical development.[87]

Naval Specialists' Assessment

The Battle of Tsushima also evoked enthusiastic responses from naval specialists worldwide. Their views soon resulted in a heated debate about the causes of the Japanese victory and even more so about the lessons that could be drawn from this experience. The debate was not theoretical as four months after the battle Britain laid down a revolutionary battleship (HMS *Dreadnought*, discussed in Chapter 6), whose novel attributes were contested vigorously at home and followed closely by all other major navies. In 1906, Alfred Thayer Mahan was one of the first to enter the fray with an analytical essay published almost simultaneously in the United States and Britain.[88] Having previously served two terms as President of the Naval War College and by then widely considered the most important American strategist of his generation, Mahan's tactical conclusions related to the ongoing *Dreadnought* project and other plans for capital ships. His main conclusions were explicit and swift, and were reached apparently on the basis of a superficial reading of the events. The renowned scholar favoured armament, and to a lesser extent also armour, over speed; a battery of mixed-calibre gun over single-calibre guns; and a large number of ordinary-sized capital ships over a small number of oversized capital ships.[89] In other words, he opposed the essence of the new British battleship.

Soon after the battle, Mahan concluded that the Japanese success had been 'the triumph of greater numbers, skilfully combined, over superior individual ship power, too concentrated for flexibility of movement'.[90] In later years, however, he delved particularly into the question of speed and its contribution to the Japanese triumph. With the benefit of a faster speed, he noted, Tōgō could choose the place of battle and control every movement. Strategically, he found, 'there was no escape from the Russian dilemma', since Rozhestvenskiĭ could not reach Vladivostok without fighting. Put differently, Tōgō's advantage in speed allowed him to reach any place in the arena before his opponent and regardless of the route he chose.[91] Mahan also linked speed with gunnery. As the speed of a naval force is determined by the speed of its slowest unit, its speed can be reduced considerably by even minor damage to the funnels of one of its ships. Since the secondary battery was particularly effective in inflicting such damage, and considering its effect on the crews, he insisted, against contemporary trends, that this battery 'is really entitled to the name primary', and certainly should not be discarded.[92] Among all the factors that make a battleship efficient, Mahan concluded, 'speed and offensive power—gun power—are at present the leading competing considerations.'[93]

Five years later, Mahan referred extensively to the battle in his *Naval Strategy* (1911). The clash at Tsushima, he asserted, displayed the principles of his strategy better than any other modern battle. In discussing the question of strategic position, he found parallels between Tōgō's uncertainty with regard to the enemy's whereabouts on the eve of the battle and Nelson on the eve of the battle of the Nile in 1798.[94] Mahan also repeated this comparison when considering maritime expeditions. He contended that 'Japan, by readiness, skill and promptitude had projected her national power across sea, forestalling the action of Russia, as Bonaparte that of Great Britain ... the positional keys of the situation were in her hands; but the defeat of Togo's fleet would have annulled all previous successes, as that of Brueys [the French commander in the Battle of the Nile] by Nelson did the achievement of Bonaparte.'[95] As for the relations between the Japanese and Russian fleets, Mahan argued, against common wisdom, that, at least prior to their engagement, 'they bore no slight resemblance to those between a pursued and pursuing fleet.' The Japanese, in fact, were on the defensive, as 'their object was to stop, to thwart, the Russian attempt', whereas the Russians were on the offensive. This meant that they had to abandon the column the moment they came under fire.[96]

Alongside his praise for Tōgō, Mahan believed history would 'take a more indulgent view' of Rozhestvenskiĭ, as time passed. Despite the 'undoubted errors of his last four days of command,' he averred, 'justice demands the combined recollection' of the various factors that hampered the voyage of 'this unfortunate admiral' and the recognition of 'the arduous task he had accomplished up to that time'. In reality, Mahan concluded, Rozhestvenskiĭ had already lost the battle in the Yellow Sea (without being there) nine months earlier, rather than 'off Tsushima nine months later'.[97] But the relations between the two battles did not end there. On 27 May 1905, the Russian admiral's course was a compromise, 'a mix-up of escape and fighting' and 'a repetition of the mistakes of the Port Arthur division'. As both battles demonstrated, Mahan summed up, the Japanese naval strategy 'was marked by the accuracy of diagnosis, concentration of purpose, and steadiness of conduct, which were strikingly wanting in their opponents'.[98]

Theodore Roosevelt was also concerned about the naval and technological implications of the battle. While serving as Assistant Secretary of the Navy only seven years earlier, he had been deeply involved in the rapid development of the US Navy which made it the world's fourth largest fleet by 1905.[99] Two months after the battle, the American president wrote to Lieutenant Commander (later Admiral) William Sims (1858–1936), the Navy's Inspector of Naval Gunnery, to discuss the reportedly successful use of medium-calibre guns in the battle and its implication for the concept of an all-big-gun warship.[100] He was highly aware of recent naval innovations and their place in the current debate, as well as of Mahan's view on this matter.[101] Sims proved to be the right person to consult. His 26-page reply suggested that Mahan's view was based on faulty information and that, in fact, the big-calibre guns were more accurate to the extent that Japan's victory would be even more decisive had it possessed all-big-gun battleships.[102] Technically, Sims was right and Roosevelt was won over.[103] Big guns, and accordingly also big battleships, were enjoying now a vogue. A few months earlier, another rising officer, Commander (later Rear Admiral) Bradley Allen Fiske (1854–1942), had written in the same spirit. He acknowledged the advantage Mahan attributed to the IJN in using small battleships 'to surround and prevent the Russians from escaping', but stressed that this could only occur *after* the Baltic Fleet 'had been whipped' by long-range gunfire.[104] However correct and persuasive, these views were not as consequential, at least for a while. Ironically, and as noted by one of Roosevelt's biographers, 'his deliberation in making the right choice played a part in slowing the adoption of the all-big-gun type.'[105]

Lieutenant Commander (and future Vice Admiral) Newton McCully was another American naval expert who wrote about the battle extensively. As one of the very few naval observers who saw the war on the Russian side, he was probably the most well-informed American of his time with regard to the IRN.[106] But, despite his acquaintance with the IRN, McCully was shocked by its unpreparedness, especially in comparison with the IJN. Official corruption, he found, 'was responsible for much of this unreadiness, government contracts being regarded as sources of private gain'.[107] In line with this corruption, McCully believed that the debacle in Tsushima, much like the IRN's earlier defeats in the war, was the outcome of a profound structural problem. 'The root of the Russian naval disaster in the war,' McCully insisted, 'is found in the Russian character, of which the government is a natural consequence.'[108] There is no country, he elaborated, 'in which a man is so free personally, and mentally so restricted. It really is a crime for a soldier, officer, or civilian to dare think, while he may be exceedingly lax in many moral relations without suffering any detriment.'[109]

In Britain, the battle stirred a heated debate about its tactical and technological implications. Admiral John 'Jacky' Fisher (1842–1920), the Royal Navy's First Sea Lord since 1904 and the man behind its concurrent reforms, was moved by the Japanese success. Indeed, the battle confirmed a good part of his vision for the Royal Navy (see Chapter 6). In discussing the admiral's role in battle, Fisher noted in his memoires that he 'got to be like Nelson . . . and the people of the fleet watch him with suspense to see what signal goes up to alter the formation of the fleet—a formation on which depends victory or defeat.' For Fisher, Admiral Tōgō, who 'won that second Trafalgar', was one such example: 'He did what is technically known as "crossing the T", which means he got the guns of his fleet all to bear, all free to fire, while those of the enemy were masked by his own ships. One by one, Rozhdestvensky's went to the bottom.' In his view, it was speed, the presence of a good admiral, and providence, that accounted for the Japanese victory.[110] Fisher's views, and his emphasis on speed, met with bitter opposition. Admiral Reginald Custance (1847–1935), for example, argued that 'superior speed confers little, if any tactical advantage. Fighting power depends upon its *offensive* rather than on its defensive form—upon weapons rather than on protection. Speed is not a weapon, and does not give protection, except in running away.'[111]

The most notable voice in British naval circles after the battle was Sir Julian Stafford Corbett (1854–1922). The foremost British naval historian and geostrategist of his time, Corbett was assigned to write the naval history of the Russo-Japanese War in 1907 and was thus distinctly familiar with the battle.[112] Four years later, Corbett referred to the lessons of Tsushima in an article seeking to defend the recently commissioned battleship HMS *Dreadnought*.[113] To maintain its global position, he argued, Britain had to resort to big and fast warships. Unlike Mahan, Corbett maintained that speed played an important role in this epoch. In his view, Admiral Tōgō chose the place to wait for the Russian armada according to the speed advantage he possessed.[114] In other words, the greater one's speed, the larger 'the size of the area within which open blockading positions may be sought'.[115] In the same article, retired Admiral Edmund Fremantle backed Corbett's notion of speed by elaborating on the horrendous impact of Rozhestvenskiĭ's slow advance. 'The chased fleet's speed is as the slowest speed,' Fremantle concluded, 'and it is true to say that chasing speed is that of the fastest speed.'[116]

Corbett referred to the Battle of Tsushima extensively also in his major exposition entitled *Some Principles of Maritime Strategy* (1911). In discussing the methods of securing command, he regarded the battle as 'a converse case' of the principle of seeking out the enemy's fleet and destroying it. Unlike his operations in 1904, Tōgō was content at Tsushima 'to have set up such a situation that the enemy must come and break it down if they were to affect the issue of the war. So he waited on the defensive, assured his enemy must come to him...'[117] The Japanese success in the battle, Corbett concluded, exemplified that the 'maxim of "seeking out" for all its moral exhilaration...must not be permitted to displace well-reasoned judgment.'[118] Similarly, he also referred to the battle when discussing strategic choices and their occasional contradictory nature. 'When Togo attacked Rojesvensky,' he noted, 'his primary object was offensive, i.e., to capture or destroy the Russian Fleet. [But] His ulterior object was to maintain the defensive function which had been assigned to the Japanese Fleet.'[119] Rozhestvenskiï's objectives, by contrast, were not as defined. Vladivostok, Corbett explained, was not an objective per se but a destination. Hence, in essence, the Russian admiral 'had no true *objective* before him except Togo's fleet'.[120] Altogether, the Japanese decision to wait for the enemy allowed Corbett to redefine the idea of command at sea. 'The primary object of the fleet,' he stated, 'is to secure communications, and if the enemy's fleet is in a position to render them unsafe it must be put out of action.'[121]

In France too, Commander René Daveluy referred frequently to the battle. In 1906, this prolific naval strategist published a comprehensive study of the war as well as a theoretical work which in three years' time would be developed into his grand three-volume magnum opus *L'esprit de la guerre navale*.[122] Translated into German and English, the two latter works of naval theory were employed extensively as naval manuals before the First World War.[123] Even as he became France's leading naval theorist, Daveluy was also mindful of practical matters. An experienced officer who had commanded the world's first functional torpedo-equipped submarine, he underscored the tactical role of the torpedo as a weapon of terror and night attacks by torpedo boats, especially for the French navy, despite the torpedo's allegedly poor performance in the battle.[124] By the same token, he stressed the importance of deploying all available means, 'while preventing the enemy from doing the same' and taking the initiative, as Tōgō did.[125] The battle, in his view, turned quickly into pursuit rather than retreat.

In other words, when one of the belligerents 'abandons all idea of resistance; his principal aim is to escape, and he will only fight to the extent is necessary to help his evasion...It offers so few chances of safety that it may be asked whether it would not be cheaper to pay with one's life than to fly, unless evasion is favored by darkness.'[126]

Germany was no different in this regard, as the Battle of Tsushima also stirred up a keen interest among its naval theorists. Grasping the significance of the battle in a period of naval expansion and great ambitions, the Naval Office hurried to prepare an assessment of the voyage and subsequent engagement. Based on very limited sources, the resulting 83-page report argued that the battle was not waged between equal adversaries, which meant that the lessons that could be derived from it were limited. The report highlighted the Russian initial unreadiness (e.g. the new *Borodino*-class warship carried 'craftsmen on board up to Skagen!'); the sailors' lack of discipline; Vice Admiral Rozhestvenskiĭ's aloofness and constant preoccupation with coaling; and the poor gunnery training.[127] As for the battle, it attributed the blame for the Russian debacle to the choice of the Korean Strait (rather than the La Pérouse Strait), Rozhestvenskiĭ's weak leadership and poor communication with his senior officers, his unfavourable starting position tactically, the overloading of the *Borodino*-class battleships, and the large number of duds among the Russian shells.[128] While hinting that Tōgō's tactics would not have necessarily been effective against a more energetic opponent, the report did acknowledge the Japanese way and spirit of fighting.[129] Aside from this classified publication, many German discussions of the battle were carried in the pages of the naval journals, *Marine-Rundschau* and *Nauticus*. In 1906, for example, a special issue of the former discussed the battle's implications. It asserted that Russia would never be a major sea power due to its geographical location.[130] During the same year, *Marine-Rundschau* also announced a competition for an essay comparing the battles of Trafalgar and Tsushima, with the two winning articles to be published by the journal in the course of 1907.[131]

6

The Battle and Naval Development

Lessons Learned and Unlearned

The Battle of Tsushima exerted a major impact on early 20th-century naval development. This should not be surprising if we accept the notion that battles are a vital element in naval evolution and consider the dearth of other large and decisive battles before and after 1905. To be sure, Tsushima was the largest major naval engagement during the 111-year period between the battles of Trafalgar (1805) and Jutland (1916), and the only large decisive engagement between Trafalgar and the Battle of Midway (1942). This is not to say that there were no other important naval battles during these long intervals: Navarino (1827), Hampton Roads (1862), Lissa (1866) and Manila (1898), among others, presented significant landmarks in the dramatic naval evolution that took place during this period. And yet, none had been as large-scale and influential as the Battle of Tsushima.

The greatest impact of the battle was obviously felt by the naval forces of Russia and Japan. Neither of them remained the same after Tsushima and both strove to learn the lessons of the engagement. Other naval forces were not very different. While they did not play an active part in the battle, they were also acutely aware of it and affected by its results. A few of them assigned naval observers to the arena, but all did their utmost to obtain insights pertaining to the warships' combat performance and to their weaponry after the battle and to validate their own doctrines.[1] Consequently, the lessons drawn from the battle played a pivotal role in the brief naval revolution and ensuing naval race that took place before the outbreak of the First World War, if not beyond. Admittedly, it is somewhat difficult to separate the battle's impact from that of the Russo-Japanese War as a whole. And yet, the Battle of Tsushima was unquestionably the most important naval engagement during the war and the lessons drawn from it greatly exceeded those of any other engagement. In this light, the present chapter examines the lessons that were learned and unlearned from the battle, and focuses on the way they were implemented and on the overall impact they exerted on naval development in the decade preceding 1914.

The Fate of the Battleship

The battle's most immediate contribution to naval development was its impact on the battleship. On the eve of the Russo-Japanese war, the status of this type of warship was in doubt. Powered by a steam engine, armed with the largest guns available and heavily armoured, battleships had been considered the dominant warships in naval warfare since their emergence in the latter half of the 19th century. Nonetheless, the race for naval supremacy led to the construction of increasingly bigger and more sophisticated battleships with a single disadvantage—their cost became so prohibitive that it burdened the national budgets of even the largest powers.[2] By 1904, there were then more than one hundred battleships flying the flag of nine navies whose value and performance had to be proven. With no proof at hand, quite a few asserted that, like dinosaurs, battleships would become extinct once they encountered smaller, cheaper, and more efficient warships armed with torpedoes. Tsushima dispelled these doubts entirely and this was its main lesson. The battleship proved to be *the* dominant vessel in the clash and the one that determined its outcome. While battleships could sink any other type of warships, only battleships could sink other fit battleships in a full daylight engagement. The battle, with six Russian battleships sunk, including the most modern ones possessed by the IRN, also demonstrated that battleships were not indestructible. That said, the performance of the Japanese Combined Fleet indicated that well-handled battleships could withstand hits by the largest guns and go through fierce engagements with relatively few casualties.

This validation of the battleship's viability did not mean the vessel was flawless. Tsushima left little doubt that further improvements could make this vessel even more powerful and resistant. As a result, the battle's most comprehensive and almost immediate lesson is found in the concept of the all-big-gun battleship. Indeed, over time, the battle became closely associated with the emergence of a new type of battleship, HMS *Dreadnought*. To be sure, this warship emerged soon after Tsushima: she was laid down in October 1905, launched in February 1906, and commissioned on 2 December 1906, some 18 months after the battle. By the same token, *Dreadnought*—the lead ship of a new class and the one that gave her name to an entire generation of battleships— was a physical manifestation of the attainment of many of the lessons drawn in the battle. She was faster (21 knots), more heavily armoured, and with much greater firepower (*ten* 305-millimetre guns) than any existing battleship, and, needless to say, any of the battleships that fought at Tsushima (Figure 35).[3]

Almost every aspect of these improvements was directly linked to the observations made and conclusions reached at Tsushima. And yet, it is often forgotten that the decision to build HMS *Dreadnought* was not the outcome of the Battle of Tsushima. In fact, this decision, as well as the ship's general design, was made some four months *before* the battle was fought.[4] A careful examination of the conception and timeline behind the building of HMS *Dreadnought* indicates that many of its features did not require the lessons of Tsushima. Fisher himself stated years later that the idea of a ship with guns of uniform calibre had been on his mind as far back as 1900 when, while in Malta, he held a discussion with the chief engineer of the Royal Navy.[5] Outside Britain, the winds were also blowing in the same direction. In 1903,

Figure 35. The post-Tsushima battleship: the all-big-gun HMS *Dreadnought*, 1907

the chief constructor of the Royal Italian Navy, Vittorio Emanuel Cuniberti, was very explicit about the new ship he envisioned. In an article published in *Jane's Fighting Ships* and entitled 'An Ideal Battleship for the British Fleet', Cuniberti proposed a battleship of 17,000 tons armed with no less than one dozen 305-millimetre guns and entirely without a secondary battery. One year later, the United States Navy, too, began to plan a battleship (the *South Carolina* class) with eight 305-millimetrer guns.[6]

As for the Russo-Japanese War, it was the August 1904 Battle of the Yellow Sea that became the initial catalyst for the concept of an all-big-gun warship, since the two fleets opened fire at such a long range that the battleships' secondary battery was rendered useless.[7] As he watched the two fleets shelling each other for hours and achieving very little, the senior British naval observer, Captain William Pakenham, composed an encomium to long-range fire after the battle. To begin with, Pakenham suggested, it was possible to open fire at a distance of 20,000 metres and to consider a firing range of 10,000 metres as being at close quarters.[8] As for the efficiency of the various guns, he wrote animatedly but unequivocally:

...the effect of the fire of every gun is so much less than that of the next larger size, that when 12-inch guns are firing, shots from 10-inch pass unnoticed, while, for all the respect they instill, 8-inch or 6-inch guns might then just as well be pea-shooters, and the 12-pounder [gun] simply does not count.[9]

The fact that only large-calibre guns were used with assured effectiveness in such a long-distance engagement had dramatic repercussions. For one thing, the development of armour, in thickness and quality, meant that only particularly large calibre guns could inflict any significant damage and even sink battleships or armoured cruisers; and for another, only ships with especially thick armour were able to withstand a hit by those guns. The logical ramification of these two observations seemed inescapable. A well-protected battleship with eight or even a dozen big guns could be the equivalent of two or even three existing pre-dreadnought battleships as large as the Japanese flagship *Mikasa*. There were also other reasons behind the decision for an all-big-gun battleship. One factor underpinning the need for an efficient and drastic solution to the problem of firepower was the wide variety of firing systems that had been created over time. This variety prevented the possibility of control and complicated the necessary uniformity. Another important reason for the need for a new type of battleship was economic. At the outbreak of the Russo-Japanese War, the Royal Navy budget was double its budget 15 years earlier, bringing the burden on the empire to new heights.[10] Appointed First Sea Lord in October 1904, Admiral John Fisher expressed his willingness for budget cuts. He actually had no intention of either reducing the fleet's firepower or overstraining its budget, but he was willing to decommission over 150 obsolete vessels. At the same time, he was aware of the necessity of providing high-quality replacements for the quantitative loss and increasing the fleet's firepower against rising German competition.[11]

Intriguingly, reports on the Battle of Tsushima reached different conclusions from earlier wartime reports. This was particularly evident with regard to the use of guns. The range of fire was mostly shorter than that of the Battle of the Yellow Sea and so the secondary battery was used effectively. Participants in the battle and armchair experts alike noted that a large part of the damage was inflicted on the Russian warships by the light guns.[12] In Britain, Admiral Edmund Fremantle, among other opponents of the all-big-gun ship, believed that the distances from which the belligerents fired during the Battle of the Yellow Sea were an exception, and opined that the idea of avoiding close range was alien to British naval tradition.[13] Nonetheless, these views and additional reports of the havoc wreaked by the secondary battery did little to change the unshakable conviction held by Fisher and his followers. By then, he was already committed in his thinking and HMS *Dreadnought* was accordingly not equipped with a secondary battery. A few years later, nonetheless, the lessons from Tsushima finally prevailed and new British battleships were armed with a secondary battery from 1910 onwards.[14] At the same time, the observation that very few shells succeeded in breaching the battleships' armour also led to an increase in the guns' calibre and to an improvement of the firing control system. Within a few years the Royal Navy increased the calibre of the primary battery from 305-millimetre to 343-millimetre (13.5-inch) guns, and in 1912 even ordered the first class of battleships to be armed with 381-millimetre (15-inch) guns. The Americans and the Japanese did not sit idly by and armed their own new capital ships with 356-millimetre (14-inch) guns. Three decades later, the gunnery race would reach its peak when the IJN armed a pair of its latest battleships, the mammoth *Yamato* and her sister ship the *Musashi*, with 460-millimetre (18.1-inch) guns.

The thickness and the quality of ship armour became another important target for improvement in the wake of the Battle of Tsushima. Unlike much of the Russo-Japanese War, at Tsushima the armament seemed to have the upper hand in the never-ending duel between armour and armament. The outcomes did not indicate an urgent need to increase the armour, but they did reveal the drawbacks of the unarmoured parts on board, including the vulnerability of the long funnels used in contemporary warships.[15] In the wake of

GREAT BATTLES

Tsushima, British analysts suggested that the Japanese ships sustained their hits better than their opponents since they had been built with the finest metallurgical technology of the time, were well compartmented, and were designed in the sturdiest fashion. That said, the Russian battleships' armour was not defective either, and in most cases the Japanese gunnery failed to breach it despite causing extensive damage that effectively put the ships out of action and often facilitated a *coup de grâce* by torpedoes fired at close range.[16] These testimonies were unequivocal proof that thick armour plating amidships, but also on the decks and around the turrets, could provide better defence against any type of shell, and might ultimately guarantee the battleship's survival. Thus, battleships built after 1905 did not have substantially thicker armour for as long as gun calibres remained the same.

The importance of speed in battleship warfare also gained particular support during the war. Admiral Tōgō's ability to execute his manoeuvres at Tsushima was attributed to his ships' speed advantage. Similarly, Vice Admiral Rozhestvenskiǐ's inability to reach Vladivostok without a fight was also the result of speed, but in this case, it was his fleet's slower speed. British observers' reports emphasized the speed factor and saw it as second only to firepower, and Fisher himself used to say that speed 'is armour'.[17] But speed came at a cost. Even a small increase in battleship speed required bigger engines, bigger fuel tanks, and consequently heavier armour to protect them. These, in turn, increased the ship's weight and lowered its speed. In other words, only a new and radically different propulsion system could break this vicious circle. In fact, such a system—the steam turbine—was already available, but its technology had never been used to propel a capital ship-scale warship.[18] If successful, it would be the key component for the entire revolution. Thus, the desire for greater speed along with greater firepower compelled Fisher to opt for this revolutionary form of propulsion, but also to make certain compromises with respect to armour as discussed below. His choices would be emulated almost instantly in almost every capital ship built in subsequent years.

The emergence of HMS *Dreadnought* was the opening shot of a race to build a dreadnought-like battleship. The name *Dreadnought* soon became a generic name for all new battleships built thereafter with a large number of heavy guns, and all previous classes would now be referred to as pre-dreadnoughts. Paradoxically, the launching of HMS *Dreadnought* meant that all the battleships that had taken part in the battle became outdated in one fell swoop, along, of course, with over 100 additional pre-dreadnought battleships possessed by seven other navies.[19] Despite gaining a new edge, Britain could not become stale. By 1911, the Royal Navy had completed the construction of 10 new battleships of five consecutive classes, each bigger than its predecessor and with each new class boasting a slight improvement in armament, armour, and speed, at a rate that astonished naval experts. Within six years of the completion of HMS *Dreadnought*, the new battleships were so superior that they were subsequently known as super dreadnoughts.[20] Commissioned in 1914, the broadside of the five Queen Elizabeth-class battleships alone was nearly three time heavier than that fired by the last pre-dreadnought class commissioned in Britain merely six years earlier, and more than twice that of HMS *Dreadnought*.[21]

The Battle of Tsushima was also associated with the emergence of the battlecruiser. The idea for a hybrid between the battleship and the armoured cruiser was entirely Fisher's and had been born before the battle.[22] An enthusiastic supporter of fast vessels, Fisher envisaged a new capital ship similar to the *Dreadnought* in firepower, but with greater speed and thinner armour.[23] His original vision was based on a pre-war scenario that emphasized the defence of imperial trade routes and engagements against inferior Russian and French cruisers.[24] Tsushima catalysed his vision while placing it in a new context. On the one hand, the highly successful use of the large Japanese armoured cruisers demonstrated the benefits of speed and the intense use of guns which compensated for their thinner armour. On the other hand, the demise of the Baltic Fleet and the earlier rapprochement with France made the threats to Britain's trade routes less urgent. Undeterred, Fisher remained convinced about the viability of this concept, estimating that a fleet composed of battlecruisers would be more powerful and economical than a fleet combining battleships and regular cruisers.[25] In line with this approach, he authorized the construction of the first three British battlecruisers of the *Invincible* class in 1905. Commissioned in 1908–9, these boasted a top speed of 25 knots and eight 305-millimetre guns with armour whose maximum thickness was half that of HMS *Dreadnought*.[26] However, a rude awakening from Fisher's dream was not long in coming. Although his original plan called for only one battleship of the *Dreadnought* class and three battlecruisers of the *Invincible* class, the Royal Navy had almost three times more *Dreadnought*-type battleships than battlecruisers at the outbreak of the First World War.[27]

Consequences for Technological Development

Naval technology was one of the main beneficiaries of Tsushima. The lessons brought forward a remarkable development in virtually every technological domain, starting with weaponry and ending with tactical control and logistics, and their impact was felt throughout the first half of the 20th century. The first and foremost domain in which significant innovations were made was in weaponry, including artillery, torpedoes, and mines. Regarded as the key factor in the battle, naval artillery attracted particular attention in subsequent years. Although the accuracy of artillery in the battle was better than in the Battle of the Yellow Sea, it was evident that even a slight improvement could provide a naval force with the upper hand in any future engagement.[28] Moreover, improvements in fire control could keep the heavy guns as the main naval weapon and allow capital ships to engage while staying beyond the growing torpedo range. The Royal Navy, for example, had begun to place a greater emphasis on naval artillery shortly before the battle, but made special efforts in this domain after 1905.[29] It was not alone in this respect. During the decade after Tsushima, all major navies made considerable efforts towards improving fire control.[30] But as the range of fire increased, the hit rate still remained fairly low a decade later.[31]

The torpedo was another weapon used effectively in the battle. To some extent, the torpedo's relatively successful performance contributed to its redemption, since its low accuracy proved to be a bitter disappointment during the first 15 months of the war. The IJN, for example, fired some 370 torpedoes but only 17 of them hit their target with an alarming success rate of no more than 4.6 per cent.[32] Incredibly, this rate was quadrupled at Tsushima.[33] Moreover, the fear of torpedoes launched by the enemy shaped both sides' combat styles to a certain extent. They avoided approaching each other too closely and sought to keep their capital ships away from night warfare, during which light vessels carrying torpedoes could gain the upper hand and use their lethal weapon to finish off crippled vessels.[34] This ultimate success of the torpedo, however indecisive, did not go unnoticed by all the leading naval powers who also maintained the momentum of its development after 1905.[35] As an ardent advocate of torpedo use, Fisher regarded it as a weapon of the future, and his trust in its rapid improvement was probably realized sooner than he imagined. Within a decade the torpedo range, which stood at about 4,000 metres in 1905, more than doubled to about 10,000 metres, while its speed increased from 19 knots to 27–8 knots at this range.[36] During the First World War, the torpedo emerged as a reliable weapon and proved to be relatively accurate, especially when launched at close range from submarines.[37]

Another naval weapon that made its combat debut in the battle was the floating naval mine. Mines had been used against warships ineffectively for centuries, but the Russo-Japanese War marked the beginning of a massive and effective use of this inexpensive and unsophisticated weapon. Following their initial successes during the early months of the war, both sides used underwater moored mines extensively while lacking suitable means for countering them. The results were horrendous, and mines became the most destructive naval weapon of all until the Battle of Tsushima. Indeed, the mining of the coastal area off Port Arthur was the direct cause for the sinking of no fewer than three battleships, five cruisers, and three destroyers, and the loss of thousands of sailors on both sides.[38] At Tsushima, however, the IJN used mines in an offensive manner for the first time and did so in the midst of an engagement rather than surreptitiously beforehand. During the first night, for example, Japanese destroyers laid lines of connected floating mines in the path of advancing Russian warships, which resulted in the sinking of the battleship *Navarin*. Four years later, this sort of attack became a standard IJN tactic, with destroyers dropping their drifting mines some 1,000–2,000 metres ahead of the enemy and then steaming away at maximum speed. The Royal Navy began to emulate this tactic in 1913 and, despite abandoning it two years later, remained cautious about its use by the Germans throughout the war, with good reason.[39] During the First World War, Britain lost 46 warships, 439 auxiliaries and minesweepers, and 260 merchant ships to mines, whether moored or drifting.[40]

With these new or improved weapons, the warship's protection needed reinforcement too. Analysis of the sinking of the six Russian battleships at Tsushima gave rise to improvements in structure. The Royal Navy introduced a torpedo bulkhead on the sides of the HMS *Dreadnought*'s magazines to protect against torpedo and mine explosions, and so did other navies afterwards.[41] With respect to tactical fleet control, Tsushima drew attention to the acute limitations but also to the advantages encapsulated by the modern era. The battle made analysts wonder about the optimal number of warships a commander could handle effectively. In an era of rising fire exchange distances, Admiral Tōgō did not directly command more than two divisions made up of a dozen warships each (in fact, and for the most part, he only directly commanded a single division), whereas Vice Admiral Rozhestvenskiĭ was practically unable to command his larger fleet once the battle began. The first navy to attempt to solve the modern admiral's inability to visualize a battle's bigger picture and control his entire fleet was the Royal Navy. In 1914, Admiral John Jellicoe (1859–1935), the commander of the Grand Fleet, adopted an idea offered by Captain Frederic Dreyer as to how to plot the position, and consequently also display the course and speed, of both his own and enemy warships.[42] Although it took more than a few years to develop this system properly, it developed to the extent of providing admirals with an important visual aid for their decision making in battle during the inter-war era.

The seminal use of wireless telegraphy during the Battle of Tsushima was another aspect of naval control. Shortly before the battle began, wireless communication was used effectively by the Japanese to announce the interception of the Russian armada and thus provide an early warning to their main force. During the battle itself, however, radio communication was not used frequently. In fact, the Russian naval force was condemned to silence because Vice Admiral Rozhestvenskiĭ believed that radiotelegraph transmissions would reveal his location and intentions.[43] In the following years, wireless telegraphy and later radiotelephony would have much more to offer than enhanced scouting. Without exception, every naval force would install wireless telegraphy in its vessels, improve its range, and learn to use it as part of the new concept of centrally controlled fleet operations.[44]

The battle also marked a watershed in terms of logistics. The inconvenient use of coal and the disadvantages associated with overloaded warships in combat provided much food for thought in this domain.[45] Soon, Lord Charles Beresford (1846–1919), the commander-in-chief of the British Mediterranean Fleet, embarked upon a campaign to improve the coaling rate of his fleet. Within two years, it resulted in raising the average coaling rate in a battleship from 162 tons to as much as 289.2 tons. The improvement achieved by the warships of the Imperial German Navy was even greater.[46] And yet, given the time expended in coaling ships at sea even after such spectacular improvements, oil seemed to offer a far more attractive alternative. Oil is more efficient than coal, and thus allowed longer sailing distances between each refuelling. Moreover, refuelling with oil was quicker and could be done while sailing, and a warship using oil required about half of the engine-room personnel.[47] Eventually, it was largely the success in obtaining reliable sources of oil in the post-war years, rather than the Baltic Fleet's ordeal, that spurred the gradual shift to oil. In 1909, the Royal Navy decided that all of its future destroyers would be oil-powered, and this decision was also implemented with regard to the new class of battleships, the *Queen Elizabeth*, within three years.[48]

The transition to the use of oil by the major navies was associated with the development of naval diesel engines. The ability to utilize this relatively new source of energy was nonetheless less due to technical innovation than to geopolitics.[49] European powers searched for it in such distant locations as the Middle East and the Persian Gulf, and by so doing began a bitter struggle for influence over those areas that has never ceased to this day. By the same token, the battle demonstrated the disadvantages associated with the use of slow civilian auxiliary and coaling ships. A decade later, the vast and continuous needs introduced by the First World War prompted the development and use of faster and purpose-made navy coalers and tankers.[50]

Repercussions on Doctrine and Its Application in the Major Fleets

The Battle of Tsushima did not provide an unequivocal answer to the late 19th-century debate surrounding the naval doctrine modern navies ought to adopt. On the one hand, advocates of the Mahanian doctrine regarded the IJN's successful use of capital ships against the mainstay of the Russian armada as supporting the notion of a single and decisive great battle won by a blue-water navy. On the other hand, advocates of the Jeune École doctrine could not ignore the effective deployment of light Japanese vessels in deadly night attacks and the extreme vulnerability of the Russian battleships. While both doctrines had their supporters, it was the former that gained the upper hand in the years after the battle. Admittedly, the reliance on battleships and armoured cruisers in the first stages of the battle was a crucial element in Japanese success and it naturally enjoyed better public relations. Moreover, due to the weather conditions, the use of light flotillas was postponed and eventually reserved for nighttime attacks, a time when their torpedoes could deliver no more than a *coup de grâce* to already battered Russian warships. The major naval forces were aware of these inadequacies of light vessels and reckoned that Tsushima corroborated their earlier decision to place their trust and money in large capital ships.

The British Royal Navy provided a quintessential example of this trend. In fact, and for a few years after the battle, it enjoyed an unprecedented position that allowed it to apply the Mahanian doctrine even further. With the demise of two of Russia's fleets, and with the emergence of the *Dreadnought* and the *Invincible* classes, the Royal Navy gained both qualitative and quantitative leads it had not possessed during the previous two decades. Britain nonetheless followed the Russo-Japanese naval campaign closely for more than technological reasons.[51] Fisher, for one, was acutely conscious of the transformation of Britain's naval and overall strategic standing in the wake of Tsushima. The battle's effect not only was bolstered by the new alliance with France but also made Britain stop worrying about maintaining the costly two-power standard in naval superiority it had adopted in 1889. In fact, after Tsushima, the Royal Navy found itself suddenly equipped 'with a comfortable margin over a Three-Power Standard', the largest it had in Europe for decades.[52] By late 1905, for example, Britain had as many as 46 battleships against France's 18, Germany's 17, and Russia's five.[53] The diminished Russian threat in 1905, along with the alliance with Japan three years earlier, allowed the Royal Navy to accelerate the process of replacing most of its outdated cruisers and gunboats and concentrate on its build-up against the German threat in the North Sea.[54]

The minor revolution Fisher initiated in 1904 and even more so in the wake of Tsushima was followed closely by the other major navies. With the completion of the HMS *Dreadnought*, the latter were forced to reconsider their plans and even halt the construction of battleships and large cruisers which suddenly became outdated. The Imperial German Navy under Admiral Alfred von Tirpitz's (1849–1930) dynamic leadership, was the first to be affected. While it began its expansion programme (the first *Flottengesetze*) in 1898, it shot up meteorically from being the world's sixth largest navy to becoming second only to the Royal Navy between 1904 and 1914. During the Russo-Japanese War, Tirpitz was anxious not to provoke a British attack on his fledging fleet and so opposed any actions that could risk the status quo, including an alliance with Russia.[55] With the enthusiastic encouragement of Kaiser Wilhelm II, Tirpitz's navy responded to the *Dreadnought* challenge with a two-year delay. The development of this warship was a significant blow at first, as Germany was forced to stop the construction of the new *Nassau* class for a year and to widen the Kiel Canal to allow the passage of larger warships.[56] However, Germany's industrial capacity could respond to the challenge, and its accelerated pace of warship construction gave rise to a great deal of concern (known as the 'naval scare') in Britain during 1908–9, but less in the Admiralty.[57] Britain, in turn, reacted by increasing its own naval allocations and accelerating its own construction.[58]

Ironically, it was only after Tsushima that Britain identified the German Imperial Navy as its main rival. In October 1906, Fisher further acknowledged that Germany was the *only* plausible foe and that Britain should maintain a fleet double Germany's in power in order to deter it.[59] Fisher did his utmost to maintain this lead by maintaining control over navy budgets. To this end, he overstated the power of the German navy and emphasized the shrinking gap between the two navies in dreadnoughts while concealing the overwhelming advantage the Royal Navy had in pre-dreadnought battleships. Accordingly, the official announcement of the two-power standard's cancellation was postponed until 1912, two years after Fisher was replaced, and when the standard was altered to a 60 per cent advantage in the number of *Dreadnought*-class battleships compared to Germany's.[60] In the naval race that took place after the battle, Britain enjoyed a slight edge after constructing the first *Dreadnought* battleship, but it inevitably lost the enormous advantage it had held earlier as its pre-dreadnought-class vessels became increasingly outdated.[61] By the time the First World War broke out, Germany had fifteen *Dreadnought*-class battleships—only seven less than Britain.[62] Still, the inability of the Imperial German Navy to compete with its British rival in both quantitative and qualitative terms in the first two years of the war discouraged Germany from fighting an all-out Tsushima-like battle. From 1916 to 1917, it belatedly accelerated the construction of submarines in an attempt to compromise the blockade and disrupt the Allies' supply lines.

The Battle of Tsushima had only a limited impact on the French Navy, although the naval race in the wake of the battle also influenced France. In the following years, the French Navy relinquished its earlier penchant for the principles of the Jeune École even further, and became committed to a battleship navy in 1909.[63] Naval spending rose in 1906 and during the next seven years were double the faltering spending at the turn of the century.[64] With this spending and the commissioning of its four Liberté-class battleships, France remained the world's second largest naval force for at least five years after Tsushima and it actively maintained this standing. And yet, with the conclusion of the Entente Cordiale a year earlier and in view of the German menace, France literally abandoned the naval race with Britain and started devoting a greater portion of its defence budget to the development of massive land forces with which to face Germany.[65] Given its allocations and changing priorities (which partly began in 1902), the French Navy did not properly counteract the challenge set by the emergence of HMS *Dreadnought*.[66] In retrospect, its move away from the principles of the Jeune École was too late and too hesitant. As a result, shortly before the First World War, the French Navy lost its position as the world's second largest naval power, with the vast majority of its capital ships becoming obsolete.[67]

The United States Navy was affected by the battle almost as much as the Royal Navy was. Sober and shrewd, President Theodore Roosevelt was a major figure behind the American reaction to the changing naval circumstances after Tsushima. Once it had completed its expansion programme, the United States Navy posed a challenge to Royal

Navy hegemony but did not constitute a genuine threat. That said, the battle did not affect these two navies in the same manner. While the Royal Navy benefited from the IRN's demise, the United States Navy was strained by the IJN's upswing. Furthermore, and while trying to calm the tensions with Japan, Roosevelt exploited the post-Tsushima state of affairs to obtain greater budgets for naval construction. In practice, he did little to alleviate American anxiety over Japan's naval rise. By the summer of 1905, the American assessment of Japan seemed to be more realistic than ever before and the defence of the Philippines more urgent than ever before.[68] Anti-Asian riots and a Japan-scare on the west coast of the United States during 1906 did not ease geopolitical worries, but did bring about a bilateral agreement with Japan one year later on the explosive issue of immigration.[69] Also in 1907, the United States Joint Army and Navy Board updated its War Plan Orange, which dealt with a possible war with Japan, and sought to fit it to the changing situation after Tsushima and the end of the war as a whole.[70] Formulated for the first time in 1903, this plan aimed to explore various ways of defending American interests in East Asia, and especially the Philippines, from Japanese attack.[71]

After Tsushima, the main American assumption was that the IJN would gain an initial military advantage in the case of hostilities, given its unrivalled combat experience and because most of the American naval forces would remain stationed in the Atlantic. In the case of a Japanese attack on the Philippines, American forces would retreat to inland strongholds. Within several weeks, naval reinforcements would arrive in the Pacific and Japanese forces would be annihilated. By 1907, American strategists regarded Japan as also capable of taking over Hawaii, blockading the Panama Canal (which was under construction), and even threatening the west coast.[72] Thereafter, and 'obsessed by the dramas of Trafalgar, Tsushima, and [later also] Jutland', the United States Navy's planning, and, even more its imagination, would be fixated upon a single and decisive battle in the Pacific strikingly similar to the IJN's decisive battle doctrine (Jpn. *Kantai kessen*).[73] The Philippines posed another problem. While the navy looked for a location in the Philippines for the construction of a large naval base defendable from both ground and naval attacks, the army opposed the idea, using insights gained from the siege of Port Arthur. As a result, both services decided to develop the port at Pearl Harbor so it could serve as the principal American base in the western Pacific, while simultaneously fortifying the Philippines for a 90- to 120-day siege.

With the impressions of the battle still fresh, Roosevelt ordered the dispatch of a 16-battleship fleet for a world tour. Leaving Hampton Roads in December 1907, these pre-dreadnought warships were used to project the naval power the United States had recently acquired (Figure 36). While cruising for a longer distance than the Baltic Fleet had covered, Roosevelt and his naval planners were mindful of the logistic difficulties the Baltic Fleet had faced and of its mistakes, and were determined not to repeat them.[74] Although this 'Great White Fleet', as it was known, did not sail for battle, its voyage was meant to convey a specific message to Japan. The United States, it aimed to signal, could and would deploy its navy anywhere, and, despite

Figure 36. Learning from the Russian experience: The 'Great White Fleet' passing off Rio de Janeiro, January 1908

Russia's naval demise far from home, would not hesitate to defend its interests in the Pacific and East Asia.[75] However, by the time the fleet sailed, Roosevelt realized that German naval expansion could pose a threat to the European order and, by extension, to the United States. The consequent need to maintain the bulk of the American naval force in the Atlantic led to a temporary rapprochement with Japan.[76] Culminating in the Root–Takahira agreement of November 1908, it was largely maintained throughout the subsequent decade.[77] At an earlier point in time, and despite Mahan's opposition, the navy had entered the dreadnought age aggressively, but without the full support of Congress.[78] When Roosevelt left office in 1909, the United States Navy had neither a close friend in the Oval Office nor an accepted policy, and it gradually lost its standing. It was only to regain and improve it after the First World War.[79]

Lessons Unlearned: The Battle and the Long-Term Naval Revolution

With the Battle of Tsushima over, quite a few believed that Japan had clinched its victory by using its newly acquired submarines. Major newspapers around the world speculated about this possibility during the first days after the battle.[80] In Russia, naval experts seemed particularly convinced and expounded this view for longer. Nikolai Klado, for example, wrote that 'It is a fact that a floating Whitehead torpedo was sighted from one of our cruisers, and it is more than probable that this torpedo came from a submarine.... even though they [submarines] may not have actually sunk any ship, the fact [of their participation] is highly important...'[81] In reality, the battle and the entire 1904–5 war missed both the submarine and the aeroplane—probably the two most crucial developments in naval warfare in the 20th century. Their absence does not necessarily mean that the battle did not play a part in promoting their development. On the contrary, operational requirements increased awareness of these new technologies as well as the pressure to develop them for full operational use.

In late 1904, both Japan and Russia had submarines, but neither regarded them as ready for operational deployment. By the end of the war, the IRN had transferred no fewer than 14 small submarines to Vladivostok by means of the Trans-Siberian Railway, but they arrived too late for combat.[82] A submarine had first been armed with a tube for launching torpedoes merely 13 years earlier, with a torpedo first launched successfully underwater six years later.[83] The United States Navy commissioned its first submarine in 1900, and the Royal Navy followed suit one year later.[84] By the outbreak of the Russo-Japanese War, all the large navies had acquired submarines, except for Germany, but they invariably defined the submarine as an experimental vessel and did not put it into operational use.[85] The difficulties the IJN faced in sinking the Russian warships hiding in the safe haven of Port Arthur gave rise to a special interest in submarines. Believing a submarine could penetrate the port and sink the Russian ships, Fisher wrote to a friend in March 1904: '... my beloved submarines ... are not only going to increase the naval power of England seven times more than present ... but they are going to bring the income tax down.'[86]

One month later, Fisher proved almost prophetic when stating that submarines on offensive missions would revolutionize the war at sea.[87] Four months before Tsushima, Fisher sent Prime Minister Arthur Balfour two 'rough papers' (entitled 'Submarines Used Defensively' and 'Submarines Used Offensively') in which he formulated his concept of 'flotilla defence'.[88] In one decade, this vision of the submarine as a defensive vessel would appear conservative, but it had very few followers at the time, and none among the belligerents at Tsushima. Neither the IJN nor the IRN used submarines during the battle or in earlier missions that would have rendered the clash in Tsushima redundant. Fisher's stimulating ideas about the submarine would eventually be implemented fully, but it would be the Imperial German Navy rather than the Royal Navy that would reap most of their benefits. Under Tirpitz's leadership, Germany embarked in 1906 on the development of efficient submarines for offensive use. Produced in large numbers during the First World War and benefiting from rapid evolution, they would begin to transform naval warfare about a decade after Tsushima.[89]

The emergence of the aeroplane was an even greater omission. The Battle of Tsushima was fought a mere 17 months after the first ever successful flight of a heavier-than-air powered aircraft by the Wright brothers. Initially, the progress made in this field was slow and sceptics in the European aviation community and in the general press fuelled profound mistrust of these two American pioneers, referring to them as bluffers as late as 1906.[90] Within a few years, however, aeroplanes not only had made a great deal of progress but also were adapted for naval use. In November 1910, another American aviator, Eugene Ely (1886–1911), accomplished a feat unimaginable a few years earlier. Ely took off in a Curtiss Pusher from a temporary platform erected over the bow of the light cruiser USS *Birmingham*, and two months later, in another flight, landed his aeroplane on a platform erected on another cruiser.[91] Scouting and reconnaissance seemed at first to be the aeroplane's innate task, but it began to display its combat potential with the outbreak of the First World War. In September 1914, the IJN seaplane carrier *Wakamiya* (an ex-Russian freighter captured in February 1905), conducted the first ever naval-launched air raid. Her four aeroplanes attacked the German protected cruiser SMS *Kaiserin Elisabeth* with bombs and altogether made 50 sorties during the siege of the Garman base in Kiachow Bay.[92] These early planes' failure to sink the cruiser did not deter naval visionaries and aeroplanes became an integral part of modern naval warfare within several years of the emergence of the first aircraft carrier in 1918.

By the Second World War, the revolution missed by the Battle of Tsushima was complete. German U-boats in the Atlantic almost choked Britain, and Japanese aeroplanes taking off from carriers struck at American battleships in Pearl Harbor and sank the imposing British battleship *Prince of Wales* and its battlecruiser consort *Repulse* on their way to Singapore in a matter of minutes. The lessons of the battle gave no inkling of that outcome, nor a model for future naval engagements. Much like the entire war of 1904–5, the clash at Tsushima concealed the fact that future wars at sea would be determined by blockades and the capacity to sink enemy merchant shipping rather than by fleet-on-fleet engagements. Instead, it served as a catalyst for developing ever larger capital ships. The example of the Battle of Tsushima did not recur. The Battle of Jutland in 1916 demonstrated the ultimate failure of Tirpitz's strategic concept, and it was far from decisive in terms of losses. Without a dramatic naval climax, the First World War was characterized, especially after Jutland, by a long war of attrition and by a struggle over supply routes where submarines, destroyers, and even Q-ships enjoyed unprecedented importance.[93]

Initially, the Battle of Tsushima had a tremendous impact on naval development. Apart from the two belligerents, the Royal Navy under Fisher drew the most forthright conclusions from the battle, even though these very lessons contained some of the seeds of the Royal Navy's future decline. In the short run, the battle catalysed the move towards a revolutionary battleship, and the Royal Navy was able to apply the data its observers faithfully gathered and construct a ship of unmatched quality. The *Dreadnought* revolution yielded a significant advantage for the Royal Navy over its German opponent, but it soon sparked a naval race that forced Fisher to allocate more resources to the construction of ever bigger capital ships. In certain domains, such as fire control and the torpedo, the impact of the lessons was more lasting. For the most part, the lessons of the battle merely consolidated earlier trends already evident during the first 15 months of the Russo-Japanese War, or even before it, rather than singly shaping naval development. Moreover, because neither the submarine nor the aeroplane had yet reached maturity, the battle had little influence in the making of a genuine revolution in naval warfare.

7

Conclusion

When the news of the battle of the Tsushima Strait spread across the globe, it gave rise to an overnight sensation. The fact that no one had expected such a one-sided and decisive victory was one reason for the excitement, but it was also the instant realization of its importance. Nonetheless, even keen observers required some time to grasp the wider significance of the event. The British naval observer, Captain William Pakenham, was one of the first to identify the essence of the Japanese triumph. In his summer 1905 report to the Admiralty, he stated: 'Whether by land or sea, battles derive their importance from the nature of the issues at stake rather than from the magnitude of the forces engaged.'[1] Still, Pakenham, like many of his contemporaries, largely viewed the outcomes of the battle through a naval lens and from a European perspective, and so as a defeat for Russia.

But was the battle the outcome of Russian failure or Japanese success? In other words, would another large naval force have suffered a similar defeat had it fought Admiral Tōgō? The analysis offered by this book suggests that both sides contributed to the extreme outcomes. Vice Admiral Rozhestvenskiĭ fulfilled all three basic categories of military failures proposed by Cohen and John Gooch in their analytical study *Military Misfortunes*.[2] As Jonathan Parshall and Anthony Tully have noted, Rozhestvenskiĭ failed to learn from the past, and especially from the experience gained from the long engagement at the Battle of the Yellow Sea nine months earlier. Moreover, he failed to anticipate what the future might bring, and he also failed to adapt to the immediate circumstances of the battle-field.[3] On the other hand, Tōgō was able to overcome all these hurdles by learning, anticipating, and adapting. These failures and their avoidance are rarely absolute, especially since one party's success is determined by the other's failure and vice versa. There is little doubt, however, that Rozhestvenskiĭ's failures in *all* three categories were horrendous. Cohen and Gooch aptly describe such a flurry of failures, when they occur together, as a 'catastrophic failure'.[4] In view of this rare amalgam of inadequacies, the prospects of another fleet, say the United States Navy, facing similar annihilation appears unlikely. However, the outcome would still be determined by the capacity, more concretely, to avoid an engagement on the same unfavourable terms that Rozhestvenskiĭ accepted when crossing the Tsushima Strait. 'A clever person solves a problem,' Albert Einstein is said to have stated, 'a wise person avoids it.' The Russian admiral, evidently, sought to solve a knotty problem but failed spectacularly.

Russia's misfortunes should not conceal its opponent's achievement. And yet, it was exigency that explains the IJN's exceptional eagerness to avoid any failure and to prepare its forces accordingly. Japan had to win this battle, since a victory in the naval clash of May 1905, more than any land or sea battle before that time, was critical to its survival. Losing the battle meant not only losing the war but also being placed at a grave risk of suffocation. This, in turn, could easily bring about the demise of its entire imperial enterprise, if not the actual takeover of the Japanese home islands. For Russia, by contrast, the clash entailed none of these risks. This sharp difference stemmed from the fact that the battle took place in the vicinity of Japan rather than Russia's heartland, and even more so from Japan's position as an island nation. When such a nation wages a war in an adjacent continent, or any other place separated by the sea, it must control that sea to allow the safe transportation of personnel and supplies. Losing this control means losing the war. Eleven years later, Britain found itself in an even more precarious situation when it sent its navy to fight at Jutland. For 1916 Germany, much like 1905 Russia, losing the battle was not necessarily a game changer. As a continental nation in control of a vast expanse of land and much less dependent on imported natural resources, command of the narrow of passage of water separating the continent from its rival was a valuable asset but certainly not vital. When examined from a strategic perspective, the Japanese victory in the Battle of Tsushima reveals itself as the least dramatic option.

Tsushima is commonly referred to as a 'great battle'. But given the Russian inadequacies and the circumstantial duress for Japan, it is certainly possible to wonder whether it can be considered a 'great battle'. There are several factors that seem to make a military engagement 'great', and they are pertinent to naval battles too. These begin with the scale of the battle, as measured in the number of sailors and warships involved, and in the decisiveness of the outcomes. Nevertheless, and as suggested by Captain Pakenham, what really makes a battle 'great' is the nature of the issues at stake and the way that the battle affects them. In other words, we have to examine both the impact the battle exerts on the course of the war ('a war-changing event') as well as the long-term repercussions it exerts on the belligerents' geopolitical situation and on naval evolution. The Russo-Japanese engagement off Tsushima seems to meet all these criteria. To start with, it was a titanic battle, bringing together some 30,000 participants and more than 150 vessels. These forces were smaller in terms of sailors (about 65 per cent) but almost twice as large in terms of vessels as the Battle of Trafalgar in 1805 and appreciably larger than any other naval engagement until the Battle of Jutland in 1916.[5]

In terms of repercussions, the impact of Tsushima seems pervasive. The battle brought the war to an end, or, at the very least, definitely expedited it. Geopolitically, it exerted a profound impact on the involvement of the belligerents in north-east Asia and the Pacific area during the subsequent years if not decades. As the battle took place during a period of escalating international tensions, in the midst of a naval race and after decades of very limited naval warfare, the lessons that were drawn from it were extremely valuable. With dozens of military observers in the arena, and tomes of post-factum reports written back home, the conclusions reached were soon implemented by some and emulated by others. And yet, within a period of less than 10 years, these lessons were overshadowed by a much greater conflict. The main lesson of the Battle of Tsushima with regard to the ascendancy of the all-big-gun battleship and its use did not materialize as expected. Instead, the submarine—a new weapon that had not taken part in the 1905 clash—came of age with horrifying effectiveness. Its incremental deployment and use for attrition undermined the very notion of a decisive battle. Instead, a new strategy emerged, which the Imperial German Navy in particular adopted. Developed in France in the mid-1880s, the Jeune École advocated the use of numerous small units against battleships and the employment of commerce raiders— by the First World War mostly submarines—for the disruption of trade and supply.[6] The year 1918, a mere 13 years after the battle, witnessed the commissioning of the first full-length flight deck aircraft carrier. This warship, the Royal Navy's HMS *Argus*, heralded an even newer crucial development in naval warfare that the Battle of Tsushima had not anticipated.

In this light, how does the Battle of Tsushima stand? Can it be compared favourably to outstanding naval clashes that occurred before and after it, such as Lepanto, Trafalgar, Jutland and Midway? Fought in 1571 between a coalition of Mediterranean Catholic states and the Ottoman Empire off the Greek coast, the Battle of Lepanto is often considered the greatest early modern naval clash. This battle was significantly larger than its 1905 counterpart in terms of the number of participants (more than 140,000 men, of whom some 90,000 were sailors and oarsmen) and vessels (more than 500, mostly galleys).[7] In other respects, however, Lepanto was not as impressive. True, it proved that the Ottomans were stoppable, but with some 10,000 dead from the Catholic coalition the victory itself was not as decisive and, more importantly, the victors failed to capitalize on their triumph. In fact, the Ottomans had already rebuilt their navy half a year after the battle and were able to reassert their hegemony in the very place the battle took place, as well as in the entire Eastern Mediterranean region. As a result, the victory's immediate impact on the struggle and its enduring geopolitical implications was very short and limited.[8] The Battle of Trafalgar is another common comparison. Fought between the British Royal Navy and the combined fleets of the French and Spanish navies exactly a century before the battle of Tsushima, it was similar in scale and in decisiveness. Nevertheless, it had little strategic impact on the war as a whole. The French Navy remained a significant rival and the war itself raged for another 10 years.[9]

During the first half of the 20th century, in turn, the two most notable naval battles were fought at Jutland in 1916 and Midway in 1942. As the largest naval battle of the First World War and the greatest single clash of all time between the British and the German fleets, the Battle of Jutland was colossal in scale, with some 105,000 participants and 250 warships involved. And yet, neither was it decisive, nor did it exert any considerable impact on the entire war or on subsequent naval evolution. Thereafter, and as a 'fleet in being', the Imperial German Navy's High Seas Fleet continued to pose a threat and the war carried on for another two and half years. The Battle of Midway, by comparison, was also gigantic, although in practice, and due to the distances between the two fleets, the number of warships and crews participating actively was similar to its Tsushima equivalent. Widely considered to be a decisive battle, with the Japanese losing five vessels (four of which were carriers) and the Americans two (including one carrier), its outcomes were not as uneven as Tsushima's.[10] Still, the greatest difference between the two battles lies in their impact. Although it has often been called 'the turning point of the Pacific', the naval engagement neither stopped the IJN nor brought the war to an end.[11] In fact, the two belligerents would clash again several times and the war would continue for an additional three years.

Thus, all things considered, it is apparent that the Battle of Tsushima was a 'great battle', perhaps even greater than other notable great battles. Nonetheless, its importance should not be restricted to the naval and the military realms alone. Alongside its naval impact, the battle had far-reaching political, cultural, and even spiritual repercussions. Its impact on Japan's navalism and imperial ambitions in Asia until 1945; its effect on Russia's decline in Asia and the weakening of the tsarist regime; its influence on the changing balance of power in Europe during the decade before the First World War; and its role as an initial inspiration to intellectuals and laypersons struggling against Western colonial rule—all these merit the description of a 'Tsushima Moment'.[12] That is, a critical juncture in modern history during which wide-ranging trends and events are initiated or catalysed with long-lasting effects.

Twentieth-century historiography has largely overlooked this 'Tsushima Moment' and its significance, much like that of the entire Russo-Japanese War.[13] Regretfully, what often makes a battle, or any other event, 'great' in historical memory is not necessarily the end product of an objective analysis or whether it satisfies stringent criteria. Instead, it is the enduring publicity a battle receives and the position the victorious party holds in 'writing' common history that ensures it either enters the pantheon of great battles or is consigned to oblivion. For these very reasons, and although it initially enjoyed the world's limelight, the Battle of Tsushima has gradually faded from memory. Remarkably, both Russia (soon transformed into the Soviet Union) and post-war Japan were strongly motivated to set it aside for an extended period.[14] Other major players in the writing of history did the same. They had their own victories to brag about and defeats to mourn. Considering its decisiveness, immediate outcomes, and long-lasting repercussions, the Battle of Tsushima deserves a more central place in historical writing. So, after all, Corbett was probably right. On the eve of the First World War, it was, indeed, 'the most decisive and complete naval victory in history.'[15]

APPENDIX

NAVAL BALANCE BEFORE AND AFTER THE BATTLE OF TSUSHIMA (26–30 MAY 1905)

Imperial Japanese Navy

THE JAPANESE COMBINED FLEET
ADM Tōgō Heihachirō

FIRST FLEET (ADM Tōgō Heihachirō on board the *Mikasa*)
   1st Battle Division (VADM Misu Sōtarō on board the *Nisshin*): *Mikasa* (BB), *Shikishima* (BB), *Fuji* (BB), *Asahi* (BB), *Kasuga* (CR), *Nisshin* (CR), *Tatsuta* (AV)
   3rd Battle Division (VADM Dewa Shigeto on board the *Kasagi*): *Kasagi* (CC), *Chitose* (CC), *Otowa* (CC), *Niitaka* (CC)
   Attached Flotillas: 1st Destroyer Division: *Harusame* (DD), *Fubuki* (DD), *Ariake* (DD), *Arare* (DD), *Akatsuki II* (DD); 2nd Destroyer Division: *Oboro* (DD), *Inazuma* (DD), *Ikazuchi* (DD), *Akebono* (DD); 3rd Destroyer Division: *Shinonome* (DD), *Usugumo* (DD), *Kasumi* (DD), *Sazanami* (DD); 14th Torpedo boat Division: *Chidori* (TB), *Hayabusa* (TB), *Manazuru* (TB), *Kasasagi* (TB)

SECOND FLEET (VADM Kamimura Hikonojō on board the *Izumo*)
   2nd Battle Division (RADM Shimamura Hayao on board the *Iwate*): *Izumo* (CR), *Azuma* (CR), *Tokiwa* (CR), *Yakumo* (CR), *Asama* (CR), *Iwate* (CR), *Chihaya* (AV)
   4th Battle Division (VADM Uryū Sotokichi on board the *Naniwa*): *Naniwa* (CC), *Takachiho* (CC), *Akashi* (CC), *Tsushima* (CC)
   Attached Flotillas: 4th Destroyer Division: *Asagiri* (DD), *Murasame* (DD), *Shirakumo* (DD), *Asashio* (DD); 5th Destroyer Division: *Shiranui* (DD), *Murakumo* (DD), *Yugiri* (DD), *Kagerō* (DD); 9th Torpedo Boat Division: *Aotaka* (TB), *Kari* (TB), *Tsubame* (TB), *Hato* (TB); 19th Torpedo Boat Division: *Kaemon* (TB), *Otoki* (TB), *Kiji* (TB)

THIRD FLEET (VADM Kataoka Shichirō on board the *Itsukushima*)
5th Battle Division (RADM Taketomi Kunikane on board the *Hashidate*): Chin'en (OBB), *Hashidate* (CC), *Itsukushima* (CC), *Matsushima* (CC), *Yaeyama* (AV)
6th Battle Division (RADM Tōgō Masamichi on board the *Suma*): *Suma* (CC), *Chiyoda* (CR), *Akitsushima* (CC), *Izumi* (CC)
7th Battle Division (RADM Yamada Hikohachi on board the *Fusō*): *Fusō* (OBB), *Tsukushi* (PG), *Takao* (PG), *Akagi* (PG), *Maya* (PG), *Chokai* (PG), *Uji* (PG)
Attached Flotillas: 15th Torpedo Boat Division: *Hibari* (TB), *Sagi* (TB), *Hashitaka* (TB), *Uzura* (TB); 1st Torpedo Boat Division: *67* (TB), *68* (TB), *69*† (TB), *70* (TB); 10th Torpedo Boat Division: *40* (TB), *41* (TB), *42* (TB), *43* (TB); 11th Torpedo Boat Division: *72* (TB), *73* (TB), *74* (TB), *75* (TB); 20th Torpedo Boat Division: *62* (TB), *63* (TB), *64* (TB), *65* (TB)

AUXILARY SQUADRON (RADM Ogura Byōichirō)
Auxiliary Cruisers Division (RADM Ogura Byōichirō): *Amerika-maru* (AX), *Dairen-maru* (AX), *Kasuga-maru* (AX), *Kumano-maru* (AX), *Manshū-maru* (AX), *Nikko-maru* (AX), *Sado-maru* (AX), *Shinano-maru* (AX), *Taichū-maru* (AX), and 8 PGs
Attached Flotillas: 16th Torpedo Boat Division: *Shirataka* (TB), *66* (TB); 17th Torpedo Boat Division: *31* (TB), *32* (TB), *33* (TB), *34*† (TB); 18th Torpedo Boat Division: *35*† (TB), *36* (TB), *60* (TB), *61* (TB)
Patrol and Guard Vessels: 2nd Torpedo Boat Division: *37* (TB), *38* (TB), *45* (TB), *46* (TB); 3rd Torpedo Boat Division: *9* (TB), *15* (TB), *20* (TB), *46*; 4th Torpedo Boat Division: *5* (TB), *6* (TB), *7* (TB), *8* (TB); 5th Torpedo Boat Division: *Fukuryū* (TB), *25* (TB), *26* (TB), *27* (TB); 6th Torpedo Boat Division: *56* (TB), *57* (TB), *58* (TB), *59* (TB); 7th Torpedo Boat Division: *11* (TB), *12* (TB), *13* (TB), *14* (TB); 8th Torpedo Boat Division: *10* (TB), *17* (TB), *18* (TB), *19* (TB); 12th Torpedo Boat Division: *50* (TB), *52* (TB), *54* (TB), *55* (TB); 13th Torpedo Boat Division: *Kotaka* (TB), *21* (TB), *24* (TB), *29* (TB), *30* (TB); 21st Torpedo Boat Division: *44* (TB), *47* (TB), *49* (TB), *71* (TB), and 20 additional small PGs and AXs

Imperial Russian Navy

THE RUSSIAN SECOND AND THIRD PACIFIC SQUADRONS
VADM Zinoviĭ Rozhestvenskiĭ

First Division (VADM Zinoviĭ Rozhestvenskiĭ on board the *Kniaz Suvorov*): *Kniaz Suvorov*† (BB), *Imperator Aleksandr III*† (BB), *Borodino*† (BB), *Orël*# (BB)

Second Division (RADM Dmitrii von Felkerzam/Captain V.I. Ber on board the *Osliabia*): *Osliabia*† (BB), *Sissoi Velikii*† (BB), *Navarin*† (BB), *Admiral Nakhimov*† (CR)

Third Division (RADM Nikolai Nebogatov on board the *Imperator Nikolai I*): *Imperator Nikolai I*# (BB), *General* Admiral Graf Apraksin# (OBB), *Admiral Seniavin*# (OBB), *Admiral Ushakov*† (OBB)

First Cruiser Division (RADM Oskar Enkvist on board the *Oleg*): *Dmitrii Donskoi*† (CR), *Vladimir Monomakh*† (CR), *Oleg*• (CC), *Aurora*• (CC)

Attached Cruisers: *Zhemchug*• (CC), *Izumrud*† (CC)

Scouting Division: *Svetlana*† (CC), *Ural*† (AX)

Destroyer Flotilla: 1st Destroyer Division: *Bedovii*# (DD), *Buinii*† (DD), *Bravii*° (DD), *Bistrii*† (DD); 2nd Destroyer Division: *Blestiashchii*† (DD), *Bezuprechnii*† (DD), *Bodrii*• (DD), *Gromkii*† (DD), *Groznii*° (DD)

Transport Squadron: *Almaz*° (PG), *Anadir*» (AX), *Irtish*† (AX), *Kamchatka*† (AX), *Koreia*• (AX), *Rus*† (AX), *Svir*• (AX), *Orël*# (AX), *Kostroma*# (AX)

Key

ADM	Admiral
VADM	Vice admiral
RADM	Rear admiral
AV	Dispatch vessel, aviso
AX	Auxiliary vessel; transport ship, hospital ship
BB	Battleship
CC	Cruiser (protected or unprotected)
CR	Armoured cruiser
DD	Destroyer
OBB	Obsolete battleship or coastal defence battleship
PG	Gunvessel or third-class cruiser
TB	Torpedo boat
†	Ship sunk or scuttled
#	Ship captured
•	Ship interned
°	Ship reaching Vladivostok
»	Ship returning to Libau

NOTES

Conventions

1. For names of ranks of military and naval officers in both tsarist Russia and imperial Japan and their corresponding British ranks, see Rotem Kowner, *Historical Dictionary of the Russo-Japanese War* (Lanham, 2017), 690 (Appendix 5).

Chapter 1

1. For the early encounters between the two nations, see George Lensen, 'Early Russo-Japanese Relations', *The Far Eastern Quarterly* 10 (1950), 2–37; George Lensen, *The Russian Push toward Japan* (Princeton, 1959); Sergey Grishachev, 'Russo-Japanese Relations in the 18th and 19th Centuries', in Dmitry V. Streltsov and Nobuo Shimotomai (eds), *A History of Russo-Japanese Relations* (Leiden, 2019), 18–41. For Russo-Japanese relations since the mid-nineteenth century, see Wada Haruki, *Nichiro sensō* (Tokyo, 2009), 1:39–103.
2. For an excellent overview of the rise of modern Japan, see Marius Jansen, *The Making of Modern Japan* (Cambridge, 2000), especially 333–455. For the structure of this oligarchy and other decision makers during the decade before the war against Russia, see Shumpei Okamoto, *The Japanese Oligarchy and the Russo-Japanese War* (New York, 1970), 11–40.
3. For the unfolding struggle over Korea and Manchuria from 1884 onwards, see George Lensen, *Balance of Intrigue* (Tallahassee, 1982).
4. Via the longer route completed in 1916.
5. For this project, see Steven Marks, *Road to Power* (Ithaca, 1991).
6. For a concise overview of the events that led to this war, see Stewart Lone, *Japan's First Modern War* (London, 1994), 12–29. The most wide-ranging overview of it in English is S.C.M. Paine, *The Sino-Japanese War of 1894–1895* (Cambridge, 2003). For its place in the road leading to the Russo-Japanese War, see Wada, *Nichiro sensō*, 1:105–209.
7. For the naval aspects of this war, see Philip Colomb, *Naval Warfare*, 3rd edn (London, 1899), 435–52.
8. Japan had 1,132 dead and 3,758 wounded, but additionally more than 12,000 soldiers who died of disease, many of them during the takeover of Taiwan, or wounds at a later stage.

9. For Russia's policy in the region, see Andrew Malozemoff, *Russian Far Eastern Policy, 1881–1904* (Berkeley, 1958).

10. For this concept and its repercussions on Japan, see Richard Thompson, 'The Yellow Peril, 1890–1924', PhD dissertation (University of Wisconsin, 1957).

11. For the first Russo-Japanese Confrontation, 1894–7, see Ian Nish, *The Origins of the Russo-Japanese War* (London, 1985), 21–34.

12. This Japanese doctrine offered Russia control of Manchuria in return for Russian recognition of Japanese hegemony in Korea.

13. Wada, *Nichiro sensō*, 1:211–321.

14. For the role of the Boxer Uprising in Russo-Japanese relations, see Nish, *The Origins*, 83–109; Wada, *Nichiro sensō*, 1:323–423.

15. For Anglo-Russian relations during this period, see Evgeny Sergeev, *The Great Game, 1856–1907* (Washington, 2013).

16. For the treaty and Anglo-Japanese relations before the war, see Ian Nish, *The Anglo-Japanese Alliance* (London, 1966).

17. For the Russian enterprise and its consequences, see Igor Lukoianov, 'The Bezobrazovtsy', in John W. Steinberg et al. (eds), *The Russo-Japanese War in Global Perspective* (Leiden, 2005–7), 1:65–86. For the uproar in Japan, see Okamoto, *The Japanese Oligarchy*, 95–6; Wada, *Nichiro sensō*, 2:48–116.

18. For the militant opposition, see Stewart Lone, *Army, Empire, and Politics in Meiji Japan* (London, 2000), 99–100. For the role of Manchuria in the Japanese decision for war, see Yōko Katō, 'What Caused the Russo-Japanese War: Korea or Manchuria?' *Social Science Japan Journal* 10 (2007), 95–103.

19. For the final negotiations, see Nish, *The Origins*, 192–205.

20. Okamoto, *The Japanese Oligarchy*, 96–102; Wada, *Nichiro sensō*, 2:215–24.

21. For the final preparations for war, see Wada, *Nichiro sensō*, 2:225–96.

22. There is a vast and diverse literature on this technological revolution. For a brief overview, see Rolf Hobson, *Imperialism at Sea* (Leiden, 2002), 24–57.

23. For this naval race, see Paul Kennedy, *Strategy and Diplomacy, 1870–1945* (London, 1983), 165–71.

24. For the emergence of the torpedo and the torpedo boat, see Robert Gardiner and Andrew Lambert (eds), *Steam, Steel, and Shellfire* (London, 1992), 134–41.

25. Theodore Ropp, *The Development of a Modern Navy* (Annapolis, 1987), 155–80; Ray Walser, France's Search for a Battle Fleet (New York, 1992), 58–90, 180–200.

26. For a contemporary exposition of the school's ideas, see Gabriel Charmes, *Naval Reform* (London, 1887). For an overview, see Arne Røksund, *The Jeune École* (Leiden, 2007).

27. For Mahan's two major books in which he explicated his naval theory, see Alfred Thayer Mahan, *The Influence of Sea Power Upon History* (Boston, 1890);

and Alfred Thayer Mahan, *The Influence of Sea Power upon the French Revolution and Empire* (Boston, 1892). For a succinct overview of his theory and its backdrop, see Azar Gat, *A History of Military Thought* (Oxford, 2001), 442–72; and Lukas Milevski, *The Maritime Origins of Modern Grand Strategic Thought* (Oxford, 2016), 29–37.

28. Gat, *A History*, 454.
29. Philip Colomb, *Naval Warfare* (London, 1891).
30. Colomb, *Naval Warfare*, 3rd edn (1899), 25.
31. Other leading navies also built a large number of battleships with similar features. By 1906, the United States had 24 battleships, Germany 25, France 20, Italy nine, Austria three, and Spain one. By 1904, on the eve of their war, Russia had 20 battleship and Japan six. For a succinct overview of the rise of the battleship during 1890–1905, see Gardiner and Lambert, *Steam, Steal, and Shellfire*, 112–26.
32. For a brief overview of the cruiser's evolution in the decade before the war, see Gardiner and Lambert, *Steam, Steel, and Sehllfire*, 126–33; John Roberts, *Battlecruisers* (Annapolis, 1997), 13–19.
33. Røksund, *The Jeune École*, 18–21.
34. For the recent emergence of destroyers and faster torpedo boats, see Gardiner and Lambert, *Steam, Steel, and Shellfire*, 141–6.
35. The best overview of the IRN's rise in the late 19th century is Nicholas Papastratigakis, *Russian Imperialism and Naval Power* (London, 2011).
36. Rossiiskii Gosudarstvennii Arkhiv Voenno-Morskogo Flota (RGAVMF), f. 417, op. 1, d. 1474, l. 40.
37. For Russian naval policy and construction in the two decades preceding the war, see J.N. Westwood, *Witnesses of Tsushima* (Tokyo, 1970), 1–26. For the priority given to the Pacific Fleet in the late 1890s, see Papastratigakis, *Russian Imperialism*, 125–58.
38. For the IJN's first decade, see J. Charles Schencking, *Making Waves* (Stanford, 2005), 9–25; David Evans and Mark Peattie, *Kaigun* (Annapolis, 1997), 1–13.
39. Lone, *Army, Empire*, 60.
40. See Hiraku Yabuki, 'Britain and the Resale of Argentine Cruisers to Japan before the Russo-Japanese War', *War in History* 16 (2009), 425–46.
41. The samurai class was dissolved, like all other classes in Japan and except for the nobility, in 1876. Nevertheless, the predominance of members of this class in politics and military affairs, among other fields, lingered decades later.
42. In 1904, the admission rate to Etajima was less than 8 per cent. See Ronald Spector, *At War at Sea* (New York, 2001), 9–10.
43. Papastratigakis, *Russian Imperialism*, 53–4; Westwood, *Witnesses of Tsushima*, 6–8.
44. For corruption within the IRN administration and among some of its officers, see Westwood, *Witnesses of Tsushima*, 11–12. For its insufficient training, see Papastratigakis, *Russian Imperialism*, 54–5.

45. See Keishi Ono, 'Japan's Monetary Mobilization for War', in Steinberg et al. (eds), *The Russo-Japanese War*, 2:253, Table 1.
46. For the military balance on the eve of the war, see Kowner, *Historical Dictionary*, 325–7.
47. In 1904 the IRN was third in terms of number of capital ships (after Britain and France), but fourth in aggregate tonnage (after Britain, France, and Germany). In terms of manpower, the IRN was the world's second naval power, after Britain's Royal Navy. With 65,054 men enlisted in 1903, it was about half of Britain's and about 50 per cent larger than the IJN (40,477 and 44,959 in 1904 and 1905, respectively). See Westwood, *Witnesses of Tshushima*, 5–6, 28; Evans and Peattie, *Kaigun*, 147; and Schencking, *Making Waves*, 104, Table 3. While seemingly relying on deficient data, another major international comparison has placed the IRN in a fifth place, after the naval forces of Britain, the USA, Germany, and France. See George Modelsky and William Thompson, *Seapower in Global Politics* (Seattle, 1988), 123.
48. Evans and Peattie, *Kaigun*, 147; and Modelsky and Thompson, *Seapower in Global Politics*, 123.
49. For similar pre-war Russian assessments of the naval power balance, see Papastratigakis, *Russian Imperialism*, 247, 255. For a retrospective assessment, see Papastratigakis, *Russian Imperialism*, 259–61.
50. For the premises underlying Japan's strategic objectives and their prioritization, see Rotem Kowner, 'The Russo-Japanese War', in Isabelle Duyvesteyn and Beatrice Heuser (eds), *The Cambridge History of Military Strategy*, 2 vols (Cambridge, 2022).
51. For the premises underlying Russia's strategic objectives and their prioritization, see Kowner, 'The Russo-Japanese War'. For the IRN's plans, see Nicolas Papastratigakis and Dominic Lieven, 'The Russian Far Eastern Squadron's Operational Plans', in Steinberg et al. (eds), *The Russo-Japanese War*, 1:222–7. See also see Pertti Luntinen and Bruce W. Menning, 'The Russian Navy at War', in Steinberg et al. (eds), *The Russo-Japanese War*, 1:230–59.
52. Julian Corbett, *Maritime Operations in the Russo-Japanese War* (London, 1914), 1:109–10.
53. During most of the conflict, until their ultimate surrender in January 1905, the Russian large warships of the Port Arthur Squadron took shelter inside the harbour of Port Arthur. However, on the eve of the war they anchored in the roadstead *off* the harbour due to the shallow waters in low tide in certain locations within.
54. Two of the Russian battleships took severe hits but the damage was repaired quickly. See Corbett, *Maritime Operations*, 1:92–108; Kowner, *Historical Dictionary*, 417–18.
55. Gunvessel, or gunboat, was a type of small-to-medium warship (under 2,000 tons), armed with small-to-medium-calibre guns, and used in the

early 20th century for guarding colonial ports, patrolling, and assisting land forces in coastal operations.

56. Corbett, *Maritime Operations*, 1:110–19; Kowner, *Historical Dictionary*, 105–6.
57. There is a large number of biographies or, rather, uncritical hagiographies devoted to Tōgō; notable among them are Naganari Ogasawara, *Life of Admiral Togo* (Tokyo, 1934); Edwin A. Falk, *Togo and the Rise of Japanese Sea Power* (New York, 1936); Georges Blond, *Admiral Togo* (New York, 1960); and the recent popular work of Jonathan Clements, *Admiral Togo: Nelson of the East* (London, 2010). In Japanese, see Ogasawara Naganari, *Tōgō gensui shōden* (Tokyo, 1921); Nakamura Kōya, *Sekai no Tōgō gensui* (Tokyo, 1934); Shimomura Toratarō, *Tōgō Heihachirō* (Tokyo, 1981); Maki Yōzō, *Tōgō Heihachirō* (Tokyo, 1985); and Tanaka Hiromi, *Tōgō Heihachirō* (Tokyo, 2013).
58. On board the *Kowshing* there were some 1,400 Chinese soldiers, of whom about 1,100 perished. For Tōgō's perspective on the sinking, see Ogasawara Naganari, *Seishō Tōgō Heihachirō den* (Tokyo: Kaizōsha, 1934), 220–42.
59. In Alexandria, for example, a Jewish family named her son after Tōgō in 1901. The son, Togo Mizrahi, would become a pioneering Egyptian director and film producer. See Ben-Ami Shillony, *The Jews and the Japanese* (Rutland, 1992), 146.
60. Tōgō's luck was not case-specific but rather part of his enduring reputation. 'Ever since he was a young man Tōgō has always been blessed with good luck', was the common view of him. In Shiba Ryōtarō, *Clouds above the Hill* (London, 2012–14), 4:227. In an audience with the emperor upon his appointment as commander-in-chief of the Combined Fleet, luck was stated to be one of the reasons, if not the main one, Navy Minister Yamamoto Gonnohyōe chose Tōgō for his new role. See Itō Masanori, *Daikaigun o omou* (Tokyo, 1956), 144. For some glimpses into Tōgō's personality, see a brief wartime interview with him in Seppings Wright, *With Togo* (London, 1905), 110–14.
61. Saigō, Yamamoto, and Tōgō belonged to samurai families from the same feudal domain of Satsuma. During the first several decades after the Meiji Restoration of 1868, this domain dominated the nation's naval affairs and its members comprised the navy's upper echelon. In fact, during the Battle of Tsushima, the commanders of the IJN's First, Second, and Third Fleets were from Satsuma, as well as the *Mikasa*'s captain, Ijichi Hikojirō, and many other senior officers. See Uzaki Kumakichi, *Satsu no kaigun Chō no rikugun* (Tokyo, 1913); and Schencking, *Making Waves*, 28–37.
62. For an overview of the land campaign, see Richard Connaughton, *The War of the Rising Sun and Tumbling Bear* (London, 2003).
63. See Oliver Wood, *From the Yalu to Port Arthur* (London, 1905).
64. See Ellis Ashmead-Bartlett, *Port Arthur* (London, 1906); and Edward Diedrich, 'The Last Iliad', PhD dissertation (New York University, 1978).

65. Coined by Arthur Herbert, 1st Earl of Torrington, in 1690, this concept of 'fleet in being' materialized during the first 11 months of war, with the Russian fleet besieged in Port Arthur posing a constant threat to Japanese war efforts. See Alfred Mahan, *Naval Strategy* (Boston, 1911), 383–401; and John B. Hattendorf, 'The Idea of a "Fleet in Being"', *Naval War College Review* 67 (2014), 43–60.

66. Corbett, *Maritime Operations*, 1:130, 134–5; Kowner, *Historical Dictionary*, 418–19.

67. Corbett, *Maritime Operations*, 1:130, 181–4.

68. Corbett, *Maritime Operations*, 1:130, 234–6. For the effect of mines during the war, see Kowner, *Historical Dictionary*, 332–4.

69. For a detailed analysis of the battle, see Corbett, *Maritime Operations*, 1:370–413.

70. For the Japanese extremely poor performance in this respect, see Corbett, *Maritime Operations*, 1:412; and Toyama Saburō, *Nichiro kaisen-shi kenkyū* (Tokyo, 1985), 1:658–62.

71. While both sides sustained severe damage, no ship was sunk. The Russians had 340 casualties versus 226 for the Japanese.

72. See Corbett, *Maritime Operations*, 1:432–48; Kowner, *Historical Dictionary*, 266–7.

73. For the siege, see Kowner, *Historical Dictionary*, 419–23.

74. The number of troops taking part in the Battle of Mukden was, according to most estimates, about 570,000. The battle ended with over 38,000 dead and 110,000 wounded on both sides, as well as some 22,000 Russian prisoners. See Kowner, *Historical Dictionary*, 341–3.

75. In such a scenario, the relatively small Russian garrison in Port Arthur (at the time of its surrender, there were in the fort some 33,200 military and naval men, about one quarter of them wounded) could hardly threaten the Japanese rear.

76. For the selection of the warships for the voyage and their lack of joint combat training, see Petr Bikov, *Russko-Iaponskaia voina 1904–1905 gg. Deystviia na more* (Moscow, 1942 [2003]), 565–8.

77. There are several seminal texts about the voyage. These include personal memoirs, such as Eugène Politovsky, *From Libau to Tsushima* (London, 1907); Vladimir Semenov, *Rasplata (The Reckoning)* (London: J. Murray; New York: E.P. Dutton, 1909); Vladimir Kostenko, *Na 'Orle' v Tsusime* (Leningrad, 1955), 151–409; and general overviews, such as Georg von Taube, *Poslednii̇ dni Vtoroi tikhookeanskoi eskadři* (St Petersburg, 1907); Georg von Taube, *Die letzten Tage des Baltischen Geschwaders* (St Petersburg, 1907); Frank Thiess, *The Voyage of the Forgotten Men* (Indianapolis, 1937); Richard Hough, *The Fleet That Had to Die* (London, 1958); and Constantine Pleshakov, *The Tsar's Last Armada* (New York, 2002).

78. For the selection of Rozhestvenskiĭ for the role, see Vladimir Gribovskiĭ, Vitse-admiral Z.P. Rozhestvenskiĭ (St Petersburg, 1999), 163–5.

79. Unlike Tōgō, the list of publications about Rozhestvenskiĭ is limited, especially in English. The most detailed biography is found in Gribovskiĭ, Vitse-admiral Z.P. Rozhestvenskiĭ. Another revealing source is his recently published letters during the voyage to East Asia. See Konstantin Sarkisov, Put' k Tsusime (St Petersburg, 2010).

80. Gribovskiĭ, Vitse-admiral Z.P. Rozhestvenskiĭ, 20–32; Pleshakov, The Tsar's, 41.

81. 'Tall, grave, virile,' one of the sailors under his command described him, 'he had so imposing an appearance that it seemed as if he could command success.' See Alexey Novikov-Priboy, Tsushima (London, 1936), 20, 131. See also Vladimir Apushkin, Russko-iaponskaia voina 1904–1905 g. (Moscow, 1910), 298; and Pleshakov, The Tsar's, 37–53.

82. For the Kaiser's commendation, see Hough, The Fleet That Had to Die, 19; and Noel F. Busch, The Emperor's Sword (New York, 1969), 87. In later years, unsubstantiated rumours circulated in the navy that the targets in that crucial gunnery exercise had been secretly rigged to fall without a direct hit. See Novikov-Priboy, Tsushima, 23.

83. For Rozhestvenskiĭ's dislike for Enkvist, see Pleshakov, The Tsar's, 287–8.

84. Some Russian sources cite 640 officers and 10,000 rank and file, e.g. Nikolai Levitskiĭ, Russko-Iaponskaia voina 1904–1905 gg. (Moscow, 1938 [2003]), 396.

85. The distress over an ambush by Japanese torpedo boats, along with fears of Japanese espionage and sabotage, was a recurrent theme throughout the voyage. See Politovsky, From Libau, 43, 101, 149, 159; Apushkin, Russko-iaponskaia voina, 305.

86. For the incident, see Richard Lebow, 'Accidents and Crises', Naval War College Review 31 (1978), 66–75.

87. For the British preparedness to use the Royal Navy to intercept Rozhest-venskiĭ's force, see T.G. Otte, 'The Fragmenting of the Old World Order', in Rotem Kowner (ed.), The Impact of the Russo-Japanese War (London, 2007), 98. See also Bikov, Russko-Iaponskaia voina, 572.

88. Lamar J. R. Cecil, 'Coal for the Fleet That Had to Die', American Historical Review 69, no. 4 (1964), 993.

89. According to the agreement, HAPAG (Hamburg-Amerikanische Packetfahrt-Actien-Gesellschaft), as the company was popularly known, was to transport a total of 300,000 tons of coal, using 52 ships. See National Archives (United Kingdom), Admiralty Papers, ADM 231/44, Papers on Naval Subjects 1906, 1:9–10. For the Russian negotiations with the company and the German government, see Cecil, 'Coal for the Fleet', 993–1005.

90. For Rozhestvenskiĭ's state in early January 1905, see Pleshakov, The Tsar's, 171–2.

91. Nicholas II to Rozhestvenskiĭ, 25 January 1905, cited in Pleshakov, The Tsar's, 183. See also Bikov, Russko-Iaponskaia voina, 576. The italics are mine.

92. Bikov, Russko-Iaponskaia voina, 574.

93. Thiess, *The Voyage*, 224–9; Pleshakov, *The Tsar's*, 172–3.

94. For morale on board the Russian ships, see Politovsky, *From Libau*, 166; and Pleshakov, *The Tsar's*, 192–3. For Rozhestvenskiĭ's state, see Pleshakov, *The Tsar's*, 75, 200.

95. Kostenko, *Na 'Orle'*, 479.

96. For Klado's rationale, see his book, *The Russian Navy in the Russo-Japanese War* (London, 1905), 160–97. In Russian, see Nikolai Klado, *Sovremennaia morskaia voina* (St Petersburg, 1905).

97. The *Admiral Ushakov*-class coast defence ships were cruiser-sized warships that sacrificed speed and range for battleship-like armour and armament. Cheaper than battleships, they were designed for defensive roles rather than participating in fully fledged battles. For the ships of this class, see Vladimir Gribovskiĭ and I.I. Chernikov, *Bronenosets 'Admiral Ushakov'* (St Peterburg, 1996); Vladimir Gribovskiĭ and I.I. Chernikov, *Bronenostsi beregovoi oboroni tipa 'Admiral Seniavin'* (St Peterburg, 2009); Vladimir Gribovskiĭ, 'Bronenosets beregovoi oboroni "General-admiral Apraksin"', *Gangut* 18 (1999), 31–45; and Stephen McLaughlin, 'The *Admiral Seniavin* Class Coast Defence Ships', *Warship International* 48, no. 1 (2011), 43–66.

98. In late 1904, quite a few naval figures urged the dispatch of the Black Sea Fleet, but to no avail. See Klado, *The Russian Navy*, 198–217.

99. Among the IJN ships, the mostly badly damaged was the battleship *Asahi*. Striking a mine off Port Arthur on 26 October 1904, she was under repair at Sasebo until late April 1905.

100. See Chiharu Inaba and Rotem Kowner, 'The Secret Factor', in R. Kowner (ed.), *Rethinking the Russo-Japanese War* (Folkestone, 2007), 86–7; Inaba Chiharu, *Baruchikku kantai o hosoku seyo* (Tokyo, 2016), *passim*.

101. Toyama Saburō, *Nichiro kaisen shinshi* (Tokyo: Tōkyō Shuppan, 1987), 230; Evans and Peattie, *Kaigun*, 110–11.

102. In 1906, as the war ended, the IJN established a new naval base in this bay.

103. Corbett, *Maritime Operations*, 2:200–2.

104. Bikov, *Russko-Iaponskaia voina*, 577–8.

105. Politovsky, *From Libau*, 255, 286.

106. Politovsky, *From Libau*, 103. For similar incidents in others ships, see Politovsky, *From Libau*, 132. After the battle, the voyage of the *Orël* was the topic of relatively a large number of memoirs, since it was the sole survivor of the four battleships of the *Borodino* class. For a recent compilation of these memoirs, see A.S. Gladkikh, R.V. Kondratenko, and K.B. Nazarenko (eds), *'Orel' v pokhode i v boiu* (St Petersburg, 2014).

107. Politovsky, *From Libau*, 287. For the rising morale, see also A. Zatertiĭ, *Bezumtsi i besplodniya zhertvi* (St Petersburg, 1907), 25.

108. The ships carried two dated 305-millimetre guns, eleven 254-millimetre guns, and four 229-millimetre guns.

109. There are more than twenty biographies of Akiyama. Notable among them are Akiyama Saneyuki-kai (ed.), *Akiyama Saneyuki* (Tokyo, 1933); Shimada Kinji, *Roshiya sensō zenya no Akiyama Saneyuki* (Tokyo, 1990); and Matsuda Jukkoku, *Tōgō Heihachirō to Akiyama Saneyuki* (Tokyo, 2008).

110. See Evans and Peattie, *Kaigun*, 112–15; Kusumi Tadao, 'Akiyama Saneyuki to Nihonkai kaisen', *Chūō kōron* 80 (August 1965), 352–8.

111. For the IJN's development of these two tactical manoeuvres, see Evans and Peattie, *Kaigun*, 74–9.

112. For the initial plan and its modification, see Corbett, *Maritime Operations*, 2:243; Toyama, *Nichiro kaisen-shi kenkyū*, 2:223–9; Evans and Peattie, *Kaigun*, 84–5, 111–14.

113. Kostenko, *Na 'Orle'*, 480.

114. For Rozhestvenskiĭ's possible considerations in choosing his ultimate route to Vladivostok, see Nicolas Klado, *The Battle of the Sea of Japan* (London, 1906), 63–4; Thiess, *The Voyage*, 288–9; and Bikov, *Russko-Iaponskaia voina*, 579–80. The only documents that provide some insight into Rozhestvenskiĭ's plans are his Order no. 182 and 227, the latter from 8 May 1905. See Admiralty, *Reports of the British Naval Attachés* (London: 1908), 4:236–7, 245; and Kostenko, *Na 'Orle'*, 496.

115. For the arrival of these transports—members of the Russian Volunteer Fleet (Rus. *Dobrovolniĭ Flot*; a state-controlled ship transport association)—to Shanghai (Usun) port and the immediate report with this regard sent by the Japanese consulate-general in the city, see Inaba, *Baruchikku kantai*, 223–6.

116. For a Japanese testimony of the anxiety about the armada's location, see Mahan, *Naval Strategy*, 56–7.

117. In 'Admiral Togo's Battleship . . .', *The Washington Times*, 26 May 1905, 1.

118. 'Confident Togo Will Lose: Capt. Von Essen Tells Why He Expects a Russian Sea Victory', *The New York Times*, 4 May 1905, 4.

119. For the prominence of the heavy guns in this battle, see Arthur Marder, *The Anatomy of British Sea Power* (New York, 1940), 531.

120. Apart from its four battleships, each carrying four 305-millimetre guns, the Japanese 1st Battle Division benefited from a single 254-millimetre gun on board the cruiser *Kasuga*. In addition, the IJN had at its disposal a few more warships with large-calibre guns, but all belonged to the 5th Battle Division and thus did not take a substantial part in the main engagement. These included the ex-Chinese ironclad *Chin'en* with four 305-millimetre guns and *Matsushima*-class protected cruisers (*Matsushima*, *Itsukushima*, and *Hashidate*) each carrying a single massive but very slow-firing 320-millimetre Canet gun.

121. See the report of Captain William Pakenham, the senior British naval observer, dated 6 May 1905: "Looking at the Russian dominance of heavy gun power, it will be a very remarkable achievement if they [the IJN] are able to do so [repeat their earlier feat of fighting against more powerful IRN warships]. In Admiralty, *Reports* (2003), 358.

122. See e.g. Politovsky, *From Libau*, 187, 217. See also 'Russian Admiral Says Togo Is the Stronger; He Hopes Rojesvensky Will Save Part of His Fleet', *The New York Times*, 17 May 1905, 4.
123. This comparison is based on data for each ship found in Hansgeorg Jentschura et al., *Warships of the Imperial Japanese Navy* (Annapolis, 1977), *passim*; and Kowner, *Historical Dictionary*, *passim*. The term 'capital ship' includes battleships, coastal battleships and armoured cruisers. Previous comparisons of a similar nature, which suggested equality in aggregate displacement or even a Russian advantage, are flawed. Apparently, they included the displacement of the Russian auxiliary ships (with 63,900 gross register tonnage), while excluding the IJN auxiliary ships (with 44,900 gross register tonnage). See Klado, *The Battle*, 26–7; Tanaka Ken'ichi and Himuro Chiharu, *Zusetsu: Tōgō Heihachirō* (Tokyo, 1995), VI-9–1.
124. The armada was marred by the speed of its auxiliary vessels, and especially the transport *Irtish* whose maximum speed was reportedly 9.5 knots. Among its warships, the new battleships could sail at 16–18 knots, the older large battleships and coastal defence ships could sail as much as 12–14 knots, whereas the old armoured cruisers *Dmitriĭ Donskoi* and *Vladimir Monomakh* could not speed more than 13 knots. See Kostenko, *Na 'Orle'*, 476. See also Piotr Olender, *Russo-Japanese Naval War* (Sandomierz, 2009–10), 2:204.
125. For this aspect, see Pakenham's report to the Admiralty dated 6 May 1905: 'All seems to have been done to bring both [the IJN fleet and its personnel] to a high state of efficiency... the chief essentials for success, well-merited confidence in leaders and courage to fight are there, and are of a kind that makes small account of odds.' In Admiralty, *Reports* (2003), 360.
126. The HAPAG transports supplied the fleet with coal and food, but did not provide it with new ammunition, so Rozhestvenskiĭ had to economize in this respect.

Chapter 2

1. See e.g. 'Expects Naval Battle Will Come This Week', *The New York Times*, 2 May 1905, 2; 'Togo's Defeat Rumored: Unconfirmed Report in Manila of a Battle South of Formosa', *The New York Times*, 25 May 1905, 1.
2. Nomura Minoru, *Kaisen-shi ni manabu* (Tokyo, 1985), 97–8.
3. In accordance with the Hague Convention of 1899, the two ships were distinguished by white external paintwork with a horizontal red band. See Pierre Boissier, *From Solferino to Tsushima* (Geneva, 1985), 331.
4. The ships comprised the *Amerika-maru*, *Manshū-maru*, *Sado-maru*, and *Shinano-maru*; and the two cruisers were *Izumi* and *Akitsushima*. See Admiralty, *Reports* (2003), 390.

5. For an analysis of the meteorological conditions shortly before and during the battle, see Hanzawa Masao, 'Kishō-kaizō ga senkyoku no jūdai tenki to natta shorei', *Kaiji shiryōkan nenpō* 19 (1991), 18–25.
6. This part is based on a synthesis of the following sources: Kaigun Gunreibu (ed.), *Meiji 37–8 nen kaisen-shi* (Tokyo, 1934), vol. 2; RGAVMF, f. 763; Admiralty, *Reports*; Corbett, *Maritime Operations*, 2:141–344.
7. Both the *Shinano-maru's* captain, John Salter, and her chief engineer, Frank Guyver Britton, were Britons. Still, the fact that this auxiliary cruiser was manned by such a high-ranking IJN officer—an ex-commander of cruisers who a year after the war was promoted to rear admiral—merely stresses further the importance that Tōgō and his staff attached to this patrol. For the profile of the Britons on board, see Dorothy Britton, 'Frank Guyver Britton (1879–1934), Engineer and Earthquake Hero', in Hugh Cortazzi (ed.), *Britain & Japan: Biographical Portraits, vol. 6* (Folkestone, 2007), 175–6.
8. There were two ships in the Russian fleet with this name. The other one was the battleship *Orël*.
9. The exact location of the intercepted Russian vessels was latitude 33°20' N and longitude 128°10' E. Drafted before the battle, the area of the Korean Strait was divided into squares, each representing 10 minutes of latitude and longitude. This radiotelegraph technology was first tested in 1897 and adopted for naval use in Japan in 1901 based on British know-how. For the early development of Japanese naval wireless communication (and specifically, for the Japanese-made 1903-type *sanroku-shiki musen-ki*), see Yamamoto Eisuke, *Kaigun denpa kankei tsuitō-shū*, 3 vols. (1955); Daqing Yang, *Technology of Empire* (Cambridge, 2010), 56–8.
10. While epoch-making, this wireless transmission was not the first in military history. Almost a year earlier, during the Battle of the Yellow Sea, the IJN had already used wireless telegraphy. See Corbett, *Maritime Operations*, 1:388. Slightly earlier, a British correspondent used wireless telegraphy to report the frontline news off Port Arthur. See Peter Slattery, *Reporting the Russo-Japanese War* (Folkestone, 2004).
11. For the prevalence of wireless communication in all the warships of the Combined Fleet in 1905, see Toyama, *Nichiro kaisen-shi kenkyū*, 2:530–1.
12. The warship relayed a prearranged code that with time would enter Japanese folklore. It consisted of tapping a key seven times to make the sound 'ta-ta-ta, ta-ta-ta-ta'. See e.g. Shiba Ryōtarō, *Clouds above the Hill* (London, 2012–14), 4:208.
13. Jpn. *Honjitsu tenki seirō naredomo nami takashi*.
14. Oide Hisashi, *Chishō Akiyama Saneyuki* (Tokyo, 1985), 191–2.
15. Admiralty, *Reports* (2003), 363; RGAVMF, f. 763, op. 1, d. 517; *Russko-Iaponskaia voina, Materiali*, 194–6.
16. On the eve of the battle, Rozhestvenskiĭ downgraded Enkvist to a commander of merely two cruisers, the *Oleg* and *Aurora*.

17. Vladimir Semenov, *The Battle of Tsu-Shima* (London, 1906), 3–5.
18. Semenov, *The Battle*, 38–42.
19. For a personal testimony about the *Izumi*'s activity during the hours before the battle by her captain, see Ishida Ichirō, 'Kaisen zengo *Izumi* no kōdō', in Todaka Kazushige (ed.), *Nihonkai kaisen no shōgen* (Tokyo: Kōjinsha, 2012), 7–15.
20. Semenov, *The Battle*, 43; Kostenko, *Na 'Orle'*, 424–5.
21. RGAVMF, f. 763, op. 1, d. 327; *Russko-Iaponskaia voina, Materiali*, 194–6; Kostenko, *Na 'Orle'*, 439–40.
22. Jpn. *Kōkoku no kōhai kono issen ni ari; kakuin issō funrei doryoku seyo.* Nelson's flags signalled a somewhat different message: 'England expects that every man will do his duty.'
23. Admiralty, *Reports* (2003), 367; Kostenko, *Na 'Orle'*, 428.
24. Semenov, *The Battle*, 53–4. For additional Russian testimony of this manoeuvre, see Klado, *The Battle*, 164.
25. Sailing in a long column, some of the Russian warships were far more distant from their target, standing at more than 9,000, 11,000, and even 13,000 metres away.
26. Semenov, *The Battle*, 55; Kostenko, *Na 'Orle'*, 430.
27. Ijichi Hikojirō, 'Gunkan Mikasa senji nisshi', 27 May 1905, Ministry of Defence, National Institute for Defence Studies, Tokyo (NIDS). For a testimony of the first minutes of the engagement on board the battleship *Asahi*, see Tsukamoto Yoshitane, *Asahi-kan yori mitaru Nihonkai kaisen* (Tokyo, 1907), 71–2.
28. The first Russian shell fell some 20 metres behind the *Mikasa* and within the next 15 minutes she was hit by five 305-milimetre shells and 14 other shells. See Admiralty, *Reports* (2003), 364, 93, 120. See also Corbett, *Maritime Operations*, 1:246–7; Toyama, *Nichiro kaisen-shi kenkyū*, 2:353–4.
29. Due to the position of the Japanese column, the three leading Russian battleships could use only their front turret, whereas, *Orël* was obscured completely. Other older ships, too, did not use their guns, at least for the first five minutes.
30. Rozhestvenskiĭ could have turned north-west and so bring a larger number of his own guns to bear, while preventing the same action from his opponent. However, this almost 90-degree turn could have led to confusion among the ships and would take his column away from its desired course to Vladivostok.
31. Admiralty, *Reports* (2003), 367–8; Levitskiĭ, *Russko-Iaponskaia voina*, 401.
32. RGAVMF, f. 763, op. 1, d. 335; *Russko-Iaponskaia voina, Materiali*, 199–202. For Rozhestvenskiĭ's injury, see Grigoriĭ Aleksandrovskiĭ, *Tsusimskii Boi* (New York, 1956), 46.
33. Semenov, *The Battle*, 113–14; Kostenko, *Na 'Orle'*, 432.

34. A. Zatertiĭ, *Za chuzhiye grekhi* (Moscow, 1907), 24. For an English translation of this testimony about the *Osliabia*'s final hour, see Westwood, *Witnesses of Tshushima*, 183–9.
35. Zatertiĭ, *Za chuzhiye grekhi*, 24–5.
36. Semenov, *The Battle*, 158.
37. For another eyewitness testimony of the *Osliabia*'s final minutes, see Vladimir Kravchenko, *Cherez tri okeana* (St Petersburg, 1910), 138.
38. Admiralty, *Reports* (2003), 371–2.
39. Kostenko, *Na 'Orle'*, 434.
40. For a personal testimony of the activity of this unit by its staff officer, see Satō Tetsutarō, 'Dai-ni kantai no kōdō', in Todaka (ed.), *Nihonkai kaisen no shōgen*, 16–23.
41. Semenov, *The Battle*, 137–8.
42. For a personal testimony about the attack by an officer of the 3rd Battle Division, see Yamaji Kazuyoshi, 'Dai-san kantai no kōdō', in Todaka (ed.), *Nihonkai kaisen no shōgen*, 24–9.
43. Kostenko, *Na 'Orle'*, 435.
44. The Japanese were surprised to discover that the *Orël* carried prisoners of a British merchantman seized earlier by the Russian force. See Boissier, *From Solferino*, 331. For the personal testimony of a Japanese officer about the events leading to the surrender of the two hospital ships, see Kamaya Chūdō, 'Rokoku byōinsen *Ariyo-ru* no hokaku, rokan *Nahimofu* oyobi *Uraji-miru Monomafu* no hokaku shobun', in Todaka (ed.), *Nihonkai kaisen no shōgen*, 76–82. For testimonies of the *Orël*'s captain and one of the medical doctors before the Investigative Commission in 1906, see Russia, *Russko-iaponskaia voina 1904–05. Deistvia flota*, (St Petersburgh, 1907, 1912–14), 5:293–300.
45. See Kravchenko, *Cherez tri okeana*, 146.
46. Levitskiĭ, *Russko-Iaponskaia voina*, 403; Bikov, *Russko-Iaponskaia voina*, 587–8.
47. See Kravchenko, *Cherez tri okeana*, 148.
48. Semenov, *The Battle*, 140–50.
49. For a testimony about the *Ural*'s sinking, see Tsukamoto, *Asahi-kan*, 87; William Pakenham, 'The Battle of Tsushima Straits', Tokio./N.A. Report 12/05, East Riding of Yorkshire Archives, 13–13a.
50. Kostenko, *Na 'Orle'*, 438.
51. For the *Imperator Aleksandr III*'s sinking, see Taube, *Posledniĭ*, 128–9; Tsukamoto, *Asahi-kan*, 91–2, including a chart of the warship's final movement on p. 97.
52. Kravchenko, *Cherez tri okeana*, 157.
53. Admiralty, *Reports* (2003), 377.
54. Kostenko, *Na 'Orle'*, 439.
55. Kravchenko, *Cherez tri okeana*, 158.
56. Semenov, *The Battle*, 159–60. See also Captain Pakenham's testimony, Admiralty, *Reports* (2003), 378.

57. For a detailed description of the end of the *Borodino*, and her earlier history, see Vladimir Gribovskiĭ, *Eskadrennyĭ bronenosets 'Borodino'* (St Petersburg, 1995).

58. Tsukamoto, *Asahi-kan*, 92.

59. Admiralty, *Reports* (2003), 379–80.

60. See Tsukamoto, *Asahi-kan*, 89; Apushkin, *Russko-iaponskaia voina*, 308–9.

61. Altogether some 906 men perished aboard the *Kniaz Suvorov*, the largest human toll of any Russian ship during the war.

62. See an eyewitness's testimony in Klado, *The Battle*, 199.

63. These four battleships were struck by 265 of the 360 152–305-millimetre shells that hit the entire force of 12 Russian capital ships (73.6 per cent of the total) during the entire battle. The *Kniaz Suvorov* alone was hit by 100 shells—the same as the number of Russian shells that hit the 12 Japanese capital ships altogether. See Vladimir Gribovskiĭ, *Rossiĭskiĭ flot Tikhogo okeana* (Moscow, 2004), Table 14.1.

64. Admiralty, *Reports* (2003), 380, 382.

65. Based on Nebogatov's official court-martial transcript published in *Morskoi Sbornik* (1907), 57, cited in Westwood, *Witnesses of Tshushima*, 231.

66. For this transfer of command before sunset, see a telegram sent by Rear Admiral Enkvist to the tsar on 5 June 1905 from Manila. In Klado, *The Battle*, 148.

67. For Rozhestvenskiĭ's presumed death, see Kravchenko, *Cherez tri okeana*, 153.

68. *Russko-Iaponskaia voina, Materiali*, 206–7.

69. For the *Aurora*'s initial encounters with torpedo boats, see Kravchenko, *Cherez tri okeana*, 161–9.

70. See RGAVMF, f. 763, op. 1, d. 330; *Russko-Iaponskaia voina, Deistviya*, 207–13; Evgeniĭ Dubrovskiĭ, *Dela o sdache iaponstam* (St Petersburg, 1907).

71. Kravchenko, *Cherez tri okeana*, 207.

72. RGAVMF, f. 870, op. 1, d. 33717; Leonid Dobrotvorskiĭ, *Uroki morskoi voini* (Kronstadt, 1907). For an animated description of Enkvist's decision making that night, see Pleshakov, *The Tsar's*, 287–95 (the speech is on p. 293).

73. A detailed description of Suzuki's exploits that night can be found in his biography. See Suzuki Kantarō Denki Hensan Iinkai (ed.), *Suzuki Kantarō den* (Tokyo, 1960), 48–52.

74. For Nebogatov's testimony, see his official court-martial transcript published in *Morskoi Sbornik* (1907), 55, and cited in Westwood, *Witnesses of Tshushima*, 233.

75. For Suzuki's own testimony of the battle, see Suzuki Kantarō, 'Dai-yon kuchi-kutai no tekikan shūgeki', in Todaka (ed.), *Nihonkai kaisen no shōgen*, 30–42.

76. Kostenko, for example, noted the presence of searchlights only on board the *Navarin*. Kostenko, *Na 'Orle'*, 458.

77. In Klado, *The Battle*, 159.

78. Toyama, *Nichiro kaisen-shi kenkyū*, 2:421.

79. See Westwood, *Witnesses of Tshushima*, 234–7.
80. For the *Sissoi Velikiǐ*'s daytime battle experience, see M.A. Bogdanov, *Eskadrenǐ bronenosets Sissoi Velikiǐ* (St Petersburg, 2004), 74–6. According to Captain Ozerov's report, the *Sissoi Velikiǐ*'s commander, she had 29 killed and 28 wounded. In Klado, *The Battle*, 214.
81. For the ship's final minutes, see Bogdanov, *Eskadrenǐ bronenosets Sissoi Velikiǐ*, 77; a brief report in Klado, *The Battle*, 214; and Toyama, *Nichiro kaisen-shi kenkyū*, 2:462. For her captain's report, see Russia, *Russko-iaponskaia voina 1904–05. Deistvia flota*, 3:353–74) (other officers are on pp. 375–84).
82. For a personal testimony about the sinking of these two cruisers, see Kamaya, 'Rokoku byōinsen', in Todaka (ed.), *Nihonkai kaisen no shōgen*, 82–8.
83. For the reports of her captain and executive officer, see Russia, *Russko-iaponskaia voina 1904–05. Deistvia flota*, 3:405–14, 415–27, respectively.
84. For the *Admiral Nakhimov*'s battle experience, see Zatertiǐ, *Za chuzhiye grekhi*, 1–3, 12–15.
85. Zatertiǐ, *Za chuzhiye grekhi*, 12–16.
86. *Admiral Seniavin* appears to be the only Russian capital ship to avoid even a single direct hit during the entire battle. By contrast, the battleship *Orël* suffered the most substantial damage among Nebogatov's ships, and had also the largest number of casualties: some 130 (43 dead and 87 wounded). For a detailed account of her state after the first day of the battle, see Kostenko, *Na 'Orle'*, 440–57.
87. For Nebogatov's testimony about his morning encounter with the Japanese main battle divisions, see his official court-martial transcript published in *Morskoi Sbornik* (1907), 67–7, cited in Westwood, *Witnesses of Tsushima*, 256–9.
88. Kostenko, *Na 'Orle'*, 466.
89. Thiess, *The Voyage*, 361–2. For the Japanese overwhelming superiority and their tactics of using their guns beyond the range of Nebogatov's ships, see Semenov, *The Price of Blood* (London & New York, 1910), 131.
90. Nebogatov's official court-martial transcript published in *Morskoi Sbornik* (1907), 43, cited in Westwood, *Witnesses of Tshushima*, 264. See also Apushkin, *Russko-iaponskaia voina*, 310.
91. Engineer-quartermaster Babushkin in Nebogatov's court martial, *Morskoi Sbornik* (1907), 67–7, cited in Westwood, *Witnesses of Tshushima*, 256–9.
92. Cited in Holger Afflerbach, 'Going Down with Flying Colours?' in Holger Afflerbach and Hew Strachan (eds), *How Fighting Ends* (Oxford, 2012), 199. For a slightly different version, see Novikov-Priboy, *Tsushima*, 249.
93. Kostenko, *Na 'Orle'*, 468.
94. For Fersen's initial request to escape and Nebogatov's rejection, see Thiess, *The Voyage*, 362.
95. Admiralty, *Reports* (2003), 381.

96. For Shvede's testimony, see Nebogatov's official court-martial transcript published in *Morskoi Sbornik* (1907), 257, cited in Westwood, *Witnesses of Tsushima*, 268. See also Klado, *The Battle*, 89–97.

97. Paine, *The Sino-Japanese War*, 229–31.

98. For personal testimonies about the surrender by an officer and a sailor on board the *Mikasa* and the *Fuji*, respectively, see Yamamoto Shinjirō, 'Nebogatofu-shō kōfuku jōkyō', in Todaka (ed,), *Nihonkai kaisen no shōgen*, 58–67; and Uchiyama Torao, 'Nichiro sensō nakaba yori jūgun no kansō', in Todaka (ed,), *Nihonkai kaisen no shōgen*, 97–8.

99. Admiralty, *Reports* (2003), 397.

100. Admiralty, *Reports* (2003), 397.

101. Bikov, *Russko-Iaponskaia voina*, 599.

102. According to Captain Fersen, the course to Vladimir Bay followed his own decision. See his testimony in Klado, *The Battle*, 154–6; and Russia, *Russko-iaponskaia voina 1904–05. Deistvia flota*, 3:491–502.

103. For the transfer of the admiral from the *Buiniĭ*, which became quite 'rickety and can't make any more headway' due to a boiler failure, to the *Bedoviĭ*, see Semenov, *The Price*, 7. For the *Bedoviĭ*'s surrender, see *Russko-Iaponskaia voina, Materiali*, 216; Admiralty, *Reports* (2003), 413; Thiess, *The Voyage*, 377–81. For Rozhestvenskiĭ's state during the 24 hours between his injury and surrender, see Pleshakov, *The Tsar's*, 299–307.

104. For a personal testimony about the sinking of the *Admiral Ushakov* by an officer on board the *Iwate*, see Takeuchi Shigetoshi, 'Rokan *Adomiraru Ushakofu* no gekichin', in Todaka (ed.), *Nihonkai kaisen no shōgen*, 68–72.

105. Bikov, *Russko-Iaponskaia voina*, 600. In the aftermath of the ship's sinking, most of her crew was taken prisoner. It had 98 casualties, 87 of them dead, including her commander. For a detailed description of the end of this ship, and her earlier history, see Gribovskiĭ and Chernikov, *Bronenosets 'Admiral Ushakov'*. For her captain's report, see Russia, *Russko-iaponskaia voina 1904–05. Deistvia flota*, 3:503–12.

106. Western sources state that this engagement took place at around 5.00 p.m. See e.g. Corbett, *Maritime Operations*, 2:329. Nonetheless, both Japanese and Russian primary sources suggest the initial encounter began in the morning. See *Russko-iaponskaia voina 1904–05. Deistvia flota*, 4:440–1; Naitō Shōichi, 'Dai-ni kuchikutai no tekikan shūgeki', in Todaka (ed.), *Nihonkai kaisen no shōgen*, 50–1.

107. For a personal testimony about the attack on *Dmitriĭ Donskoi* by a Japanese officer on board the destroyer *Oboro* of the 2nd Destroyer Division, see Naitō, 'Dai-ni kuchikutai', 50–7.

108. See the testimony of the ship's chaplain, Petr N. Dobrovolskiĭ, in Klado, *The Battle*, 149–54; and that of N.N. Dmitriev, *Bronenosets 'Admiral Ushakov'* (St Petersburg, 1906).

109. Admiralty, *Reports* (2003), 381; Thiess, *The Voyage*, 372–3.

110. For her captain's report, see Russia, *Russko-iaponskaia voina 1904–05. Deistvia flota*, 3:453–66.

111. For her captain's testimony before the Commission, see Russia, *Russko-iaponskaia voina 1904–05. Deistvia flota*, 5:289–92. For a testimony about the *Irtish*'s last minutes, see G.K. Graf, *Moriaki; ocherki 12 'zhizni morskikh'* (Paris, 1930), 108–10.

112. For this three-ship force's escape to Manila, see Kravchenko, *Cherez tri okeana*, 204–25; 'Russian Ships Safe in Manila Bay', *The New York Times*, 4 June 1905, 1. See also Rear Admiral Enkvist's own telegram to the tsar on 5 June 1905 from Manila, in Klado, *The Battle*, 148–9. For reports of the captains of the *Oleg, Aurora*, and *Zhemchug*, see Russia, *Russko-iaponskaia voina 1904–05. Deistvia flota*, 2:67–110, 111–26, and 189–96, respectively.

113. According to the contemporary concepts of neutrality in the international law (The Law of Neutrality), it was the duty of a neutral nation to intern a belligerent warship (together with its officers and crew) that would not or could not depart a neutral port or roadstead where it was not entitled to remain.

114. For three reports on the experience of the *Koreia*, see Klado, *The Battle*, 186–201.

115. For her captain's report, see Russia, *Russko-iaponskaia voina 1904–05. Deistvia flota*, 2:213–20.

116. For her captain's report, see Russia, *Russko-iaponskaia voina 1904–05. Deistvia flota*, 2:241–56.

117. For her captain's report, see Russia, *Russko-iaponskaia voina 1904–05. Deistvia flota*, 2:257–62.

118. For the *Bravii*'s escape, see a telegram of her commander, in Klado, *The Battle*, 156–7. For her captain's report, see Russia, *Russko-iaponskaia voina 1904–05. Deistvia flota*, 2:267–84.

119. For a report of the commander of the *Groznii*, see Klado, *The Battle*, 183–6; Russia, *Russko-iaponskaia voina 1904–05. Deistvia flota*, 3:469–72.

120. For a testimony of the first minutes of the engagement on board the battleship *Asahi*, see Tsukamoto, *Asahi-kan*, 128–36.

121. Twelve additional auxiliary ships of the armada had left the fleet shortly before the battle and so were saved. The *Merkuri* and *Tambov* left for Saigon on 18 May; the *Rion, Dnieper, Livonia, Kuronia, Meteor, Vladimir, Voronezh*, and *Yaroslavl* left for the mouth of the Yangtze on 25 May; whereas the *Terek* and *Kuban* were dispatched to diversionary operations off the south-eastern coast of the Japanese archipelago.

122. These torpedo boats were nos. 34 and 35, which were sunk during the night attacks, and no. 69 which foundered after colliding with the destroyer *Akatsuki*.

123. The Russian losses included 125,910 tons sunk, 48,941 tons captured, and 23,879 tons interned. The total figure includes 146,905 tons of warships and 51,916 tons of auxiliary ships. The Russian and Japanese aggregate displacements are calculated based on Kowner, *Historical Dictionary, passim*, and Jentschura et al., *Warships*, 124.

124. The larger Russian figure quoted above appeared in the British official history of the war and is quoted also in Corbett, *Maritime Operations*, 2:333. For the figure of Russian crew members reaching safe haven, see Iu. Chernov, 'Tsushima', in Ivan Rostunov (ed.), *Istoriia russko-iaponskoi voiny* (Moscow, 1977), 3. Nonetheless, there is minor disagreement about the exact number of casualties in the battle. The IJN medical report seems to provide the most detailed account of the casualties on both sides with a breakdown for each ship and rank. Yet, while reporting 4,625 dead (including 180 officers) and 745 wounded on the Russian side, and 117 dead (including 39 officers) and 580 wounded on the Japanese side, it does not include some of the Russian auxiliary vessels and certain Japanese light vessels of secondary importance. See National Archives of Japan, Japan Center for Asian Historical Record (JACAR), 'Meiji 37-8 nen gokuhi kaisenshi', Section II, 5:70–5. The larger Russian figure quoted above appeared in British official history of the war and is quoted also in Corbett, *Maritime Operations*, 2:333. For slightly different figures, see United States, *Epitome of the Russo-Japanese War* (Washington, 1907), 165. Russian sources tended to quote even higher death tolls. Vladimir Kostenko, for example, mentioned 5,044 dead on the Russian side, 5,982 captured, 2,110 disarmed, 870 who arrived in Vladivostok, and another 544 released to Russia (on board the hospital ship *Kostroma*). See Kostenko, *Na 'Orle'*, 490, 46.

125. See e.g. H.P. Willmott, *Sea Warfare* (New York, 1981), 32; H.P. Willmott, *The Last Century of Sea Power* (Bloomington, 2009), 1:115.

126. Levitskiĭ, *Russko-Iaponskaia voina*, 400; and Bikov, *Russko-Iaponskaia voina*, 587–8.

127. The 12 Japanese capital ships (1st and 2nd Battle Divisions) fired 446 305-millimetre, 50 254-millimetre, 1,199 203-millimetre, 9,464 152-millimetre, and 7,526 76-millimetre shells (altogether 11,159 152–305-millimetre shells). See N.J.M. Campbell, 'The Battle of Tsu-Shima', Parts 1, 2, 3, and 4, in Antony Preston (ed.), *Warship* (London, 1978), 46–49, 127–35, 186–92, 258–65, 4:260. Among these, the six armoured cruisers of the 2nd Battle Division fired 915 203-millimetre, 3,716 152-millimetre, and 3,480 76-millimetre shells. The 12 Russian capital ships fired 782 305-millimetre, 535 254-millimetre, 261 229-millimitre, 280 203-millimetre, 5,084 152-millimetre, and 1,250 120-millimetre shells (altogether 8,195 120–305-millimetre shells, namely, 73.4 per cent of the Japanese shells of similar calibres). See Gribovskiĭ, *Rossiĭskiĭ flot Tikhogo okeana*, Table 14.1.

128. See e.g. Olender, *Russo-Japanese Naval War*, 2:223.

129. For the Russian accuracy, see Olender, *Russo-Japanese Naval War*, 2:224 (the figures for the Japanese guns are calculated based on data on pp. 225–6).

130. The United States Navy's hit rate was 2.5 per cent and 1.3 per cent in the battles of Manila and Santiago of 1898, respectively. The Imperial German Navy and the British Royal Navy did not fare much better at the Battle of

Jutland of 1916, with a hit rate of 3.4 per cent and 2.8 per cent, respectively. See Jim Leeke, *Manila and Santiago* (Annapolis, 2009); and Vincent O'Hara, and Leonard Heinz, *Clash of the Fleets* (Annapolis, 2017), 182. Unaware of the actual Japanese hitting rate, Pakenham stated in his report that the 'Japanese shooting has produced an astonishing effect, and the excellence of their marksmanship is likely to be overstated. It is believed the standard attained in at least one other navy is far higher than any to which the Japanese even now aspire'. The National Archive, Foreign Office Papers 46/592, 'The Russo-Japanese War: Battle of Tsushima Straits', Pakenham Report, f. 219

131. A few scholars have speculated that the IJN's use of better rangefinders during the battle was the source of its advantage. However, the range of fire and the similarity of equipment suggest that training and actual combat experience were the main elements of the Japanese higher hit rate. See Iain Russel, 'Rangefinders at Tsushima', *Warship* 49 (1989), 30–6; and Peter Ifland, 'Finding Distance—The Barr & Stroud Rangefinders', *Journal of Navigation* 56 (2003), 315–21.

132. There are many Russian testimonies about the 'terrible havoc' the Japanese small-calibre guns made on the Russian ships. See e.g. Klado, *The Battle*, 166; Kostenko, *Na 'Orle'*, 442–3.

133. Semenov, *The Battle*, 62–3.

134. For an evaluation and breakdown of the Japanese and Russian gun hits, see Olender, *Russo-Japanese Naval War*, 2:225–6.

135. Focusing solely on the 152–305-millimetre shells that hit the 12 main capital ships in each of the fleets, another source suggests a similar ratio. That is, the Russian ships were hit by 360 shells whereas the Japanese were hit by as few as 100 shells (27.8 per cent of the Russian hits). See Gribovskiĭ, *Rossiĭskiĭ flot Tikhogo okeana*, Table 14.1.

136. For the Russian shells, see Semenov, *The Battle*, 77.

137. Mayuzumi Haruo, *Kaigun hōsen shidan* (Tokyo, 1972), 117–21; Kostenko, *Na 'Orle'*, 520–1.

138. Newton McCully, *The McCully Report* (Annapolis, 1977), 249–50; Kostenko, *Na 'Orle'*, 523–4. Kostenko argued, however, that the use of this type of shell for destroying armoured ships 'reached the goal only due to the large number of hits', and that had the IJN 'used armour-piercing shells, then the three *Borodino*-class battleships would have been sunk much earlier and would not have required as many hits' (521, 522).

139. According to Russian sources, the impact of the Japanese bursting charge was as much as seven times stronger than the impact of shells of similar size. See Semenov, *The Battle*, 77. For the improvements made in the Japanese projectiles based on the experience of the engagements of 1904, see Admiralty, *Reports* (2003), 384.

140. Developed in 1888 on the basis of a form of picric acid used in France and Britain, this new explosive became mass-produced in Japan in 1899. Soon

after the end of the war, its developer, the naval engineer Shimose Masachika, was bestowed various honours in recognition of his wartime contribution, including the Order of the Rising Sun in 1906. For descriptions of the heat this explosive generated, see Corbett, *Maritime Operations*, 2:249. For Russian impressions of Shimose HC shells, see Kostenko, *Na 'Orle'*, 519.

141. For the breakdown of the Japanese and Russian torpedo launching and hits, see Olender, *Russo-Japanese Naval War*, 2:235–6.

142. See Klado, *The Battle*, 122–3. Klado listed the Japanese superiority in torpedo craft as the third in five 'probable causes for the disaster' (p. 126).

143. Fred Jane, *The Imperial Russian Navy* (London, 1899), 327.

144. Stephen McLaughlin, *Russian & Soviet Battleships* (Annapolis, 2003), 113–14.

145. Among the four Japanese battleships, three were protected by Harvey armour, but by the late 1890s, with the introduction of the stronger Krupp armour, this steel armour was rendered obsolete.

146. See e.g. Klado, *The Battle*, 129–30; Kostenko, *Na 'Orle'*, 501.

147. For an overview, see Dmitrii Likharev, 'Shells vs. Armour', *War & Society* 36 (2017), 184.

148. A large number of sources emphasized this point and its devastating impact, e.g. Admiralty, *Reports* (2003), 385; Klado, *The Battle*, 122; Taube, *Poslednii*, 89; Kostenko, *Na 'Orle'*, 505–8; Thiess, *The Voyage*, 111–12; Alfred Thayer Mahan, 'Reflections, Historic and Other', *US Naval Institute Proceedings* 32 (1906), 465.

149. David Brown, *The Grand Fleet* (Annapolis, 1999), 27.

150. See the response of the ex-Director of Naval Construction of the French Navy, Louis-Émile Bertin, 'The Fate of the Russian Ships at Tsushima', in *Jane's Fighting Ships (1904–7)*, reprinted in Hogue, *The Fleet That Had to Die*, 233.

151. That said, for decades after Tsushima, the IJN and the Soviet navy would insist on heavy armour for their warships. See J.N. Westwood, *Russian Naval Construction, 1904–45* (Basingstoke, 1994), 204.

152. For a Russian testimony about this inferiority in battle, see Klado, *The Battle*, 173. According to some assessments, the Russian warships lost as much as three knots due to fouling. See e.g. David Brown, *Warrior to Dreadnought* (Annapolis, 1997), 170. See also David Brown, 'The Russo-Japanese War', *Warship* (1996), 66–77.

153. An increasing lack of homogeneity, seen in ships' incompatibility in speed, armament, and protection, was a notable feature of the Russian programme of battleship construction since the early 1890s. See Sergei Vinogradov, 'Battleship Development in Russia from 1905 to 1917', *Warship International* 35 (1998), 268–9.

154. Mahan, 'Reflections', 405.

155. Apushkin, *Russko-iaponskaia voina*, 307.

156. Kostenko, *Na 'Orle'*, 442. For a Russian eye-witness testimony about the difficulty of aiming in the fog at the 'dirty olive color' Japanese warships, see Kostenko, *Na 'Orle'*.

157. For this observation, see Mahan, *Naval Strategy*, 417. For the naval intelligence available to Rozhestvenskiĭ before and during the battle, see Evgeny Sergeev, *Russian Military Intelligence in the War with Japan* (London, 2007), 148–9; Inaba, *Baruchikku kantai*, 171–226, *passim*. See also Bruce Menning, 'Miscalculating One's Enemies', *War in History* 13, no. 2 (2006), 147–8.
158. For a similar verdict of Rozhestvenskiĭ, see Kostenko, *Na 'Orle'*, 478.
159. Taube, *Posledniĭ*, 14.
160. For Nebogatov's leadership, see Thiess, *The Voyage*, 360.
161. See Mayuzumi, *Kaigun hōsen shidan*, 231.
162. For harsh criticism about the dearth of training in the Russian force, see Klado, *The Battle*, 79–80.
163. For the role of Japanese education system in this indoctrination, see Ury Eppstein, 'School Songs, the War and Nationalist Indoctrination in Japan', in Kowner (ed.), *Rethinking*, 185–201.
164. See Rotem Kowner, 'The War as a Turning Point', in Kowner (ed.), *The Impact*, 39–41.
165. For this view, see Mahan, *Naval Strategy*, 398 ('if twenty only of the numbers under his command reached Vladivostok, the Japanese communications would be seriously endangered. This is a clear "Fleet in Being" theory, and quite undiluted').
166. Mahan, *Naval Strategy*, 398.
167. Olender, *Russo-Japanese Naval War*, 2:185.
168. Some naval strategists have reckoned that a fleet's power is eroded by as much as 10 per cent for each thousand miles it sails from its base. See e.g. Norman Friedman, *The U.S. Maritime Strategy* (Annapolis, 1988), 72, no. 10.
169. For this crucial difference between the two services, see Luntinen and Menning, 'The Russian Navy', 258.
170. After the war, naval experts suggested a number of options about the preferable way of handling the auxiliary vessels, including their dispatch to Vladivostok via a route east of Japan. See Mahan, *Naval Strategy*, 419; Klado, *The Battle*, 73–5.
171. Thiess, *The Voyage*, 360.
172. In Admiralty, *Reports* (2003), 382.
173. For further angles on Tōgō's key tactical and strategic decisions during the battle, see Ronald Andidora, 'Admiral Togo: An Adaptable Strategist', *Naval War College Review* 44 (1991), 52–62.
174. Julian Corbett, *Some Principles of Maritime Strategy* (London, 1911), 319, 338.

Chapter 3

1. For the poem, see Donald Keene, *Emperor of Japan* (New York, 2002), 645.
2. Interestingly, the news on the triumph in the Battle of Mukden prompted the gathering of twice as many people. See Sakurai Ryōju, *Taishō seijishi no shuppatsu* (Tokyo, 1997), 22–5.

3. See e.g. 'Kaigun dai-shōri' ('The navy's great victory'), *Tōkyō Niroku Shimbun*, 29 May 1905, 1; 'Dai-kaisen' ('The great naval battle'), *Hōchi Shimbun*, 30 May 1905, 2.

4. Lone, *Army, Empire*, 117. Often forgotten, Russia too was broke and required loans. See William C. Fuller, *Civil–Military Conflict in Imperial Russia, 1881–1914* (Princeton, 1985), 160.

5. Elting Morison, *The Letters of Theodore Roosevelt* (Cambridge, 1951–4), 4:1221–2. See also Komura Jutarō to General Kodama Gentarō, 9 June 1905. In Japan, Gaimushō, *Nihon gaikō bunsho: Nichiro sensō* (Tokyo, 1958–60), 5:252–4.

6. The naval force assembled in Aomori Bay in the northern part of the main island of Honshu. It consisted of the four armoured cruisers, *Azuma, Kasuga, Nisshin*, and *Yakumo* under Vice Admiral Dewa Shigetō, four cruisers under Rear Admiral Tōgō Masamichi, and four coastal defence ships under Kataoka, as well as nine destroyers and 12 torpedo boats. See Great Britain. *Official History of the Russo-Japanese War*, 5 vols (London, 1906–10), 3:834.

7. For the takeover of Sakhalin, see Hara Teruyuki (ed.), *Nichiro sensō to Saharin-tō* (Sapporo, 2011); Marie Sevela, 'Chaos versus Cruelty', in Kowner (ed.), *Rethinking*, 93–108.

8. For these efforts, see Robert Valliant, 'The Selling of Japan', *Monumenta Nipponica* 29 (1974), 415–38; Rotem Kowner, 'Becoming an Honorary Civilized Nation', *The Historian* 64 (2001), 19–38.

9. See Rotem Kowner, 'Japan's "Fifteen Minutes of Glory"', in Yulia Mikhailova and M. William Steele (eds), *Japan and Russia* (Folkestone, 2008), 47–70.

10. For a personal account of one of the prisoners, see Kostenko, *Na 'Orle'*, 469–70; for the general treatment of Russian POWs during the conflict, see Rotem Kowner, 'Imperial Japan and its POWs', in Guy Podoler (ed.), *War and Militarism in Modern Japan* (Folkestone, 2009), especially 86–7.

11. Blond, *Admiral Togo*, 237; see also Thiess, *The Voyage*, 385.

12. The most notable artistic depiction of the visit was made by the Japanese painter Fujishima Takeji (1867–1943). The painting is available online at https://en.wikipedia.org/wiki/Zinovy_Rozhestvensky#/media/File:Admiral_Togo_Visiting_Zinovy_Rozhestvensky_by_Fujishima_Takeji_(Reimeikan).jpg.

13. The other hospital ship, the *Orёl*, remained in Japan as a prize. For the negotiations and debate about these ships, see Boissier, *From Solferino*, 331–2; House of Representatives, *Papers Relating to Foreign Relation of the United States* (Washington, 1906), 1: 595–6, 790–1.

14. There is extensive literature on the Portsmouth Peace Conference and its repercussions. See e.g. Eugene Trani, *The Treaty of Portsmouth* (Lexington, 1969); Okamoto, *The Japanese Oligarchy*, 150–63; Norman Saul, 'The Kittery Peace', in Steinberg et al. (eds), *The Russo-Japanese War*, 1:485–507; Steven Ericson and Allen Hockley (eds), *The Treaty of Portsmouth and Its Legacies* (Hanover, 2008); and Francis Wcislo, *Tales of Imperial Russia* (Oxford, 2011), 204–14.

15. Okamoto, *The Japanese Oligarchy*, 167–95.

16. Semenov, *The Price*, 82.
17. Okamoto, *The Japanese Oligarchy*, 196–223; Shumpei Okamoto, 'The Emperor and the Crowd', in Tetsuo Najita and J. Victor Koschmann (eds), *Conflict in Modern Japanese History* (Princeton, 1982), 262–70; Lone, *Army, Empire*, 117–20.
18. For an overview of the war's impact on Japan, see Kowner, 'The War as a Turning Point', 29–46.
19. For the Japanese post-war agreements, see Peter Berton, *Russo-Japanese Relations, 1905–17* (London, 2011); and E.W. Edwards, 'The Far Eastern Agreements of 1907', *The Journal of Modern History* 26, no. 4 (1954), 340–55.
20. Schencking, *Making Waves*, 111.
21. See e.g. *Jiji shimpō*, 21 October 1905; 'Editorial', *The Yamato Shimbun*, no. 1870, 13 November 1905, 1. See also Chapter 5 in the present volume. For the atmosphere among the British naval observers in Japan that helped eliciting the association between and Nelson, see Richard Dunley, '"The Warrior Has Always Shewed Himself Greater Than His Weapons": The Royal Navy's Interpretation of the Russo-Japanese War 1904–5', *War & Society* 34 (2015) 248–62.
22. Schencking, *Making Waves*, 111.
23. For the naval review, see Takashi Fujitani, *Splendid Monarchy* (Berkeley, 1996), 134–6; Blond, *Admiral Togo*, 240–2.
24. There have been sundry speculations and theories about the source of the explosion, ranging from humid gunpowder to a terrorist attack. See Toyoda Jō, *Kikan Mikasa no shōgai* (Tokyo, 2016), 368–402.
25. Pleshakov, *The Tsar's*, 316.
26. By the same token, the Army Day was celebrated every year on 10 March, the date of the victory in the 1905 land battle of Mukden. For the emergence of these two dates, see Harada Keiichi, 'Irei to tsuito: sensō kinenbi kara shūsen kinenbi e', in Kurasawa Aiko et al. (eds), *Sensō no seijigaku* (Tokyo, 2005), 296–307.
27. The aggregate displacement of the Russian ships captured at the Battle of Tsushima was 48,941 tons (among them 32, 641 tons of warships). The IJN had also captured five semi-sunken Russian battleships in Port Arthur which were commissioned after the war. For the IRN's structure and vessels in 1906, see The Editors, 'The Progress of Navies: Foreign Navies', in John Leyland and T.A. Brassey (eds), *The Naval Annual, 1906* (Portsmouth, 1906), 23–5. Cf. 'Sea Strength of the Naval Powers', *Scientific American* 93, no. 2 (July 8, 1905), 26.
28. See Evans and Peattie, *Kaigun*: 147. This specific position is also corroborated by Modelsky and Thompson, *Seapower in Global Politics*, 123, although their proportional distribution of global sea power suggested that the IJN had never been in a higher position than sixth place.
29. Schencking, *Making Waves*, 117–22, 128–34.
30. For the popularity of cards containing naval images, primarily warships, both during and after the Russo-Japanese War, see *Japanese Philately* 41:4 (August 1986), 152–8.

31. Yoshitake Oka, 'Generational Conflict after the Russo-Japanese War', in Tetsuo Najita and J. Victor Koschmann (eds), *Conflict in Modern Japanese History* (Princeton, 1982), 214–15.

32. Schencking, *Making Waves*, 123–8. For this new image, see Shōichi Saeki, 'Images of the United States as a Hypothetical Enemy', in Akira Iriye (ed.), *Mutual Images* (Cambridge, 1975), 100–14.

33. See Tal Tovy and Sharon Halevy, 'America's First Cold War', in Kowner (ed.), *The Impact*, 137–52.

34. For the term 'budgetary navy', see Ian Nish, 'Japan and Naval Aspects of the Washington Conference', in William Beasley (ed.), *Modern Japan* (Berkeley, 1975), 69.

35. For the plan, see Evans and Peattie, *Kaigun*, 153 (for the expansion between 1905–22, see pp. 152–98).

36. For a reconstruction of this document, which was destroyed in 1945, see Shimanuki Takeharu, 'Nichiro sensō ikō ni okeru kokubō hōshin shoyō heiryoku', *Gunji Shigaku* 8, no. 4, (1973), 2–11.

37. For the plan, see Sanematsu Yuruzu, 'Hachi-hachi kantai to Katō Tomosaburō', *Rekishi to jinbutsu* 6 (August 1976), 58–65; Evans and Peattie, *Kaigun*, 150–1; Fumio Takahashi, 'The First War Plan Orange and the First Imperial Japanese Defense Policy: An Interpretation from the Geopolitical Strategic Perspective', NIDS Security Reports 5 (2004), 68–103.

38. During the seven years starting in 1914, navy expenditures rose 5.8-fold and their share in national expenditures rose from 12.9 to 32.5 per cent. See J. Charles Schencking, 'The Imperial Japanese Navy and the First World War: Unprecedented Opportunities and Harsh Realities', in Tosh Minohara, Tze-ki Hon, and Evan Dawley (eds), *The Decade of the Great War* (Leiden: Brill, 2014), 97, Table 4.1.

39. For this passement made by the British Naval Attaché in Tokyo in January 1909, see Arthur Marder, *From the Dreadnought to Scapa Flow* (London, 1961), 236.

40. Tadokoro Masayuki, 'Why did Japan Fail to Become the "Britain" of Asia?' in Steinberg et al. (eds), *The Russo-Japanese War*, 2:321.

41. For the post-war navy expenditures and expansion programmes, see Keishi Ono, 'The War, Military Expenditures and Postbellum Fiscal and Monetary Policy in Japan', in Kowner (ed.), *Rethinking*, 139–57.

42. Lone, *Army, Empire*, 175–84.

43. For the IJN's expanding political role and its inter-service rivalry between 1906 and 1914, see Masuda Tomoko, 'Kaigun gunbi kakuchō o meguru seiji katei', in *Kindai Nihon kenkyū*, vol. 4: *Taiheiyō sensō* (Tokyo, 1982), 411–33; J. Charles Schencking, 'The Politics of Pragmatism and Pageantry', in Sandra Wilson (ed.), *Nation and Nationalism in Japan* (London, 2002), 565–90.

44. For the impact of the war on Japanese militarism, see Kowner, 'The War as a Turning Point', 33–5. For the role of the war in shaping the concept of

bushidō, see Oleg Benesch, *Inventing the Way of the Samurai* (Oxford, 2014), 103–10, 114–18.

45. For the post-war legacy of the battle as a naval and spiritual milestone for the Japan Maritime Self-Defence Force and supporting naval circles, see Alessio Patalano, *Post-War Japan as a Sea Power* (London, 2015), 41–6, 73, 90.

46. For this concept, see Benesch, *Inventing*, 84–5, 109, 147.

47. For the rising sense of invincibility and the role of the war as a prelude to a future war, see Sandra Wilson, 'The Russo-Japanese War and Japan', in David Wells and Sandra Wilson (eds), *The Russo-Japanese War in Cultural Perspective* (Basingstoke, 1999), 182–3; and Frederick Dickinson, 'Commemorating the War in Post-Versailles Japan', in Steinberg et al. (eds), *The Russo-Japanese War*, 1:539–42.

48. Jō Eiichirō, *Jijū bukan Jō Eiichirō nikki* (Tokyo, 1982), 4–5; Emiko Ohnuki-Tierney, *Kamikaze, Cherry Blossoms, and Nationalisms* (Chicago, 2002), 159–66.

49. For this argument, see Evans and Peattie, *Kaigun*, 132; and Jonathan Parshall and Anthony Tully, *Shattered Sword* (Dulles, 2005), 72–3, 403.

50. See e.g. Minoru Genda, 'Tactical Planning in the Imperial Japanese Navy', *Naval War College Review* 22, no. 2 (1969), 45.

51. For the origin of this ratio, see Carlos Rivera, 'Big Stick and Short Sword', PhD dissertation (Ohio State University, 1995), 230–1.

52. See e.g. Thomas Buckley, *The United States and the Washington Conference, 1921–1922* (Knoxville, 1970); Sadao Asada, *From Mahan to Pearl Harbor* (Annapolis, 2006), 74–88 (for abrogation of the treaty, see pp. 192–5).

53. See Admiral Nagumo Chūichi's statement three weeks before the attack on Pearl Harbor, in Nobutaka Ike (ed.), *Japan's Decision for War* (Stanford, 1967), 247.

54. Hiroyuki Agawa, *The Reluctant Admiral* (Tokyo, 1979), 2.

55. For the IJN strategy in late 1941, see Evans and Peattie, *Kaigun*, 480–1.

56. Shigeru Fukudome, 'Hawaii Operation', *U.S. Naval Institute Proceedings* 81 (1955), 1315–31.

57. Alvin Coox, 'The Pearl Harbor Raid Revisited', *The Journal of American–East Asian Relations* 3, no. 3 (1994), 218.

58. Donald Goldstein and Katherine Dillon (eds), *The Pearl Harbor Papers* (Washington, 1999), 122.

59. For the reasons behind the choice of that day for departure, see Parshall and Tully, *Shattered Sword*, 69.

60. Evans and Peattie, *Kaigun*, 129.

61. Patalano, *Post-War Japan*, 137.

62. For this argument, see Parshall and Tully, *Shattered Sword*, 404–5.

63. For the IJN's offensive, and at time unique, approach to the use of carriers on the eve of the Second World War, see Rotem Kowner, 'Passing the Baton', *Education About Asia* 19 (2014), 68–73.

64. See Atsushi Oi, 'Why Japan's Anti-Submarine Warfare Failed', in David Evans (ed.), *The Japanese Navy in World War II* (Annapolis, 1986), 387.

65. Evans and Peattie, *Kaigun*, 130, 266–72, 383.
66. For the commemoration of the war in post-1905 Japan, see Dickinson, 'Commemorating the War', 1:523–43; Ben-Ami Shillony and Rotem Kowner (ed.), 'The Memory and Significance of the Russo-Japanese War', in Kowner (ed.), *Rethinking*, 1–9.
67. For the IJA's and IJN's respective resentment over the public indifference towards the army and navy memorial days, see Harada, 'Irei to tsuito', 300.
68. See Yuriĭ Pestushko and Yaroslav A. Shulatov, 'Russo-Japanese Relations from 1905 to 1916', in Streltsov and Shimotomai (eds), *A History of Russo-Japanese Relations*, 109.
69. For various indications of the flagging interest by 1906, see Isao Chiba, 'Shifting Contours of Memory and History', in Steinberg et al. (eds), *The Russo-Japanese War*, 2:361.
70. Today, this Memorial of the Battle of the Sea of Japan (Jpn. *Nihonkai kaisen kinenhi*) is part of Tonosaki park (Tonosaki Kokutei Kōen), in Kamitsushima town.
71. The other War God was the IJA's Major Tachibana Shūta, who was killed in the Battle of Liaoyang. For more on Hirose, see Naoko Shimazu, *Japanese Society at War* (Cambridge, 2009), 197–229.
72. Among other honours, Tōgō was made a Member of the British Order of Merit in 1906. Twenty years later, he was awarded the Collar of the Supreme Order of the Chrysanthemum, an honour which, at the time, was only shared with the Emperor and Prince Kan'in Kotohito. See Falk, *Togo*, 431–3; Clements, *Admiral Togo*, 208–24.
73. For the most part, Tōgō opposed the erection of statues of himself. Nonetheless, in 1927 he was persuaded to allow the erection of such a statue, alongside Nogi's statue, at the Tōgō Park (Tōgō Kōen), in the grounds of Chichibu Ontake Shrine, near Chichibu, Saitama, and took part in the unveiling ceremony. See Ōkuma Asajirō, *Shinsui Horiuchi Bunjirō shōgun o itamu* (Fukuoka, 1942), 5.
74. At an earlier point in time, Ogasawara was heavily involved with the creation of the IJN myth of its first *gunshin*, Hirose Takeo. See Shimazu, *Japanese Society at War*, 200–2.
75. Herbert Bix, *Hirohito and the Making of Modern Japan* (New York, 2000), 108–11.
76. Falk, *Togo*, 457–8.
77. Upon Tōgō's death, his domestic lionization reached a zenith alongside renewed international interest, as is evidenced by a flurry of publications in Japanese and English. See e.g. Nakamura Koya, *Sekai no Tōgō gensui* (Tokyo, 1934); Abe Shinzō, *Tōgō gensui jikiwashū* (Tokyo, 1935); Kaigun Heigakkō, *Tōgō gensui keikōroku* (Tokyo, 1935); Ogasawara, *Life of Admiral Togo* (1934); Ronald Bodley, *Admiral Togo* (London, 1935); Falk, *Togo* (New York, 1936); and Koya Nakamura, *Admiral Togo* (Tokyo, 1937).

78. A key figure in the campaign was Shiba Sometarō, the editor of *The Japan Times* during the 1920s. See his 'Save the Mikasa', *The Japan Times*, 14 June 1923; 'Save the Mikasa!' *The Japan Times*, 21 July 1923.
79. For the establishment of the Society (Jpn. Mikasa Hozonkai), see '"Save the Mikasa" Men Meeting to Organize Today', *The Japan Times*, 24 March 1924; Ogasawara Naganari, *Seishō Tōgō Heihachirō den*, 490–6.
80. Ozaki Chikara, *Seishō Tōgō to reikan Mikasa* (Tokyo, 1935), 100–1. For the Society and its publications, see NIDS, *Senshi–Nichiro sensō*-11.
81. Edan Corkill, 'How *The Japan Times* Saved a Foundering Battleship, Twice', *The Japan Times*, 18 December 2011.
82. For the ceremony, see Dickinson, 'Commemorating the War', 536–7.
83. Tatsushi Hirano et al., 'Recent Developments in the Representation of National Memory and Local Identities', *Japanstudien* 20 (2009), 252.
84. Jpn. *Fukutsu shi no Nihonkai kaisen kinenhi*.
85. Abe Masahiro, the person behind the monument, was a local veterinarian who erected it at his own expense.
86. For this revived memory, see Chiba, 'Shifting Contours', 2:365.
87. See Saburo Ienaga, 'Glorification of War in Japanese Education', *International Security* 18, no. 3 (1993–94), 119–20.
88. 'Togo shrine dedicated', *Nippu Jiji*, 27 May 1940, 1. Curiously, and for a short time before the war, Tōgō worship also took place on American soil, as part of the Daijingu Temple of Hawaii, a Shinto shrine in Honolulu. See Wilburn Hansen, 'Examining Prewar Tôgô Worship in Hawaii', *Nova Religio* 14 (2010), 67–92.
89. For the history of the two shrines, see *Nogi jinja-Tōgō jinja* (Tokyo, 1993).
90. Toyoda, *Kikan Mikasa*, 491.
91. For the state of the site during the early years of the occupation, see Elmer Potter, *Nimitz* (Annapolis, 1976), 397–8, 466.
92. For Rubin's visit and letter, see Toyoda, *Kikan Mikasa*, 497–8.
93. John S. Rubin, 'Flagship Mikasa then and Now', *Nippon Times*, 24 September 1955.
94. For the post-war efforts to restore the *Mikasa*, see Patalano, *Post-War Japan*, 45–7.
95. For this notion, see Patalano, *Post-War Japan*, 37.
96. For Itō's campaign, see Alessio Patalano, 'A Symbol of Tradition and Modernity', *Japanese Studies* 34 (2014), 61–82.
97. Nimitz's acquaintance with Tōgō began shortly after the Battle of Tsushima and the former also attended the latter's funeral. See Potter, *Nimitz*, 56–7, 158, 397–8; and Brayton Harris, *Admiral Nimitz* (New York, 2012), 13, 48.
98. Directed by Watanabe Kunio, the film offered a pioneering portrayal of the Emperor Meiji. See Chiba, 'Shifting Contours', 2:371–4.
99. The film had the highest number of viewers (around 20 million) and was the highest-grossing film in Japanese film history at the time. Its viewership record was only broken 44 years later with the 2001 release of Miyazaki Hayao's animated fantasy film *Spirited Away* (Jpn. *Sen to Chihiro no kamikakushi*).

The monthly *Bungei Shunjū* had been involved in drumming up public interest in the Memorial Ship Mikasa since 1957. See NIDS, *Senshi–Nichiro senso-7*. For Nimitz's article in the *Bungei Shunjū*, see Potter, *Nimitz*, 466–7; and Harris, *Admiral Nimitz*, 210. Nimitz's legacy did not end there. In 2009, sailors from the aircraft carrier USS *Nimitz* volunteered to paint the *Mikasa*. For further information on Nimitz's involvement in the Mikasa restoration, see Papers of Chester W. Nimitz, Archives Branch, Naval History and Heritage Command, Washington, D.C., Box 63, folders 499–503.

101. Among other supporters, the Japan Sumo Association toured the country to raise funds, and altogether more than half a million Japanese contributed to the project. The main source on the restoration project is the 32-page booklet published by the Mikasa Preservation Society, *Memorial Ship Mikasa* (Yokosuka, Japan, 1981).

102. After an initial surge of visitors, their number fluctuated between 150,000 and 200,000 annually throughout the 1970s and the 1980s, but declined considerably in the following decade. See Hirano et al., 'Recent Developments', 252.

103. Elmer B. Potter and Chester Nimitz (eds), *The Great Sea War* (Englewood Cliffs, 1960); Chester Nimitz and Elmer B. Potter, *Nimittsu no taiheiyō no kaisen-shi* (Tokyo, 1962).

104. For Nimitz's donation of the royalties of the Japanese translation of his book, see Potter, *Nimitz*, 467; and Harris, *Admiral Nimitz*, 175.

105. Another Tōgō Shrine and a small museum were opened on 27 May 1971 in the town of Fukutsu, in the vicinity of the 1934 memorial monument.

106. Harald Salomon, 'Japan's Longest Days', in King-fai Tam et al., *Chinese and Japanese Films on the Second World War* (Abingdon, 2015), 126.

107. Salomon, 'Japan's Longest Days', 121; and Marie Thorsten and Geoffrey M. White, 'Binational Pearl Harbor?', *The Asia-Pacific Journal* 8 (2010), Issue 52, no. 2.

108. The story was simultaneously reprinted in six volumes. See Shiba Ryōtarō, *Saka no ue no kumo* (Tokyo, 1969–72). A four-volume English translation of the novel has also been published recently, with the last of these being largely devoted to the battle. See Shiba Ryōtarō, *Clouds above the Hill* (London, 2012–14).

109. For Shiba's literary legacy and its impact on Japan's war memory, see Donald Keene, *Five Modern Japanese Novelists* (New York, 2003), 85–100; and Hidehiro Nakao, 'The Legacy of Shiba Ryotaro', in Roy Starrs (ed.), *Japanese Cultural Nationalism at Home and in the Asia Pacific* (Folkestone, 2004), 99–115.

110. For Shiba's historical perspective, see Tomoko Aoyama, 'Japanese Literary Response to the Russo-Japanese War', in Wells and Wilson (eds), *The Russo-Japanese War in Cultural Perspective*, 79–82; and Alexander Bukh, 'Historical Memory and Shiba Ryōtarō', in Sven Saaler and Wolfgang Schwentker (eds), *The Power of Memory in Modern Japan* (Folkestone, 2008), 96–115.

111. See Nomura Naokuni, *Gensui Tōgō Heihachirō* (Tokyo, 1968); Yonezawa Fujiyoshi, *Tōgō Heihachirō* (Tokyo, 1972); and Togawa Yukio, *Nogi to Tōgō* (Tokyo, 1972).

112. Yoshimura Akira, *Umi no shigeki* (Tokyo, 1972). The book has been reissued in several editions and numerous reprints, most recently in 2003.

113. This serialized manga was also published in book form. See Ueda Shin and Takanuki Nobuhito, *Jitsuroku Nihonkai kaisen* (Tokyo, 2000).

114. Egawa Tatsuya, *Nichiro sensō monogatari* (Tokyo, 2001–6). Starting in 2001, the story was serialized in a leading manga weekly for five years and then reissued gradually in 22 independent volumes.

115. For the differences between Egawa's and Shiba's works, see Yukiko Kitamura, 'Serial War: Egawa Tatsuya's Tale of the Russo-Japanese War', in John W. Steinberg et al. (eds), *The Russo-Japanese War*, 2:427–30.

116. Following the novel's success and due to the author's prominence, the city of Matsuyama opened a museum commemorating the novel (the Saka no Ue no Kumo Museum) in 2007, which is housed in a building designed by the famed Japanese architect Ando Tadao.

117. The 13 episodes were highly popular in Japan, with an average viewership rating of 14.5 per cent, and two episodes reaching as much as 19.6 per cent.

118. Hirose Takeo, 'Nichiro sensō o megutte', in Roshiashi Kenkyūkai (ed.), *Nichiro 200 nen* (Tokyo, 1993), 106.

119. See Toyoda Jō, 'Tōgō Heihachirō', in Bungei Shunjū (ed.), *Nihon no ronten* (Tokyo, 1992), 594–601; and Ienaga, 'Glorification of War', 129–31.

120. For an overview of these textbooks, see Elena Kolesova and Ryota Nishino, 'Talking Past Each Other?' *Aoyama Journal of International Studies* 2 (2015), 22–3.

121. For the ceremony, see Hirano et al., 'Recent Developments', 252.

122. The presumed link with these two foreign warships has also been maintained on the Memorial Ship Mikasa's webpage. They are 'the world's three largest memorial ships,' the webpage text states, 'because they bravely fought in historic naval battles to protect their respective nation's independence.' Available online at https://www.kinenkan-mikasa.or.jp/mikasa/big3.html (accessed 1 March 2020).

123. Patalano, *Post-War Japan*, 90.

124. See Colin Joyce, 'Japan proudly flies battle flag again', *The Telegraph*, 6 January 2005.

125. For this monument and the 'pacifist' aspects of the battle's recent commemoration, see Hirano et al., 'Recent Developments', 253–7.

126. By the same token, the commander of the United States Seventh Fleet is invited every year to take part as a guest of honour in the commemoration ceremony on board the *Mikasa* despite the fact that the US navy did not take part in the battle. See Tsukada Shūichi, 'Taiken naki sensō no kioku no genba', *Mita shakaigaku* 23 (2018), 94.

127. This trend can be seen in the celebration of the humane treatment of German POWs in the Bando Camp, Shikoku, in both the restored site and the subsequent feature film (*Baruto no gakuen*, 2006). Another facet of it is the recent public reverence for the Japanese consul Sugihara Chiune. Granting visas to Jewish refugees in Lithuania in 1940, this diplomat and his deeds are presently commemorated in several museums, including the 'Port of Humanity' (Jpn. *Jindo no minato*) in the city of Tsuruga. For the movement to reform Japan's historical image, see Masami Saito et al., 'Dissecting the Wave of Books on Nippon Kaigi', *The Asia-Pacific Journal* 16 (2018).

128. In 2015, 253,000 guests visited the Memorial Ship Mikasa. During the same year, the Mikasa Preservation Society had as many as 3,790 members. See Tsukada, 'Taiken', 89–90.

129. For the use of this narrative in recent ceremonies on board the *Mikasa* that also deplores Japan's weak reaction to the 'unlawful invasion of China' and the unsettled state of affairs with North Korea and Russia, see Tsukada, 'Taiken', 93.

130. In this spirit, the committee that stood behind the erection of the new monument suggested in 2004 that 'present-day Japan has lost its self-confidence'. Accordingly, national pride could be fostered by 'handing on the inheritance of 27 May and engraving it in the hearts of the Japanese people. Only then will our country, Nippon, be able to recover its great hopes and dreams. Our committee continues to plead for a return to the old Japan and considers this an opportunity to reassert [the values of] "Bushidō JAPAN", "genuine nationalism", and the creation of a proud Japan as objectives for future generations.' Cited in Hirano et al., 'Recent Developments', 254.

Chapter 4

1. Anna Akhmatova, *Sochineniia* (Moscow, 1986), 1:284. See also Apushkin, *Russko-iaponskaia voina*, 315.

2. See e.g. a report of the American ambassador George von Lengerke Meyer, 2 June 1905, in Tyler Dennet, *Roosevelt and the Russo-Japanese War* (New York, 1925), 217. It is possible that the loss of Port Arthur in early January 1905 had given the Russian public a similar shock, but now, due to the revolution, reactions were more open and evident.

3. British diplomat Arthur Henry Hardinge in a message to the Secretary of State for Foreign Affairs Lansdowne, 5 June 1905, in G.P. Gooch and Harold Temperley (eds), *British Documents on the Origins of the War* (London, 1926–38), 4:83. See also 'Feeling in St Petersburg', *The Times*, 1 June 1905, 5.

4. Aleksandr Kuprin, *Shtabs-Kapitan Ribnikov* (St Petersburg, 1906). For an English translation, see Aleksandr Kuprin, 'Captain Ribnikov', in Gerri Kimber et al. (eds), *The Poetry and Critical Writings of Katherine Mansfield* (Edinburgh, 2014), 165.

5. For Russian journalism during the war against Japan and the Revolution of 1905, see Louise McReynolds, *The News under Russia's Old Regime* (Princeton, 1991), 168–222.

6. *Peterburgskaia Gazeta*, no. 127, 31 May 1905.

7. S. Galai, 'The Impact of War on the Russian Liberals in 1904–5', *Government and Opposition* 1 (1965), 105–6.

8. Galai, 'The Impact', 106.

9. *Russkoe Slovo*, no. 254, 23 June 1905.

10. For the attitudes of Jews in Russia and beyond towards the war, see Shillony, *The Jews and the Japanese*, 143–50.

11. See e.g. 'HaMilchama al HaYam', *Ha-Tsfira*, 30 May 1905, 1; 'HaMilchama', *HaSman*, 2 June 1905, 1. For an overview of the battle, expressing appreciation for Japanese patriotism and hope for Russian resurrection, see 'Acharei Milchemet HaYapanim VehaRussim al pnei HaYam', *Ha-Tsfira*, 4 June 1905, 1.

12. 'Hamilchama', *Machsike Hadas*, 2 June 1905, 6. At the time, Lviv was part of the Austria–Hungary Empire.

13. See Raymond Esthus, *Double Eagle and the Rising Sun* (Durham, 1988), 5.

14. Grand Duke Alexander, *Once a Grand Duke* (New York, 1932), 223. According to the author, the news about the battle arrived by a messenger during a picnic party at the Gatchina Palace on the unlikely date of 27 May 1905.

15. Nicholas II, *Dnevnik imperatora Nikolaia II* (Berlin, 1923), 201.

16. Nicholas II, *Dnevnik*, 201.

17. For the tsar's pre-war perceptions of Japan, see Rotem Kowner, 'Nicholas II and the Japanese Body', *The Psychohistory Review* 26 (1998), 211–52. For the tsar's view of the war on the eve of the Battle of Tsushima, see Raymond Esthus, 'Nicholas II and the Russo-Japanese War', *Russian Review* 40 (1981), 403.

18. Esthus, 'Nicholas II', 404. See also Sergei Witte's perspective in this respect in his *The Memoirs of Count Witte* (Garden City, 1921), 132. For a slightly different version of this perspective, see Wcislo, *Tales of Imperial Russia*, 189.

19. Esthus, 'Nicholas II', 404. Russia was far from losing Siberia. With some one million Russian soldiers assembled in northern Manchuria by June 1905 and Japan suffering great losses and seeking peace, the prospects for Russia to further losing substantial territory were very low.

20. Boris A. Romanov (ed.), 'Konets russko-iaponskoĭ voiny (Voennoe soveshchanie 24 Maia 1905 goda v Tsarskom Sele)', *Krasnyi arkhiv* 3 (1928), 201.

21. Esthus, 'Nicholas II', 405.

22. Aleksei Kuropatkin, *The Russian Army and the Japanese War* (New York, 1909), 1:241–2.

23. For major overviews of the Revolution of 1905, see Sidney Harcave, *First Blood* (New York, 1964); and Abraham Ascher, *The Revolution of 1905* (Stanford, 1988).

24. For the development of a domestic crisis in Russia from February to May 1905 and the eruption of the 'Tsushima crisis', see Roberta Manning, *The Crisis of the Old Order in Russia* (Princeton, 1982), 89–105.
25. For the events on board the *Potemkin*, see John Bushnell, *Mutiny Amid Repression* (Bloomington, 1993), 55–65; Neal Bascomb, *Red Mutiny* (Boston, 2007); and Iu. Kardashev, *Vosstanie: Drama na Tendre* (Kirov, 2008). For the death toll, see Robert Weinberg, *The Revolution of 1905 in Odessa* (Bloomington, 1993), 136.
26. By the end of August 1905, Russian manpower at the Manchurian theatre reached 788,000 men, 562 battalions. See Levitskii, *Russko-Iaponskaia voina*, 386.
27. See Jonathan Frankel, 'The War and the Fate of the Tsarist Autocracy', in Kowner (ed.), *The Impact*, 63.
28. Menshikov is associated with the first textual reference to the *Protocols of the Elders of Zion* in 1902. See Cesare De Michelis, *The Non-Existent Manuscript* (Lincoln, 2004), 23–37.
29. Mikhail O. Menshikov, 'Polyaki i Tsusima', *Novoe Vremia*, 18 February 1908.
30. Frankel, 'The War', 65.
31. Abraham Ascher, *P.A. Stolypin* (Stanford, 2001), 137–49.
32. Witte, *The Memoirs*, 132.
33. John Leyland, 'The Russo-Japanese Naval Campaign', in J. Leyland and T.A. Brassey (eds), *The Naval Annual, 1906* (Portsmouth, 1906), 116.
34. Roderick McLean, 'Dreams of a German Europe', in Annika Mombauer and Wilhelm Deist (eds), *The Kaiser* (Cambridge, 2004), 119–42.
35. See Rotem Kowner, 'The High Road to World War I? Europe and Outcomes of the Russo-Japanese War', in Chiharu Inaba, John Chapman, and Masayoshi Matsumura (eds), *Rethinking the Russo-Japanese War: The Nichinan Papers* (Folkestone, 2007), 294–7.
36. For the annexation and the breakdown of the equilibrium in south-east Europe, see David Stevenson, *Armaments and the Coming of War* (Oxford, 1996), 112–64.
37. Robert Seton-Watson, *Sarajevo* (London, 1926), 36.
38. For the Russo-Japanese rapprochement in the years before the First World War, see Berton, *Russo-Japanese Relations*, 2–7; and Pestushko and. Shulatov, 'Russo-Japanese Relations', 101–18.
39. Although secret, the text of the agreement was communicated to both France and Britain. See Berton, *Russo-Japanese Relations*, 3.
40. See Mikhail Petrov, *Podgotovka Rossiĭ k mirovoi voine na more* (Moscow, 1926), 95, 103; and Donald Mitchell, *A History of Russian and Soviet Sea Power* (New York, 1974), 269.
41. For the structure and vessels of the IRN in 1906, see The Editors, 'The Progress of Navies', 25–8.
42. Peter Gatrell, *Government, Industry, and Rearmament in Russia* (New York, 1994), 71.

43. For the IRN's relative position in 1906–10, see Evans and Peattie, *Kaigun*, 147. Its position as the world's sixth largest navy in 1906 is corroborated also by Modelsky and Thompson, *Seapower in Global Politics*, 123. In aggregate tonnage, the IRN lost more than half of its pre-war displacement. By 1 June 1905, it was about 224,000 tons, below that of the IJN and the Italian Regia Marina (in fifth and sixth place). For the world media's attention to this fact, see 'Sea Strength of the Naval Powers', *Scientific American* 93, no. 2 (8 July 1905), 26; and 'Russia Seventh of Naval Powers, Was Third until Admiral Togo Won His Victory', *The New York Times*, 2 June 1905, 1.

44. Klado, *The Battle*, 130.

45. See Aleksei Shishov, *Rossiia i Iaponiia* (Moscow, 2001), 340–5.

46. Writers would often portray him 'either as a bullying incompetent taking advantage of the Tsar's favour, or as a tragic victim of tsarist mismanagement'. See Westwood, *Witnesses of Tshushima*, xi.

47. Pleshakov, *The Tsar's*, 321–6.

48. For the decision to reinstate Rozhestvenskiĭ, dated from 29 January 1906, see RGAVMF, Fund 406, inventory 9, case 3560, sheet 1–13 vol.

49. For the view that the tsar stood behind the trial, see Pleshakov, *The Tsar's*, 326–7.

50. 'Rojestvensky Talks: Admiral Who Lost to Togo Blame English', *The Spokane Press*, 3 January 1906, 1. See also Pleshakov, *The Tsar's*, 328–30.

51. Among the officers put on trial were Rozhestvenskiĭ's two staff officers, Captain Konstantin Clapier de Colongue (1859–1945) and Colonel Vladimir Filippovskiĭ, as well as Commander Vladimir Semenov. See Thiess, *The Voyage*, 388–9. For their testimonies before the Commission, see Russia, *Russko-iaponskaia voina 1904–05. Deistvia flota*, 4:79–84; 106–9, 85–105, respectively.

52. 'Rojestvensky Guilty: Admiral Enters Plea to Save Members of His Staff', *New York Tribune*, 5 July 1906, 1. For his testimony before the commission, see Russia, *Russko-iaponskaia voina 1904–05. Deistvia flota*, 4: 9–42. For his reports sent to the Naval Ministry from Sasebo (July 1905) and submitted on 20 March 1906, see Russia, *Russko-iaponskaia voina 1904–05. Deistvia flota*, 3:597–616, and 617–32, respectively.

53. 'Rojestvensky Freed: Court Martial Acquits Admiral', *New York Tribune*, 11 July 1906, 3. See also Pleshakov, *The Tsar's*, 331–3.

54. Cited in Gribovskiĭ, *Vitse-admiral Z.P. Rozhestvenskiĭ*, 309.

55. For Enkvist's testimony before the Commission, see Russia, *Russko-iaponskaia voina 1904–05. Deistvia flota*, 4:61–9.

56. For Nebogatov's testimony before the Commission, see Russia, *Russko-iaponskaia voina 1904–05. Deistvia flota*, 4:43–60.

57. Richard Plaschka, *Matrosen, Offiziere, Rebellen, Krisenkonfrontationen zur See* (Vienna, 1984), 1:283.

58. Denis Warner and Peggy Warner, *The Tide at Sunrise* (New York, 1974), 518.

59. Commander Shvede, the captain of the *Orël* at the time of her surrender was acquitted since his badly damaged ship was found to be unfit for further fighting. In fact, he had replaced the mortally wounded Captain Nikolai Yung only several hours earlier.

60. Nebogatov's surrender and consequent trial led to a long-lasting debate about his decision. See e.g. Generalmajor D. C. von Zepelin, 'Die Kapitulation des "Bjödowy" und der Schiffe Nebogatows', *Marine-Rundschau* (1907), 186–96; Hans-Otto Rieve, 'Admiral Nebogatov—Schuld oder Schicksal', *Marine-Rundschau* 1 (1964), 1–11; Alexander Meurer, *Seekriegsgeschichte in Umrissen* (Leipzig, 1941), 402; Warner and Warner, *The Tide at Sunrise*, 516–19; Vladimir Gribovskiĭ, 'Krostniĭ put' otriada Nebogatova', *Gangut* 3 (1992), 34.

61. Afflerbach, 'Going Down with Flying Colours?', 200.

62. See Kowner, *Historical Dictionary*, 368, 513.

63. See Gribovskiĭ, 'Krostniĭ put', 34.

64. Vinogradov, 'Battleship Development', 269.

65. Rudnev's fame in tsarist Russia was brief, however. Unwilling to take disciplinary measure against his mutinous crew, he was placed on the inactive list by the end of 1905. Two years later, Emperor Meiji awarded him the Order of the Rising Sun, 2nd class. No Russian participants at the battle of Tsushima won this honour. See Kowner, *Historical Dictionary*, 460–1.

66. See Petrov, *Podgotovka Rossiĭ*, 99–100; Kornelliĭ Shatsillo, *Russkiĭ imperializm i razvitieflota nakanune pervoi mirovoi voiny* (Moscow, 1968), 173–4.

67. See Evgenii Podsoblyaev, 'The Russian Naval General Staff', *Journal of Military History* 66 (2002), 42–3.

68. Along with the *Novoe Vremia*, the main venues in this post-Tsushima discourse were *Sankt-Peterburgskie vedomosti*, *Slovo*, and *Voenni Golos*, and the naval magazine *Morskoi sbornik*. For a sample of these early articles, see Podsoblyaev, 'The Russian Naval General Staff', 46 n.31. See also the six-article series of criticism on naval reform by E.K. Brut, 'Reforma flota', *Novoe Vremia*, 5–18 February 1908.

69. The most important overviews of IRN's reorganization and rebuilding in the aftermath of the Battle of Tsushima are still Petrov, *Podgotovka Rossiĭ*, especially 90–129; and Shatsillo, *Russkiĭ imperializm*. In English, see Peter Gatrell, 'After Tsushima: Economic and Administrative Aspects of Russian Naval Rearmament', *Economic History Review* 43 (1990), 255–72; Podsoblyaev, 'The Russian Naval General Staff', 37–69; and Tony Demchak, 'Rebuilding the Russian Fleet', *Journal of Slavic Military Studies* 26 (2013), 25–40. For a general overview of the evolution of the IRN until the First World War, see Mitchell, *A History*, 267–82.

70. Cited in Podsoblyaev, 'The Russian Naval General Staff', 51.

71. Cited in Podsoblyaev, 'The Russian Naval General Staff', 51.

72. For the programme, see Petrov, *Podgotovka Rossiĭ*, 110–19.

73. Petrov, *Podgotovka Rossiĭ*, 133–6; Westwood, *Russian Naval Construction*, 51–3.

74. For the initial discussions of the expedition soon after the debacle in Tsushima, see William Barr, 'Tsarist Attempt at Opening the Northern Sea Route: The Arctic Ocean Hydrographic Expedition, 1910–1915', *Polarforschung* 45 (1972), 54–5. See also N.A. Transehe, 'The Siberian Sea Road: The Work of the Russian Hydrographical Expedition to the Arctic 1910–1915', *Geographical Review* 15, no. 3 (1925), 367–98; I.Ye. Kuksin, 'The Arctic Ocean Hydrographic Expedition 1910–1915', *Polar Geography and Geology* 15 (1991), 299–309.

75. By Russian definition, the Northern Sea Route is a portion of the Northeast Passage as it does not include the Barents Sea and therefore does not reach the Atlantic Ocean. For this route and its history, see Marcus Matthias Keupp, 'The Northern Sea Route: Introduction and Overview', in M.M. Keupp (ed.), *The Northern Sea Route* (Wiesbaden, 2015), 7–20.

76. See Andreas Renner, 'Markt, Staat, Propaganda: Der Nördliche Seeweg in Russlands Arktisplänen', *Osteuropa* 70, no. 5 (2020), 39–59.

77. Podsoblyaev, 'The Russian Naval General Staff', 67.

78. For the development of Russia's battleships in the decade after the Battle of Tsushima, see Vinogradov, 'Battleship Development', 118–41.

79. The first German, American, Japanese, and French dreadnoughts were commissioned in October 1909, March 1910, March 1912, and November 1913, respectively.

80. N. Nordman, 'Nashi morskie budzheti', *Morskoi Sbornik* 379, no. 12 (1913), 77. For the portion of battleships, reaching 64 per cent according to some calculations, see Vinogradov, 'Battleship Development', 284. For the total military budget, see Fuller, *Civil–Military Conflict*, 227.

81. For this conclusion, see Petrov, *Podgotovka Rossii*, 184.

82. For Russia's planned naval construction for the period 1917–29 on the eve of the First World War, see Vinogradov, 'Battleship Development', 286, Table 1.2.

83. For a brief review of the Baltic Fleet during the First World War, see O'Hara and Heinz, Clash of the Fleets, 60–6, 116–36, 190–4, 244–57, 304–5.

84. For the mutiny, see Paul Avrich, *Kronstadt, 1921* (Princeton, 1970).

85. Cited in George Hudson, 'Soviet Naval Doctrine under Lenin and Stalin', *Soviet Studies* 28 (1976), 43.

86. Jürgen Rohwer and Mikhail Monakov, *Stalin's Ocean-Going Fleet* (Portland, 2001) 69–109.

87. Milan Hauner, 'Stalin's Big-Fleet Program', *Naval War College Review* 57, No. 2 (2004), 115.

88. For the commemoration of the war in Russia, see Dmitrii Oleinikov, 'The War in Russian Historical Memory', in Steinberg et al. (eds), *The Russo-Japanese War*, 1:509–22; and Shillony and Kowner. 'The Memory', 1–9.

89. Cited in Aaron Cohen, 'Long Ago and Far Away', *Russian Review* 69 (2010), 388.

90. For media references to Tsushima in describing the failure of the Russian government in its meddling in the Balkan Crisis in 1912, see David McDonald, *United Government and Foreign Policy in Russia* (Cambridge, 1992), 189.

91. Cited in David Wells, 'The Russo-Japanese War in Russian Literature', in Wells and Wilson (eds), *The Russo-Japanese War in Cultural Perspective*, 124. Tolstoy was remarkable, nonetheless, for expressing also his respect for the Japanese fighting qualities in the wake of the battle. See Barry Scherr, 'The Russo-Japanese War and the Russian Literary Imagination', in Steinberg et al. (eds), *The Russo-Japanese War*, 1:440.

92. There are several overviews of this specific impact of the Russo-Japanese War in general and the Battle of Tsushima in particular, e.g. Wells, 'The Russo-Japanese War'; Rosamund Bartlett, 'Japonisme and Japanophobia', *Russian Review* 67 (2008), 24–9; and Susanna Lim, *China and Japan in the Russian Imagination* (Abingdon, 2013), 149–61.

93. For the poem in both Russian and English translation, see Wells, 'The Russo-Japanese War', 117–18 (for additional poems on Tsushima in contemporary Russia, see pp. 109, 114–16).

94. Andrei Bely, *Petersburg* (St Petersburg, 1913). For an English translation, see Andrei Bely, *Petersburg* (Bloomington, 1978).

95. For a similar literal expression of fear of the 'yellow peril' following the battle, see symbolist novelist Dmitriĭ Merezhkovskiĭ's article entitled *Griadushchiĭ kham* (*The Approaching Boor*, 1906). For Merezhkovskiĭ's views, see Lim, *China and Japan*, 156–8.

96. Semenov's books include the trilogy *Rasplata*, *Boi Pri Tsusime*, and *Tsena Krovi* (St Petersburg, 1906) and the posthumously published *Flot i Morskoe Vedomstvo do Tsushimi i Posle* (St Petersburg, 1911). For the trilogy's English translation, see *The Battle of Tsu-Shima* (1906); *Rasplata (The Reckoning)* (1909); and *The Price of Blood* (1910).

97. For Klado's analysis of the causes for the Russian debacle in the battle, see Klado, *The Battle*, 126–30.

98. *Novoe Vremia*, 26 May 1908, cited in Cohen, 'Long Ago and Far Away', 400.

99. The imperial family donated at least 50,000 roubles for its construction (some 18 per cent of the total cost). See Cohen, 'Long Ago and Far Away', 397.

100. For Russian fascination with Japan in the decade before the First World War, see Bartlett, 'Japonisme and Japanophobia', 30–3; Lim, *China and Japan*, 161–9.

101. For the making of the Great War as a 'national war' and contrasting it with the war against Japan, see Christopher Stroop, 'Thinking the Nation through Times of Trial', in Murray Frame et al. (eds), *Russian Culture in War and Revolution* (Bloomington, 2014), 2:207; and William Fuller, *Strategy and Power in Russia* (New York, 1992), 408–9.

102. The most extensive study of the Soviet view of the Russo-Japanese War is Shimizu Takehisa, *Soren to Nichiro sensō* (Tokyo, 1973).

103. Cited in Isaac Deutscher, *Stalin* (London, 1949), 528. For Lenin's views of the war, see Shimizu, *Soren*, 45–140.

104. Vladimir Lenin, 'The Debacle', from *Proletariĭ*, no. 3, 9 June 1905; in Vladimir Lenin, *Collected Works* (Moscow, 1960–7), 7:389.

105. One of the figures the Soviets commemorated in the 1920s was Petr Schmidt, the naval officer who in November 1905 led a large uprising within the fleet units in Sevastopol, the headquarters and main base of the Black Sea Fleet, and following its suppression was executed by the authorities. See Robert Zebroski, 'Lieutenant Peter Petrovich Schmidt: Officer, Gentleman, and Reluctant Revolutionary', *Jahrbücher für Geschichte Osteuropas* 59 (2011), 28–50.

106. The decision for this demolition was made, allegedly, by Sergei Kirov (1886–1934), the powerful First Secretary of the Leningrad Regional Committee of the All-Union Communist Party, in all likelihood independently of the central government.

107. For the enthusiast reception of the book in 1932 and its long-lasting popularity, see Oleinikov, 'The War', 515–16.

108. The first Russian edition of volumes one and two sold 925,000 and 520,700 copies, respectively. See translators' note in Aleksei Novikov-Priboi, *Tsushima* (London, 1936), i.

109. Aleksei Novikov-Priboi, *Tsushima*, 2 vols. (Moscow, 1935–36); Aleksei Novikov-Priboi, *Nihonkai sensen* (Tokyo, 1933–35); Alexey Novikoff-Priboy, *La tragédie de Tsoushima* (Paris, 1934); Alexey Novikoff-Priboy, *Tsushima* (London, 1936).

110. See J.N. Westwood, 'Novikov-Priboi as Naval Historian', *Slavic Review* 28 (1969), 297–303.

111. For the escalation in Russo-Japanese relations during the 1930s, see Ryōchi Tobe, 'Japan's Policy toward the Soviet Union, 1931–1941', in Streltsov and Shimotomai (eds), *A History of Russo-Japanese Relations*, 201–17; and Anastasia Lozhkina, Yaroslav Shulatov, and Kirill Cherevko, 'Soviet–Japanese Relations after the Manchurian Incident, 1931–1939', in Streltsov and Shimotomai (eds), *A History of Russo-Japanese Relations*, 218–37.

112. Nikolai Levitskiĭ, *Russko-Iaponskaia voina 1904–1905 gg.* (Moscow, 1936); Aleksandr Svechin, *Strategiia XX veka na pervom etape* (Moscow, 1937). For an English translation of Stepanov's novel, see Aleksandr Stepanov, *Port Arthur, Historical Narrative* (Moscow, 1947).

113. In 1943, the process of rehabilitation of imperial symbols reached a new stage with the reintroduction of shoulder plates for military personnel. It was an incredible turn considering that earlier the term '*zoloto-pogonniki*' (gold-shoulder-platers) was used derisively to refer to soldiers of the White movement. Furthermore, thereafter veterans were allowed to wear their imperial decorations received during the First World War and even the Russo-Japanese War.

114. Levitskiĭ, *Russko-Iaponskaia voina* (Moscow, 2003), 397.
115. Levitskiĭ, *Russko-Iaponskaia voina*, 399–400. Based on detailed tables comparing the two fleets, Levitskiĭ concluded that 'the rate of fire of the Russian artillery was 2–3 times less than the Japanese; the Japanese fleet exceeded the Russian one by 2.5 times the amount of metal emitted per minute; [and] the explosive charge in the Japanese shells was 5–6 times greater than in the Russian shells.'
116. Levitskiĭ, *Russko-Iaponskaia voina*, 404.
117. Levitskiĭ, *Russko-Iaponskaia voina*, 405.
118. Bikov, *Russko-Iaponskaia voina*, 565.
119. Bikov, *Russko-Iaponskaia voina*, 587–8.
120. Interestingly, both Levitskiĭ and Bikov referred only briefly to Nebogatov's surrender and none of them vilified him. Cf. Apushkin's negative outlook a few years after the battle in his *Russko-iaponskaia voina*, 310–12.
121. Bikov, *Russko-Iaponskaia voina*, 605.
122. Bikov, *Russko-Iaponskaia voina*, 605.
123. The best account of these clashes is still Alvin Coox, *Nomonhan: Japan against Russia* (Stanford, 1985).
124. See L. Gench, 'Tridtsat piat let nazad. Teper', *Krokodil* 3 (1939), 3, cited in Yulia Mikhailova, 'Japan's Place in Russian and Soviet National Identity', in Mikhailova and Steele (eds), *Japan and Russia*, 84. Volochaefka and Spask were two sites in which Bolshevik partisans defeated IJN troops during the Siberian Intervention of 1918–22.
125. Andrew Grajdanzev, 'Japan in Soviet Publications', *Far Eastern Survey* 13, no. 24 (1944), 224–5.
126. Cited in Deutscher, *Stalin*, 528.
127. Derevyanko was a signatory to the Japanese Instrument of Surrender and then the Soviet representative at the headquarters of the Supreme Commander for the Allied Powers (SCAP) in Tokyo. See Potter, *Nimitz*, 398, 466.
128. The last veteran, a sailor on board the *Svetlana*, died in 1975. See Oleinikov, 'The War', 510, 521.
129. This wave began with Sergei Bondarchuk's four-part *Voina i mir* (*War and Peace*) in 1966–7, the most expensive film made in the Soviet Union; the historical drama film *Beg* (*The Flight*). For a concurrent transition in the image of the White Movement, see Alexander Fedorov, 'The Image of the White Movement in the Soviet Films of 1950s–1980s', *European Journal of Social and Human Sciences* 9 (2016), 28–31.
130. See Viktor V. Kuz'minkov and Viktor N. Pavlyatenko, 'Soviet–Japanese Relations from 1960 to 1985', in Streltsov and Shimotomai (eds), *A History of Russo-Japanese Relations*, 425–34.
131. 'Japan: Treasure off Tsushima', *Time* 116, no. 16, 20 October 1980. One of the ship's 2-3-millimetre guns was brought out of the water and is now on display on Mogihama beach, Tsushima.

132. In 2007, some mosaics which had been removed from the previous church just before its demolition and discovered in 1995 were returned to the site.
133. Cited in Kolesova and Nishino, 'Talking Past', 25.
134. Kolesova and Nishino, 'Talking Past', 25–6.
135. See e.g. Aleksandr Chubaryan, *Istoriia Rossii XX-nachalo XXI veka. 11 klass* (Moscow, 2007), 32.
136. Cited in Leonid Smorgunov, 'Strategies of Representation', in Mikhailova and Steele (eds), *Japan and Russia*, 204.
137. Jiji Press English News Service (17 February 2005), 1. For mutual visits and joint exercises conducted by the Russian and Japanese navies, see Vladimir Solntsev, 'Russia, Japan to Hold Joint Naval Exercises', *TASS News Wire* (1 June 1998), 1; Vladimir Solntsev, 'Russian Navy to Attend Joint Exercise with Japan', *TASS News Wire* (15 September 2001), 1.
138. Six years later, Korean representatives handed Russian authorities in Seoul the flag of the cruiser *Variag*. After the Battle of Chemulpo, it was raised from the sea floor, and had been kept in a local museum. See 'Historic Ship's Flag Returns Home to Russia', *Naval History* 25 (February 2011), 11.
139. For Russo-Japanese relations during the 2000s, see Hidetake Kawaraji, 'Japanese–Russian Relations in the 21st Century, 2001–2015', in Streltsov and Shimotomai (eds), *A History of Russo-Japanese Relations*, 521–34; and Dmitry Streltsov, 'The Territorial Issue in Russian–Japanese Relations', in Streltsov and Shimotomai (eds), *A History of Russo-Japanese Relations*, 577–606.
140. See Hirano et al., 'Recent Developments', 252, 255.
141. For a brief overview of these books, see David Schimmelpenninck van der Oye, 'Rewriting the Russo-Japanese War: A Centenary Retrospective', *Russian Review* 67 (2008), 81.
142. Nine per cent of the respondents mentioned Tsushima, whereas 8 per cent mentioned Port Arthur or the Variag. See Cohen, 'Long Ago and Far Away', 411.

Chapter 5

1. Yang, *Technology of Empire*, 35.
2. See Kowner, *Historical Dictionary*, 589–90; Michael Sweeney and N.T. Roelsgaard, *Journalism and The Russo-Japanese War* (Lanham, 2020).
3. See e.g. Slattery, *Reporting the Russo-Japanese War*; Philip Towle, 'British War Correspondents and the War', in Kowner (ed.), *Rethinking*, 319–31; Michael S. Sweeney, '"Delays and Vexation"', *Journalism and Mass Communication Quarterly* 75 (1998), 548–59.
4. Despite considerable technological improvement made during the war, telegrams sent from Japan to Europe and the United States still travelled for some seven to ten hours, or even longer, depending on delays in relays or technical problems. Cf. Yang, *Technology of Empire*, 37; Jorma Ahvenainen, *The Far Easter Telegraphs* (Helsinki, 1981).

5. See e.g. '17 Ships off the Saddle Islands', *Exeter and Plymouth Gazette*, 27 May 1905, 6; 'Rozhdestvensky's Possible Routes', *Birmingham Mail*, 27 May 1905, 2.

6. *The Sphere*, 21, no. 279, 27 May 1905, 1.

7. 'The Great Naval Battle', *Newcastle Evening Chronicle*, 29 May 1905, 4; 'Rodjestvensky's Fleet Annihilated', *Liverpool Echo*, 29 May 1905, 8. see also 'Great Naval Battle in Korean Straits; Japanese Success', *Eastern Daily Press*, 29 May 1905, 5.

8. 'Reported Japanese Success', *The Times*, 29 May 1905, 5; 'Great Japanese Victory', *The Times*, 30 May 1905, 5.

9. See e.g. 'The Japanese losses so far are reported to be one cruiser and ten torpedo-boats' in 'The Japanese Losses', *The Daily Telegraph & Courier*, 30 May 1905, 9.

10. *The Times*, 2 June 1905. See also 'Britons Eulogize Togo: Jubilation over Japan's Victory, Which Is Compared to Trafalgar', *The New York Times*, 30 May 1905, 2.

11. See, however, 'The Destruction of Russian Armada off Japan by Admiral Togo's Fleet, *The Sphere*, 3, 6–7, June 1905, 1.

12. See e.g. 'Russian Fleet is Sighted', *Daily Capital*, 27 May 1905, 1; 'Rojestvensky's Fleet Keeps in Public Eye', *Waterbury Evening Democrat*, 27 May 1905, 1; 'Russian Fleet Has Reassembled on China Coast', *The Washington Times*, 27 May 1905, 1.

13. 'Russia Has Laugh on Japan: Rojestvensky's Fleet Evades the Japanese and is Seen Sailing through Japan's Fishpond', *Bismark Daily*, 27 May 1905, 1.

14. 'Naval Battle is Expected', *The Bemidji Daily Pioneer*, 27 May 1905, 1.

15. See e.g. 'Issue of Great Battle in the Korean Strait Is Not Yet Confirmed: Rumors That Fight Has Taken Place Already', *The St. Louis Republic*, 28 May 1905, 1; 'Fleets May Be in Battle: Togo in Good Position', *The Sun* (New York), 28 May 1905, 1; 'Naval Battle Now Raging?', *Daily Press*, 28 May 1905, 1.

16. *Los Angeles Times*, 28 May 1905, 1.

17. *The San Francisco Call*, 29 May 1905, 1, 5.

18. *New York Tribune*, 29 May 1905, 1.

19. *The Washington Times*, 29 May 1905, 1.

20. See e.g. 'Nineteen Russian Warship Are Sunk or Captured: Destruction of Remnant of the Fleet Continues', *The San Francisco Call*, 30 May 1905, 1; 'Part of Russia's Grand Armada Destroyed or Captured in Battle', *The Washington Times*, 30 May 1905, 1.

21. See e.g. 'Comparative Strength of the Rival Fleets', *New York Tribune*, 29 May 1905, 2; 'Dispatches from World Centers Bearing on the Great Sea Fight', *The Washington Times*, 29 May 1905, 2.

22. 'Flying Shells Strike Rojestvensky; Five of the Fugitives Elude Togo; Saturday's Big Battle Described; Borodino's End', *Baltimore Evening Herald*, 30 May 1905, 1.

23. Marion Rodgers, *Mencken: The American Iconoclast* (Oxford, 2006), 97.

24. H.L. Mencken, *Newspaper Days* (New York, 1941), 274–5. See also Sweeney and Roelsgaard, *Journalism*, 35.

25. See e.g. 'Togo and Rojestvensky Clash in Korea Straits: Both Fleets Crippled', *The St. Louis Republic*, 29 May 1905, 1; 'Russian Fleet is Smashed by Togo', *The Topeka State Journal*, 29 May 1905, 1; and 'Brief Reports Tell Togo's Story of Great Achievement', *The San Francisco Call*, 30 May 1905, 1.

26. See e.g. 'Central Figure in Orient is Admiral Togo of Japan', *The San Francisco Call*, 21 February 1904, 24.

27. 'Togo and Nelson', *Evening Star* (Washington, DC), 2 June 1905, 4; 'The Victorious Sun-Flag', *The Washington Times*, 4 June 1905, 34. This comparison would soon appear in books, e.g. Giuseppe Gavotti, *Tre grandi uomini di Mare* (Savona, 1911).

28. *The Washington Times*, 29 May 1905, 1.

29. *The Washington Times*, 30 May 1905, 1. For similar news, see also 'Wounded in the Head: Serious Injuries to Admiral Rojestvensky', *The Evening News* (Washington, DC), 30 May 1905, 1.

30. See e.g. 'Czar's Fleet Wiped Out', *The Evening World*, 29 May 1905, 1.

31. The news of the surrender appeared first on the pages of a German-language newspaper, based on reports from Berlin. See 'Der Zusammen-bruch', *Indiana Tribüne*, 30 May 1905, 3. On the same day, it was followed by 'Nebogatoff's Surrender Humiliating', *The Hawaiian Star*, 30 May 1905, 1 and some other evening editions.

32. See e.g. 'Threw Wounded Men Overboard', *Los Angeles Herald*, 3 June 1905, 2; 'A Contemptible Spectacle: Correspondent's Description of Nebogatoff's Surrender', *The New York Times*, 3 June 1905, 2.

33. See e.g. 'Treachery on Russian Ships', *The Evening World* (New York), 2 June 1905, 1; 'Rojestvensky's Skull Broken', *The Washington Times*, 31 May 1905, 1; 'Rojestvensky at Sasebo: His Skull Fractured, But the Doctors Say He Will Recover', *The New York Times*, 1 June 1905, 2; 'Rojestvensky Is Reported to Be Now Out of Danger', *The San Francisco Call*, 3 June 1905, 2.

34. See e.g. 'La flotte russe', *L'Intransigeant*, 28 May 1905, 2; 'La flotte russe dans le détroit de Corée' *L'Intransigeant*, 29 May 1905, 2.

35. Patrick Beillevaire, 'The Impact of the War on the French Political Scene', in Kowner (ed.), *The Impact*, 128–31.

36. 'Un désastre Russe: L'escadre Rodjestvensky anéantie', *Le Petit Parisien*, 30 May 1905, 1.

37. 'La bataille navale: Un désastre Russe', *Le Journal*, 30 May 1905, 1. See also 'La flotte Russe anéantie', *L'Aurore*, 30 May 1905, 1; 'La bataille du détroit de Corée: Catastrophe Navale', *Le Figaro*, 30 May 1905, 1.

38. 'Après le désastre: le bilan d'une bataille historique', *Le Petit Parisien*, 31 May 1905, 1; 'La poursuite continue le sort de Rodjestvinsky', *Le Journal*, 31 May 1905, 1; 'La défaite navale de Tsoushima', *L'Aurore*, 31 May 1905, 1; 'La défaite navale russe', *Le Figaro*, 31 May 1905, 4; 'Premiers rapports de Togo, *La Dépêche*, 31 May 1905, 3.

39. 'Le désastre Russe: la guerre doit finir', *Le Croix*, 31 May 1905, 1.
40. See, however, 'Les causes de la défaite russe', *Le Journal*, 3 June 1905, 1.
41. 'Roschdjestwensky geschlagen!', *Berliner Tageblatt*, 29 May 1905, 1; 'Der Sieg der Japaner zur See', *Berliner Tageblatt*, 29 May 1905, 1 (evening edition); 'Die baltische Flotte vernichtet!', *Berliner Volks-Zeitung*, 29 May 1905, 1. See also 'Sieg der japanischen Flotte', *Königlich privilegirte Berlinische Zeitung*, 29 May 1905, 1.
42. 'Der russisch-japanische Krieg: eine Seeschlacht', *Norddeutsche Allgemeine Zeitung*, 30 May 1905, 1; 'Die Seeschlacht bei Tsuschima', *Berliner Tageblatt*, 30 May 1905, 1. For a map, see 'Die Seeschlacht in der Tsuschima-Straße', *Berliner Volks-Zeitung*, 30 May 1905, 1.
43. Hitler to the Japanese ambassador to Berlin, Mushanokōji Kintomo, 15 September 1937. Cited in J.W.M. Chapman, 'Japan in Poland's Secret Neighborhood War', *Japan Forum* 7 (1995), 269.
44. 'Roschdjestwensky, Fölkersahm und Nebogatow gefangen?', *Berliner Tageblatt*, 31 May 1905, 1. See also 'Die Katastrophe in der Koreastraße', *Berliner Volks-Zeitung*, 31 May 1905, 1.
45. See e.g. 'Rußland und Japan', *Berliner Börsen-Zeitung*, 1 June 1905, 1; 'Kriegskunft und Staatskunft', *Königlich privilegirte Berlinische Zeitung*, 1 June 1905, 1.
46. *Simplicissimus*, 17 October 1905, 338. For the magazine's views of the war in Asia, see Peter Hugill, 'German Great-Power Relations in the Pages of "Simplicissimus"', *Geographical Review* 98 (2008), 13–16.
47. For the popular response to the battle in the non-Western world, see Pankaj Mishra, *From the Ruins of Empire* (New York, 2012), 7–13.
48. For the attitude of the Muslim world to the Russo-Japanese War, see Fernand Farjenel, 'Le Japon et l'Islam', *Revue du monde musulman* 1 (1907), 101–14; Klaus Kreiser, 'Der japanische Sieg über Rußland (1905)', *Die Welt des Islams* 21 (1981), 209–39; Hashem Rajabzadeh, 'Russo-Japanese War as Told by Iranians', *Annals of Japan Association for Middle East Studies* 3 (1988), 144–66; Rina Bieganiec, 'Distant Echoes', in Kowner (ed.), *Rethinking*, 444–55.
49. Steven Marks, '"Bravo, Brave Tiger of the East!"', in Steinberg et al. (eds), *The Russo-Japanese War*, 1:609–27; and Paul Rodell, 'Inspiration for Nationalist Aspirations?', in Steinberg et al. (eds), *The Russo-Japanese War*, 1:629–54.
50. R.P. Dua, *The Impact of the Russo-Japanese (1905) War on Indian Politics* (Delhi, 1966); Tilak Raj Sareen, 'India and the War', in Kowner (ed.), *The Impact*, 137–52; and Marks, '"Bravo, Brave Tiger of the East!"'
51. *Habl al-Matîn*, 14 August 1905, cited in Rajabzadeh, 'Russo-Japanese War', 155.
52. For the newspaper's coverage of the war, see Li Anshan, 'The Miscellany and Mixed', in Steinberg et al. (eds), *The Russo-Japanese War*, 2:498.
53. The other battles are the fall of Singapore and Midway in 1942, the landing in Inchon in 1950, and Dien Bien Phu in 1954. See *Time* magazine, Asian edition, 'The Battles that Changed the Continent', 23 August 1999.

54. Letters to George von Lengerke Meyer, 24 May 1905, and to Cecil Spring Rice, 16 June 1905, cited in Saul, 'The Kittery Peace', 1:493.
55. Morison, The Letters, 4:1198. See also Japan, Gaimushō, Nihon gaikō bunsho, 5:731; and Okamoto, The Japanese Oligarchy, 119.
56. For an overview of the impact of the Russo-Japanese War on the United States, see Tovy and Halevy, 'America's First Cold War', 137–52.
57. See Japan, Gaimushō, Nihon gaikō bunsho, 5:731.
58. See Raymond Esthus, Theodore Roosevelt and Japan (Seattle, 1966), 40.
59. For Roosevelt's earlier concern about Japan, see John White, The Diplomacy of the Russo-Japanese War (Princeton, 1964), 162.
60. For Roosevelt's role in this naval expansion, see Lawrence Sondhaus, Naval Warfare 1815–1914, Warfare and History (London, 2001), 206.
61. Letter to Cecil Spring Rice, 16 June 1905, cited in John Chapman, 'British Naval Estimation of Japan and Russia', Suntory Center Discussion Paper no. IS/04/475 (2004), 44.
62. See e.g. Charles à Court Repington, The War in the Far East (London, 1905), 579.
63. Cited in Otte, 'The Fragmenting', 99.
64. Nish, The Anglo-Japanese Alliance, 292 (for British attitudes to Japan in 1907, see pp. 363–4).
65. On the Russian interest and activities in East Asia soon after the Russo-Japanese War, see Ian Nish, Alliance in Decline (London, 1972), 19–20.
66. George Monger, The End of Isolation (London, 1963), passim; Beryl Williams, 'Great Britain and Russia', in F.H. Hinsley (ed.), British Foreign Policy (Cambridge, 1977), 143–7.
67. Cited in Williams, 'Great Britain and Russia', 134.
68. Diary entry, 29 May 1905, in Maurice Paléologue, Un grand tournant de la politique mondiale (Paris, 1934), 336.
69. For the French attitude to the war, see Beillevaire, 'The Impact', 124–36.
70. See E.C. Kiesling, 'France', in Richard Hamilton and Holger Herwig (eds), The Origins of World War I (Cambridge, 2003), 244.
71. See George Kennan, The Fateful Alliance (New York, 1984).
72. Cited in John Röhl, Wilhelm II (Cambridge, 2014), 272.
73. Röhl, Wilhelm II, 285.
74. Dennet, Roosevelt, 218–19; and Röhl, Wilhelm II, 365–7.
75. For the treaty, see Röhl, Wilhelm II, 377–80.
76. For Germany's changing position during and following the war, see Matthew Seligman, 'Germany, the Russo-Japanese War, and the Road to the Great War', in Kowner (ed.), The Impact, 126–22.
77. See Mishra, From the Ruins, 7.
78. In Sultan Abdülhamid, Siyasî hatıratım (Istanbul, 1987), 165, cited in Halit D. Akarca, 'A Reinterpretation of the Ottoman Neutrality', in Kowner (ed.), Rethinking, 389.

79. Mohandas Gandhi, 'Japan and Russia', *Indian Opinion*, 10 June 1905, in *Collected Works of Mahatma Gandhi* (New Delhi, 1960), 4:466. See also Jonathan Hyslop, 'An "Eventful" History of Hind Swaraj', *Public Culture* 23 (2011), 299–319.

80. Vishnu Priya-o-Ananda Bazar Patrika, *Reports Bengal*, 8 July 1905, 1:587, cited in Gita Dharampal-Frick, 'Der Russisch-Japanische Krieg und die indische Nationalbewegung', in Maik Sprotte et al. (eds), *Der Russisch-Japanische Krieg* (Wiesbaden, 2007), 270.

81. Jawaharlal Nehru, *An Autobiography* (London, 1936), 16, 18. See also Marie Seton, *Panditji: A Portrait of Jawaharlal Nehru* (London, 1967), 24.

82. For Sun's enthusiasm over the Japanese victories during the war, see Harold Schiffrin, 'The Impact of the War on China', in Kowner (ed.), *The Impact*, 173.

83. Cited in Schiffrin, 'The Impact', 173.

84. See e.g. the pride the Korean political activist Yun Chi-ho expressed of Japan for 'vindicating the honor of the yellow race (1864–1945)' in Guy Podoler and Michael Robinson, 'On the Confluence of History and Memory', in Kowner (ed.), *The Impact*, 192.

85. Alfred Zimmern, *The Third British Empire* (London, 1926), 82.

86. For this prophecy, see Sidney Gulick, *The White Peril in the Far East* (New York, 1905), 5.

87. For the rise of fears of racial struggle under Japanese leadership, see Akira Iriye, *Across the Pacific* (New York, Harcourt, Brace and World, 1967), 103–4; Akira Iikura, 'The Anglo-Japanese Alliance and the Question of Race', in Phillips Payson O'Brien (ed.), *The Anglo-Japanese Alliance* (London, 2004), 228–31; Marilyn Lake and Henry Reynolds, *Drawing the Global Colour Line* (Cambridge, 2012), 166–89. For the Japanese reaction, see Sven Saaler, 'The Russo-Japanese War and the Emergence of the Notion of the "Clash of Races" in Japanese Foreign Policy', in John W.M. Chapman and Chiharu Inaba (eds), *Rethinking the Russo-Japanese War, 1904–05* (Folkestone, 2007), 279–82.

88. Mahan, 'Reflections'. Earlier, some two weeks after the battle, Mahan penned a brief analysis of the battle which was published simultaneously in *Collier's Weekly* and *The Times* (London). See Mahan, 'The Battle of the Sea of Japan', *Collier's Weekly* 35 (17 June 1905), 11–12.

89. For a critical review of Mahan's conclusions, see Wayne Hughes, 'Mahan, Tactics and Principles of Strategy', in John Hattendorf (ed.), *The Influence of History on Mahan* (Newport, 1991), 25–6.

90. Mahan, 'The Battle of the Sea of Japan', 12.

91. Mahan, 'Reflections', 1337.

92. Mahan, 'Reflections', 1338.

93. Mahan, 'Reflections', 1344.

94. Mahan, *Naval Strategy*, 137–8.

95. Mahan, *Naval Strategy*, 215.

96. Mahan, *Naval Strategy*, 268, 278.

97. Mahan, *Naval Strategy*, 410, 412.

98. Mahan, *Naval Strategy*, 420, 421.

99. For the United States Navy's position, see Evans and Peattie, *Kaigun*, 147.

100. Theodore Roosevelt to William S. Sims, 27 July 1905, in Morison, *The Letters*, 4:1289.

101. Sims, unlike Mahan, could read recent reports on the battle, such as R.D. White, 'With the Baltic Fleet at Tsushima', *US Naval Institute Proceedings* 32, no. 2 (1906), 597–620.

102. Matthew Oyos, 'Theodore Roosevelt and the Implements of War', *The Journal of Military History* 60 (1996), 648; William M. McBride, *Technological Change and the United States Navy* (Baltimore, 2000), 75–7. Sim elaborated his views in an article published the same year. See William Sims, 'The Inherent Tactical Qualities of the All-Big-Gun, One Caliber Battleship of the High Speed, Large Displacement and Gun Power', *US Naval Institute Proceedings* 32, no. 4 (1906), 1337–66.

103. With Sims's reply, Azar Gat concludes, 'it became clear, not least to Mahan himself, that the ageing authority was out of touch.' See Gat, *A History*, 468; and Hughes, 'Mahan, Tactics', 26.

104. Bradley A. Fiske, 'Compromiseless Ships', United States Naval Institute Proceedings 31 (July 1905), 552. For an analysis of the Fiske–Mahan exchange, see also McBride, *Technological Change*, 71–4.

105. Oyos, 'Theodore Roosevelt', 648.

106. For his report of the battle, see McCully, *The McCully Report*, 237–42.

107. McCully, *The McCully Report*, 243.

108. McCully, *The McCully Report*, 253.

109. McCully, *The McCully Report*, 253.

110. John Fisher, *Memories, by Admiral of the Fleet, Lord Fisher* (London, 1919), 107.

111. Reginald Custance, 'Lessons from the Battle of Tsu Sima', Blackwood's *Edinburgh Magazine* 179 (February 1906), 164, quoted in Marder, *From the Dreadnought*, 60–1. Italics in the original text.

112. See 'Introduction', in Corbett, *Maritime Operations*, 1:x–xv. For his biography, see Donald Schurman, *Julian S. Corbett, 1854–1922* (London, 1981). For Corbett's view of naval strategy and history, see Donald Schurman, *The Education of a Navy* (London, 1965), 147–84; and Milevski, *The Maritime*, 37–43.

113. Julian Corbett, 'The Strategical Value of Speed in Battleships', *Journal of the Royal United Services Institute* (July 1911), 824–39.

114. For a similar view on speed, see Admiral John Hopkins, 'Comments on Tsushima', 232.

115. Corbett, 'The Strategical', 831.

116. In Corbett, 'The Strategical', 837.

117. Corbett, *Some Principles*, 170–1.

118. Corbett, *Some Principles*, 171.

119. Corbett, *Some Principles*, 309.

120. Corbett, *Some Principles*, 334. Italics in the original text.
121. Corbett, *Some Principles*, 323.
122. René Daveluy, *Les leçons de la guerre russo–japonaise* (Paris, 1906); René Daveluy, *Étude sur la stratégie navale* (Paris, 1906); René Daveluy, *L'esprit de la guerre navale* (Paris, 1909–10).
123. René Daveluy, *Studie über die See-Strategie* (Berlin, 1907); René Daveluy, *The Genius of Naval Warfare* (Annapolis, 1910–11).
124. 'At Tsushima the Japanese fired some sixty of them, but the distance was too great for them to be able to reach the mark.' In Daveluy, *The Genius*, 2:27 (see also 2:71, 103).
125. Daveluy, *The Genius*, 2:25, 52.
126. Daveluy, *The Genius*, 2:67–8.
127. See 'Die Schlacht in der japanischen See', undated, in Bundesarchiv, Militärarchiv Freiburg, BAMA RM 5/5784 (*geheime Denkschrift*). For the background to this report, see also Cord Eberspaecher, 'The Road to Jutland?', in Kowner (ed.), *The Impact*, 301–2.
128. 'Die Schlacht'.
129. 'Die Schlacht'.
130. 'Der Kampf um die Seeherrschaft', *Marine-Rundschau* (1906) Heft 1 (special issue). See Frank Jacob, *Tsushima 1905* (Paderborn, 2017), 136–7.
131. In Eberspaecher, 'The Road to Jutland?', 298.

Chapter 6

1. Although several countries had sent naval observers to observe the war either on the Japanese or the Russian side, during the Battle of Tsushima, only a single foreign observer took part in it. He was Britain's Captain William Pakenham on board the IJN battleship *Asahi*. For Pakenham's background, his initial experience in the Russo-Japanese War, and his part in the battle, see Quintin Barry, *Command of the Sea* (Warwick, 2019), 118–28, 261–79.
2. In Britain, for example, the Royal Navy was allocated no less than 28.8 per cent of the national budget in 1904–5. See Norman Friedman, *Fighting the Great War at Sea* (Barnsley, 2014), 75–6.
3. For the *Dreadnought*'s specifications, see Oscar Parkes, *British Battleships, 'Warrior' 1860 to 'Vanguard' 1950* (Annapolis, 1990), 447.
4. David Brown, *Warrior to Dreadnought* (Annapolis, 1997), 186, 189–90. Arthur Marder has suggested that Fisher had the essentials of the dreadnought design firmly fixed as early as October 1904, two months after the Battle of the Yellow Sea. See Marder, *From the Dreadnought*, 59.
5. Some attribute the idea of a battleship based on a primary battery alone to a conversation Fisher held as early as 1882. See e.g. Richard Hogue, *Dreadnought* (New York, 1964), 15–16.

6. For Cuniberti's article, see James George, *History of Warships* (Annapolis, 1998), 91; for the American plans, see Marder, *From the Dreadnought*, 57.

7. Corbett, *Maritime Operations*, 1:385–6, 388.

8. Admiral Fisher himself mentioned Pakenham's report in a letter to Edward Grey in 1908. See Arthur Marder, *Fear God and Dread Nought* (London, 1956), 156.

9. Cited in Marder, *The Anatomy*, 531. For similar impressions of the impact and accuracy of the heavy guns in the battle, following visits to the returning Russian battleships on 15 and 17 August 1904, see the report of Lieutenant Commander Albert Hopman (1865–1942), the German naval observer in Port Arthur, in a letter sent to Kaiser Wilhelm II on 23 September 1904, in Albert Hopman, *Das ereignisreiche Leben eines 'Wilhelminers'* (Munich, 2004), 115–16.

10. On the governmental pressures to cut naval budgets in Britain, see Charles Fairbanks, 'The Origins of the Dreadnought Revolution', *International History Review* 13 (1991), 262.

11. For Fisher's readiness to cut the number of warships but not the fleet's firepower, see Eric Grove, *Big Fleet Actions* (London, 1995), 47.

12. See e.g. Klado, *The Battle*, 166; Kostenko, *Na 'Orle'*, 442–3; Semenov, *The Battle*, 62–3.

13. See Philip Towle, 'The Evaluation of the Experience of the Russo-Japanese War', in Bryan Ranft (ed.), *Technical Change and the British Naval Policy* (London, 1977), 69. For a similar view, see the Commander-in-Chief of the China Station, Vice Admiral Hedworth Meux's (1856–1929) 1908 reference to the Japanese and Russian battleship procurement after Tsushima, in Towle, 'The Evaluation', 71.

14. Completed in Britain in 1910, the *Orion* class was armed with sixteen 102-millimetre guns, and five years later the *Queen Elizabeth* class was armed with a dozen 152-millimetre guns.

15. The Russo-Japanese War, the British politician William Palmer, 2nd Earl of Selborne, asserted, 'proved the resisting power of ships is greater than was supposed, and only the hardest knocks count'. Cited in Marder, *From the Dreadnought*, 58–9.

16. On the invulnerability of Russian battleship armour at Tsushima, see Evans and Peattie, *Kaigun*: 125.

17. For the discussion on the importance of speed in the Royal Navy, see Towle, 'The Evaluation', 72–3. Fisher's view on speed is quoted in Marder, *From the Dreadnought*, 59.

18. For the rise of this technology, see Alexander Richardson, *The Evolution of the Parsons Steam Turbine* (London, 1911); Crosbie Smith, 'Dreadnought Science', in Robert Blyth et al. (eds), *The Dreadnought and the Edwardian Age* (Farnham, 2011), 137–49.

19. For the controversy HMS *Dreadnought* provoked in Britain, see Marder, *From the Dreadnought*, 56–70.
20. O'Hara and Heinz, Clash of the Fleets, 17.
21. The first battleship class to be referred to as super-dreadnought was the *Orion*. Its four ships were all commissioned in 1912.
22. For this concept and its emergence, see Roberts, *Battlecruisers*, 10–45.
23. On Fisher's support of the battlecruiser, see Jon Sumida, *In Defense of Naval Supremacy* (Winchester, 1989), 37–61.
24. For Fisher's warning against a Russo-French combined threat and surprise attack on Malta and Egypt during 1900–1, see John W.M. Chapman, 'British Naval Estimation of Japan and Russia, 1894–1905', Suntory Center Discussion Paper no. IS/04/475 (2004), 17–55.
25. For Fisher's attraction to the battlecruiser concept, see Nicholas Lambert, *Sir John Fisher's Naval Revolution* (Columbia, 1999); Nicholas Lambert, 'Admiral Sir John Fisher and the Concept of Flotilla Defence, 1904–1909', in Phillips P. O'Brien (ed.), *Technology and Naval Combat in the Twentieth Century and Beyond* (London, 2001), 70–2.
26. Roberts, *Battlecruisers*, 24–8.
27. Other navies did not overlook the gamble involved in the investment in this type of warship. Among them, only the German and Japanese navies decided to build battlecruisers before the First World War.
28. For the accuracy rate in the battle, see Chapter 2 ('Analysis') in this book.
29. By 1904, the Royal Navy had developed the first targeting device. It also unified the fire from all the gun turrets by remote control using analogous computing machines to align the position of the ship with the target. On the improvement in gunnery systems, see Sumida, *In Defense*, chs 3–5; and Peter Padfield, *The Battleship Era* (London, 1972), 183–5.
30. Jon Sumida, 'British Capital Ship Design and Fire Control in the Dreadnought Era', *Journal of Modern History* 51 (1979), 212–17, 222–9; Friedman, *Fighting the Great War*, 78–81; Trent Hone, *Learning War* (Annapolis, 2018), 55–91.
31. The hit rate at the Battle of Jutland was 3.4 per cent for the Germans and 2.8 per cent for the British. See O'Hara and Heinz, *Clash of the Fleets*, 182.
32. Marder, *From the Dreadnought*, 329. For reports on even lower success rates (about 2 per cent), see Edwyn Gray, *The Devil's Device* (London, 1975), 175; and Lambert, 'Admiral Sir John Fisher', 74.
33. For the accuracy rate in the battle, see Chapter 2 ('Analysis') in this book.
34. For the role of torpedo boats during the war and the battle in particular, see McCully, *The McCully Report*, 246.
35. For this development, see Norman Friedman, *The British Battleship, 1906–1946* (Annapolis, 2015), 48–53.
36. Friedman, *Fighting the Great War*, 78.
37. For the evolution of torpedo range and speed, see Marder, *From the Dreadnought*, 329.

38. For details of the losses both belligerents suffered, see Corbett, *Maritime Operations*, 2:446.
39. Friedman, *Fighting the Great War*, 74.
40. O'Hara and Heinz, *Clash of the Fleets*, 275.
41. Friedman, *The British Battleship*, 53–4.
42. Friedman, *Fighting the Great War*, 77, 85.
43. Corbett, *Maritime Operations*, 2:224.
44. Friedman, *Fighting the Great War*, 89–93.
45. For the Russian ordeal of using coal during the voyage, see Politovsky, *From Libau*, 257.
46. James Goldrick, 'Coal and the Advent of the First World War at Sea', *War in History* 21 (2014), 330–31.
47. Friedman, *The British Battleship*, 58–9; Goldrick, 'Coal and the Advent', 331.
48. The need for new energy resources in the Royal Navy became evident in 1912 with the appointment of Fisher as chairman of a royal committee reviewing the possibility of supplying oil to the fleet. See Winston Churchill, *The World Crisis* (London, 1923), 137–8.
49. Towards the First World War, the German navy also began to use oil as a secondary fuel for its larger ships. It still relied on coal, however, fearing its lack of a stable supply of oil, as well as assuming that the ship's coal storages served as additional shielding against torpedoes, particularly below the water level. See Michael Epkenhans, 'Technology, Shipbuilding and Future Combat in Germany, 1880–1914', in O'Brien (ed.), *Technology and Naval Combat*, 61–2.
50. On the development of purpose-made supply ships during the first decades of the 20th century, see Thomas Wildenberg, *Gray Steel and Black Oil* (Annapolis, 1996).
51. For Fisher's interest in the war, see R.F. Mackay, *Fisher of Kilverstone* (Oxford, 1973), 307.
52. See Nicholas Rodger, 'Anglo-German Naval Rivalry, 1860–1914', in Michael Epkenhans et al. (eds), *Jutland* (Lexington, 2015), 14.
53. Phillips O'Brien, *British and American Naval Power* (Westport, 1998), 31.
54. Some 90 obsolete and small ships were sold off and a further 64 vessels were put into reserve.
55. For Tirpitz's opposition against any alliance with Russia during 1904–5, see Patrick Kelly, *Tirpitz and the Imperial German Navy* (Bloomington, 2011), 251–2.
56. For the effects of the war and the *Dreadnought* revolution on the German navy, see Holger Herwig, *'Luxury' Fleet: The Imperial German Navy, 1888–1918* (London, 1980), 33–68; Holger Herwig, 'The German Reaction to the Dreadnought Revolution', *International History Review* 13 (1991), 273–83; and Hans Steltzer, *Die deutsche Flotte* (Darmstadt, 1989), 238–55.
57. See Matthew Seligman, 'Intelligence Information and the 1909 Naval Scare', *War in History* 17 (2010), 37–59.

58. On the naval crisis in Britain in 1908–9, see O'Brien, *British and American*, 33–44, 73–97.

59. Fisher's position on the German fleet is presented in Herwig, *'Luxury' Fleet*, 50.

60. Marder, *From the Dreadnought*, 182–3; O'Brien, *British and American*, 25–46.

61. For a similar conclusion reached by Wilhelm II soon after HMS *Dreadnought*'s completion, see German Emperor William II, *The Kaiser's Memoirs* (New York, 1922), 235. For the British–German naval race after the war, see James Goldrick, 'The Battleship Fleet: The Test of War, 1895–1919', in J.R. Hill (ed.), *The Oxford Illustrated History of the Royal Navy* (Oxford, 1995), 280–318.

62. On the eve of the First World War, France had ten *Dreadnoughts* (as well as 21 pre-*Dreadnoughts*), Italy had three (15), Austro-Hungary had six (6), Russia had four (11), Japan had two (8), and the United States had ten (25). See George, *History of Warships*, 99; Richard Hough, *The Great War at Sea* (Oxford, 1983), 55.

63. On the commitment to battleships for the French navy after Tsushima, see Paul Halpern, 'The French Navy, 1880–1914', in O'Brien (ed.), *Technology and Naval Combat*, 46–7.

64. Stevenson, *Armaments*, 29.

65. Whereas French defence expenditure reduced slightly in 1905, its army expenditure increased. For French defence expenditures in the early 20th century, see Stevenson, Armaments, 4; and David Herrmann, *The Arming of Europe and the Making of the First World War* (Princeton, 1996), 237.

66. On the reasons for French technological inferiority, and the failure of the *Danton* class in particular, in the naval race of 1906, see Ray Walser, *France's Search for a Battle Fleet* (New York, 1992), 141–8; and Halpern, 'The French Navy', 45–6.

67. On British estimation of French naval power in 1909, see O'Brien, *British and American*, 31–2.

68. In fact, fears within the navy of the Japanese takeover of Hawaii, and even an attack on the Pacific coast, emerged as early as 1897 and were followed by drafts for counteracting it. See Scott Mobley, *Progressives in Navy Blue* (Annapolis, 2018), 253.

69. For the American–Japanese Gentlemen's Agreement of 1907, see Charles Neu, *An Uncertain Friendship* (Cambridge, 1967), 69–80, 163–80.

70. Edward Miller, *War Plan Orange* (Annapolis, 1991), 19–25.

71. See Mobley, *Progressives in Navy Blue*, 253.

72. Tovy and Halevy, 'America's First Cold War', 142.

73. Miller, *War Plan Orange*, 160.

74. In a discussion with the German Admiral Alfred von Tirpitz, Roosevelt boasted that 'there were fleets of the white race which were totally different from the fleet of the poor Rozhesvenski'. Cited in Samuel Carter, *The Incredible Great White Fleet* (New York, 1971), 19. See also James Reckner, *Teddy Roosevelt's Great White Fleet* (Annapolis, 1988), 14.

75. For this 14-month circumnavigation of the Earth, see Robert Hart, *The Great White Fleet* (Boston, 1965); Reckner, *Teddy Roosevelt's*; and Lake and Reynolds, *Drawing the Global Colour Line*, 190–209 (for Roosevelt's aims vis-à-vis Japan, see p. 24); Neu, *An Uncertain Friendship*, 110–14. For the fleet's visit in Japan, see Reckner, *Teddy Roosevelt's*, 79–80.

76. See William Braisted, 'The United States Navy's Dilemma in the Pacific, 1906–1909', *Pacific Historical Review* 26 (1957), 235–44.

77. Reckner, *Teddy Roosevelt's*, 158–9.

78. For Mahan's warning about the inherent risks found in concentrating the resources of a navy around a small number of warships of massive power, see Alfred Mahan, 'Retrospect upon the War between Japan and Russia', *National Review* (May 1906), 142. See also Robert Seager, *Alfred Thayer Mahan* (Annapolis, 1977), 525–7.

79. For the post-Russo-Japanese War state of the United States Navy, see O'Brien, *British and American*, 62–7.

80. See e.g. 'Under-sea Fighting craft bear brunt of combat when Slav fleet is checked in the straits', in 'American-Built Submarines Sink the Russian Warships', *The San Francisco Call*, 31 May 1905, 3; 'Submarines Boat Used?', *The New York Times*, 31 May 1905, 1; 'Submarines Story Doubted', *The New York Times*, 31 May 1905, 2; Les rapports officiels des Japonais', *L'Aurore*, 1 June 1905, 1; 'L'oeuvre de sous-marins japonais', *L'Aurore*, 2 June 1905, 1.

81. Klado, *The Battle*, 124 (see also p. 192).

82. For the early history of submarines, see Alex Roland, *Underwater Warfare in the Age of Sail* (Bloomington, 1978); and Richard Compton-Hall, *Submarine Boats* (London, 1983).

83. For the introduction of submarines into the Royal Navy, see Nicholas Lambert, *Sir John Fisher's Naval Revolution* (Columbia, 1999), 38–72; and Antony Preston, *The Royal Navy Submarine Service* (Annapolis, 2001), 24–43.

84. For early submarines in the IRN service, see Norman Polmar and Jurrien Noot, *Submarines of the Russian and Soviet Navies, 1718–1990* (Annapolis, 1991), 10–22.

85. For IRN use of submarines during the war against Japan, see Bikov, *Russko-Iaponskaia voina*, 583–4; Mitchell, *A History*, 233.

86. In a letter to Arnold While, 12 March 1904, in Arthur Marder, *Fear God and Dread Nought* (London, 1952), 305.

87. In a letter of 20 April 1904, in Marder, *Fear God* (1952), 308–9.

88. Add. Mss. 49710, reprinted in Nicholas Lambert (ed.), *The Submarine Service, 1900–1918* (Aldershot, 2001), 109–12. For Fisher's view of the offensive possibilities of the submarine, see Marder, *From the Dreadnought*, 332–3.

89. For the German decision to develop high-seas submarines from 1906 onwards, see Alfred von Tirpitz, *Erinnerungen* (Leipzig, 1920), 517–19; and William II, *The Kaiser's Memoirs*, 236–7. With the outbreak of the First World War, the submarine became an efficient offensive vessel. On 22 September

1914, the German submarine U-9 sank three British armoured cruisers, HMS *Aboukir, Hogue,* and *Cressy* in less than an hour in an early demonstration of its lethal potential. During the entire war, Germany built 346 submarines (in addition to the 28 it had on the eve of the war). Together, they sank some 104 warships and more than 5,000 merchant ships. Cf. George, *History of Warships,* 159. The German limited triumph in this domain does not mean that other naval powers, including the IRN, did not use submarines successfully during that war. See Ian Ona Johnson, 'Strategy on the Wintry Sea: The Russo-British Submarine Flotilla in the Baltic, 1914–1918', *International Journal of Military History and Historiography* 40 (2020), 187–212.

90. For the repercussions of the Russo-Japanese War on the early development of the aeroplane, see Rotem Kowner, 'The Impact of the War on Naval Warfare', in Kowner (ed.), *The Impact,* 284.

91. John Moore, 'The Short, Eventful Life of Eugene B. Ely', *U.S. Naval Institute Proceedings* 107 (1981), 58–63.

92. For the *Wakamiya,* see Evans and Peattie, *Kaigun,* 180.

93. The last recorded incident of a battleship sinking another battleship took place on 25 October 1944 when the USN *Mississippi* hit the IJN *Yamashiro* with a salvo at 18,000 metres. Half a year later, the world's largest battleship *Yamato* was also sunk by multiple hits of bombs and torpedoes dropped by about 380 aeroplanes.

Conclusion

1. William Pakenham, 'The Battle of the Sea of Japan,' in Admiralty, *Reports* (2003), 362.

2. Eliot Cohen and John Gooch, *Military Misfortunes* (New York, 1990), 59–163.

3. Parshall and Tully, *Shattered Sword,* 402–3.

4. Cohen and Gooch, *Military Misfortunes,* 27, 197–230.

5. There were some 46,000 seamen on board 73 warships (60 of which were ships of the line) at the Battle of Trafalgar. The figures were calculated based on Mark Adkin, *The Trafalgar Companion* (London, 2005), 307–93.

6. For the emergence of the idea to use submarines instead of swarms of torpedo boats for coastal defence, see Roksund, *The Jeune École,* 134, 173, 189–221.

7. John Guilmartin, *Gunpowder and Galleys* (Cambridge, 1974), 242–5; Roger Crowley, *Empires of the Sea* (London, 2008), 256.

8. In 1573, the Ottomans got hold of Cyprus and a year later they retook Tunis. See Guilmartin, *Gunpowder,* 250–1; David Abulafia, *The Great Sea* (New York, 2012), 451; Lord Kinross, *The Ottoman Centuries* (New York, 1977), 272.

9. '... of all the great victories,' Julian Corbett noted on Trafalgar, 'there is not one which to all appearance was so barren of immediate result ... It gave to England finally the dominion of the seas, but it left Napoleon dictator of the Continent.' In Julian Corbett, *The Campaign of Trafalgar* (London, 1910), 408.

10. For a similar conclusion about the indecisiveness of this battle, at least in comparison with Tsushima, see Parshall and Tully, *Shattered Sword*, 428; Geoffrey Till, 'Trafalgar, Tsushima, and Onwards', *The Japan Society Proceedings* 144 (2006), 45–6.

11. Paul Dull, *A Battle History of the Imperial Japanese Navy* (Annapolis, 1978), 166; Gordon Prange et al., *Miracle at Midway* (New York, 1982), 395.

12. The first to suggest this idea has been David Schimmelpenninck van der Oye, in his 'Rewriting the Russo-Japanese War', 87.

13. Since 2004, however, there has been a marked change in the historical treatment of this war. See e.g. Gerhard Krebs, 'World War Zero?', *The Asia-Pacific Journal* 10, issue 21, no. 2 (2012).

14. See Shillony and Kowner, 'The Memory'.

15. Corbett, *Maritime Operations*, 2:333.

SELECT BIBLIOGRAPHY

Archival Sources

Germany

Bundesarchiv, Militärarchiv Freiburg (BAMA)

Japan

National Archives of Japan, Japan Center for Asian Historical Record (JACAR), Tokyo
Ministry of Defence, National Institute for Defence Studies (NIDS), Tokyo
Ministry of Foreign Affairs, Diplomatic Archive, Tokyo

Russia

Rossiiskii Gosudarstvenniĭ Arkhiv Voenno-Morskogo Flota (RGAVMF), St Petersburg

United Kingdom

The National Archives, Kew, Greater London
    Admiralty Papers
    Foreign Office Papers
East Riding of Yorkshire Archives, Beverley
    Pakenham, Sir William Christopher, Admiral: Reports, Correspondence, Letters and Photographs, 1904–1911 (PKM/2)

United States

Archives Branch, Naval History and Heritage Command, Washington, DC.
    Papers of Chester W. Nimitz, Box 63.

Newspapers

Austria–Hungary

Machsike Hadas (Lviv)

France

La Croix (Paris)
L'Aurore (Paris)
La Dépêche (Toulouse)
Le Figaro (Paris)
Le Gaulois (Paris)
Le Journal (Paris)
Le Petit Parisien (Paris)
L'Intransigeant (Paris)

Germany

Berliner Börsen-Zeitung (Berlin)
Berliner Tageblatt (Berlin)
Berliner Volks-Zeitung (Berlin)
Königlich privilegirte Berlinische Zeitung (Berlin)
Norddeutsche Allgemeine Zeitung (Berlin)
Simplicissimus (Berlin)

Great Britain

Birmingham Mail (Birmingham)
Daily Telegraph & Courier (London)
Eastern Daily Press (Norwich)
Exeter and Plymouth Gazette (Exeter)
Liverpool Echo (Liverpool)
Newcastle Evening Chronicle (Newcastle)
The Sphere (London)
The Times (London)

Japan

Chūō Shimbun (Tokyo)
Hōchi Shimbun (Tokyo)
Japan Mail (Yokohama)
Japan Times (Tokyo)
Jiji Shimpō (Tokyo)
Tōkyō Asahi Shimbun (Tokyo)

Tōkyō Nichi Nichi Shimbun (Tokyo)
Tōkyō Niroku Shimbun (Tokyo)
Yomiuri Shimbun (Tokyo)
Yorozu Chōhō (Tokyo)

Russia

Ha-Tsfira (Warsaw)
Hasman (Vilnius)
Morskoi Sbornik (St Petersburg)
Novoe Vremia (St Petersburg)
Peterburgskaia Gazeta (St Petersburg)
Russkoe Slovo (St Petersburg)
Sankt-Peterburgskie vedomosti (St Petersburg)
Voenni Golos (St Petersburg)

United States

Baltimore Evening Herald (Baltimore)
Bismark Daily (North Dakota)
Hawaiian Star (Honolulu)
Littell's Living Age (Boston)
Los Angeles Times (Los Angeles)
New York Tribune (New York)
Nippu Jiji (Honolulu)
Puck (New York)
St. Louis Republic (Missouri)
The Bemidji Daily Pioneer (Minnesota)
The Daily Capital (Salem, Oregon)
The Daily Press (Virginia)
The Evening News (Washington, DC)
The Evening World (New York)
The New York Times (New York)
The San Francisco Call (San Francisco)
The Spokane Press (Washington)
The Washington Times (Washington, DC)
Topeka State Journal (Kansas)
Waterbury Evening Democrat (Connecticut)
Yamato Shimbun (Honolulu)

Official Histories and Reports: General and Maritime Operations

France. *Opérations maritimes de la Guerre Russo–japonaise: historique officiel publié par l'État-major général de la marine japonaise*, trans. Henri Rouvier (Paris: R. Chapelot, 1910–11).

Germany. *Der Japanisch–Russische Seekrieg 1904–1905. Amtliche Darstellung des Japanischen Admiralstabes*, 3 vols (Berlin: E. S. Mittler, 1910–11).

Great Britain. Admiralty. *Reports of the British Naval Attachés*, 5 vols (London: Public Records Office, 1908; rep. Nashville, TN: Battery Press, 2003).

Great Britain. Admiralty War Staff. *Japanese Official Naval History of the Russo-Japanese War*, 2 vols (London: His Majesty's Stationery Office, 1913–14).

Great Britain. *Official History of the Russo-Japanese War*, 5 vols (London: His Majesty's Stationery Office, 1906–10).

Japan, Gaimushō. *Nihon gaikō bunsho: Nichiro sensō*, 5 vols (Tokyo: Gaimushō, 1958–60).

Japan. Kaigun Gunreibu. *Meiji 37–8 nen kaisen-shi*, 2 vols (Tokyo: Naikaku Insatsukyoku, 1934).

Japan. Kaigun Gunreibu. *Meiji 37–8 nen kaisen-shi*, 4 vols (Tokyo: Shun'yōdō, 1909–10).

Japan. Kaigun Gunreibu. *Nihonkai daikaisen-shi* (Tokyo: Naikaku Insatsukyoku, 1935).

Japan. Rikugunshō. *Meiji gunjishi*, 2 vols (Tokyo: Hara Shobō, 1966).

Russia. Morskoi Generalniĭ Shtab. *Voenno-Istoricheskaia kommissiia po opisaniiu deistviĭ flota v voinu 1904–05 gg., Russko-iaponskaia voina 1904–05 gg.*, 7 vols (St Petersburg: Tip. V.D. Smirnova, 1912–18).

Russia. *Russko-iaponskaia voina 1904–05. Deistvia flota. Dokumenti*, 13 vols (St Petersburg: Tip. V.D. Smirnova, 1907, 1912–14) [five of these volumes are devoted to the Second Pacific Fleet and the Battle: *2-ia Tikhookeanskaia Eskadra, Boj 14–15 maia 1905 goda*].

Russia. *Russko-iaponskaia voina 1904–05 gg. Materiali dlia opisaniia deistviĭ flota. Khronologicheskiĭ perechen' voennie deistviĭ flota v 1904–05 gg.*, 2 vols, edited by N.V. Novikov (St Petersburg: Tip. V.D. Smirnova, 1910–12).

Russia. Voenno-istoricheskaia Komissiia po opisaniiu. *Russko-iaponskaia voina 1904–1905 gg.*, 9 vols (St Petersburg: A.S. Suvorina, 1910–13).

United States. War Department. *Epitome of the Russo-Japanese War* (Washington: G.P.O., 1907).

Primary Sources

Alexander Mikhailovich [Romanov], Grand Duke. *Once a Grand Duke* (New York: Farrar and Rinehart, 1932).

Ashmead-Bartlett, Ellis. *Port Arthur: The Siege and Capitulation* (London: W. Blackwood and Sons, 1906).

Bely, Andrei. *Petersburg* (St Petersburg: M.M. Stasiulevicha, 1913).

Bely, Andrei. *Petersburg*, trans. and annot. John E. Malmstad and Robert A. Maguire (Bloomington: Indiana University Press, 1978).

Bertin, Louis-Émile. 'The Fate of the Russian Ships at Tsushima', in *Jane's Fighting Ships* (1904–7), reprinted in Richard Hogue, *The Fleet That Had to Die* (London: Viking, 1958), 233.

Bikov, Pëtr D. *Russko-iaponskaia voina 1904–1905 gg. Deistviia na more* (Moscow: Voienno-morskoie izdatel'stvo NKVMF Soyuza SSR, 1942; rep. St Petersburg: Terra Fantastica, 2003).

Bikov, Pëtr D. *Russko-Iaponskaia voina 1904–1905 gg. Deystviia na more* (Moscow: Voenmorizdat, 1938; rep. Moscow: Eksmo, Izografus, 2003).

Cassell's History of the Russo-Japanese War, 5 vols (London: Cassell, 1905).

Charmes, Gabriel. *Naval Reform*, trans. J.E. Gordon-Cumming (London: W.H. Allen, 1887).

Churchill, Winston S. *The World Crisis* (London: Thornton-Butterworth, 1923).

Colomb, Philip H. *Essays on Naval Defence* (London: W.H. Allen, 1893).

Colomb, Philip H. *Naval Warfare: Its Ruling Principles and Practice Historically Treated* (London: W.H. Allen, 1891).

Colomb, Philip H. *Naval Warfare: Its Ruling Principles and Practice Historically Treated*, 3rd edn (London: W.H. Allen, 1899).

Corbett, Julian S. *Maritime Operations in the Russo-Japanese War, 1904–5*, 2 vols (London, 1914; rep. Annapolis, MD: Naval Institute Press, 1994).

Corbett, Julian S. *Some Principles of Maritime Strategy* (London: Longmans, Green, 1911).

Corbett, Julian S. 'The Strategical Value of Speed in Battleships', *Journal of the Royal United Services Institute* (July 1911), 824–39.

Custance, Reginald. 'Lessons from the Battle of Tsu Sima', *Blackwood's Edinburgh Magazine* 179 (February 1906).

Daveluy, René. *Étude sur la stratégie navale* (Paris: Berger-Levrault, 1906).

Daveluy, René. *L'esprit de la guerre navale*, 3 vols (Paris: Berger-Levrault, 1909–10).

Daveluy, René. *Les Leçons de la guerre Russo-japonaise: la lutte pour l'empire de la mer, exposé et critique* (Paris: A. Challamel, 1906).

Daveluy, René. *Studie über die See-Strategie*, trans. Ferdinand Lavaud (Berlin: Boll & Pickardt, 1907).

Daveluy, René. *The Genius of Naval Warfare*, 2 vols, trans. Philip R. Alger (Annapolis, MD: United States Naval Institute, 1910–11).

Dmitriev, N.N. *Bronenosets "Admiral Ushakov"* (St Petersburg: Ekonomicheskaia Tipo-Litografiia, 1906; rep. St Petersburg: Korabli I srazheniia, 1997).

Dobrotvorskiĭ, Leonid. *Uroki morskoi voini* (Kronstadt: Kotlin, 1907).

Dubrovskiĭ, Evgeniĭ. *Dela o sdache iaponstam (1) minonostsa "Bedoviĭ" I (2) eskadriĭ Nebogatova* (St Petersburg: S.l., 1907).

Egawa Tatsuya. *Nichiro sensō monogatari: Honjitsu tenki seirō naredomo nami takashi*, 22 vols (Tokyo: Shōgakukan, 2001–6).

Fisher, John Arbuthnot. *Memories, by Admiral of the Fleet, Lord Fisher* (London: Hodder and Stoughton, 1919).

Fiske, Bradley A. 'Compromiseless Ships', *United States Naval Institute Proceedings* 31 (July 1905), 549–53.

Gandhi, Mohandas K. *Collected Works of Mahatma Gandhi*, 97 vols (New Delhi: Government of India, 1960–80).

Gavotti, Giuseppe. *Tre grandi uomini di Mare: De Ruyter, Nelson, Togo* (Savona: D. Bertolotto, 1911).

Goldstein, Donald M., and Katherine V. Dillon (eds). *The Pearl Harbor Papers: Inside the Japanese Plans* (Washington, DC: Brassey's, 1999).

Gooch, G.P., and H. Temperley (eds). *British Documents on the Origins of the War, 1898–1914*, 11 vols (London: HMSO, 1926–38).

Graf, G.K. *Moriaki; ocherki 12 'zhizni morskikh'* (Paris: Imprimérie de Navarre, 1930).

Grew, Edwin Sharpe. *War in the Far East; a History of the Russo-Japanese Struggle*, 6 vols (London: Virtue, 1905).

Gulick, Sidney. *The White Peril in the Far East: An Interpretation of the Significance of the Russo-Japanese War* (New York: F.H. Revell, 1905).

Hare, James H. *A Photographic Record of the Russo-Japanese War* (New York: P.F. Collier, 1905).

Hopkins, John O. 'Comments on Tsushima', in *Jane's Fighting Ships* (1904–7), reprinted in Richard Hogue, *The Fleet That Had to Die* (London: Viking, 1958), 230–2.

Hopman, Albert. *Das ereignisreiche Leben eines "Wilhelminers: tagebücher, briefe, aufzeichnungen 1901 bis 1920*, ed. Michael Epkenhans (Munich: R. Oldenbourg Verlag, 2004).

House of Representatives. *Papers Relating to Foreign Relation of the United States, vol. 1: House Documents* (Washington: G.P.O., 1906).

Ishida Ichirō. 'Kaisen zengo *Izumi* no kōdō', in Todaka Kazushige (ed.), *Nihonkai kaisen no shōgen* (Tokyo: Kōjinsha, 2012), 7–15.

Jō Ei'ichirō. *Jijū bukan Jō Ei'ichirō nikki* (Tokyo: Yamakawa Shuppansha, 1982).

Kaigun rekishi hozonkai. *Nihon kaigun-shi*, 11 vols (Tokyo: Kaigun rekishi Hozonkai, 1995).

Kamaya Chūdō. 'Rokoku byōinsen *Ariyo-ru* no hokaku, rokan *Nahimofu* oyobi *Uraji-miru Monomafu* no hokaku shobun', in Todaka Kazushige (ed.), *Nihonkai kaisen no shōgen* (Tokyo: Kōjinsha, 2012), 73–88.

Klado, Nikolai [Nicolas]. *The Battle of the Sea of Japan*, trans. J.H. Dickinson and F.P. Marchant (London: Hodder and Stoughton, 1906).

Klado, Nikolai [Nicolas]. *The Russian Navy in the Russo-Japanese War*, trans. J.H. Dickinson (London: Hurst and Blackett, 1905).

Klado, Nikolai. *Sovremennaia morskaia voina: morskie zametki o Russko-Iaponskoĭ voine* (St Petersburg: A.S. Suvorina, 1905).

Kostenko, Vladimir P. *Na 'Orle' v Tsusime* (Leningrad: Sudostroenie, 1955).

Kravchenko, Vladimir. *Cherez tri okeana* (St Petersburg: Tip. I. Fleĭtmana, 1910).

Kuprin, Aleksandr. 'Captain Ribnikov', in Gerri Kimber et al. (eds), *The Poetry and Critical Writings of Katherine Mansfield* (Edinburgh: Edinburgh University Press, 2014), 151–82.

Kuprin, Aleksandr. *Shtabs-Kapitan Ribnikov* (St Petersburg: *"Mir Bozhiĭ"* Magazine №1/1906, Tip. I.N. Skorokhodov, 1906).

Kuropatkin, Aleksei. *The Russian Army and the Japanese War*, 2 vols, trans. A.B. Lindsay (New York: E.P. Dutton, 1909).

Lenin, Vladimir Il'ich. *Collected Works*, 41 vols (Moscow: Foreign Languages Publishing House, 1960–7).

Levitskiĭ, Nikolai A. *Russko-Iaponskaia voina 1904–1905 gg.* (Moscow: *Gosudarstvennoe Voennoe Izdatel'stvo Narkomata Oboroni Soyuza SSR*, 1936).

Levitskiĭ, Nikolai A. *Russko-Iaponskaia voina 1904–1905 gg.*, 3rd edn (Moscow: *Gosudarstvennoe Voennoe Izdatel'stvo Narkomata Oboroni Soyuza SSR*, 1938; rep. Moscow: Eksmo, Izografus, 2003).

Leyland, John. 'The Russo-Japanese Naval Campaign', in John Leyland and T.A. Brassey (eds), *The Naval Annual, 1906* (Portsmouth: J. Griffin, 1906), 93–117.

McCully, Newton A. *The McCully Report: The Russo-Japanese War, 1904–05* (Annapolis, MD: Naval Institute Press, 1977).

McCutcheon, John T. *The Mysterious Stranger and Other Cartoons by John T. McCutcheon* (New York: McClure, Phillips & Co. 1905).

Mahan, Alfred Thayer. *Naval Strategy: Compared and Contrasted with the Principles and Practice of Military Operations on Land* (Boston, MA: Little, Brown, and Co., 1911).

Mahan, Alfred Thayer. 'Reflections, Historic and Other, Suggested by The Battle of The Japan Sea', *US Naval Institute Proceedings* 32, no. 2 (1906), 447–71; *Royal United Services Institution Journal* 50, no. 345 (1906), 1327–46.

Mahan, Alfred Thayer. 'Retrospect upon the War between Japan and Russia', *National Review* (May 1906), reprinted in A.T. Mahan, *Naval Administration and Warfare* (London: Sampson Low, Marston, 1908), 133–73.

Mahan, Alfred Thayer. 'The Battle of the Sea of Japan', *Collier's Weekly* 35 (17 June 1905), 11–12.

Mahan, Alfred Thayer. *The Influence of Sea Power Upon History, 1660–1783* (Boston, MA: Little, Brown, 1890).

Mahan, Alfred Thayer. The Influence of Sea Power upon the French Revolution and Empire, 1793–1812 (Boston, MA: Little, Brown, 1890).

Merezhkovskiĭ, Dmitriĭ S. 'Griadushchiĭ kham', in *Polnoe sobranie sochineniĭ*, 24 vols (Moscow: Tipografiia Tva I.D. Sytina, 1914), 14:7–11.

Morison, Elting E. *The Letters of Theodore Roosevelt*, 8 vols (Cambridge, MA: Harvard University Press, 1951–4).

Naitō Shōichi. 'Dai-ni kuchikutai no tekikan shūgeki', in Todaka Kazushige (ed.), *Nihonkai kaisen no shōgen* (Tokyo: Kōjinsha, 2012), 43–57.

Nehru, Jawaharlal. *An Autobiography: With Musings on Recent Events in India* (London: John Lane, 1936).

Nicholas II. *Dnevnik imperatora Nikolaia II, 1890–1906 gg.* (Berlin: Knigoizgatel'stvo "Slovo", 1923).

Novikoff-Priboy, Alexey. *La tragédie de Tsoushima*, trans. V. Soukhomline and S. Campaux (Paris: Payot, 1934).

Novikoff-Priboy, Alexey. *Tsushima*, trans. Eden Paul and Cedar Paul (London: G. Allen & Unwin, 1936).

Novikoff-Priboy, Alexey. *Tsushima: Nihonkai kaisen* (Tokyo: Tōkyō Sōgensha, 1956).

Novikov-Priboi, Aleksei. *Nihonkai sensen* (Tokyo: Kaizōsha, 1933–5).

Novikov-Priboi, Aleksei. *Tsushima*, 2 vols (Moscow: Gosudarstvennoe Izdatel'stvo Khudozhestvennoĭ Literatury, 1935–6).

Ōkuma Asajirō. *Shinsui Horiuchi Bunjirō shōgun o itamu* (Fukuoka: Ōkuma Asajirō, 1942).

Ozaki Chikara. *Seishō Tōgō to reikan Mikasa* (Tokyo: Mikasa Hozonkai, 1935).

Paléologue, Maurice. *Un grand tournant de la politique mondiale, 1904–1906* (Paris: Pilon, 1934).

Politovsky, Eugène S. *From Libau to Tsushima*, trans. F.R. Godfrey (London: John Murray, 1907).

Repington, Charles à Court. *The War in the Far East, 1904–1905: By the Military Correspondent of "The Times"* (London: J. Murray; New York: E. P. Dutton, 1905).

Satō Tetsutarō. 'Dai-ni kantai no kōdō', in Todaka Kazushige (ed.), *Nihonkai kaisen no shōgen* (Tokyo: Kōjinsha, 2012), 16–23.

Semenov, Vladimir. *Flot i Morskoe Vedomstvo do Tsushimi i Posle* (St Petersburg: Tip. T-va M.O. Volf, 1911).

Semenov, Vladimir. *Rasplata (Rasplata, Boi Pri Tsusime, Tsena Krovi)*, 3 vols (St Petersburg: Tip. T-va M.O. Volf, 1906).

Semenov, Vladimir. *Rasplata [The Reckoning]* (London: J. Murray; New York: E.P. Dutton, 1909).

Semenov, Vladimir. *The Battle of Tsu-Shima between the Japanese and Russian Fleets, Fought on 27th May 1905*, trans. A.B. Lindsay (London: J. Murray; New York: E.P. Dutton, 1906).

Semenov, Vladimir. *The Price of Blood; The Sequel to "Rasplata" and "The Battle of Tsushima"* (London: J. Murray; New York: E.P. Dutton, 1910).

Shiba Ryōtarō. *Clouds above the Hill: A Historical Novel of the Russo-Japanese War*, trans. Juliet Winters Carpenter and Paul McCarthy, 4 vols (London: Routledge, 2012–14).

Shiba Ryōtarō. *Saka no ue no kumo*, 6 vols (Tokyo: Bungei Shunjū, 1969–72).

Sims, William S. 'The Inherent Tactical Qualities of the All-Big-Gun, One Caliber Battleship of the High Speed, Large Displacement and Gun Power', *US Naval Institute Proceedings* 32, no. 4 (1906), 1337–66.

Stepanov, Aleksandr. *Port Arthur, Historical Narrative*, trans. J. Fineberg (Moscow: Foreign Language Publishing House, 1947).

Sultan Abdülhamid, *Siyasî hatıratım* (Istanbul: Dergâh Yayınları, 1987).

Suzuki Kantarō. 'Dai-yon kuchikutai no tekikan shūgeki', in Todaka Kazushige (ed.), *Nihonkai kaisen no shōgen* (Tokyo: Kōjinsha, 2012), 30–42.

Svechin, Aleksandr A. *Strategiia XX veka na pervom etape: Planirovanie voini i operatsii na sushe i na more v 1904–1905 gg.* (Moscow: Akademiia General'nogo Shtaba RKKA, 1937).

Takeuchi Shigetoshi. 'Rokan *Adomiraru Ushakofu* no gekichin', in Todaka Kazushige (ed.), *Nihonkai kaisen no shōgen* (Tokyo: Kōjinsha, 2012), 68–72.

Taube, G. *Poslednĭi dni Vtoroi tikhookeanskoi eskadrĭ* (St Petersburg: A.S. Suvorina, 1907).

Taube, Georg Freiherr von. *Die letzten Tage des Baltischen Geschwaders* (St Petersburg: Sankt Petersburger Herold, 1907).

The Editors. 'The Progress of Navies: Foreign Navies', in John Leyland and T.A. Brassey (eds), *The Naval Annual, 1906* (Portsmouth: J. Griffin, 1906), 8–27.

The Russo-Japanese War Fully Illustrated, 3 vols (Tokyo: The Kinkodo Publishing Company, 1904–5).

Tirpitz, Alfred von. *Erinnerungen* (Leipzig: K.F. Koehler, 1920).

Tsuboya Zenshirō. *Nichiro sen'eki kaigun shashinshū* (Tokyo: Hakubunkan, 1905).

Tsukamoto Yoshitane. *Asahi-kan yori mitaru Nihonkai kaisen* (Tokyo: Sōrōkaku Shobō, 1907).

Uchiyama Torao. 'Nichiro sensō nakaba yori jūgun no kansō', in Todaka Kazushige (ed.), *Nihonkai kaisen no shōgen* (Tokyo: Kōjinsha, 2012), 89–98.

Ueda Shin, and Takanuki Nobuhito. *Jitsuroku Nihonkai kaisen: Nichiro sensō kiseki no tekizen dai kaitō* (Tokyo: Tachikaze Shobō, 2000).

White, R.D. 'With the Baltic Fleet at Tsushima', *US Naval Institute Proceedings* 32, no. 2 (1906), 597–620.

William II, German Emperor. *The Kaiser's Memoirs*, trans. Thomas R. Ybarra (New York: Harper and Brothers, 1922).

Wilson, H.W. *Japan's Fight for Freedom*, 3 vols (London: The Amalgamated Press, 1904–6).

Witte, Sergei Iu. *The Memoirs of Count Witte*, trans. Abraham Yarmolinsky (Garden City, NY: Doubleday, Page, 1921).

Wood, Oliver Ellsworth. *From the Yalu to Port Arthur: An Epitome of the First Period of the Russo-Japanese War* (London: K. Paul, Trench, Trübner, 1905).

Wright, Seppings H.C. *With Togo: The Story of Seven Months' Active Service under His Command* (London: Hurst-Blackett, 1905).

Yamaji Kazuyoshi. 'Dai-san kantai no kōdō', in Todaka Kazushige (ed.), *Nihonkai kaisen no shōgen* (Tokyo: Kōjinsha, 2012), 24–9.

Yamamoto Shinjirō. 'Nebogatofu-shō kōfuku jōkyō', in Todaka Kazushige (ed.), *Nihonkai kaisen no shōgen* (Tokyo: Kōjinsha, 2012), 58–67.

Yoshimura Akira. *Umi no shigeki*, 2 vols (Tokyo: Shinchōsha, 1972).

Zatertĭi, A. [Novikov-Priboĭ, Aleksei]. *Bezumtsi i besplodniya zhertvi* (St Petersburg: S.l., 1907).

Zatertĭi, A. [Novikov-Priboĭ, Aleksei]. *Za chuzhiye grekhi* (Moscow: S.l., 1907).

Zepelin, Generalmajor a. D. C. von. 'Die Kapitulation des "Bjödowy" und der Schiffe Nebogatows vor dem Kriegsgericht, 2. Der Prozeß Nebogatow', *Marine-Rundschau* (February, 1907), 186–96.

Zimmern, Alfred. *The Third British Empire* (London: Humphrey Milford, 1926).

Secondary Sources

Abe Shinzō. *Tōgō gensui jikiwashū* (Tokyo, Chūō Kōronsha, 1935).

Abulafia, David. *The Great Sea: A Human History of the Mediterranean* (New York: Penguin, 2012).

Adkin, Mark. *The Trafalgar Companion: A Guide to History's Most Famous Sea Battle and the Life of Admiral Lord Nelson* (London: Aurum Press, 2005).

Afflerbach, Holger. 'Going Down with Flying Colours? Naval Surrender from Elizabethan to Our Own Times', in Holger Afflerbach and Hew Strachan (eds), *How Fighting Ends: A History of Surrender* (Oxford: Oxford University Press, 2012), 187–210.

Agawa, Hiroyuki. *The Reluctant Admiral: Yamamoto and the Imperial Navy* (Tokyo: Kodansha, 1979).

Ahvenainen, Jorma. *The Far Eastern Telegraphs: The History of/Telegraphic Communications between the Far East, Europe, and America before the First World War* (Helsinki: Suomalainen Tiedeakatemia, 1981).

Akarca, Halit D. 'A Reinterpretation of the Ottoman Neutrality during the War', in Rotem Kowner (ed.), *Rethinking the Russo-Japanese War, 1904–05* (Folkestone: Global Oriental, 2007), 383–92.

Akiyama Saneyuki-kai (ed.). *Akiyama Saneyuki* (Tokyo: Akiyama Saneyuki-kai, 1933).

Aleksandrovskiĭ, Grigoriĭ B. *Tsusimskii Boi* (New York: Rossiya Pub. Co., 1956; rep. Moscow: Veche, 2012).

Andidora, Ronald. 'Admiral Togo: An Adaptable Strategist', *Naval War College Review* 44 (1991), 52–62.

Aoyama, Tomoko. 'Japanese Literary Response to the Russo-Japanese War', in David Wells and Sandra Wilson (eds), *The Russo-Japanese War in Cultural Perspective, 1904–05* (Basingstoke: Macmillan, 1999), 60–85.

Apushkin, Vladimir A. *Russko-iaponskaia voina 1904–1905 g.* (Moscow: Obrazovanie, 1910; rep. St Petersburg: Izd-vo S.-Peterb. un-ta, 2005).

Asada, Sadao. *From Mahan to Pearl Harbor: The Imperial Japanese Navy and the United States* (Annapolis, MD: Naval Institute Press, 2006).

Ascher, Abraham. *P.A. Stolypin: The Search for Stability in Late Imperial Russia* (Stanford, CA: Stanford University Press, 2001).

Ascher, Abraham. *The Revolution of 1905*, 2 vols (Stanford, CA: Stanford University Press, 1988).

Avrich, Paul. *Kronstadt, 1921* (Princeton, NJ: Princeton University Press, 1970).

Barr, William. 'Tsarist Attempt at Opening the Northern Sea Route: The Arctic Ocean Hydrographic Expedition, 1910–1915', *Polarforschung* 45 (1972), 51–64.

Barry, Quintin. *Command of the Sea: William Pakenham and the Russo-Japanese Naval War, 1904–1905* (Warwick: Helion & Company, 2019).

Bartlett, Rosamund. 'Japonisme and Japanophobia: The Russo-Japanese War in Russian Cultural Consciousness', *The Russian Review* 67 (2008), 8–33.

Bascomb, Neal. *Red Mutiny: Eleven Fateful Days on the Battleship Potemkin* (Boston, MA: Houghton Mifflin, 2007).

Beillevaire, Patrick. 'The Impact of the War on the French Political Scene', in Rotem Kowner (ed.), *The Impact of the Russo-Japanese War* (London: Routledge, 2007), 124–36.

Benesch, Oleg. *Inventing the Way of the Samurai: Nationalism, Internationalism, and Bushido in Modern Japan* (Oxford: Oxford University Press, 2014).

Berton, Peter. *Russo-Japanese Relations, 1905–17: From Enemies to Allies* (London: Routledge, 2011).

Bieganiec, Rina. 'Distant Echoes: The Reflection of the War in the Middle East Perspective', in Rotem Kowner (ed.), *Rethinking the Russo-Japanese War, 1904–05* (Folkestone: Global Oriental, 2007), 444–55.

Bix, Herbert. *Hirohito and the Making of Modern Japan* (New York: HarperCollins, 2000).

Blond, Georges. *Admiral Togo*, trans. Edward Hyams (New York: Macmillan, 1960).

Bodley, Ronald V.C. *Admiral Togo* (London: Jarrolds, 1935).

Bogdanov, M.A. *Eskadrennĭ bronenosets Sissoi Velikiĭ* (St Petersburg: M.A. Leonov, 2004).

Boissier, Pierre. *From Solferino to Tsushima: History of the International Committee of the Red Cross* (Geneva: Henry Dunant Institute, 1985).

Braisted, William Reynolds. 'The United States Navy's Dilemma in the Pacific, 1906–1909', *Pacific Historical Review* 26 (1957), 235–44.

Britton, Dorothy. 'Frank Guvyer Britton (1879–1934), Engineer and Earthquake Hero', in Hugh Cortazzi (ed.), *Britain & Japan: Biographical Portraits*, vol. 6 (Folkestone: Global Oriental, 2007), 174–81.

Brown, David K. *The Grand Fleet: Warship Design and Development 1906–1922* (Annapolis, MD: Naval Institute Press, 1999).

Brown, David K. 'The Russo-Japanese War: Technical Lessons as Perceived by the Royal Navy', *Warship* (1996), 66–77.

Brown, David K. *Warrior to Dreadnought: Warship Development 1860–1905* (Annapolis, MD: Naval Institute Press, 1997).

Buckley, Thomas H. *The United States and the Washington Conference, 1921–1922* (Knoxville: University of Tennessee Press, 1970).

Bukh, Alexander. 'Historical Memory and Shiba Ryōtarō: Remembering Russia, Creating Japan', in Sven Saaler and Wolfgang Schwentker (eds), *The Power of Memory in Modern Japan* (Folkestone: Global Oriental, 2008), 96–115.

Busch, Noel F. *The Emperor's Sword: Japan vs. Russia in the Battle of Tsushima* (New York: Funk & Wagnalls, 1969).

Bushnell, John S. *Mutiny amid Repression: Russian Soldiers in the Revolution of 1905–1906* (Bloomington: Indiana University Press, 1993).

Campbell, N.J.M. 'The Battle of Tsu-Shima', Parts 1, 2, 3, and 4, in Antony Preston (ed.), *Warship* (London: Conway Maritime Press, 1978), 46–49, 127–35, 186–92, 258–65.

Carter, Samuel. *The Incredible Great White Fleet* (New York: Macmillan, 1971).

Cecil, Lamar J. R. 'Coal for the Fleet That Had to Die', *American Historical Review* 69, no. 4 (1964), 990–1005.

Chapman, John W.M. 'British Naval Estimation of Japan and Russia, 1894–1905', Suntory Center Discussion Paper no. IS/04/475 (2004), 17–55.

Chapman, John W.M. 'Japan in Poland's Secret Neighbourhood War', *Japan Forum* 7 (1995), 225–83.

Chernov, Iu.I. 'Tsushima', in Ivan Rostunov (ed.), *Istoriia russko-iaponskoi voini 1904–1905 gg.* (Moscow: Nauka, 1977), 332–47.

Chiba, Isao. 'Shifting Contours of Memory and History, 1904–1980', in John W. Steinberg et al. (eds), *The Russo-Japanese War in Global Perspective*, 2 vols (Leiden: Brill, 2005–7), 2:357–78.

Chubaryan, Aleksandr O. *Istoriia Rossii XX–nachalo XXI veka. 11 klass*, 4th edn (Moscow: Prosveshenie, 2007).

Clements, Jonathan. *Admiral Togo: Nelson of the East* (London: Haus Publishing, 2010).

Cohen, Aaron J. 'Long Ago and Far Away: War Monuments, Public Relations, and the Memory of the Russo-Japanese War in Russia, 1907–14', *Russian Review* 69 (2010), 388–411.

Cohen, Eliot A., and John Gooch. *Military Misfortunes: The Anatomy of Failure in War* (New York: Free Press, 1990).

Compton-Hall, Richard. *Submarine Boats: The Beginnings of Underwater Warfare* (London: Conway Maritime Press, 1983).

Connaughton, Richard Michael. *The War of the Rising Sun and Tumbling Bear: Russia's War with Japan*, rev. edn (London: Cassell, 2003).

Coox, Alvin D. *Nomonhan: Japan against Russia, 1939*, 2 vols (Stanford, CA: Stanford University Press, 1985).

Coox, Alvin D. 'The Pearl Harbor Raid Revisited', *The Journal of American–East Asian Relations* 3, no. 3 (1994), 211–27.

Corbett, Julian S. *The Campaign of Trafalgar* (London: Longmans, Green & Co., 1910).

Crowley, Roger. *Empires of the Sea: The Siege of Malta, the Battle of Lepanto, and the Contest for the Center of the World* (London: Faber and Faber, 2008).

De Michelis, Cesare G. *The Non-Existent Manuscript: A Study of the Protocols of the Sages of Zion*, trans. Richard Newhouse (Lincoln: University of Nebraska Press, 2004).

Demchak, Tony E. 'Rebuilding the Russian Fleet: The Duma and Naval Rearmament', *Journal of Slavic Military Studies* 26 (2013), 25–40.

Dennet, Tyler. *Roosevelt and the Russo-Japanese War: A Critical Study of American Policy in Eastern Asia in 1902–1905* (New York: Doubleday, 1925).

Deutscher, Isaac. *Stalin: A Political Biography* (London: Oxford University Press, 1949).

Dharampal-Frick, Gita 'Der Russisch-Japanische Krieg und die indische Nationalbewegung', in Maik Hendrik Sprotte, Wolfgang Seifert, and Heinz-Dietrich Löwe (eds), *Der Russisch-Japanische Krieg, 1904/05* (Wiesbaden: Harrassowitz, 2007), 259–75.

Dickinson, Frederick R. 'Commemorating the War in Post-Versailles Japan', in John W. Steinberg et al. (eds), *The Russo-Japanese War in Global Perspective*, 2 vols (Leiden: Brill, 2005–7), 1:523–43.

Diedrich, Edward C. 'The Last Iliad: The Siege of Port Arthur in the Russo-Japanese War, 1904–1905', PhD dissertation (New York University, 1978).

Dua, R.P. *The Impact of the Russo-Japanese (1905) War on Indian Politics* (Delhi: S. Chand, 1966).

Dull, Paul S. *A Battle History of the Imperial Japanese Navy (1941–1945)* (Annapolis, MD: Naval Institute Press, 1978).

Dunley, Richard. '"The Warrior Has Always Shewed Himself Greater Than His Weapons": The Royal Navy's Interpretation of the Russo-Japanese War 1904–5', *War & Society* 34 (2015) 248–62.

Eberspaecher, Cord. 'The Road to Jutland? The War and the Imperial German Navy', in Rotem Kowner (ed.), *The Impact of the Russo-Japanese War* (London: Routledge, 2007), 290–305.

Edwards, E.W. 'The Far Eastern Agreements of 1907', *The Journal of Modern History* 26, no. 4 (1954), 340–55.

Epkenhans, Michael. 'Technology, Shipbuilding and Future Combat in Germany, 1880–1914', in Phillips P. O'Brien (ed.), *Technology and Naval Combat in the Twentieth Century and Beyond* (London: Frank Cass, 2001), 53–68.

Eppstein, Ury. 'School Songs, the War and Nationalist Indoctrination in Japan', in Rotem Kowner (ed.), *Rethinking the Russo-Japanese War, 1904–05* (Folkestone: Global Oriental, 2007), 185–201.

Ericson, Steven, and Allen Hockley (eds). *The Treaty of Portsmouth and Its Legacies* (Hanover: Dartmouth College Press, 2008).

Esthus, Raymond A. *Double Eagle and the Rising Sun: The Russian and Japanese at Portsmouth in 1905* (Durham, NC: Duke University Press, 1988).

Esthus, Raymond A. 'Nicholas II and the Russo-Japanese War', *Russian Review* 40 (1981), 396–411.

Esthus, Raymond A. *Theodore Roosevelt and Japan* (Seattle: University of Washington Press, 1966).

Evans, David C., and Mark R. Peattie. *Kaigun: Strategy, Tactics, and Technology in the Imperial Japanese Navy, 1887–1941* (Annapolis, MD: Naval Institute Press, 1997).

Fairbanks, Charles H. 'The Origins of the Dreadnought Revolution: A Historiographical Essay', *International History Review* 13 (1991), 246–72.

Falk, Edwin A. *Togo and the Rise of Japanese Sea Power* (New York: Longmans, Green, 1936).

Farjenel, Fernand. 'Le Japon et l'Islam', *Revue du monde musulman* 1 (1907), 101–14.

Fedorov, Alexander. 'The Image of the White Movement in the Soviet Films of 1950s–1980s', *European Journal of Social and Human Sciences* 9 (2016), 23–42.

Frame, M. et al. (eds). *Russian Culture in War and Revolution, 1914–22, Vol. 1, Popular Culture, the Arts, and Institutions* (Bloomington: IN: Slavica, 2014).

Frankel, Jonathan. 'The War and the Fate of the Tsarist Autocracy', in Rotem Kowner (ed.), *The Impact of the Russo-Japanese War* (London: Routledge, 2007), 54–77.

Friedman, Norman. *Fighting the Great War at Sea: Strategy, Tactics and Technology* (Barnsley: Seaforth, 2014).

Friedman, Norman. *The British Battleship, 1906–1946* (Annapolis, MD: Naval Institute Press, 2015).

Friedman, Norman. *The U.S. Maritime Strategy* (Annapolis, MD: Naval Institute Press, 1988).

Fujitani, Takashi. *Splendid Monarchy: Power and Pageantry in Modern Japan* (Berkeley: University of California Press, 1996).

Fukudome, Shigeru. 'Hawaii Operation', *U.S. Naval Institute Proceedings* 81 (1955), 1315–31.

Fuller, Jr, William C. *Civil–Military Conflict in Imperial Russia, 1881–1914* (Princeton, NJ: Princeton University Press, 1985).

Fuller, Jr, William C. *Strategy and Power in Russia, 1600–1914* (New York: Free Press, 1992).

Galai, S. 'The Impact of War on the Russian Liberals in 1904–5', *Government and Opposition* 1 (1965), 85–109.

Gardiner, Robert, and Andrew Lambert (eds). *Steam, Steel, and Shellfire: The Steam Warship, 1815–1905* (London: Conway Maritime Press, 1992).

Gat, Azar. *A History of Military Thought* (Oxford: Oxford University Press, 2001).

Gatrell, Peter. 'After Tsushima: Economic and Administrative Aspects of Russian Naval Rearmament, 1905–1913', *Economic History Review* 43 (1990), 255–72.

Gatrell, Peter. *Government, Industry, and Rearmament in Russia: The Last Argument of Tsarism* (New York: Cambridge University Press, 1994).

Genda, Minoru. 'Tactical Planning in the Imperial Japanese Navy', *Naval War College Review* 22, no. 2 (1969), 45–50.

George, James L. *History of Warships* (Annapolis, MD: Naval Institute Press, 1998).

Goldrick, James. 'Coal and the Advent of the First World War at Sea', *War in History* 21 (2014), 322–37.

Goldrick, James. 'The Battleship Fleet: The Test of War, 1895–1919', in J.R. Hill (ed.), *The Oxford Illustrated History of the Royal Navy* (Oxford: Oxford University Press, 1995), 280–318.

SELECT BIBLIOGRAPHY

Gooch, John. *The Plans of War: The General Staff and British Military Strategy, c.1900–1916* (London: Routledge and K. Paul, 1974).

Grajdanzev, Andrew J. 'Japan in Soviet Publications', *Far Eastern Survey* 13, no. 24 (1944), 223–6.

Gray, Edwyn. *The Devil's Device: The Story of Robert Whitehead, Inventor of the Torpedo* (London: Seeley, Service, & Co., 1975).

Gribovskiĭ, Vladimir. 'Bronenosets beregovoi oboroni "General-admiral Apraksin"', *Gangut* 18 (1999), 31–45.

Gribovskiĭ, Vladimir. *Eskadrennyĭ bronenosets "Borodino"* (St Petersburg: Gangut, 1995).

Gribovskiĭ, Vladimir. 'Krëstnyĭ put' otriada Nebogatova', *Gangut* 3 (1992), 16–34.

Gribovskiĭ, Vladimir. *Rossiĭskiĭ flot Tikhogo okeana, 1898–1905: istoriĭa sozdaniĭa i gibeli* (Moscow: Voen. kniga, 2004).

Gribovskiĭ, Vladimir. *Vitse-admiral Z.P. Rozhestvenskiĭ* (St Petersburg: Tsitadel, 1999). Reprinted under the title *Posledniĭ parad admirala* (Moscow: Veche, 2013).

Gribovskiĭ, Vladimir, and I.I. Chernikov. *Bronenosets "Admiral Ushakov"* (St Petersburg: Sudostroenie, 1996).

Gribovskiĭ, Vladimir, and I.I. Chernikov. *Bronenostsi beregovoi oboroni tipa "Admiral Seniavin"* (St Petersburg: Leko, 2009).

Grishachev, Sergey V. 'Russo-Japanese Relation in the 18th and 19th Centuries: Exploration and Negotiation', in Dmitry V. Streltsov and Nobuo Shimotomai (eds), *A History of Russo-Japanese Relations: Over Two Centuries of Cooperation and Competition* (Leiden: Brill, 2019), 18–41.

Grove, Eric. *Big Fleet Actions: Tsushima, Jutland, Philippine Sea* (London: Arms and Armour, 1995).

Guilmartin, John F. *Gunpowder and Galleys: Changing Technology & Mediterranean Warfare at Sea in the Sixteenth Century* (Cambridge: Cambridge University Press, 1974).

Halpern, Paul. 'The French Navy, 1880–1914', in Phillips P. O'Brien (ed.), *Technology and Naval Combat in the Twentieth Century and Beyond* (London: Frank Cass, 2001), 36–52.

Hansen, Wilburn. 'Examining Prewar Tôgô Worship in Hawaii Toward Rethinking Hawaiian Shinto as a New Religion in America', *Nova Religio: The Journal of Alternative and Emergent Religions* 14 (2010), 67–92.

Hanzawa Masao. 'Kishō-kaizō ga senkyoku no jūdai tenki to natta shorei (IV): Nihonkai kaisen no kaiyō kishōgakuteki kaiseki', *Kaiji shiryōkan nenpō* 19 (1991), 18–25.

Hara Teruyuki (ed.). *Nichiro sensō to Saharin-tō* (Sapporo: Hokkaido University Press, 2011).

Harada Keiichi. 'Irei to tsuito: sensō kinenbi kara shūsen kinenbie', in Kurasawa Aiko et al. (eds), *Sensō no seijigaku* (Tokyo: Iwanami, 2005), 291–316.

Harcave, Sidney. *First Blood: The Russian Revolution of 1905* (New York: Macmillan, 1964).

Harris, Brayton. *Admiral Nimitz: The Commander of the Pacific Ocean Theater* (New York: Palgrave Macmillan, 2012).

Hart, Robert A. *The Great White Fleet: Its Voyage Around the World, 1907–1909* (Boston, MA: Little, Brown, 1965).

Hattendorf, John B. 'The Idea of a "Fleet in Being" in Historical Perspective', *Naval War College Review* 67 (2014), 43–60.

Hauner, Milan L. 'Stalin's Big-Fleet Program', *Naval War College Review* 57, no. 2 (2004), 87–120.

Herrmann, David G. *The Arming of Europe and the Making of the First World War* (Princeton, NJ: Princeton University Press, 1996).

Herwig, Holger H. *"Luxury" Fleet: The Imperial German Navy, 1888–1918* (London: George Allen & Unwin, 1980).

Herwig, Holger H. 'The German Reaction to the Dreadnought Revolution', *International History Review* 13 (1991), 273–83.

Hirano, Tatsushi, Sven Saaler, and Stefan Säbel. 'Recent Developments in the Representation of National Memory and Local Identities: The Politics of Memory in Tsushima, Matsuyama, and Maizuru' *Japanstudien* 20 (2009), 247–77.

Hirose Takeo. 'Nichiro sensō o megutte', in Roshiashi Kenkyūkai (ed.), *Nichiro 200 nen–rinkoku Roshia to no Kōryūshi* (Tokyo: Sairyūsha, 1993).

Hobson, Rolf. *Imperialism at Sea: Naval Strategic Thought, the Ideology of Sea Power, and the Tirpitz Plan, 1875–1914* (Leiden: Brill, 2002).

Hogue, Richard. *Dreadnought: A History of the Modern Battleship* (New York: Macmillan, 1964).

Hogue, Richard. *The Fleet That Had to Die* (London: Viking, 1958).

Hone, Trent. *Learning War: The Evolution of Fighting Doctrine in the U.S. Navy 1898–1945* (Annapolis, MD: Naval Institute Press, 2018).

Hough, Richard A. *The Great War at Sea, 1914–1918* (Oxford: Oxford University Press, 1983).

Hudson, George E. 'Soviet Naval Doctrine under Lenin and Stalin', *Soviet Studies* 28 (1976), 42–65.

Hughes, Wayne P. 'Mahan, Tactics and Principles of Strategy', in John B. Hattendorf (ed.), *The Influence of History on Mahan* (Newport, RI: Naval War College Press, 1991), 25–36.

Hugill, Peter J. 'German Great-Power Relations in the Pages of "Simplicissimus", 1896–1914', *Geographical Review* 98 (2008), 1–23.

Hyslop, Jonathan 'An "Eventful" History of Hind Swaraj: Gandhi between the Battle of Tsushima and the Union of South Africa', *Public Culture* 23 (2011), 299–319.

Ienaga, Saburo. 'Glorification of War in Japanese Education', *International Security* 18, no. 3 (1993–4), 113–33.

Ifland, Peter. 'Finding Distance—The Barr & Stroud Rangefinders', *Journal of Navigation* 56 (2003), 315–21.

Iikura, Akira. 'The Anglo-Japanese Alliance and the Question of Race', in Phillips Payson O'Brien (ed.), *The Anglo-Japanese Alliance, 1902–1922* (London: RoutledgeCurzon, 2004), 222–35.

Ike, Nobutaka (ed.). *Japan's Decision for War: Records of the 1941 Policy Conference* (Stanford, CA: Stanford University Press, 1967).

Inaba Chiharu. *Baruchikku kantai o hosoku seyo: kaigun jōhō-bu no Nichiro sensō* (Tokyo: Seibunsha, 2016).

Inaba, Chiharu, and Rotem Kowner. 'The Secret Factor: Japanese Network of Intelligence Gathering on Russia during the War', in Rotem Kowner (ed.), *Rethinking the Russo-Japanese War, 1904–05* (Folkestone: Global Oriental, 2007), 78–92.

Iriye, Akira. *Across the Pacific: An Inner History of American–East Asian Relations* (New York, Harcourt, Brace and World, 1967).

Itō Masanori. *Daikaigun o omou* (Tokyo: Bungei Shunjū Shinsha, 1956).

Jacob, Frank. *Tsushima 1905: Ostasiens Trafalgar* (Paderborn: Ferdinand Schöningh, 2017).

Jane, Fred T. *The Imperial Japanese Navy* (London: W. Thacker, 1904).

Jane, Fred T. *The Imperial Russian Navy* (London: W. Thacker, 1899).

Jansen, Marius B. *The Making of Modern Japan* (Cambridge, MA: Belknap Press of Harvard University Press, 2000).

Jentschura, Hansgeorg, Dieter Jung, and Peter Mickel. *Warships of the Imperial Japanese Navy, 1869–1945*, trans. David Brown and Antony Preston (Annapolis, MD: Naval Institute Press, 1977).

Johnson, Ian Ona. 'Strategy on the Wintry Sea: The Russo-British Submarine Flotilla in the Baltic, 1914–1918', *International Journal of Military History and Historiography* 40 (2020), 187–212.

Kaigun Heigakkō. *Tōgō gensui keikōroku* (Tokyo: Dai-Nihon Tosho, 1935).

Kardashev, Iu.P. *Vosstanie: Drama na Tendre; Posledstviia vosstaniia; Komanda korablia* (Kirov: Viatka, Dom Pechati, 2008).

Katō, Yōko. "What Caused the Russo-Japanese War: Korea or Manchuria?" *Social Science Japan Journal* 10 (2007), 95–103.

Kawaraji, Hidetake. 'Japanese–Russian Relations in the 21st Century, 2001–2015', in Dmitry V. Streltsov and Nobuo Shimotomai (eds), *A History of Russo-Japanese Relations: Over Two Centuries of Cooperation and Competition* (Leiden: Brill, 2019), 521–34.

Keene, Donald. *Emperor of Japan: Meiji and His World, 1852–1912* (New York: Columbia University Press, 2002).

Keene, Donald. *Five Modern Japanese Novelists* (New York: Columbia University Press, 2003).

Kelly, Patrick J. *Tirpitz and the Imperial German Navy* (Bloomington: Indiana University Press, 2011).

Kennan, George F. (1984). *The Fateful Alliance: France, Russia, and the Coming of the First World War* (New York: Pantheon Books, 1984).

Kennedy, Paul. *Strategy and Diplomacy, 1870–1945* (London: George Allen & Unwin, 1983).

Keupp, Marcus Matthias. 'The Northern Sea Route: Introduction and Overview', in M.M. Keupp (ed.), *The Northern Sea Route: A Comprehensive Analysis* (Wiesbaden: Springer, 2015), 7–20.

Kiesling, Eugenia C. 'France', in Richard F. Hamilton and Holger H. Herwig (eds), *The Origins of World War I* (Cambridge: Cambridge University Press, 2003), 227–65.

Kinross, Patrick Balfour, Baron. *The Ottoman Centuries: The Rise and Fall of the Turkish Empire* (New York: Morrow, 1977).

Kitamura, Yukiko. 'Serial War: Egawa Tatsuya's Tale of the Russo-Japanese War', in John W. Steinberg et al. (eds), *The Russo-Japanese War in Global Perspective*, 2 vols (Leiden: Brill, 2005–7), 2:417–31.

Kolesova, Elena, and Ryota Nishino. 'Talking Past Each Other? A Comparative Study of the Descriptions of the Russo-Japanese War in Japanese and Russian History Textbooks, ca. 1997–2010', *Aoyama Journal of International Studies* 2 (2015), 5–39.

Kowner, Rotem. 'Becoming an Honorary Civilized Nation: Remaking Japan's Military Image during the Russo-Japanese War, 1904–1905', *The Historian* 64 (2001), 19–38.

Kowner, Rotem. *Historical Dictionary of the Russo-Japanese War*, 2nd edn (Lanham, MD: Rowman & Littlefield, 2017).

Kowner, Rotem. 'Imperial Japan and its POWs: The Dilemma of Humaneness and National Identity', in Guy Podoler (ed.), *War and Militarism in Modern Japan* (Folkestone: Global Oriental, 2009), 80–110.

Kowner, Rotem. 'Japan's "Fifteen Minutes of Glory": Managing World Opinion during the War with Russia, 1904–05', in Yulia Mikhailova and M. William Steele (eds), *Japan and Russia: Three Centuries of Mutual Images* (Folkestone: Global Oriental, 2008), 47–70.

Kowner, Rotem. 'Nicholas II and the Japanese Body: Images and Decision Making on the Eve of the Russo-Japanese War', *The Psychohistory Review* 26 (1998), 211–52.

Kowner, Rotem. 'Passing the Baton: The Asian Theater of World War II and the Coming of Age of the Aircraft Carrier', *Education About Asia* 19, no. 2 (2014), 68–73.

Kowner, Rotem. 'The High Road to World War I? Europe and Outcomes of the Russo-Japanese War', in Chiharu Inaba, John Chapman, and Masayoshi Matsumura (eds), *Rethinking the Russo-Japanese War: The Nichinan Papers* (Folkestone: Global Oriental, 2007), 293–314.

Kowner, Rotem. 'The Impact of the War on Naval Warfare', in R. Kowner (ed.), *The Impact of the Russo-Japanese War* (London: Routledge, 2007), 269–89.

Kowner, Rotem. 'The Russo-Japanese War', in Isabelle Duyvesteyn and Beatrice Heuser (eds.), *The Cambridge History of Military Strategy*, 2 vols (Cambridge: Cambridge University Press, 2022).

Kowner, Rotem. 'The War as a Turning Point in Modern Japanese History', in R. Kowner (ed.), *The Impact of the Russo-Japanese War* (London: Routledge, 2007), 29–46.

Krebs, Gerhard. 'World War Zero? Re-Assessing the Global Impact of the Russo-Japanese War 1904–05', *The Asia-Pacific Journal* 10, issue 21, no. 2 (2012).

Kreiser, Klaus. 'Der japanische Sieg über Rußland (1905) und sein Echo unter den Muslimen', *Die Welt des Islams* 21 (1981), 209–39.

Kuksin, I.Ye. 'The Arctic Ocean Hydrographic Expedition 1910–1915', *Polar Geography and Geology* 15 (1991), 299–309.

Kusumi Tadao. 'Akiyama Saneyuki to Nihonkai kaisen', *Chūō kōron* 80 (August 1965), 352–8.

Kuz'minkov, Viktor V., and Viktor N. Pavlyatenko. 'Soviet–Japanese Relations from 1960 to 1985: An Era of Ups and Downs', in Dmitry V. Streltsov and Nobuo Shimotomai (eds), *A History of Russo-Japanese Relations: Over Two Centuries of Cooperation and Competition* (Leiden: Brill, 2019), 419–39.

Lake, Marilyn, and Henry Reynolds. *Drawing the Global Colour Line: White Men's Countries and the International Challenge of Racial Equality* (Cambridge: Cambridge University Press, 2012).

Lambert, Nicholas A. 'Admiral Sir John Fisher and the Concept of Flotilla Defence, 1904–1909', in Phillips P. O'Brien (ed.), *Technology and Naval Combat in the Twentieth Century and Beyond* (London: Frank Cass, 2001), 69–90.

Lambert, Nicholas A. *Sir John Fisher's Naval Revolution* (Columbia: University of South Carolina Press, 1999).

Lambert, Nicholas A. (ed.). *The Submarine Service, 1900–1918* (Aldershot: Ashgate, 2001).

Lebow, Richard Ned. 'Accidents and Crises: The Dogger Bank Affair', *Naval War College Review* 31 (1978), 66–75.

Leeke, Jim. *Manila and Santiago: The New Steel Navy in the Spanish American War* (Annapolis, MD: Naval Institute Press, 2009).

Lensen, George Alexander. *Balance of Intrigue: International Rivalry in Korea and Manchuria, 1884–99*, 2 vols (Tallahassee, FL: Diplomatic Press, 1982).

Lensen, George Alexander. 'Early Russo-Japanese Relations', *The Far Eastern Quarterly* 10 (1950), 2–37.

Lensen, George Alexander. *The Russian Push toward Japan: Russo-Japanese Relations, 1697–1875* (Princeton, NJ: Princeton University Press, 1959).

Li Anshan. 'The Miscellany and Mixed: The War and Chinese Nationalism', in John W. Steinberg et al. (eds), *The Russo-Japanese War in Global Perspective*, 2 vols (Leiden: Brill, 2005–7), 2:491–512.

Likharev, Dmitrii V. 'Shells vs Armour: Material Factors of the Battle of Tsushima in the works of Russian Memoirists and Historians', *War & Society* 36, no. 3 (2017), 182–93.

Lim, Susanna Soojung. *China and Japan in the Russian Imagination, 1685–1922* (Abingdon: Routledge, 2013).

Lloyd, Arthur. *Admiral Togo* (Tokyo: Kinkodo; London: Probsthain, 1905).

Lone, Stewart. *Army, Empire, and Politics in Meiji Japan: The Three Careers of General Katsura Taro* (London: Palgrave Macmillan, 2000).

Lone, Stewart. *Japan's First Modern War: Army and Society in the Conflict with China, 1894–95* (London: Macmillan, 1994).

Lozhkina, Anastasia S., Yaroslav A. Shulatov, and Kirill E. Cherevko. 'Soviet–Japanese Relations after the Manchurian Incident, 1931–1939', in Dmitry V. Streltsov and Nobuo Shimotomai (eds), *A History of Russo-Japanese Relations: Over Two Centuries of Cooperation and Competition* (Leiden: Brill, 2019), 218–37.

Lukoianov, Igor V. 'The Bezobrazovtsy', in John W. Steinberg et al. (eds), *The Russo-Japanese War in Global Perspective*, 2 vols (Leiden: Brill, 2005–7), 1:65–86.

Luntinen, Pertti, and Bruce W. Menning. 'The Russian Navy at War, 1904–05', in John W. Steinberg et al. (eds), *The Russo-Japanese War in Global Perspective*, 2 vols (Leiden: Brill, 2005–7), 1:229–59.

McBride, William M. *Technological Change and the United States Navy, 1865–1945* (Baltimore, MD: The Johns Hopkins University Press, 2000).

McDonald, David M. 'Tsushima's Echoes: Asian Defeat and Tsarist Foreign Policy', in John W. Steinberg et al. (eds), *The Russo-Japanese War in Global Perspective*, 2 vols (Leiden: Brill, 2005–7), 1:545–64.

McDonald, David M. *United Government and Foreign Policy in Russia, 1900–1914* (Cambridge, MA: Harvard University Press, 1992).

Mackay, R.F. *Fisher of Kilverstone* (Oxford: Clarendon Press, 1973).

McLaughlin, Stephen. *Russian & Soviet Battleships* (Annapolis, MD: Naval Institute Press, 2003).

McLaughlin, Stephen. 'The Admiral Seniavin Class Coast Defense Ships', *Warship International* 48, no. 1 (2011), 43–66.

McLean, Roderick R. 'Dreams of a German Europe: Wilhelm II and the Treaty of Björkö 1905', in Annika Mombauer and Wilhelm Deist (eds), *The Kaiser: New Research on Wilhelm II´s Role in Imperial Germany* (Cambridge: Cambridge University Press, 2004), 119–42.

McReynolds, Louise. *The News under Russia's Old Regime: The Development of a Mass-Circulation Press* (Princeton, NJ: Princeton University Press, 1991).

Maki Yōzō. *Tōgō Heihachirō*, 2 vols (Tokyo: Bungei Shunjū, 1985).

Malozemoff, Andrew. *Russian Far Eastern Policy, 1881–1904, with Special Emphasis on the Causes of the Russo-Japanese War* (Berkeley: University of California Press, 1958).

Manning, Roberta T. *The Crisis of the Old Order in Russia: Gentry and Government* (Princeton, NJ: Princeton University Press, 1982).

Marder, Arthur J. *Fear God and Dread Nought: The Correspondence of Admiral of the Fleet Lord Fisher of Kilverstone: The Making of an Admiral, 1854–1904* (London: Jonathan Cape, 1952).

Marder, Arthur J. *Fear God and Dread Nought: The Correspondence of Admiral of the Fleet Lord Fisher of Kilverstone: Years of Power, 1904–1914* (London: Jonathan Cape, 1956).

Marder, Arthur J. *From the Dreadnought to Scapa Flow: The Royal Navy in the Fisher Era, 1904–1919* (London: Oxford University Press, 1961).

Marder, Arthur J. *The Anatomy of British Sea Power: A History of British Naval Policy in the Pre-Dreadnought Era* (New York: Knopf, 1940).

Marks, Steven. '"Bravo, Brave Tiger of the East!" The War and the Rise of Nationalism in British Egypt and India', in John W. Steinberg et al. (eds), *The Russo-Japanese War in Global Perspective*, 2 vols (Leiden: Brill, 2005–7), 1:609–27.

Marks, Steven. *Road to Power: The Trans-Siberian Railroad and the Colonization of Asian Russia, 1850–1917* (Ithaca, NY: Cornell University Press, 1991).

Mencken, H.L. *Newspaper Days, 1899–1906* (New York: Alfred A. Knopf, 1941).

Menning, Bruce W. 'Miscalculating One's Enemies: Russian Military Intelligence before the Russo-Japanese War', *War in History* 13, no. 2 (2006), 141–70.

Meurer, Alexander. *Seekriegsgeschichte in Umrissen. Seemacht und Seekriege vornehmlich vom 16. Jahrhundert ab* (Leipzig: Verlag v. Hase & Koehler, 1941).

Mikasa Preservation Society. *Memorial Ship Mikasa* (Yokosuka: Mikasa Preservation Society, 1981).

Mikhailova, Yulia. 'Japan's Place in Russian and Soviet National Identity: From Port Arthur to Khalkhin Gol', in Yulia Mikhailova and M. William Steele (eds), *Japan and Russia: Three Centuries of Mutual Images* (Folkestone: Global Oriental, 2008), 71–90.

Milevski, Lukas. *The Maritime Origins of Modern Grand Strategic Thought* (Oxford: Oxford University Press, 2016).

Miller, Edward S. *War Plan Orange: The U.S. Strategy to Defeat Japan, 1897–1945* (Annapolis, MD: Naval Institute Press, 1991).

Mishra, Pankaj. *From the Ruins of Empire: The Intellectuals Who Remade Asia* (New York: Farrar, Straus and Giroux, 2012).

Mitchell, Donald W. *A History of Russian and Soviet Sea Power* (New York: Macmillan, 1974).

Mobley, Scott. *Progressives in Navy Blue: Empire, and the Transformation of U.S. Naval Identity, 1873–1898* (Annapolis, MD: Naval Institute Press, 2018).

Modelsky, George, and William R. Thompson. *Seapower in Global Politics, 1494–1993* (Seattle: University of Washington Press, 1988).

Monger, George W. *The End of Isolation: British Foreign Policy, 1900–1907* (London: T. Nelson, 1963).

Moore, John H. 'The Short, Eventful Life of Eugene B. Ely', *U.S. Naval Institute Proceedings* 107 (1981), 58–63.

Nakamura, Kōya. *Admiral Togo: A Memoir* (Tokyo: Togo Gensui Publishing Society, 1937).

Nakamura, Kōya. *Sekai no Tōgō gensui* (Tokyo: Tōgō Gensui Hensankai, 1934).

Nakao, Hidehiro. 'The Legacy of Shiba Ryotaro', in Roy Starrs (ed.), *Japanese Cultural Nationalism at Home and in the Asia Pacific* (Folkestone: Global Oriental, 2004), 99–115.

Neu, Charles E. *An Uncertain Friendship: Theodore Roosevelt and Japan, 1906–1909* (Cambridge, MA, Harvard University Press, 1967).

Nimitz, Chester, and Elmer B. Potter. *Nimittsu no taiheiyō no kaisen-shi*, trans. Sanematsu Yuzuru Tominaga Kengo (Tokyo: Kōbunsha, 1962).

Nish, Ian. *Alliance in Decline: A Study in Anglo-Japanese Relations, 1908–1923* (London: Athlone Press, 1972).

Nish, Ian. 'Japan and Naval Aspects of the Washington Conference', in William Beasley (ed.), *Modern Japan* (Berkeley: University of California Press, 1975), 67–80.

Nish, Ian. *The Anglo-Japanese Alliance: The Diplomacy of Two Island Empires, 1894–1907* (London: Athlone Press, 1966).

Nish, Ian. *The Origins of the Russo-Japanese War* (London: Longman, 1985).

Nogi jinja-Tōgō jinja. *Nogi Maresuke to Tōgō Heihachirō* (Tokyo: Shinjinbutsu Ōraisha, 1993).

Nomura Minoru. *Kaisen-shi ni manabu* (Tokyo: Bungei Shunjū, 1985).

Nomura Naokuni (ed.). *Gensui Tōgō Heihachirō* (Tokyo: Nihon Kaibō Kyōkai, 1968).

Nordman, N. 'Nashi morskie budzheti', *Morskoi Sbornik* 379, no. 12 (December 1913), 63–84.

O'Brien, Phillips P. *British and American Naval Power: Politics and Policy, 1900–1936* (Westport, CT: Praeger, 1998).

Ogasawara Naganari. *Life of Admiral Togo*, trans. Jukichi Inouye and Tozo Inouye (Tokyo: Seito Shorin Press, 1934).

Ogasawara Naganari. *Seishō Tōgō Heihachirō den* (Tokyo: Kaizōsha, 1934).

Ogasawara Naganari (ed.). *Tōgō gensui shōden* (Tokyo: Shun'yōdō, 1921).

O'Hara, Vincent P., and Leonard R. Heinz. *Clash of Fleets: Naval Battles of the Great War, 1914–18* (Annapolis, MD: Naval Institute Press, 2017).

Ohnuki-Tierney, Emiko. *Kamikaze, Cherry Blossoms, and Nationalisms: The Militarization of Aesthetics in Japanese History* (Chicago, IL: University of Chicago Press, 2002).

Oi, Atsushi. 'Why Japan's Anti-Submarine Warfare Failed', in David C. Evans (ed.), *The Japanese Navy in World War II*, 2nd edn (Annapolis, MD: Naval Institute Press, 1986), 385–414.

Oide Hisashi. *Chishō Akiyama Saneyuki: aru sen'nin sanbō no shōgai* (Tokyo: Kōjinsha, 1985).

Oka, Yoshitake. 'Generational Conflict after the Russo-Japanese War', in Tetsuo Najita and J. Victor Koschmann (eds), *Conflict in Modern Japanese History: The Neglected Tradition* (Princeton, NJ: Princeton University Press, 1982), 197–225.

Okamoto, Shumpei. 'The Emperor and the Crowd: The Historical Significance of the Hibiya Riots', in Tetsuo Najita and J. Victor Koschmann (eds), *Conflict in Modern Japanese History: The Neglected Tradition* (Princeton, NJ: Princeton University Press, 1982), 262–70.

Okamoto, Shumpei. *The Japanese Oligarchy and the Russo-Japanese War* (New York: Columbia University Press, 1970).

Oleinikov, Dmitrii. 'The War in Russian Historical Memory', in John W. Steinberg et al. (eds), *The Russo-Japanese War in Global Perspective*, 2 vols (Leiden: Brill, 2005–7), 1:509–22.

Olender, Piotr. *Russo-Japanese Naval War, 1904–1905*, 2 vols (Sandomierz: Stratus, 2009–10).

Ono, Keishi. 'Japan's Monetary Mobilization for War', in John W. Steinberg et al. (eds), *The Russo-Japanese War in Global Perspective*, 2 vols (Leiden: Brill, 2005–7), 2:251–69.

Ono, Keishi. 'The War, Military Expenditures and Postbellum Fiscal and Monetary Policy in Japan', in Rotem Kowner (ed.), *Rethinking the Russo-Japanese War, 1904–05* (Folkestone: Global Oriental, 2007), 139–57.

Otte, T.G. 'The Fragmenting of the Old World Order: Britain, The Great Powers, and the War', in Rotem Kowner (ed.), *The Impact of the Russo-Japanese War* (London: Routledge, 2007), 91–108.

Oyos, Matthew. 'Theodore Roosevelt and the Implements of War', *The Journal of Military History* 60 (1996), 631–55.

Padfield, Peter. *The Battleship Era* (London: Rupert Hart-Davis, 1972).

Paine, S.C.M. *The Sino-Japanese War of 1894–1895: Perception, Power, and Primacy* (Cambridge: Cambridge University Press, 2003).

Papastratigakis, Nicholas. *Russian Imperialism and Naval Power: Military Strategy and the Build-Up to the Russo-Japanese War* (London: I.B. Tauris, 2011).

Papastratigakis, Nicholas, and Dominic Lieven. 'The Russian Far Eastern Squadron's Operational Plans', in John W. Steinberg et al. (eds), *The Russo-Japanese War in Global Perspective*, 2 vols (Leiden: Brill, 2005–7), 1:203–27.

Parkes, Oscar. *British Battleships, "Warrior" 1860 to "Vanguard" 1950: A History of Design, Construction, and Armament* (Annapolis, MD: Naval Institute Press, 1990).

Parshall, Jonathan, and Anthony Tully. *Shattered Sword: The Untold Story of the Battle of Midway* (Dulles, VA: Potomac Books, 2005).

Patalano, Alessio. '"A Symbol of Tradition and Modernity": Itō Masanori and the Legacy of the Imperial Navy in the Early Postwar Rearmament Process', *Japanese Studies* 34 (2014), 61–82.

Patalano, Alessio. *Post-War Japan as a Sea Power: Imperial Legacy, Wartime Experience and the Making of a Navy* (London: Bloomsbury, 2015).

Pestushko, Yuriĭ S., and Yaroslav A. Shulatov. 'Russo-Japanese Relations from 1905 to 1916: from Enemies to Allies', in Dmitry V. Streltsov and Nobuo Shimotomai (eds), *A History of Russo-Japanese Relations: Over Two Centuries of Cooperation and Competition* (Leiden: Brill, 2019), 101–18.

Petrov, Mikhail A. *Podgotovka Rossii k mirovoi voine na more* (Moscow: Gosudarstvennoe voennoe izdatel'stvo, 1926).

Plaschka, Richard G. *Matrosen, Offiziere, Rebellen, Krisenkonfrontationen zur See, 1900–1918*, 2 vols (Vienna: H. Böhlau, 1984).

Pleshakov, Constantine. *The Tsar's Last Armada: The Epic Voyage to the Battle of Tsushima* (New York: Basic Books, 2002).

Podoler, Guy, and Michael Robinson. 'On the Confluence of History and Memory: The Significance of the War for Korea', in Rotem Kowner (ed.), *The Impact of the Russo-Japanese War* (London: Routledge, 2007), 183–98.

Podsoblyaev, Evgenii F. 'The Russian Naval General Staff and the Evolution of Naval Policy, 1905–1914', *Journal of Military History* 66 (2002), 37–69.

Polmar, Norman, and Jurrien Noot. *Submarines of the Russian and Soviet Navies, 1718–1990* (Annapolis, MD: Naval Institute Press, 1991).

Potter, Elmer B. *Nimitz* (Annapolis, MD: Naval Institute Press, 1976).

Potter, Elmer B., and Chester Nimitz (eds). *The Great Sea War: The Story of Naval Action in World War II* (Englewood Cliffs, NJ: Prentice-Hall, 1960).

Prange, Gordon W., Donald M. Goldstein, and Katherine V. Dillon. *Miracle at Midway* (New York: McGraw-Hill, 1982).

Preston, Antony. *The Royal Navy Submarine Service: A Centennial History* (Annapolis, MD: Naval Institute Press, 2001).

Rajabzadeh, Hashem. 'Russo-Japanese War as Told by Iranians', *Annals of Japan Association for Middle East Studies* 3, no. 2 (1988), 144–66.

Reckner, James R. *Teddy Roosevelt's Great White Fleet* (Annapolis, MD: Naval Institute Press, 1988).

Renner, Andreas. 'Markt, Staat, Propaganda: Der Nördliche Seeweg in Russlands Arktisplänen', *Osteuropa* 70, no. 5 (2020), 39–59.

Richardson, Alexander. *The Evolution of the Parsons Steam Turbine* (London: Engineering, 1911).

Rieve, Hans-Otto. 'Admiral Nebogatov–Schuld oder Schicksal', *Marine-Rundschau* 1 (1964), 1–11.

Rivera, Carlos R. 'Big Stick and Short Sword: The American and Japanese Navies as Hypothetical Enemies', PhD dissertation (Ohio State University, 1995).

Roberts, John. *Battlecruisers* (Annapolis, MD: Naval Institute Press, 1997).

Rodell, Paul A. 'Inspiration for Nationalist Aspirations? Southeast Asia and Japan's Victory', in John W. Steinberg et al. (eds), *The Russo-Japanese War in Global Perspective*, 2 vols (Leiden: Brill, 2005–7), 1:629–54.

Rodger, Nicholas A.M. 'Anglo-German Naval Rivalry, 1860–1914', in Michael Epkenhans, Jörg Hillmann, and Frank Nägler (eds), *Jutland: World War I's Greatest Naval Battle* (Lexington: University Press of Kentucky, 2015), 7–21.

Rodgers, Marion Elizabeth. *Mencken: The American Iconoclast* (Oxford: Oxford University Press, 2006).

Röhl, John C. G. *Wilhelm II: Into the Abyss of War and Exile, 1900–1941*, trans. Sheila de Bellaigue and Roy Bridge (Cambridge: Cambridge University Press, 2014).

Rohwer, Jürgen, and Mikhail S. Monakov. *Stalin's Ocean-Going Fleet: Soviet Naval Strategy and Shipbuilding Programmes, 1935–1953* (Portland, OR: Frank Cass, 2001).

Røksund, Arne. *The Jeune École: The Strategy of the Weak* (Leiden: Brill, 2007).

Roland, Alex. *Underwater Warfare in the Age of Sail* (Bloomington: Indiana University Press, 1978).

Romanov, Boris A. (ed.). 'Konets russko-iaponskoĭ voini (Voennoe soveshchanie 24 maia 1905 goda v Tsarskom Sele)', *Krasnyi arkhiv* 3 (1928), 182–204.

Ropp, Theodore. *The Development of the Modern Navy: French Naval Policy, 1871–1914* (Annapolis, MD: Naval Institute Press, 1987).

Russel, Iain. 'Rangefinders at Tsushima', *Warship* 49 (1989), 30–6.

Saaler, Sven. 'The Russo-Japanese War and the Emergence of the Notion of the "Clash of Races" in Japanese Foreign Policy', in John W.M. Chapman and Chiharu Inaba (eds), *Rethinking the Russo-Japanese War, 1904–05: The Nichinan Papers* (Folkestone: Global Oriental, 2007), 274–89.

Saeki, Shōichi. 'Images of the United States as a Hypothetical Enemy', in Akira Iriye (ed.), *Mutual Images: Essays in American–Japanese Relations* (Cambridge, MA: Harvard University Press, 1975), 100–14.

Saito, Masami, Motokazu Nogawa, and Tadanori Hayakawa. 'Dissecting the Wave of Books on Nippon Kaigi, the Rightwing Mass Movement that Threatens Japan's Future', *The Asia-Pacific Journal* 16, issue 19, no. 1 (2018) [https://apjjf.org/2018/19/Saito.html].

Sakurai Ryōju. *Taishō seijishi no shuppatsu: rikken dōshikai no seiritsuto sono shūhen* (Tokyo: Yamakawa Shuppansha, 1997).

Salomon, Harald. 'Japan's Longest Days: Tōhō and the Politics of War Memory, 1967–1972' in King-fai Tam, Timothy Y. Tsu, and Sandra Wilson (eds), *Chinese and Japanese Films on the Second World War* (Abingdon: Routledge, 2015), 121–35.

Sanematsu, Yuruzu. 'Hachi-hachi kantai to Katō Tomosaburō', *Rekishi to jinbutsu* 6 (August 1976), 58–65.

Sareen, Tilak Raj. 'India and the War', in Rotem Kowner (ed.), *The Impact of the Russo-Japanese War* (London: Routledge, 2007), 137–52.

Sarkisov, Konstantin. *Put'k Tsusime: po neopublikovannym pis'mam vitse-admirala Z.P. Rozhestvenskogo* (St Petersburg: Izdatel'stvo Avrora, 2010).

Satō Ichirō. *Kaigun gojūnenshi* (Tokyo: Masu Shobō, 1943).

Satō Kasumi (ed.). *Zusetsu: Nichiro sensō heiki zensentōshū: Ketteiban* (Tokyo: Gakushū Kenkyūsha, 2006).

Saul, Norman E. 'The Kittery Peace', in John W. Steinberg et al. (eds), *The Russo-Japanese War in Global Perspective*, 2 vols (Leiden: Brill, 2005–7), 1:485–507.

Schencking, J. Charles. *Making Waves: Politics, Propaganda, and the Emergence of the Imperial Japanese Navy, 1868–1922* (Stanford, CA: Stanford University Press, 2005).

Schencking, J. Charles. 'The Imperial Japanese Navy and the First World War: Unprecedented Opportunities and Harsh Realities', in Tosh Minohara, Tze-ki Hon, and Evan Dawley (eds), *The Decade of the Great War: Japan and the Wider World in the 1910s* (Leiden: Brill, 2014), 83–106.

Schencking, J. Charles. 'The Politics of Pragmatism and Pageantry: Selling a National Navy at the Elite and Local Level in Japan, 1890–1913', in Sandra Wilson (ed.), *Nation and Nationalism in Japan* (London: RoutledgeCurzon, 2002), 565–90.

Scherr, Barry P. 'The Russo-Japanese War and the Russian Literary Imagination', in John W. Steinberg et al. (eds), *The Russo-Japanese War in Global Perspective*, 2 vols (Leiden: Brill, 2005–7), 1:425–46.

Schiffrin, Harold Z. 'The Impact of the War on China', in Rotem Kowner (ed.), *The Impact of the Russo-Japanese War* (London: Routledge, 2007), 169–82.

Schimmelpenninck van der Oye, David. 'Rewriting the Russo-Japanese War: A Centenary Retrospective', *Russian Review* 67 (2008), 78–87.

Schurman, Donald M. *Julian S. Corbett, 1854–1922: Historian of British Maritime Policy from Drake to Jellicoe* (London: Royal Historical Society, 1981).

Schurman, Donald M. *The Education of a Navy: The Development of British Naval Strategic Thought, 1867–1914* (London: Cassell, 1965).

Seager, Robert. *Alfred Thayer Mahan: The Man and His Letters* (Annapolis, MD: Naval Institute Press, 1977).

Seligman, Matthew S. 'Germany, the Russo-Japanese War, and the Road to the Great War', in Rotem Kowner (ed.), *The Impact of the Russo-Japanese War* (London: Routledge, 2007), 109–23.

Seligman, Matthew S. 'Intelligence Information and the 1909 Naval Scare: The Secret Foundations of a Public Panic', *War in History* 17 (2010), 37–59.

Sergeev, Evgeny. *Russian Military Intelligence in the War with Japan, 1904–05: Secret Operation on Land and at Sea* (London: Routledge, 2007).

Sergeev, Evgeny. *The Great Game, 1856–1907: Russo-British Relations in Central and East Asia* (Washington, DC: Woodrow Wilson Center Press; Baltimore, MD: The Johns Hopkins University Press, 2013).

Seton, Marie. *Panditji: A Portrait of Jawaharlal Nehru* (London: Dobson, 1967).

Seton-Watson, Robert W. *Sarajevo: A Study in the Origins of the Great War* (London: Hutchinson, 1926).

Sevela, Marie. 'Chaos versus Cruelty: Sakhalin as a Secondary Theater of Operations', in Rotem Kowner (ed.), *Rethinking the Russo-Japanese War, 1904–05* (Folkestone: Global Oriental, 2007), 93–108.

Shatsillo, Kornelliĭ F. *Russkiĭ imperializm i razvitieflota nakanune pervoi mirovoi voini, 1906–1914 gg.* (Moscow: Nauka, 1968).

Shillony, Ben-Ami. *The Jews and the Japanese: The Successful Outsiders* (Rutland, VT: C.E. Tuttle, 1992).

Shillony, Ben-Ami, and Rotem Kowner. 'The Memory and Significance of the Russo-Japanese War from a Centennial Perspective', in Rotem Kowner (ed.), *Rethinking the Russo-Japanese War, 1904–05* (Folkestone: Global Oriental, 2007), 1–9.

Shimada Kinji. *Roshiya sensō zenya no Akiyama Saneyuki*, 2 vols (Tokyo: Asahi Shinbunsha, 1990).

Shimanuki Takeharu. 'Nichiro sensō ikō ni okeru kokubō hōshin shoyō heiryoku, yōhei kōryō no hensen', *Gunji Shigaku* 8, no. 4, (1973), 2–11.

Shimazu, Naoko. *Japanese Society at War: Death, Memory and the Russo-Japanese War* (Cambridge: Cambridge University Press, 2009).

Shimizu Takehisa. *Soren to Nichiro sensō* (Tokyo: Hara Shobō, 1973).

Shimomura Toratarō. *Tōgō Heihachirō* (Tokyo: Kōdansha, 1981).

Shishov, Aleksei V. *Rossiia i Iaponiia (Istoriia voennie konfliktov)* (Moscow: Veche, 2001).

Slattery, Peter. *Reporting the Russo-Japanese War: Lionel James's First Wireless Transmission to the Times* (Folkestone: Global Oriental, 2004).

Smith, Crosbie. 'Dreadnought Science: The Cultural Construction of Efficiency and Effectiveness', in Robert J. Blyth, Andrew Lambert, and Jan Rüger (eds), *The Dreadnought and the Edwardian Age* (Farnham: Ashgate, 2011), 135–64.

Smorgunov, Leonid. 'Strategies of Representation: Japanese Politicians on Russian Internet and Television', in Yulia Mikhailova and M. William Steele (eds), *Japan and Russia: Three Centuries of Mutual Images* (Folkestone: Global Oriental, 2008), 192–207.

Sondhaus, Lawrence. *Naval Warfare 1815–1914: Warfare and History* (London: Routledge, 2001).

Spector, Ronald H. *At War at Sea: Sailors and Naval Combat in the Twentieth Century* (New York: Viking, 2001).

Steltzer, Hans G. *Die deutsche Flotte: Ein historischer Überblick von 1640 bis 1918* (Darmstadt: Societäts Verlag, 1989).

Stevenson, David. *Armaments and the Coming of War: Europe, 1904–1914* (Oxford: Clarendon Press, 1996).

Streltsov, Dmitry V. 'The Territorial Issue in Russian–Japanese Relations: An Overview', in Dmitry V. Streltsov and Nobuo Shimotomai (eds), *A History of Russo-Japanese Relations: Over Two Centuries of Cooperation and Competition* (Leiden: Brill, 2019), 577–606.

Stroop, Christopher A. 'Thinking the Nation through Times of Trial: Russian Philosophy in War and Revolution', in Murray Frame et al. (eds), *Russian Culture in War and Revolution, 1914–22*, 2 vols (Bloomington, IN: Slavica, 2014), 2:199–220.

Sumida, Jon T. 'British Capital Ship Design and Fire Control in the Dreadnought Era: Sir John Fisher, Arthur Hungerford Pollen, and the Battle Cruiser', *Journal of Modern History* 51 (1979), 205–30.

Sumida, Jon T. *In Defense of Naval Supremacy: Finance, Technology, and British Naval Policy, 1889–1914* (Winchester, MA: Unwin Hyman, 1989).

Suzuki Kantarō Denki Hensan Iinkai (ed.). *Suzuki Kantarō den* (Tokyo: Suzuki Kantarō Denki Hensan Iinkai, 1960).

Sweeney, Michael, and Natascha Toft Roelsgaard, *Journalism and the Russo-Japanese War* (Lanham, MD: Lexington, 2020).

Sweeney, Michael S. '"Delays and Vexation": Jack London and the Russo-Japanese War', *Journalism and Mass Communication Quarterly* 75 (1998), 548–59.

Tadokoro, Masayuki. 'Why did Japan Fail to Become the "Britain" of Asia?' in John W. Steinberg et al. (eds), *The Russo-Japanese War in Global Perspective*, 2 vols (Leiden: Brill, 2005–7), 2:295–323.

Takahashi Norio. *Chizu de shiru Nichiro sensō* (Tokyo: Buyōdō, 2009).

Takahashi, Fumio. 'The First War Plan Orange and the First Imperial Japanese Defense Policy: An Interpretation from the Geopolitical Strategic Perspective', *NIDS Security Reports* 5 (2004), 68–103.

Tanaka Hiromi. *Tōgō Heihachirō* (Tokyo: Yoshikawa Kōbunkan, 2013).

Tanaka Ken'ichi, and Himuro Chiharu. *Zusetsu: Tōgō Heihachirō; me de miru Meiji no kaigun* (Tokyo: Tōgō Jinja–Tōgō-kai, 1995).

Thiess, Frank. *The Voyage of the Forgotten Men (Tsushima)*, trans. Fritz Sallagar (Indianapolis, IN: Bobbs-Merrill, 1937).

Thompson, Richard Austin. 'The Yellow Peril, 1890–1924', PhD dissertation (University of Wisconsin, 1957).

Thorsten, Marie, and Geoffrey M. White. 'Binational Pearl Harbor? Tora! Tora! Tora! and the Fate of (Trans)national Memory', *The Asia-Pacific Journal* 8 (2010), issue 52 no. 2 [online] available at https://apjjf.org/-Geoffrey-M.-White/3462/article.html.

Till, Geoffrey. 'Trafalgar, Tsushima, and Onwards: Japan and the Decisive Naval Battles of the Twenty-First Century', *The Japan Society Proceedings* 144 (2006), 42–56.

Tobe, Ryōchi. 'Japan's Policy toward the Soviet Union, 1931–1941: The Japanese–Soviet Non-Aggression Pact', in Dmitry V. Streltsov and Nobuo Shimotomai (eds), *A History of Russo-Japanese Relations: Over Two Centuries of Cooperation and Competition* (Leiden: Brill, 2019), 201–17.

Togawa Yukio. *Nogi to Tōgō* (Tokyo: Kadokawa Shoten, 1972).

Tovy, Tal, and Sharon Halevy. 'America's First Cold War: The Emergence of a New Rivalry', in Rotem Kowner (ed.), *The Impact of the Russo-Japanese War* (London: Routledge, 2007), 137–52.

Towle, Philip. 'The Evaluation of the Experience of the Russo-Japanese War', in Bryan Ranft (ed.), *Technical Change and the British Naval Policy, 1860–1939* (London: Hodder and Stoughton, 1977), 65–79.

Towle, Philip. 'British War Correspondents and the War', in Rotem Kowner (ed.), *Rethinking the Russo-Japanese War, 1904–05: Centennial Perspectives* (Folkestone: Global Oriental, 2007), 319–31.

Toyama Saburō. *Nichiro kaisen shinshi* (Tokyo: Tōkyō Shuppan, 1987).

Toyama Saburō. *Nichiro kaisen-shi kenkyū: senkiteki kōsatsu o chūshin toshite*, 2 vols (Tokyo: Kyōiku Shuppan Sentā, 1985).

Toyoda Jō. *Kikan Mikasa no shōgai* (Tokyo: Kōjinsha, 2016).

Toyoda Jō. '"Tōgō Heihachirō" wa kyōikushō ni noserarete shikarubeki riyū ga aru', in Bungei Shunjū (ed.), *Nihon no ronten* (Tokyo: Bungei Shunjū, 1992), 594–601.

Trani, Eugene P. *The Treaty of Portsmouth: An Adventure in American Diplomacy* (Lexington: University Press of Kentucky, 1969).

Transehe, N.A. 'The Siberian Sea Road: The Work of the Russian Hydrographical Expedition to the Arctic 1910–1915', *Geographical Review* 15, no. 3 (1925), 367–98.

Tsukada Shūichi. 'Taiken naki sensō no kioku no genba: Nihonkai kaisen kinen shikiten no kansatsu yori', *Mita shakaigaku* 23 (2018), 87–98.

Uzaki Kumakichi. *Satsu no kaigun Chō no rikugun* (Tokyo: Seikōsha, 1913).

Valliant, Robert B. 'The Selling of Japan: Japanese Manipulation of Western Opinion, 1900–1905', *Monumenta Nipponica* 29 (1974), 415–38.

Vinogradov, Sergei E. 'Battleship Development in Russia from 1905 to 1917', *Warship International* 35 (1998), 267–90.

Vinogradov, Sergei E. 'Battleship Development in Russia from 1905 to 1917', *Warship International* 36 (1999), 118–41.

Wada Haruki. *Nichiro sensō: kigen to kaisen*, 2 vols (Tokyo: Iwanami, 2009).

Walser, Ray. *France's Search for a Battle Fleet: Naval Policy and Naval Power, 1898–1914* (New York: Garland Press, 1992).

Warner, Denis, and Peggy Warner. *The Tide at Sunrise: A History of the Russo-Japanese War 1904–1905* (New York: Charterhouse, 1974).

Wcislo, Francis W. *Tales of Imperial Russia: The Life and Times of Sergei Witte, 1849–1915* (Oxford: Oxford University Press, 2011).

Weinberg, Robert E. *The Revolution of 1905 in Odessa: Blood on the Steps* (Bloomington: Indiana University Press, 1993).

Wells, David. 'The Russo-Japanese War in Russian Literature', in David Wells and Sandra Wilson (eds), *The Russo-Japanese War in Cultural Perspective, 1904–05* (Basingstoke: Macmillan, 1999), 108–33.

Westwood, J.N. 'Novikov-Priboi as Naval Historian', *Slavic Review* 28 (1969), 297–303.

Westwood, J.N. *Russian Naval Construction, 1904–45* (Basingstoke: Palgrave Macmillan, 1994).

Westwood, J.N. *Witnesses of Tsushima* (Tokyo: Sophia University, 1970).

White, John A. *The Diplomacy of the Russo-Japanese War* (Princeton, NJ: Princeton University Press, 1964).

Wildenberg, Thomas. *Gray Steel and Black Oil: Fast Tankers and Replenishment at Sea in the US Navy, 1912–1992* (Annapolis, MD: Naval Institute Press, 1996).

Williams, Beryl. 'Great Britain and Russia, 1905 to the 1907 Convention', in F. H. Hinsley (ed.), *British Foreign Policy under Sir Edward Grey* (Cambridge: Cambridge University Press, 1977), 133–48.

Willmott, H.P. *Sea Warfare: Weapons, Tactics and Strategy* (New York: Hippocrene Books, 1981).

Willmott, H.P. *The Last Century of Sea Power*, 2 vols (Bloomington: Indiana University Press, 2009).

Wilson, Sandra. 'The Russo-Japanese War and Japan: Politics, Nationalism and Historical Memory', in David Wells and Sandra Wilson (eds), *The Russo-Japanese War in Cultural Perspective, 1904–05* (Basingstoke: Palgrave Macmillan, 1999), 160–96.

Yabuki, Hiraku. 'Britain and the Resale of Argentine Cruisers to Japan before the Russo-Japanese War', *War in History* 16 (2009), 425–46.

Yamamoto Eisuke et al. *Kaigun denpa kankei tsuitō-shū: Gojū-shūnen kinen*, 3 vols (Denpa kankei mokkosha kenshō irei-kai, 1955).

Yang, Daqing. *Technology of Empire: Telecommunications and Japanese Expansion in Asia, 1883–1945* (Cambridge, MA: Harvard University Asia Center, 2010).

Yonezawa Fujiyoshi. *Tōgō Heihachirō* (Tokyo: Shin Jinbutsu Ōraisha, 1972).

Zebroski, Robert. 'Lieutenant Peter Petrovich Schmidt: Officer, Gentleman, and Reluctant Revolutionary', *Jahrbücher für Geschichte Osteuropas* 59 (2011), 28–50.

PICTURE AND MAP
ACKNOWLEDGEMENTS

Fig. 1. Wikipedia Common, https://commons.wikimedia.org/wiki/File:Knyaz %27Suvorov1904Reval.jpgl; https://commons.wikimedia.org/wiki/File:%D0% 90%D1%81%D0%B0%D1%85%D0%B8.jpg

Fig. 2. Wikipedia Common, https://en.wikipedia.org/wiki/Russian_cruiser_ Oleg#/media/File:Russian_Cruiser_Oleg_LOC_16924u.jpg https://en.wikipedia.org/wiki/Shirakumo-class_destroyer#/media/File:IJN_ Shirakumo_in_England_Meiji_35.jpg

Fig. 3. James Hare, *A Photographic Record of the Russo–Japanese War* (New York, 1905), 39. Author's private collection.

Fig. 4. Courtesy of the Library of Congress, Prints and Photographs Division (reproduction number, LC - FP 2 - JPD, no. 1597).

Fig. 5. Unknown author. Wikipedia Common, https://upload.wikimedia.org/ wikipedia/commons/8/81/Japanese_battleship_Shikishima_on_Battle_of_the _Yellow_Sea.jpg

Fig. 6. Wikipedia Common, https://commons.wikimedia.org/wiki/File:Port_ Arthur_from_Gold_Hill.jpg

Fig. 7. Courtesy of the Library of Congress, http://chroniclingamerica.loc.gov/ lccn/sn88085187/1904-09-21/ed-1/seq-1/

Fig. 8. Tsar Nicholas II on board the cruiser *Svetlana*. Author's private collection.

Fig. 9. Courtesy of the British Newspaper Archive.

Fig. 10. Tsuboya Zenshirō, *Nichiro sen'eki kaigun shashinshū* (Tokyo, 1905), 89. Author's private collection.

Fig. 11. Wikipedia Common, https://upload.wikimedia.org/wikipedia/commons/ b/b8/MIKASAPAINTING.jpg

Fig. 12. Tsuboya, *Nichiro sen'eki kaigun shashinshū*, 104. Author's private collection.

Fig. 13. Tsuboya, *Nichiro sen'eki kaigun shashinshū*, 94. Author's private collection.

Fig. 14. Tsuboya, *Nichiro sen'eki kaigun shashinshū*, n.p. Author's private collection.

Fig. 15. Tsuboya, *Nichiro sen'eki kaigun shashinshū*, 100. Author's private collection.

Fig. 16. Edwin Sharpe Grew, *War in the Far East*, 6 vols. (London, 1905), 5:160. Author's private collection.

Fig. 17. Courtesy of the Library of Congress, Prints and Photographs Division (reproduction number, LC- LC-USZ62-68815).

Fig. 18. Courtesy of Sven Saaler (private collection).

Fig. 19. *Puck*, 22 September 1909, cover. Courtesy of the Library of Congress, Prints and Photographs Division (Illus. in AP101.P7 1909).

Fig. 20. Photo taken by the author, June 2019.

Fig. 21. Courtesy of the Library of Congress, Library of Congress, Prints and Photographs Division (reproduction number, LC- LC-H261- 488).

Fig. 22. Ogasawara Naganari, *Seishō Tōgō Heihachirō den*, ix. Author's private collection.

Fig. 23. Wikipedia Common, https://ja.wikipedia.org/wiki/%E6%97%A5%E6%9C%AC%E6%B5%B7%E6%B5%B7%E6%88%A6%E7%B4%80%E5%BF%B5%E7%A2%91#/media/

Fig. 24. Photo taken by the author, June 2019.

Fig. 25. Photo taken by the author, June 2019.

Fig. 26. Photo taken by the author, June 2019. The original drawing is printed in H.W. Wilson, *Japan's Fight for Freedom* (London, 1904–6), 3: 1385.

Fig. 27. The Miriam and Ira D. Wallach Division of Art, Prints and Photographs: Picture Collection, The New York Public Library. 'Admiral Rodjestvensky and four officers of the *Biedovy* on trial before the naval council of war at Cronstadt', Accessed January 1, 2020. http://digitalcollections.nypl.org/items/510d47e1-0d01-a3d9-e040-e00a18064a99

Fig. 28. The heroes of the *Kniaz Suvorov*. Courtesy of Felix Brenner (private collection).

Fig. 29. Wikipedia Common, https://commons.wikimedia.org/wiki/File:Tsushima_obelisk_(Saint_Petersburg).jpg

Fig. 30. Photo taken by the author, August 2011.

Fig. 31. *The Sphere* (London), vol. 21, no. 279 (27 May 1905), cover. Courtesy of the British Newspaper Archive.

Fig. 32. Courtesy of the Library of Congress, Prints and Photographs Division, https://chroniclingamerica.loc.gov/lccn/sn85066387/1905-05-29/ed-1/

Fig. 33. John McCutcheon, *The Mysterious Stranger and Other Cartoons by John T. McCutcheon* (New York. 1905). John T. McCutcheon, *Chicago Tribune*, 30 May 1905, 1. Wikipedia Common, https://upload.wikimedia.org/wikipedia/commons/c/c1/McCutcheonTogoTakingPlace.jpg

Fig. 34. Museum of Fine Arts, Boston, Leonard A. Lauder Collection of Japanese Postcards, 2002.3761

Fig. 35. Wikipedia Common, https://commons.wikimedia.org/wiki/File:British_Battleships_of_the_First_World_War;_HMS_Dreadnought_Q21183.jpg

Fig. 36. Wikipedia Common, https://en.wikipedia.org/wiki/Great_White_Fleet#/media/File:Kosmos_esquadra_americana_2.jpg

Map 1. Adapted from 'Map Showing the Strategic Situation in the East', *The Topeka State Journal* (25 May 1904), 1. Courtesy of the Library of Congress, https://chroniclingamerica.loc.gov/lccn/sn82016014/1904-05-25/ed-1/seq-8/

Map 2. Based on Tanaka and Himuro, *Zusetsu: Tōgō Heihachirō*, 112; Satō, *Zusetsu: Nichiro sensō*, 152–3.

Map. 3. Based on Norio Takahashi, *Chizu de shiru Nichiro sensō*, 49.

Map 4. Based on Evans and Peattie, *Kaigun*, Map 4–4.

Map 5. Based on *Satō, Zusetsu: Nichiro sensō*, 156, Map 2.

Map 6. Based on Toyama, *Nichiro kaisen-shi kenkyū* (map appendix); Evans and Peattie, *Kaigun*, Map 4–5.

Map 7. Based on Toyama, *Nichiro kaisen-shi kenkyū* (map appendix); Evans and Peattie, *Kaigun*, Map 4–6.

Map 8. Based on Satō, *Zusetsu: Nichiro sensō*, 160.

INDEX

Note: Figures and Tables are indicated by an italic "*f*" and "*t*", respectively, following the page number.

For the benefit of digital users, indexed terms that span two pages (e.g., 52–53) may, on occasion, appear on only one of those pages.

Baltic Fleet 8*f*, 22, 24–7, 28*f*, 30*f*, 31–5, 37, 38*t*, 42*f*, 50, 54, 57, 63, 70, 74, 77–9, 81, 93, 116, 121, 125, 127–9, 132–5, 137, 143–4, 149, 151, 156–7, 161, 173, 177, 183, 25, 26*f*, 27–9, 30*f*, 34, 40, 79, 123, 127, 133, 136, 143–4, 149, 156, 160, 165, 183
Baltic region 117
Baltic Sea 10, 27, 29, 129
Baltimore Evening Herald 147
Baranov, Nikolai 122
barnacles 76
Barrow-in-Furness 105
Battle Division, 1st 8*f*, 15*t*, 38*t*, 43*f*, 44, 46, 50, 52, 57, 95
Battle Division, 2nd 38*t*, 48, 51–2, 57
Battle Division, 3rd 53
Battle Division, 4th 44, 53, 57
Battle Division, 5th 52, 63
Battle Division, 6th 52
Battle of Chemulpo 16, 138, 140
Battle of Hampton Roads 166, 183
Battle of Jutland 48, 166, 182, 186, 189–92
Battle of Lepanto 191
Battle of Liaoyang 23
Battle of Lissa 166
Battle of Manila 166
Battle of Midway 93, 95–6, 166, 191–2
Battle of Mukden 24, 83, 116, 137
Battle of Nanshan 20
Battle of Navarino 166
Battle of Shaho 23
Battle of Sandepu 24
Battle of the Nile 160
Battle of the Yalu River 3, 19
Battle of the Yellow Sea 21, 22*f*, 23, 34–5, 48, 72–3, 78, 132, 160, 169–70
Battle of Trafalgar 46, 87, 110, 149, 152, 155, 162, 165–6, 182, 190–1
Battle of Tsushima 1, 16, 19, 21, 25, 38*t*, 74, 76, 83, 86, 88, 90–1, 93, 95, 98, 103*f*, 103–6, 108–10, 112, 114, 117–20, 125, 128–30, 132, 134, 139–41, 143, 159, 163, 165–6, 168, 170–1, 173, 175, 177–8, 181, 184, 186–7, 189–93; armament 72–5; armour and structure 75–6; casualties 71, 216n. 124; communication and detection 77; consequences, international naval ranking 231n. 43; consequences, Japan 87–98; consequences, Russia 115–30; impact on naval development 165–87; leadership and preparedness 77–8; list of ships 195–7; losses 71; memory, Japan 98–112; memory, Russia 130–42;

motivation 78–80; number of shells shot 216n. 127; plans before the battle 33–9; power balance on the eve of the battle 38*t*, 195–7; reactions, foreign decision makers 152–8; reactions, international media 143–52; reactions, Japan 83–7; reactions, naval specialists 158–65; reactions, Russia 112–15; speed 76–7; stages 41–71; strategy 81; tactics 80–1; tonnage of ships captured 221n. 27; tonnage of ships losses 71, 215n. 123; weather 41, 43, 54, 70, 74, 77, 80, 218n. 156, *See also* firing rate, gunnery, leadership, motivation
Battle of Tsushima, memorials. *See* Church of Christ the Saviour, Fukutsu, Japan–Russia Friendship Hill, Memorial Ship Mikasa, Tōgō Shrine, Tsushima obelisk
Battle of Ulsan 22
battle plan 33–5, 81
battlecruiser 90–1, 97, 173, 186
See also Invincible class, *Repulse*
Battles of Khalkhin Gol 137
battleship 7, 8*f*, 9–10, 12, 14, 15*t*, 16, 20, 21*f*, 22*f*, 23, 31–2, 35, 37, 38*t*, 39, 43–5, 47*f*, 50–1, 53–4, 55, 56*f*, 56–8, 59*f*, 62–4, 65*f*, 66–7, 70, 72, 75–6, 80, 88, 90–1, 93–5, 97, 101, 117, 120, 123, 126*f*, 127–9, 132, 133*f*, 134–5, 159, 161, 163, 165, 167–8, 169*f*, 168–73, 175–81, 183, 186–7, 190, low-freeboard battleship, 62 *See also* all-big-gun battleship, *Asahi, Borodino, Fuji, Gangut* class, *Hatsuse, Imperator Nikolai I, Imperator Aleksandr III, Kniaz Suvorov, Kniaz Potëmkin Tavricheskiĭ, Mikasa, Musashi, Navarin, Nassau* class, *Orël, Osliabia, Petropavlovsk, Prince of Wales, Sissoi Velikiĭ, Slava, South Carolina* class, *Tsesarevich, Yamato, Yashima*
Bedoviĭ 65, 122
Beiyang Fleet 3, 64, 93
Bely, Andrei 131
Beresford, Charles 177
Berlin Treaty of 1878 119
Berliner Tageblatt 151
Berliner Volks-Zeitung 151
Bezuprechniĭ 67
Big Five 86
Big Shipbuilding Programme 127
Bikov, Pëtr 137
Birmingham 186
Bistriĭ 67
Black Sea Fleet 10, 25, 31, 117, 119–20

U-boat 186
Ueda Shin 108
Ulleungdo 58, 63, 66
Ulsan 22, 46f, 67, 69f
umi no shigeki 108
United States Navy 86, 90, 94, 154, 168,
181–3, 185, 188
See also Great White Fleet, War Plan
Orange, Washington Treaty
United States Seventh Fleet 105
United States Third Fleet 138
United States 4, 7, 83–4, 91, 143, 146, 150f,
152–3, 159, 181, 183
unprotected cruisers 10, 15t, 38t
Ural 43, 53, 55
Uryū Sotokichi 16, 57
Utsuryō-tō. *See* Ulleungdo

Vaigach 127
Variag 16, 125, 138
Versailles Peace Conference 86
Vickers Naval Construction Yard 105
Victory 105, 110
Vigo 29, 30f, 132
Vitgeft, Vilgelm 21
Vladimir 215n. 121
Vladimir Bay 65
Vladimir Monomakh 31, 43, 53, 62, 69f, 98
Vladivostok Independent Cruiser
Squadron 22
Vladivostok 3, 14–16, 20, 29, 30f, 33–5,
54, 58, 63–5, 66f, 67–8, 78, 81, 123,
127, 131, 137, 144, 147, 149, 159, 163,
172, 185
Voronezh 215n. 121
Volochaevka 137

Wakamiya 186
War Council 115
War Plan Orange 182
warships. *See* aircraft carrier, armed yacht,
armoured cruisers, battlecruiser,
battleship, capital ship, cruiser,
destroyer, dreadnought, gunvessel,
Pre-Dreadnought, protected cruiser,

super dreadnought, submarine, torpedo
boat, unprotected cruisers
Washington Naval Conference of 1921–22.
See Washington Treaty
Washington Times 35, 147, 149
Washington Treaty 94, 101
Washington 115, 152, 154
watertight compartment 75
weather. *See* Battle of Tsushima
Weihaiwei 3, 122
Wilhelm II, Kaiser 4, 25, 157, 179
wireless telegraphy 143, 177
Witte, Sergei 118
World War I. *See* First World War
World War II. *See* Second World War
Wright brothers 186
Wusong 68

Yakumo 48, 49f, 66
Yalu Delta 6
Yalu River 3, 16, 19–20
Yamagata Aritomo 89f
Yamamoto Gonnohyōe 19, 32, 89f
Yamamoto Isoroku 95–6
Yamamoto Isoroku, Commander in chief
of the Combined Fleet (film). See *Rengō
kantai shirei Chōkan Yamamoto Isoroku* 107
Yamanashi Katsunoshin 105
Yamato damashii 93
Yamato class 97
Yamato 170
Yangtze River 35, 157
Yaroslavl 215n. 121
Yashima 15t
Yellow peril 4
Yellow Sea, Battle of. *See* Battle of the
Yellow Sea
Yokohama 87–8
Yoshimura Akira 108
Young School. *See* Jeune École

Z flag 46, 47f, 96, 110, 111f
Zemstvo 114
Zhemchug 43, 49f, 53, 60, 68, 69f
Zhytomyr 114